I0510438

The Undefendable Trial I

Volume I

By

James Coghill

© Copyright 2018 All Rights Reserved

Table of Contents

Preface

"While the truncheon may be used in lieu of conversation, words will always retain their power. Words are the means to meaning and for those who will <u>listen</u> the enunciation of truth, and the truth is there is something terribly wrong with this country. For when a nations' judiciary no longer concerns itself with the pursuit of truth, it turns a deaf ear on the people it derives its power from and made itself an enemy of the public." (James P. Coghill)

In March 2003 I drove from Tucson Arizona to Phoenix Arizona to pick up a friend of mine named Jacob Franks. When we arrived in Tucson I told Jake that he could use my GoPed to look for employment as long as he remained within a 4 block area around the RV Park where I was living. I told him that I didn't want him making any long trips on it because I was concerned for his safety.

After arranging a job interview for Jake the next morning for a job where I was working, upon my return home with groceries and good news I found Jake talking on my cell phone. Not wanting to interrupt him I sat down in a chair and waited for him to finish his conversation. As I listened to what he was saying I recognized that he was speaking with an attorney. I then looked to my left and found my GoPed on the floor in pieces. When Jake's conversation was concluded I asked him what was going on. He told me that he was at the intersection of 4th Street and Broadway where he attempted to ride the GoPed through a crosswalk where the traffic lights had not yet been installed. It was then that an automobile came around the corner and hit him, which launched him across the hood of the car. This resulted in a mild sprain of his right ankle. However when the police arrived they requested an ambulance to pick him up and take him to a hospital in the event there were other injuries. In addition the police gave Jake a ticket for riding a GoPed in a crosswalk.

Around 6:30 AM we both got up. I began to get into my uniform and he began to get dressed for the interview. As he was getting dressed he put on a wrinkled shirt as big as a trash bag. I told him that this was a professional interview for an office position and that this kind of clothing was not acceptable. He then walked down the hallway and yelled at me, "It's the only shirt I've got man." It was

3

the only shirt he had because his aunt had burned all his clothes when she threw him out prior to his arrival at my place. I told him he could wear a white shirt and tie of mine, which he did. Afterwards he came back to my bedroom and said, "After the interview I want you to take me to Walgreen's and buy my pain medication." I informed Jake that he alone was responsible for his own actions and therefore I was not responsible for buying his pain medication. Then Jake exploded into an argument and I told him that I was not going to put up with this. I told him that we were finished and that he should take off my shirt and tie, put on his own clothes and that I was taking him back to Phoenix immediately. He then walked out and I assumed that he had gone for a walk to blow off steam. Realizing that I still had about an hour and a half before I had to go to work I decided to give Jake some time to come back and that I would deal with him when that happened. Jake then returned and asked me if I was going to take him to the interview and I told him that I wasn't and that if he wanted to go to the interview he would have to make it on his own. He then entered my motorhome and was inside for about 20 minutes. I assumed that he was packing his possessions up and putting them into my car so that I could take him back to Phoenix however this is not what happened. What he was doing during this time is unknown, however I do know he changed his clothes and left, leaving all his possessions behind.

The next thing to occur was the arrival of two police officers one male and the other female. I was in the yard raking debris at the time. They appeared to be lost so I asked them if I could help them. They asked me if this was lot 7 and I told them that it was. They asked me if I knew Jacob Franks and I said that I did. I then asked them, "What has he gotten himself into now?" They replied that Jake was very upset with them for giving him a ticket for riding my GoPed in a crosswalk yesterday. I told them that I was aware of this and informed them that he had no job to pay for the ticket. They asked if they could see my GoPed and I pulled it out of the trunk of my car. They asked if they could discuss this matter inside my motorhome and I told them I had no problem with that. Upon entry into my motorhome they observed my computer and informed me that a complaint had been filed with them stating that I had child pornography that had been stored on CD-ROM. They asked me if I had such materials and I replied that I did not. During this time I received better offers for employment in other cities and I took them because as the police had told me I was free to go. Jake on the other hand hacked and defaced my websites destroying eight years of work and was arrested for burglary in Phoenix a month later.

About a year later I was arrested and at my arraignment I pled not guilty. Shortly afterward I was offered a plea bargain consisting of a fine for $15,000, five years in prison, lifetime probation and registration as a sex offender which I rejected. It is important to note that these charges were pressed against me before the Pima County Sheriff's office had even conducted computer forensics on my computer. When the computer forensics report was finally delivered to me several unique things were discovered.

1. All of the files that I had been charged with had been deleted from the hard drive of my computer. All 15 charges arose from compact discs.
2. There was no evidence to support the conclusion that any of the contraband files or any file titles similar to them had been downloaded using my computer. This by necessity proves that the contraband files had to come from a computer other than my own.
3. There was no evidence to support the conclusion that any of the contraband files or any file titles similar to them had been viewed. This is conclusive proof that there was no possible way that I could have known the files had been inserted into my CD collection consisting of over 650 discs.

With this evidence on my side I felt confident that it would not be difficult to win this trial so I continued to fight in spite of the fact that I was facing a 155 year sentence in prison. During trial, the prosecutor introduced into testimony the presence of adult pornography, which is perfectly legal and presented it to the jury as prior bad act evidence and proof of my ability to download material from the Internet along with many other illegal practices that are quite common in courtrooms everywhere in this country. As you read this see how many of them you can find. Where page numbers are cited they are in reference to the page numbers in this book.

```
 1        BEFORE THE PIMA COUNTY GRAND JURY NUMBER 181

 2                     TUCSON, ARIZONA

 3

 4

 5   THE STATE OF ARIZONA,

 6             Plaintiff,

 7   vs.                          NO.   181-GJ-634
                                  NO.   CR-20042573
 8   JAMES NMN COGHILL,

 9             Accused.                 FILED AUG 0 4 2004
     ----------------------------

10

11

12               TRANSCRIPT OF PROCEEDINGS

13        Official Court Reporter's transcript of
     proceedings had before the Pima County Grand Jury, in
14   secret session, on the 15th day of July, 2004, on
     the Fifth Floor, Pima County Administration Building,
15   Tucson, Arizona.

16

17   APPEARANCES:

18             Brad Roach, Esq.,
               Deputy County Attorney.
19

20

21

22

23

     MARY JO M. BAIR, RMR
24   CERTIFIED COURT REPORTER #50116
     Pima County Superior Court
25   Tucson, Arizona   85701
```

SUPERIOR COURT, PIMA COUNTY

1   GRAND JURORS PRESENT:

2

3   BEVERLY JO BEATTIE

4   JEAN ALVINA DODGE

5   BRYANT JEROME FARNSWORTH, JR.

6   LORRAINE LOURDES HIDALGO (Bailiff)

7   SHANE ANN KNEPP

8   RONNIE BRYANT LOWRIE

9   DEBRA JEANNE MAYS

10   PATRICIA EILEEN MURPHY

11   THERESA JEAN REED

12   KENNETH W. SELLERS (The Foreperson)

13   CARMELLA LOPEZ VALADEZ

14

15

16

17

18

19

20

21

22

23

24

25

SUPERIOR COURT, PIMA COUNTY

```
 1              P R O C E E D I N G S

 2

 3              THE FOREPERSON:  We are back on the record.

 4    There were no cases or matters discussed during the

 5    recess.

 6              Number 181-GJ-634.  11 grand jurors present.

 7    Those absent are Cormier, Kalloch, McDonald, Opitz,

 8    and Samuels.

 9              The accused is James Coghill.

10              The proposed charges, Counts 1 through 15,

11    sexual exploitation of a minor under 15.

12              The witness is Detective Englander.

13

14                    JEFF ENGLANDER,

15    having been duly sworn, was examined and testified as

16    follows:

17                   DIRECT EXAMINATION

18    BY MR. ROACH:

19       Q.   Would you state your name and occupation,

20    please?

21       A.   My name is Jeff Englander.  I'm a detective

22    with the Pima County Sheriff's Department.

23       Q.   In that capacity do you have some

24    information for the grand jury concerning a James

25    Coghill?
```

1   A.   I do.

2   Q.   That concern some events that occurred on or

3   about April 1st, 2003?

4   A.   Yes.

5   Q.   And can you give us the information that you

6   have?

7   A.   Mr. Coghill was living in a -- an actually

8   mobile mobile home, a small trailer, with another

9   individual who stayed with him for a short period of

10   time. That individual staying with Mr. Coghill called

11   us to report Mr. Coghill had in his possession

12   multiple CD-ROMs, compact disks that had computer

13   movie files on them containing child pornography.

14   Q.   What did you do once you got that

15   information?

16   A.   We went out to the house and ultimately

17   served a search warrant on the residence and retrieved

18   many, many of the described compact disks from the

19   residence.

20   Q.   And where were these compact disks you

21   retrieved located?

22   A.   They weren't exactly rooms. It was a very

23   small trailer, but directly inside the main door to

24   the right was a small desk, sitting area, and there

25   was a computer there, and there were at that computer

1 desk and in that general area several stacks of CDs,

2 also some of the folding type that you can carry music

3 CDs in your car, but obviously these had data CDs in

4 them.

5   Q.   And did you get a chance to analyze those

6 CDs to see what their content was?

7   A.   I did.

8   Q.   And what did you find?

9   A.   Many, many movies of child pornography and

10 adult pornography, but a considerable amount of child

11 pornography on the CDs.

12   Q.   And the counts that we have charged -- or

13 you are going to present to us today, did you -- well,

14 first explain to us. You said these movies were

15 contained on compact disks. How is it a movie is

16 stored on a compact disk?

17   A.   At some point in time the user of the

18 computer will transfer the file or save it onto the

19 compact disk for storage. This particular computer

20 had a very small amount of storage inside of a small

21 hard drive, and the user was using the compact disks

22 as the majority of the storage for some of these

23 files, which can be rather large, so as a process they

24 were being stored there rather than on the computer.

25   Q.   And do each one of these, the 15 specific

SUPERIOR COURT, PIMA COUNTY

11

1   counts or movies that we are talking about here, did

2   they all come from the same disk?

3   A.   They did not.   They came from several

4   different CDs.

5   Q.   But for ease of presentation you have

6   compiled all those images under one CD to present to

7   the grand jury?

8   A.   Correct.

9   Q.   And does that CD have in order files that

10 were named -- and I will go through them.   The first

11 file that we are going to see on the CD is Roygold

12 style dash Lucy dot mpg?

13   A.   Yes.

14   Q.   And what does dot mpg mean?

15   A.   The letters after the dot indicate the type

16 of file for the computer system.   Mpg denotes that

17 it's a movie file.   It's one particular type of movie

18 file.   There are several other ones, but mpg or mpeg

19 are a standardized Windows movie file.

20   Q.   The second image we will see is entitled

21 Roygold style BabyJ 3yo girl eatscum2 dot mpg?

22   A.   Correct.

23   Q.   Third count, Roygold underscore, which is an

24 underline?

25   A.   Correct.

SUPERIOR COURT, PIMA COUNTY

1   Q.   Ilikeit dot mpg?

2   A.   Correct.

3   Q.   Okay. Fourth is a Vicky complete dot mpg?

4   A.   Yes.

5   Q.   The fifth one is Roygold Rushian 2 preteen

6 boys sucking 1 teen boy, parentheses 2, mpg?

7   A.   Correct.

8   Q.   Count 6, reel kiddy movie dash Vicky

9 sucking, in parentheses new, dot mpg?

10   A.   Yes.

11   Q.   Number 7, Vicky underscore good, close

12 parentheses, daughter underscore 2 dot mpg?

13   A.   Correct.

14   Q.   Eighth, Roygold style dash RCA3, parentheses

15 1, parentheses 1, mpg?

16   A.   Yes.

17   Q.   Nine, Roygold underscore tvg013bound dot

18 mpg?

19   A.   Correct.

20   Q.   Ten, BabyJ dash Babycum dot mpg?

21   A.   Yes.

22   Q.   Eleven, BabyJ dash captive dot avi?

23   A.   Yes.

24   Q.   Is avi --

25   A.   Another standard Windows movie file format

SUPERIOR COURT, PIMA COUNTY

1   like mpg.

2   Q.   Count 12, BabyJ dash Lol dash 01 dot avi?

3   A.   Yes.

4   Q.   Thirteen, BabyJ dash Teddy dot mpg?

5   A.   Yes.

6   Q.   And 14, Roygold BabyJ compilation, and a

7   bunch of letters and numbers, dot mpg?

8   A.   Correct.

9   Q.   And Number 15, Roygold Style dash Open

10 underscore 11 dash trade only, comma, no exceptions

11 explanation point, explanation point, explanation

12 point dot mpg?

13   A.   Yes.

14   Q.   Okay. And the CD you have, are those images

15 in that order?

16   A.   Correct.

17   Q.   And can you see on the CD, does it actually

18 have the title of the file it came from?

19   A.   It has the file name, as well as the count

20 number.

21   Q.   Before we start the file that you brought

22 us, some of these are varying lengths?

23   A.   Correct. Some are a minute long, some less.

24 Some are 13, 14, 15 minutes long.

25   Q.   Okay. So what I will ask you to do is to

                 SUPERIOR COURT, PIMA COUNTY

```
 1  play the movies, and for some of the longer ones, once
 2  a good portion of it has been shown, I will ask you to
 3  just continue to the next one.
 4          Can you start with the first one?
 5      A.  Sure.  Is it all ready.  If I come down
 6  here?
 7      Q.  Please.
 8      A.  Pardon me for one minute.
 9      Q.  All right.  Can you go to the next one,
10  please?
11          You can go to the next one.
12          You can go to the next one.
13          You can go on to the next one.
14          You can go on to the next one.
15          You can go on to the next one.
16          You can go on to the next one.
17          You can go on to the next one.
18          You can go on to the next one.
19          You can go on to the next one.
20          You can go on to the next one.
21          You can go on to the next one.
22          You can go on to the next one.
23          You can go on to the next one.
24          Apparently you accidentally duplicated
25  number 14 twice?
```

1   A.   Right. It's correct, but I would have to go
2   back and do it, if you want to, now.
3   Q.   Okay. Go back and find the other one, the
4   image in Count 15.
5   A.   This is 15. The one we saw is 14. This is
6   15. I apologize.
7   Q.   Okay.
8   Turn on the lights.
9   Let me clarify, first, some of the
10   indictment counts. All the counts that are Roygold,
11   what is that, Roygold Style?
12   A.   Roygold is a name associated with child
13   pornography images and movies for years and years
14   since the '70s. It's actually the R and the X symbols
15   and the Y. Some say Gaygold and some Roygold. There
16   are a bunch of different theories of that, but it's a
17   common associated term to be used in child
18   pornography.
19   Q.   On each of the counts in the indictment, the
20   charges themselves, if you choose to show it, do you
21   need to put all of them that just have RY, and if you
22   choose to indict on the correct file name on all
23   those, which is Count 1, 2, 3, 4, 5, 6, 14, and 15,
24   would be R and then the at sign Y? Is that how it
25   would be correctly spelled?

SUPERIOR COURT, PIMA COUNTY

```
 1      A.   Correct.

 2      Q.   And I noticed one other typographical error

 3 on Count 7.   The proposed indictment has Vicky

 4 underscore good, close parentheses.   The correct

 5 spelling of number 7 would have, again, Vicky

 6 underscore good underscore daughter?

 7      A.   Correct.

 8           MR. ROACH:   Thank you.   No further

 9 questions.

10           MS. KULSETH:   For the record, we will make

11 those pen and ink changes now.

12           MR. ROACH:   I have no further questions.

13           THE FOREPERSON:   Any member of the grand

14 jury have any questions for the witness?

15           You are excused, but we may have more

16 questions later.   Please wait until we have finished

17 this case.

18           (The witness exits the grand jury room.)

19           THE FOREPERSON:   Does anyone have any legal

20 questions for the deputy county attorney?

21           Is there any member of the grand jury who is

22 a witness, has a direct or indirect interest in the

23 case, or who has any knowledge of the suspect which

24 would bias or prejudice their ability to serve?

25           Let the record show none.
```

SUPERIOR COURT, PIMA COUNTY

1   The court reporter and the deputy county

2   attorney are excused.

3   (The grand jury deliberated in secret

4   session, out of the presence of the deputy county

5   attorney and court reporter.)

6   THE FOREPERSON: Number 181-GJ-634. The

7   accused is James Coghill.

8   By a vote of 11 to zero the grand jurors

9   returned a true bill.

10   MS. KULSETH: If we can go off the record

11 briefly so the detective can dismantle the equipment.

12   THE FOREPERSON: We will go off the record

13 for the purposes to clean up his equipment.

14   I will remind the jurors not to discuss any

15 legal matters or cases under consideration while we

16 are off the record.

17   (The grand jury stood in recess.)

18

19

20

21

22

23

24

25

SUPERIOR COURT, PIMA COUNTY

```
 1
 2
 3                    C E R T I F I C A T E
 4
 5
 6         I, Mary Jo M. Bair, do hereby certify that as
 7    an Official Court Reporter for the Pima County
 8    Superior Court I reported the foregoing proceedings to
 9    the best of my skill and ability; and that the same
10    was transcribed under my supervision via
11    computer-aided transcription; and that the foregoing
12    pages of typewritten matter are a true, correct, and
13    complete transcript of all the proceedings had as set
14    forth in the title page hereto.
15
16
17    _____
18    MARY JO M. BAIR, RMR
      CERTIFIED COURT REPORTER #50116
19    Pima County Superior Court
      Tucson, Arizona 85701
20
21
22
23
24
25


              SUPERIOR COURT, PIMA COUNTY
```

IN THE SUPERIOR COURT OF THE STATE OF ARIZONA
IN AND FOR THE COUNTY OF PIMA

STATE OF ARIZONA,   )
)
            Plaintiff,   )   CAUSE NO. _____
)
      vs.   )   GRAND JURY MINUTES
)
JAMES NMN COGHILL,   )   181-GJ-634
)
            Defendant.   )
_____)

The above defendant having been accused of the crimes of:

COUNT ONE: (SEXUAL EXPLOITATION OF A MINOR UNDER FIFTEEN, A CLASS TWO
FELONY, A DANGEROUS CRIME AGAINST CHILDREN)

On or about the 1st day of April, 2003, JAMES NMN COGHILL knowingly
committed sexual exploitation of a minor by distributing, transporting,
exhibiting, receiving, selling, purchasing, electronically transmitting,
possessing or exchanging any visual depiction in which a minor, under
fifteen years of age, is engaged in exploitive exhibition or other sexual
conduct, to wit: a video and/or movie showing a prepubescent girl
masturbating and having a dildo inserted into her anus, located on CD in
file entitled "Rygold style - Lucy.mpg", in violation of A.R.S. §§ 13-
3553 (A) (2) and (C), 13-3557, 13-603, 13-604.01, 13-701, 13-702, 13-
702.01, 13-801, 13-804 and 13-811. [Field 2878] [13-3553A2] [M] [C]

COUNT TWO: (SEXUAL EXPLOITATION OF A MINOR UNDER FIFTEEN, A CLASS TWO
FELONY, A DANGEROUS CRIME AGAINST CHILDREN)

On or about the 1st day of April, 2003, JAMES NMN COGHILL knowingly
committed sexual exploitation of a minor by distributing, transporting,
exhibiting, receiving, selling, purchasing, electronically transmitting,
possessing or exchanging any visual depiction in which a minor, under
fifteen years of age, is engaged in exploitive exhibition or other sexual
conduct, to wit: a movie and/video depicting a prepubescent female
performing oral sex on an adult male, contained on CD on file "Rygold
style BabyJ 3yo girl eats cum2.mpg", in violation of A.R.S. §§ 13-3553 (A)
(2) and (C), 13-3557, 13-603, 13-604.01, 13-701, 13-702, 13-702.01, 13-
801, 13-804 and 13-811. [Field 2878] [13-3553A2] [M] [C]

COUNT THREE: (SEXUAL EXPLOITATION OF A MINOR UNDER FIFTEEN, A CLASS TWO
FELONY, A DANGEROUS CRIME AGAINST CHILDREN)

On or about the 1st day of April, 2003, JAMES NMN COGHILL knowingly
committed sexual exploitation of a minor by distributing, transporting,
exhibiting, receiving, selling, purchasing, electronically transmitting,
possessing or exchanging any visual depiction in which a minor, under
fifteen years of age, is engaged in exploitive exhibition or other sexual
conduct, to wit: A movie and/or video depicting a prepubescent female
performing oral sex upon an adult male, contained on CD on a file entitled
"rygold_ilikeit.mpg", in violation of A.R.S. §§ 13-3553 (A) (2) and (C),
13-3557, 13-603, 13-604.01, 13-701, 13-702, 13-702.01, 13-801, 13-804 and
13-811. [Field 2878] [13-3553A2] [M] [C]

COUNT FOUR: (SEXUAL EXPLOITATION OF A MINOR UNDER FIFTEEN, A CLASS TWO FELONY, A DANGEROUS CRIME AGAINST CHILDREN)

On or about the 1st day of April, 2003, JAMES NMN COGHILL knowingly committed sexual exploitation of a minor by distributing, transporting, exhibiting, receiving, selling, purchasing, electronically transmitting, possessing or exchanging any visual depiction in which a minor, under fifteen years of age, is engaged in exploitive exhibition or other sexual conduct, to wit: a movie and/or video depicting an adult male attempting to vaginally penetrate a prepubescent female, contained on CD on file "Vicky complete.mpg", in violation of A.R.S. §§ 13-3553 (A) (2) and (C), 13-3557, 13-603, 13-604.01, 13-701, 13-702, 13-702.01, 13-801, 13-804 and 13-811. [Field 2878] [13-3553A2] [M] [C]

COUNT FIVE: (SEXUAL EXPLOITATION OF A MINOR UNDER FIFTEEN, A CLASS TWO FELONY, A DANGEROUS CRIME AGAINST CHILDREN)

On or about the 1st day of April, 2003, JAMES NMN COGHILL knowingly committed sexual exploitation of a minor by distributing, transporting, exhibiting, receiving, selling, purchasing, electronically transmitting, possessing or exchanging any visual depiction in which a minor, under fifteen years of age, is engaged in exploitive exhibition or other sexual conduct, to wit: a movie and/or video depicting two prepubescent males masturbating each other and an adult male, contained on CD on file "hygold russian 2 preteen boys sucking 1 teen boy(2).mpg", in violation of A.R.S. §§ 13-3553 (A) (2) and (C), 13-3557, 13-603, 13-604.01, 13-701, 13-702, 13-702.01, 13-801, 13-804 and 13-811. [Field 2878] [13-3553A2] [M] [C]

COUNT SIX: (SEXUAL EXPLOITATION OF A MINOR UNDER FIFTEEN, A CLASS TWO FELONY, A DANGEROUS CRIME AGAINST CHILDREN)

On or about the 1st day of April, 2003, JAMES NMN COGHILL knowingly committed sexual exploitation of a minor by distributing, transporting, exhibiting, receiving, selling, purchasing, electronically transmitting, possessing or exchanging any visual depiction in which a minor, under fifteen years of age, is engaged in exploitive exhibition or other sexual conduct, to wit: A movie and/or video depicting a prepubescent female performing oral sex on an adult male, contained on CD in file "Reel Kiddy Mov - Vicky Sucking (New).mpg", in violation of A.R.S. §§ 13-3553 (A) (2) and (C), 13-3557, 13-603, 13-604.01, 13-701, 13-702, 13-702.01, 13-801, 13-804 and 13-811. [Field 2878] [13-3553A2] [M] [C]

COUNT SEVEN: (SEXUAL EXPLOITATION OF A MINOR UNDER FIFTEEN, A CLASS TWO FELONY, A DANGEROUS CRIME AGAINST CHILDREN)

On or about the 1st day of April, 2003, JAMES NMN COGHILL knowingly committed sexual exploitation of a minor by distributing, transporting, exhibiting, receiving, selling, purchasing, electronically transmitting, possessing or exchanging any visual depiction in which a minor, under fifteen years of age, is engaged in exploitive exhibition or other sexual conduct, to wit: a movie and/or video depicting an adult male ejaculating into the mouth of a prepubescent female, contained on CD in file "vicky_good_daughter_2.mpg", in violation of A.R.S. §§ 13-3553 (A) (2) and (C), 13-3557, 13-603, 13-604.01, 13-701, 13-702, 13-702.01, 13-801, 13-804 and 13-811. [Field 2878] [13-3553A2] [M] [C]

COUNT EIGHT: (SEXUAL EXPLOITATION OF A MINOR UNDER FIFTEEN, A CLASS TWO
FELONY, A DANGEROUS CRIME AGAINST CHILDREN)

On or about the 1st day of April, 2003, JAMES NMN COGHILL knowingly
committed sexual exploitation of a minor by distributing, transporting,
exhibiting, receiving, selling, purchasing, electronically transmitting,
possessing or exchanging any visual depiction in which a minor, under
fifteen years of age, is engaged in exploitive exhibition or other sexual
conduct, to wit: a movie and/or video depicting a prepubescent female
masturbating, then performing oral sex on an adult male, contained on CD
in file "Rygold Style - RCA3 (1) (1).mpg", in violation of A.R.S. §§ 13-
3553 (A) (2) and (C), 13-3557, 13-603, 13-604.01, 13-701, 13-702, 13-
702.01, 13-801, 13-804 and 13-811. [Field 2878] [13-3553A2] [M] [C]

COUNT NINE: (SEXUAL EXPLOITATION OF A MINOR UNDER FIFTEEN, A CLASS TWO
FELONY, A DANGEROUS CRIME AGAINST CHILDREN)

On or about the 1st day of April, 2003, JAMES NMN COGHILL knowingly
committed sexual exploitation of a minor by distributing, transporting,
exhibiting, receiving, selling, purchasing, electronically transmitting,
possessing or exchanging any visual depiction in which a minor, under
fifteen years of age, is engaged in exploitive exhibition or other sexual
conduct, to wit: a movie and/or video depicting a prepubescent female
striping, displaying her genitals and performing oral sex on an adult
male, contained on CD in file "Rygold_tvg013bound.mpg", in violation of
A.R.S. §§ 13-3553 (A) (2) and (C), 13-3557, 13-603, 13-604.01, 13-701, 13-
702, 13-702.01, 13-801, 13-804 and 13-811. [Field 2878] [13-3553A2] [M]
[C]

COUNT TEN: (SEXUAL EXPLOITATION OF A MINOR UNDER FIFTEEN, A CLASS TWO
FELONY, A DANGEROUS CRIME AGAINST CHILDREN)

On or about the 1st day of April, 2003, JAMES NMN COGHILL knowingly
committed sexual exploitation of a minor by distributing, transporting,
exhibiting, receiving, selling, purchasing, electronically transmitting,
possessing or exchanging any visual depiction in which a minor, under
fifteen years of age, is engaged in exploitive exhibition or other sexual
conduct, to wit: a movie and/or video depicting an adult male ejaculating
into the mouth of a partially clothed prepubescent female, contained on CD
in file "BabyJ - babycum.mpg", in violation of A.R.S. §§ 13-3553 (A) (2)
and (C), 13-3557, 13-603, 13-604.01, 13-701, 13-702, 13-702.01, 13-801,
13-804 and 13-811. [Field 2878] [13-3553A2] [M] [C]

COUNT ELEVEN: (SEXUAL EXPLOITATION OF A MINOR UNDER FIFTEEN, A CLASS TWO FELONY, A DANGEROUS CRIME AGAINST CHILDREN)

On or about the 1st day of April, 2003, JAMES NMN COGHILL knowingly committed sexual exploitation of a minor by distributing, transporting, exhibiting, receiving, selling, purchasing, electronically transmitting, possessing or exchanging any visual depiction in which a minor, under fifteen years of age, is engaged in exploitive exhibition or other sexual conduct, to wit: a movie and/or video depicting a bound prepubescent female vaginally, anally and digitally penetrated by an adult male, contained on CD in file "BabyJ-Captive.avi", in violation of A.R.S. §§ 13-3553 (A) (2) and (C), 13-3557, 13-603, 13-604.01, 13-701, 13-702, 13-702.01, 13-801, 13-804 and 13-811. [Field 2878] [13-3553A2] [M] [C]

COUNT TWELVE: (SEXUAL EXPLOITATION OF A MINOR UNDER FIFTEEN, A CLASS TWO FELONY, A DANGEROUS CRIME AGAINST CHILDREN)

On or about the 1st day of April, 2003, JAMES NMN COGHILL knowingly committed sexual exploitation of a minor by distributing, transporting, exhibiting, receiving, selling, purchasing, electronically transmitting, possessing or exchanging any visual depiction in which a minor, under fifteen years of age, is engaged in exploitive exhibition or other sexual conduct, to wit: a movie and/or video depicting a prepubescent female performing oral sex on an adult male, contained on CD in file "BabyJ-Lol-01.avi", in violation of A.R.S. §§ 13-3553 (A) (2) and (C), 13-3557, 13-603, 13-604.01, 13-701, 13-702, 13-702.01, 13-801, 13-804 and 13-811. [Field 2878] [13-3553A2] [M] [C]

COUNT THIRTEEN: (SEXUAL EXPLOITATION OF A MINOR UNDER FIFTEEN, A CLASS TWO FELONY, A DANGEROUS CRIME AGAINST CHILDREN)

On or about the 1st day of April, 2003, JAMES NMN COGHILL knowingly committed sexual exploitation of a minor by distributing, transporting, exhibiting, receiving, selling, purchasing, electronically transmitting, possessing or exchanging any visual depiction in which a minor, under fifteen years of age, is engaged in exploitive exhibition or other sexual conduct, to wit: a movie and/or video depicting a prepubescent female performing oral sex on an adult male, contained on CD in file "BabyJ-Teddy.mpg", in violation of A.R.S. §§ 13-3553 (A) (2) and (C), 13-3557, 13-603, 13-604.01, 13-701, 13-702, 13-702.01, 13-801, 13-804 and 13-811. [Field 2878] [13-3553A2] [M] [C]

COUNT FOURTEEN: (SEXUAL EXPLOITATION OF A MINOR UNDER FIFTEEN, A CLASS TWO FELONY, A DANGEROUS CRIME AGAINST CHILDREN)

On or about the 1st day of April, 2003, JAMES NMN COGHILL knowingly committed sexual exploitation of a minor by distributing, transporting, exhibiting, receiving, selling, purchasing, electronically transmitting, possessing or exchanging any visual depiction in which a minor, under fifteen years of age, is engaged in exploitive exhibition or other sexual conduct, to wit: a movie and/or video depicting a prepubescent female taking off her underwear, masturbating and being vaginally penetrated by an adult male, contained on CD in file "Rygold BabyJ Compilation776394eof0380a88af26e53b9debe739083.mpg", in violation of A.R.S. §§ 13-3553 (A) (2) and (C), 13-3557, 13-603, 13-604.01, 13-701, 13-702, 13-702.01, 13-801, 13-804 and 13-811. [Field 2878] [13-3553A2] [M] [C]

COUNT FIFTEEN: (SEXUAL EXPLOITATION OF A MINOR UNDER FIFTEEN IN THE SECOND DEGREE, A CLASS THREE FELONY, A PREPARATORY DANGEROUS CRIME AGAINST CHILDREN)

On or about the 1st day of April, 2003, JAMES NMN COGHILL knowingly committed sexual exploitation of a minor in the second degree by attempting to distribute, transport, exhibit, receive, sell, purchase, electronically transmit, possess or exchange any visual depiction in which a minor, under fifteen years of age, is engaged in exploitive exhibition or other sexual conduct, to wit: videos and/or a movies depicting multiple scenes of prepubescent males and females engaged in various sexual acts with each other as well as six males contained in "Rygold Style - Open_11 - Trade Only, No Exceptions!!!.mpg", in violation of A.R.S. §§ 13-3553 (A)(2) and (C), 13-3557, 13-603, 13-604.01 (I), 13-701, 13-702, 13-702.01, 13-801, 13-804 and 13-811. [Field 2881] [13-3553A2] [M] [C]

PCSO 030401051

at a session of the grand jury of the County of Pima with ___||___ members present, deliberated upon the evidence and with ___||___ jurors voting by a vote of ___||___ to ___0___ , returned ___TRUE BILL_____ .

_____
Foreperson of the Grand Jury

Date ____7/15/04_____

June 4, 2004

Denial of due process, no grand jury invitation.
On or about June 4, 2004, the Pima County Grand Jury was convened against Defendant. Defendant was never notified at his home of record of the date, time and place of the hearing.

> ARS 21-412 Evidence on behalf of person under investigation.
> "The person under investigation shall have the right to advice of counsel during the giving of any testimony by him before the grand jury, provided that such counsel may not communicate with anyone other than his client."

Without notification of the date, time and place of the grand jury proceedings it is impossible to exercise this right. Therefore due process has been denied from the defendant.

> Lambright v. Lewis, 932 F.SUPP. 1547 (ARIZ. 1996)
> "State trial courts violation of state law constitutes violation of Federal constitutional right to due process."

> U.S. v. Deters, 143 F.3d 577 (10th CIR. 1998)
> "When government action deprives a person of life, liberty or property without fair procedures it violates procedural due process."
> "Once due process is denied all jurisdiction ceases per 5 USC § 556(d), 557, 706.

> Judges have no immunity per:
> Owen v. City of Independence, 100 S.CT. 1398
> Maine v. Thiboutot, 100 S.Ct. 2502
> Hafer v. Melon, 502 U.S. 21
> Title 42 USC § 1983
> 18 USC § 241/242
> 28 USC § 1746."

The above is made applicable in the state by instrumentality rule with, "28 USC § 3001/3002 (15)(A)(C) wherefore any alleged jurisdiction has already been voided by the denial of due process.

Page 9-3 Englander perjures his testimony to that in trial.

Page 10-8 Grand Jury never saw the original evidence. They saw a compilation disk that was fabricated by Detective Englander.

No handwriting evidence presented.

No fingerprint evidence presented.

On or about June 28, 2004 defendant was arrested. No Miranda.

Defense counsel fails to determine if judge and prosecutor are bonded and properly installed to the positions they hold.

On August 21, 2004, 25 men assaulted defendant during extradition at the Imperial County Jail in El Centro, California.

Canter v. Jones, 293 F3d 981 (7th Cir.2002)
Prison officials have a duty to protect prisoners from violence at the hands of other inmates.

Calderon-Ortiz v. Laboy Alvarado, 300 F3d.60 (1st Cir.2002)
An inmate may sue a correctional facility under the 8th Amendment for failure to provide adequate protection to inmates from attack by other inmates.

Defense counsel did nothing more than call the jail. Defendant had been deliberately placed in the Security Threat Group of general population.

The above is made applicable in the state by instrumentality rule with, "28 USC § 3001/3002 (15)(A)(C) wherefore any alleged jurisdiction has already been voided by the denial of due process.

Defense counsel at first court appearance informs defendant that he had been arrested without fingerprint analysis or computer forensics being done. That the grand jury was never told anything about fingerprints obtained from the contraband CD ROM's or the results of the computer forensics report because they still had not been analyzed. Defense counsel raised no objections to this evidence being withheld from the grand jury even after they had retained the evidence for over a year before defendant was arrested.

On October 27, 2004, Defense motion for admission of Tom Coghill as defense co-counsel ad hoc vicae was denied for failure to comply with rule 33(d) rules of Supreme Court ARS 17A. Defense counsel raised no objections to motion denied.

U.S. v. Gonzalez-Lopez, July 26, 2006
"The 6th amendment provides that in all criminal prosecutions, the accused shall enjoy the right... to have the assistance of counsel for his defense. We have previously held that an element of this right is the right of the defendant who does not require appointed counsel to choose who will represent him... Where the right to be assisted by counsel of one's choice is wrongly denied, therefore it is unnecessary to conduct an ineffectiveness or prejudicial inquiry to establish a 6th amendment violation. Deprivation is complete when the defendant is erroneously prevented from being represented by the lawyer he wants, regardless of the quality of the representation he received.

On November 3, 2004, defendant was denied his 5th amendment right to assist counsel in the pre-trial questioning of witnesses by the Pima County Attorney's Office. Defense counsel raised no objections over his client's constitutional rights being violated.

U.S. v. Deters, 143 F.3d 577 (10th CIR. 1998)
"When government action deprives a person of life, liberty or property without fair procedures it violates procedural due process."

On November 4, 2004, defendant was denied his 5th amendment right to assist counsel in the pre-trial questioning of witnesses by the Pima County Attorney's Office a second time. Defense counsel raised no objections over his client's constitutional rights being violated.

U.S. v. Deters, 143 F3d 577 (10th CIR 1998)
"When government action deprives a person of life, liberty or property without fair procedures it violates procedural due process."

On November 8, 2004, defendant was denied 5th amendment right to assist counsel in the pre-trial questioning of witnesses by the Pima County Attorney's Office a third time. Defense counsel raised no objections over the denial of his client's constitutional rights.

U.S. v. Deters, 143 F3d 577 (10th CIR 1998)
"When government action deprives a person of life, liberty or property without fair procedures it violates procedural due process."

On May 26, 2005, a motion is filed for release of evidence to defense expert for examination. The court ordered the evidence released.

> Rule 15.1(b) Provision of evidence for expert examination.
> Supplemental disclosure scope.
> "Except as provided by Rule 39(b) the prosecutor shall make available to the defendant the following material and information within the prosecutors possession or control:
>
> (5) A list of all papers, photographs or tangible objects that the prosecutor intends to use at trial or which were obtained from or purportedly belong to the defendant.
>
> Rule 15.1(e) provides:
> Additional disclosure upon request and specification. Unless otherwise ordered by the court, the prosecutor shall within 30 days of a written request make available to the defendant for examination, testing and reproduction the following:
>
> (1) Any item specified in the list submitted under Rule 15.1(b).

On June 20, 2005, the Court files an order to release the evidence to defense expert for examination and testing. Item (1) specifically states, "Not further copying of said materials shall be made absent a Court Order form the Court after a hearing specifying the need for copying." No such hearing ever took place.

On September 20, 2005, the State filed a response to written motion to continue trial stating they "disagreed that the CD's were not made available to defense expert."

On September 27, 2005, Defense Counsel filed a second motion to continue trial. In this motion Defense Counsel states, "for reason the disks were not made available." In violation of:

> ARCP 15.1(e)
> ARS 13-35.1
> ARE 1003
> ARS 13-2409
> Court Order dated 06/20/05

Lambright v. Lewis
U.S. v. Deters
5 USC
28 USC
Judges are not immune

On January 9, 2006, Defense Counsel was forced to file a third motion to continue status conference, stating, "the Pima County Sheriff's Department has failed to turn over the CD disks to the defendant as ordered on December 12, 2005." In violation of:

ARS 13-2409
Court Order dated 06/20/05
Lambright v. Lewis
U.S. v. Deters
5 USC
28 USC
Judges are not immune

On May 2, 2005, the prosecutor copies the hard drives and CD ROM's, in violation of court order, using data compression software to create an image of the evidence that was locked in such a way that defense expert could only look at file titles and dates of file creation. Because the evidence presented to defense expert consisted of locked, data compressed copies, defense expert was unable to use advanced computer forensics software to do a detailed analysis of the evidence. It was impossible for defense expert to use advanced computer forensic software to analyze the copies of the hard drives which forced defense expert to use the forensics report generated by the Pima County Sheriff's Department.

ARS 13-35.1 (J)
"(J) Except as provided below, nothing in this rule shall be construed to require the prosecutor to reproduce or release for testing or examination any items listed in Rule 15.1(b)(5) if the production or possession of the items is otherwise prohibited by ARS 13-35.1. Reproduction of or release for examination and testing shall be subject, in addition to such other terms and conditions ordered by the court in any particular case, to the following restrictions: **(1) the item shall not be further reproduced or distributed except as allowed in the courts order;**

The courts order was to release the evidence to defense expert for examination and testing, not to copy it and distribute it to defense expert. Defendant upon discovering a similar law to Rule 15.1(J) (1) in California asked defense counsel to investigate and determine if an Arizona law similar to the California law existed. Defense counsel failed to comply with clients request. No objection to the violation of Rule 15.1(J) (1) was made to the court because defense counsel had no knowledge of this rule or refused to use it in his client's defense.

Lambright v. Lewis, 932 F. SUPP. 1547 (ARIZ. 1996)
U.S. v. Deters, 143 F.3d 577 (10th CIR. 1998)

On January 13, 2006, Defense Counsel filed a fourth motion to continue trial stating that defense expert received copies of the disks, in violation of:

ARCP 15.(e)
ARS 13-35.1
ARS 13-2407
ARS 13-2409
ARE 1003
Court Order dated 06/20/05
Lambright v. Lewis
U.S. v. Deters
5 USC
28 USC
Judges are not immune

On March 13, 2006, the State modified the indictment without going back to the Grand Jury. In the amendment the file names for all 15 counts were changed to fictitious file names because the @ symbol is missing from all the file names. In addition, the element of the offense of all counts was charged without going back to Grand Jury. New indictment is void. Compare the two indictments.

On March 20, 2006, Defense Counsel stated on the record the following:
Page 3 Line 14 to Page 5 Line 15
By this copying in this manner the Prosecutor, Shawn A Jensvold, effectively sabotaged Defense's examination of the evidence in violation of:
ARS 13-2407 Tampering with public record; classification.
A.   A person commits tampering with a public record if, with the intent to defraud or deceive, such person knowingly:

1. Makes or completes a written instrument, knowing that it has been falsely made, which purports to be a public record or true copy thereof or alters or makes a false entry in a written instrument which is public record or a true copy of a public record; or

2. Presents or uses a written instrument which is or purports to be public record, knowingly that it has been falsely made, with intent that it be taken as genuine; or

3. Records, register or files in a governmental office or agency a written statement which has been falsely made, completed or altered or in which a false entry has been made or which contains a false statement or false information, or

4. Destroys, mutilates, conceals, removes or otherwise impairs the availability of any public record; or

5. Refuses to deliver a public record in such persons possession upon proper request of a public servant entitled to receive such record for examination or other purposes.

B. In this section" public records" means all official books, papers, written instruments or records created, issued, received or kept by others for the information of government.

C. Tampering with a public record is a class 6 felony.

and,

ARS 13-2409 Obstructing criminal investigations or prosecutions; Classification.

A person who knowingly attempts by means of bribery, misrepresentation or force or threats of force to obstruct, delay or prevent the communication of information of testimony relating to a violation of any criminal statute to a peace officer, magistrate, prosecutor or grand jury or who knowingly, injures another in his person or property on account of the giving by the latter or by any other person of any such information or testimony to a peace officer, magistrate, prosecutor or grand jury is guilty of a Class 5 felony.

```
 1         IN THE SUPERIOR COURT OF THE STATE OF ARIZONA

 2              IN AND FOR THE COUNTY OF PIMA

 3
     THE STATE OF ARIZONA,            )
 4                                    )
              Plaintiff,              )
 5                                    )
     vs.                              )    CR-20042573
 6                                    )
                                      )    2 CA-CR 2006-0215
 7   JAMES PRENTISS COGHILL,          )
                                      )
 8            Defendant.              )
                                      )
 9

10   BEFORE:   THE HONORABLE TED B. BOREK
               Judge of the Superior Court
11             Division 24                          DEFENSE

12

13   APPEARANCES:  SHAWN JENSVOLD
                    JONATHAN MOSHER
14                  Deputy County Attorneys
                    on behalf of the State;
15
                    JAMES LAGATTUTA
16                  on behalf of the Defendant.

17

18            REPORTER'S TRANSCRIPT ON APPEAL

19                 JURY TRIAL DAY ONE

20   _____

21                 TUCSON, ARIZONA

22                 MARCH 28, 2006

23                                        SEP19'06 PDA AM10:14

24   Reported By:   CHERYL L. AUSTIN, OFFICIAL

25   RMR, CRR, Certified Reporter #50029
```

1

INDEX

5

6

7

8

9

10

11

12

13

14

15

16

17

18

19

20

21

22

23

24

25

PIMA COUNTY SUPERIOR COURT

```
 1              P R O C E E D I N G S
 2         THE COURT:  This is State of Arizona vs. James
 3  Coghill.
 4         Your client's not here?
 5         MR. LAGATTUTA:  Oh, I'm sorry.  He's outside.
 6         THE COURT:  Bring him in.
 7         (Pause.)
 8         THE COURT:  Okay, this is State of Arizona vs.
 9  James Coghill.  It's CR-20042573.
10         Appearances, please.
11         MR. JENSVOLD:  Shawn Jensvold for the State.
12         MR. LAGATTUTA:  Good morning, your Honor.  Jim
13  Lagattuta with James Coghill, present, out of custody.
14         THE COURT:  Thanks.
15         Mr. Coghill, I spoke with the lawyers in
16  chambers just a few minutes ago.  I gave counsel a copy
17  of a book that has the preliminary instructions in it,
18  and, you know, there's a couple of things that we have to
19  put on or discuss here in court.  So we're in here to do
20  that now.  It has to do with the motions in limine that
21  the State had filed, and so I want to talk that up before
22  we bring the jury in.  Or we could probably do it also
23  later, unless it's going to affect any kind of opening.
24         MR. JENSVOLD:  It might.
25         THE COURT:  Okay.  Why don't we -- I will tell
```

PIMA COUNTY SUPERIOR COURT

1 you that, just as a preliminary thing, your motion in

2 limine has to do mentioning of other pornography files.

3 My reaction is to defer because I need to hear the

4 evidence to see how they fit into the scope of things.

5 Just looking at things here, I don't fully know the

6 answers to that, whether or not some of these things

7 would in fact be relevant. I would think they might be

8 under certain circumstances, but I'm not sure. So I

9 wanted to give you my impression after reading that.

10   I would suspect there's not an objection to some

11 modification of No. 3, the introduction of prior felony

12 if the defendant testifies. And so why don't we take 3

13 first. That might be the easiest.

14   MR. JENSVOLD: You were right. It's actually

15 three felony convictions, and they're all related; either

16 burglary or auto theft. He does have three and not two.

17   MR. LAGATTUTA: Right. Okay. So, yeah, we

18 don't object. In fact, I would ask -- I think you said

19 that to me in a letter. This may have been before you

20 were on the case. I don't have it with me for some

21 reason. I didn't bring that portion of the file.

22   Before we start, if you could just give me the

23 list of the dates and the times of the convictions, and

24 then we're fine.

25   THE COURT: One way to handle it, I understand

```
1    your interest in not prejudicing the defendant, you could
2    say this in terms of prior felony conviction not related
3    to a sex offense rather than even mentioning it was for
4    auto theft.
5           MR. JENSVOLD:  Well, this is for Jacob Franks,
6    the State's witness.
7           THE COURT:  Oh, this is for Mr. Franks, the
8    State's witness?
9           MR. JENSVOLD:  Right.
10          THE COURT:  So if he testifies, you'll have
11   that, and you would indicate what it is that his
12   conviction is?
13          MR. JENSVOLD:  I'm fine with saying what it is.
14          THE COURT:  Okay.  And you have no objection to
15   that?
16          MR. LAGATTUTA:  No.  In fact, I was going to ask
17   myself.
18          And then in looking down the line, I hope that
19   we can rely on this ruling to know that we will be able
20   to get a jury instruction at the end of the case about
21   the instruction that talks --
22          THE COURT:  We have one on credibility of
23   witnesses and the effect of a felony conviction, sure.
24   And we will take up all the jury instructions somewhere
25   down the line, depending where we are and when we think
```

PIMA COUNTY SUPERIOR COURT

1   we can make a good shot at what they all are going to be.
 2   And you have a chance before they go to the jury to make
 3   any argument requesting additional instructions.
 4   With regard to the mentioning -- this is No. 1,
 5   pornography files, Mr. Jensvold, do you want to add to
 6   what you have here?
 7   MR. JENSVOLD: Well, the only thing I would add
 8   is -- the evidence in this case is there were many more
 9   child pornography files than were charged. And Detective
10   Englander and, I assume, Detective Roach, whoever charged
11   this case, had discussed how many files charged. But the
12   mere existence of other child porn files, it's the
13   State's position that that weighs on -- it goes -- it
14   goes against the defense's proposed argument, which I
15   believe is going to be it's Mr. Franks' material other
16   than Mr. Coghill's.
17   Other evidence will show this is Mr. Coghill's
18   RV, he had been there for two months, and Mr. Franks had
19   only been there a week, although there will be evidence
20   that Mr. Franks lived with Mr. Coghill on occasions prior
21   to that. But not to go into not showing any other files
22   or anything, but just to indicate that there were many
23   more of these files present within the defendant's RV.
24   THE COURT: Okay. And the defense's position?
25   MR. LAGATTUTA: Well, your Honor, that's

PIMA COUNTY SUPERIOR COURT

```
 1    evidence of uncharged criminal activity.  What we're
 2    talking about I think in Section No. 1 is the State wants
 3    to be able to say:  Hey, look, we charged Mr. Coghill
 4    with 15 crimes, but we could have charged him with 350
 5    crimes.  That's just not fair because otherwise we
 6    would -- we would be able to prepare a defense against
 7    the other so-and-so number of crimes that are being
 8    mentioned and talked about.
 9           We don't have any intention of talking about
10    other crimes other than those proposed in the Complaint.
11    In fact, we have the right to be on notice about what it
12    is we're being actually charged with.  So, No. 1, which
13    is -- it's actually different.
14           No. 2 I think proposed some unique problem
15    because actually what the State is saying is:  Yeah,
16    there are other crimes, jury, you can consider that; we
17    just didn't go ahead and charge them.  And I think that's
18    contrary to the rules and far too prejudicial.  And in
19    addition to that, had we known, for example, that some of
20    these other things that are mentioned here were to be
21    charged as crimes, in the interview process, you know, we
22    would have gone to further lengths to determine whether
23    they were in violation of the statute, which we had no
24    opportunity to do.
25           THE COURT:  Okay.  I'm going to defer with the
```

PIMA COUNTY SUPERIOR COURT

1   idea that it would be precluded unless somehow it comes

 2   up in the scope of examination, or what have you, and

 3   cross-examination that, you know, that would appear to

 4   make it relevant. And I just have to do that at this

 5   point because when you look at 404 (B), I think that it

 6   certainly could come up to demonstrate what was -- what

 7   the State says.

 8   But on the other hand, we have the other four

 9   charges here. But if there's suggestion there wasn't

10   anything else, the State could come in and say there

11   was -- and part of my reason for deferring on this in

12   this sense also is I don't know how the stuff presumably

13   got there, you know, as far as the knowledge of the

14   computer in order to get it downloaded.

15   And, you know, I think that if there is

16   additional things that are somehow connected to that kind

17   of thing, well, then it may be relevant. And if it's not

18   charged, they're not charged. I have to hear more. For

19   now, for voir dire, you can't get into saying there's

20   more things. But as the evidence goes along, I may allow

21   that to come out.

22   MR. LAGATTUTA: Your Honor, just so I'm clear,

23   because this relates to the other arguments, too,

24   somewhat of a slippery slope because I think what it does

25   is allows the prosecution, you know, a lot more latitude

PIMA COUNTY SUPERIOR COURT

```
1    than the rules do.  Because in this case, one of the
2    main -- the main issue is whether or not my client
3    knowingly possessed these discs, which are CD-ROM discs.
4    And if other issues are brought out that there are other
5    potential crimes or other potential articles of child
6    pornography that were inside this motor home or
7    somewhere, then we all of a sudden not only have to
8    defend against these new charges, but the State gets the
9    unfair advantage of saying our indictment only had 15
10   counts, but it could have had more.
11          And the other thing is this issue of possession
12   and knowing possession is going to be very central to the
13   case.  And if the Court is saying, "Well, I want to hear
14   some of the evidence about how everything was going in
15   there," I would just point out that I think it's
16   important to be cautious about when you hear this
17   evidence whether to decide automatically, simply because
18   my client was the owner of this motor home where the
19   evidence was found, where the liability -- criminal
20   liability automatically shifts to him, because there is
21   another person involved in the case.
22          THE COURT:  Well, I stand where I am.  Don't
23   mention in the opening and voir dire, and I'm going to
24   defer on ruling on whether or not any of these things
25   would be relevant to how the case develops.
```

PIMA COUNTY SUPERIOR COURT

```
 1          MR. LAGATTUTA:  Just so -- does that include --
 2     are you telling the prosecutor to instruct his witnesses
 3     not to go into those areas?  Because sometimes what
 4     happens is we discuss these things, and then the witness
 5     doesn't know about it, and all of a sudden it pops out
 6     and --
 7          THE COURT:  Well, I would agree with that right
 8     at this point.
 9          MR. JENSVOLD:  I'll make a note.
10          THE COURT:  Now, on cross-examination that's a
11     different thing.  So if you open the door --
12          MR. LAGATTUTA:  I understand that.
13          THE COURT:  If you open the door somehow or
14     other, then that's where -- that's another reason why I'm
15     deferring.
16          MR. LAGATTUTA:  Okay.
17          THE COURT:  Because I want to be clear about
18     that.
19          MR. LAGATTUTA:  All right.
20          THE COURT:  And then the second part of this was
21     introductory of compact discs, defendant computer located
22     within -- that's kind of the same thing, and I'm not sure
23     whether -- what your distinction there is, Mr. Jensvold?
24          MR. JENSVOLD:  I would agree that at least the
25     whole theory behind -- my theory behind doing this is the
```

PIMA COUNTY SUPERIOR COURT

1   time in which Mr. Franks was in the motor home is going

2   to be key; the argument as to whether he had, you know,

3   time to do all this kind of thing.

4   As for the adult pornography, in both

5   Mr. Franks' and Mr. Coghill's interviews, they both admit

6   to having downloaded or watched adult pornography. And

7   so mainly -- well, there's a distinction between the

8   first argument about just the general adult pornography

9   files being on the computer and the stuff that's within,

10   you know, the specific KaZaA light My Share folder issue,

11   which the State's position is right now, as far as I can

12   tell, there's a pattern of use through the KaZaA program

13   that quite frankly corresponds to Mr. Franks that

14   includes various music files as well as a block of time

15   where there was some pornography viewed. But it appears

16   to all be adult pornography or significantly different

17   than the type of files that were charged in this case,

18   and --

19   THE COURT: So if -- see, again, it's hard for

20   me to rule without hearing the evidence on these things.

21   It seems to me that you're saying that you agree that

22   Franks brought down adult pornography.

23   MR. JENSVOLD: He didn't bring it down. He was

24   looking at it on the computer.

25   THE COURT: Okay. Well, I just have to hear

PIMA COUNTY SUPERIOR COURT

```
 1    also, because I can't sit here now and know the
 2    significance of the computer downloading and how it might
 3    relate.  And, you know, I know there are firewalls and
 4    stuff like that that you end up getting into, so it's
 5    just impossible for me to rule right now on these things
 6    until I hear what the evidence is and whether or not
 7    somehow or other the fact that adult pornography comes
 8    down out of the same kind of area on the computer -- and
 9    I'm not being articulate very well with this.  You've got
10    computer experts to describe that would connect up to one
11    of these people or the other one.  That's the kind of
12    stuff I need to hear.
13           If it comes from the same kind of place, it
14    might be relevant that it would have to come out or it
15    could come out.
16           MR. LAGATTUTA:  Your Honor, here's the main
17    distinction from my perspective, both -- two contentions.
18    The adult pornography that the county attorney is talking
19    about that is allegedly found in the motor home and
20    whatnot, this is not -- oddly enough, it's not against
21    the law to possess those.
22           THE COURT:  Sure.
23           MR. LAGATTUTA:  So this is kind of a whole
24    different realm.  This is really more sort of 404 (B)
25    evidence where if the county attorney is saying:  Well,
```

PIMA COUNTY SUPERIOR COURT

1   you know, if Mr. Cog- -- if we can show Mr. Coghill had

2   possession of certain adult pornography, then that may

3   tend to lead us to believe that he may have had

4   possession of some other things that may have been a

5   crime. First of all, there isn't an expert in the case

6   that can make that statement.

7   Second of all, that isn't the type of disclosure

8   that we -- we have never had that so far in the case in

9   terms of how we understand the witnesses are going to

10   testify the theory of the case is. So I think it's

11   inappropriate to bring it in now. And again, it's --

12   it's another slippery slope because it just opens the

13   door to, I think, a lot of prejudicial information that

14   comes before the jury. I mean, I think we all recognize

15   that, you know, pornography is not a subject that's

16   easily and well received by everybody. In this case, it

17   doesn't really need to be.

18   There's another portion of it that also I think

19   the Court needs to consider, and that is I tried looking

20   through most of the interviews last night of the taped

21   interviews. When I talked to -- my recollection talking

22   to some of the officers, they gathered a lot of material

23   out of this motor home. I don't recall all of them

24   telling me that they actually viewed all these things.

25   So I think we're in a position where at least even some

PIMA COUNTY SUPERIOR COURT

1   of the things mentioned in the motion, I don't know that

2   a foundation can be laid that -- of the search was made,

3   a disc was found that had a name on it that sounds --

4   sounds dirty, but it really might not be because it's

5   never been viewed. Now all of a sudden this information

6   is in front of the jury, and it's not substantiated.

7   THE COURT: Well, I'm going to right now say

8   don't get into the adult pornography either, and then

9   I'll have to -- you know, in your openings and what have

10   you. But as you bring in your witnesses -- except I hear

11   that he's made an admission with regard to downloading.

12   I think that's -- I wouldn't preclude that. You know, if

13   he's downloaded these things, and he said that he has

14   done some downloading, that's an admission that I think

15   is admissible.

16   MR. JENSVOLD: For Mr. Franks or -- because,

17   frankly, they both -- both Mr. Coghill and Mr. Franks

18   admit that they were downloading pornography.

19   THE COURT: I think that relates to the

20   defendant. That's where I'm talking about. Someone who

21   is not on trial I'm not concerned about, quite honestly.

22   So, you know, that's your ballgame for him, and that's

23   not -- as Mr. Lagattuta points out, that's not a

24   violation of any kind of law to download adult

25   pornography, and so you can go into that.

PIMA COUNTY SUPERIOR COURT

```
 1        But as far as -- and, again, I'm just going to
 2   defer until I hear because I'm not sure how it might in
 3   fact be connected up as far as adult pornography.
 4   Somehow or other there's a connection in the way the
 5   computer -- you can download the stuff from the computer
 6   as far as adult and child pornography, then it might be
 7   relevant.  Otherwise, it may not be.  So I have to hear
 8   more evidence, you know, an awful lot more about the
 9   case.
10        MR. JENSVOLD:  Just so I'm clear, Mr. Coghill,
11   in the interview with Detective Englander, says:  Yeah, I
12   downloaded pornography, stored it in a particular file,
13   but it's all adult porn.  He denies he had any child
14   porn.  He's admitting to something that's not charged,
15   but it's very closely related to -- sort of a denial of
16   the charges in this case as well.
17        MR. LAGATTUTA:  Well, your Honor, my quick point
18   is this:  There is no relation -- there's no one --
19   there's no one in this case that can come in and say that
20   there is a relation between a person who does the viewing
21   of adult -- a person who does a legal activity and this
22   illegal activity.  There's no one that can cross that
23   bridge.  No witnesses in this case are qualified to do
24   that.
25        So now we're on a slope where the prosecution
```

PIMA COUNTY SUPERIOR COURT

1   brings out this argument specifically, if you think about
2   it, to prejudice my client by saying here's someone who
3   does something. It's actually perfectly legal, but it
4   somehow may be related to his tendency to commit a crime.
5   There's no bridge there. It sounds similar, but there's
6   no bridge.
7   THE COURT: The bridge to me is if it's somehow
8   in the computer. Are you going to have any evidence that
9   the computer connection --
10   MR. JENSVOLD: Yes.
11   THE COURT: You --
12   MR. JENSVOLD: And just to respond. Detective
13 Englander went CD by CD. That evidence had been
14 disclosed where he found contraband and adult
15 pornography. The complete hard drive has been disclosed
16 way prior to today.
17   THE COURT: Again, that's part of the link. And
18 if the link is somehow or other the computer -- that, you
19 know, the downloading would demonstrate that the
20 capability of downloading child porn from the places,
21 then I have to hear the evidence.
22   Again, I'm going to -- well, for the purposes of
23 voir dire and what have you, don't get into any adult
24 pornography, and then don't get into it with your
25 witnesses until you raise it with me to see whether or

PIMA COUNTY SUPERIOR COURT

```
 1   not it's gotten to the point where I think it's relevant
 2   and should clearly be allowed to come in.  You're saying
 3   it's your motions.  I'm siding with the defense with
 4   regard to disclosing and submitting evidence on that
 5   until I've heard enough evidence to know whether or not
 6   it can come in.  Okay?  So preclude but defer right at
 7   this point.
 8           Anything further?
 9           MR. LAGATTUTA:  Your Honor, as to the suggestion
10   or the offer the Court made about my client's father, Tom
11   Coghill, he is a licensed member of two bars.  I don't
12   have a case agent, per se, or assistant from my office.
13   The Court made the offer that if he were not to actually
14   testify in the case, that he could assist me during the
15   jury selection.  I'm wondering if he could stay for the
16   balance of the trial?
17           THE COURT:  Well, my inclination was just for
18   the jury selection, and that's out of the -- and
19   Mr. Jensvold hasn't been heard on that.  My idea is you
20   would -- you can often have someone who is a jury
21   consultant, for example, to come in.  And I think family
22   members are here, and you'd like to have somebody with
23   his experience as a lawyer sit with you for the jury
24   selection part, just to eliminate the crowdedness in the
25   courtroom, that I would be inclined to that.
```

PIMA COUNTY SUPERIOR COURT

1   But I don't know if the State would agree or
2 disagree with that, and certainly if he's going to be a
3 witness I don't think he can.
4   MR. LAGATTUTA: Right. This would be a choice
5 we would make. My question is: Given the fact that -- I
6 think we would normally be entitled to -- if I had a
7 private investigator, if I had a case agent or an
8 assistant from my office, I think the Court would
9 normally allow them to at least sit at the table and --
10 during the balance of the trial.
11   MR. JENSVOLD: I don't have a problem with that.
12 The only problem I would have is him testifying at this
13 late of date, especially considering -- I don't think --
14 I'm not sure whether his testimony would be necessary the
15 way Mr. Lagattuta has phrased it so far.
16   THE COURT: Where is he licensed to practice?
17   THE DEFENDANT: Missouri and Illinois.
18   MR. LAGATTUTA: Missouri and Illinois.
19   THE COURT: So you don't have any objection if
20 he's in here as a case agent?
21   MR. JENSVOLD: No, that's fine.
22   THE COURT: Okay. With that, the choice is to
23 have him with you during the course of the trial. And
24 you can introduce him as your assistant, I suspect. You
25 don't have to get into his qualifications and what have

PIMA COUNTY SUPERIOR COURT

1 you. But -- and without objection, he can stay, but it
2 is a choice. If he's here -- he's either here as a
3 witness or -- in which case the rule has been invoked;
4 he's going to be outside. Otherwise, he can be here as
5 your assistant.
6   MR. LAGATTUTA: Very good. Thank you.
7   THE COURT: So which are you going to do?
8   MR. LAGATTUTA: I'm going to ask him, and I'll
9 be back in two seconds.
10   (Pause.)
11   MR. LAGATTUTA: My legal assistant.
12   THE COURT: Then, Mr. Coghill -- I understand
13 that's your name?
14   MR. THOMAS COGHILL: Right.
15   THE COURT: And given a choice here --
16   MR. THOMAS COGHILL: Thank you.
17   THE COURT: Given a choice to Mr. Lagattuta --
18 it's Mr. Colburn?
19   MR. THOMAS COGHILL: Coghill. That's the firm.
20 I am not one of the two names, your Honor.
21   THE COURT: You realize you're here to only help
22 him, so you don't have a right to do any examination or
23 anything like that. But really in deference to all the
24 family members here, I wanted you to have a chance to be
25 in here because we're going to have full folks. You can

```
 1    assist with the jury selection.

 2            MR. THOMAS COGHILL:  I appreciate that.

 3            THE COURT:  And the State didn't object to that

 4    either.

 5            So, Peter, if there's nothing else, we can you

 6    can bring the jurors.

 7                (Whereupon, the prospective jury panel

 8                entered the courtroom.)

 9            THE COURT:  We're going to need to keep the

10    front row open at first.  Some people are going to be

11    standing at first, but bear with us and we'll move things

12    on here.

13            We have more jurors than we have seats, and I

14    apologize for that.  We're going to try to move quickly

15    through this.  But if you are in a medical situation that

16    you absolutely need to have a seat, please come on in and

17    we'll ask one of the people to be seated.  You do need to

18    keep the front open and take parts on both sides as you

19    come in.

20            Need to keep the front row open.  Sorry, sir.

21    Just if you stand on the side, sir.  See where those

22    seats are?  We need to have those for jurors that we're

23    going to call in a few minutes.  I know it's going to be

24    crowded.  We have more of you than I have seats for right

25    now.  We will try to move expeditiously through.  But if
```

PIMA COUNTY SUPERIOR COURT

1 you could come in, we're going to have a few more seats
2 open up here.
3   Just sort of move to the side and stand there.
4 I appreciate it. For a number of you, Peter has asked
5 you to come last, and we'll have seats pretty quickly.
6 But if you could bear with us and bear with me here,
7 please.
8   Peter, we've got everybody?
9   Ladies and gentlemen, this is time set for trial
10 in Cause No. CR-20042573.
11   The State ready to proceed?
12   MR. JENSVOLD: Yes, your Honor.
13   THE COURT: Defense ready to proceed?
14   MR. LAGATTUTA: Good morning, your Honor. We're
15 ready to proceed.
16   THE COURT: Okay. You all can be seated,
17 please.
18   And I'm going to ask all the jurors now to
19 stand, please, if you can.
20   (Whereupon, the prospective jury panel was
21   sworn.)
22   THE COURT: Thanks. You can be seated now, if
23 you have a seat. I really apologize for the seating that
24 we have, but we have more people today for this trial
25 than we have seats.

PIMA COUNTY SUPERIOR COURT

1   So we're going to try to call 26 of you forward.

 2   As you come forward, you can come forward on either side.

 3   Peter will direct you to where we have seats. We'll be

 4   seated here from right to left in the back row, right to

 5   left here, and then in the row right behind the bar for

 6   the rest of you. And the others, as we proceed along, I

 7   think you'll see that we may have some people that we'll

 8   be excusing.

 9   So with that, Marty, please call the first 26.

10   THE CLERK: Ronda Buchanan, Edward Massey,

11   Richard Theiss, Siebo Friesenborg, Charles Loding, Donald

12   Escalante, Patty Perez, Andrea Taylor, Teresa Carrillo.

13   THE COURT: Ms. Carrillo here?

14   THE CLERK: Teresa Carrillo, Irene Noriega,

15   Ronald Smith, Lisa Richardson, Denise Coffey, Stephanie

16   Levy, Robert Storie, Tamara Nichelson, Matthew Alexander,

17   Amy Fee, Victor Cardenas, Esmeralda Villalobos, Maria

18   Gonzales, Nyla Contreras, Esperanza Saucedo, Mary O'Hara,

19   Reed Peterson, James Salmen.

20   THE COURT: Thanks. I know some of you don't

21   have seats still. I'm just going to ask you to bear with

22   us. I think it will move along, and we'll find seats as

23   people move out of here. You can take a couple of seats

24   here. And if anyone is in a situation where you

25   absolutely have to have a seat, tell Peter and we'll try

PIMA COUNTY SUPERIOR COURT

1   to get an exchange.

2   Ladies and gentlemen, we're going to now ask

3   jurors that have been called a number of questions about

4   yourselves. These questions aren't designed to pry

5   unnecessarily into your personal lives, and I hope they

6   don't do that. Technically, this process is called "voir

7   dire," and it simply means to see or to speak. We ask

8   you just to tell us the truth.

9   It's necessary for the lawyers or me to ask you

10   some questions to find out if you have any knowledge

11   about this case or about any of the persons who might be

12   involved in the case. We also ask these questions to

13   find out if you have any preconceived opinions about the

14   case which you might find it difficult to lay aside. And

15   also to find out if you have had any personal or family

16   experiences that might cause you to identify yourselves

17   with any of the parties.

18   In other words, we need to ask these questions

19   to do all we can to assure each of the parties that the

20   jurors who will be selected to decide the case can be

21   fair and impartial. So please don't withhold any

22   information in order to be seated on the jury, and do not

23   be concerned with whether your answer is right or wrong.

24   This isn't any sort of test. Please just be honest and

25   candid in your answers, and do not be concerned with what

PIMA COUNTY SUPERIOR COURT

1   you feel the lawyers or I might want to hear from you.

2   Now, if I ask you a question or the lawyers ask

3   you a question of the whole panel and your answer is no,

4   then you need do nothing. However, if your answer is

5   yes, please raise your hand, and when I call on you I

6   will ask you some additional questions. When I call on

7   you, please state your name before answering if I don't

8   do that. Sometimes I do, as I have a list. However,

9   Cheryl, the court reporter here, needs to hear the names

10   of the persons who are answering the questions, and so we

11   need to have the name on the record.

12   Now, if at any time I ask a question, but for

13   whatever reason you don't want to answer that in open

14   court, please raise your hand anyway. When I call on

15   you, say you have a yes answer and prefer to answer it in

16   private. That can be done at the appropriate time. I'll

17   ask the juror probably with the lawyers also to come up,

18   and we'll probably talk to you here at the bench. And if

19   necessary, we can also go into the office that I have

20   behind me here.

21   Now, I have a mike here, and I hope it's on at

22   the right times and off at the right times, so I ask

23   jurors to help with this. If I'm having a bench

24   conference and it's on and it should be off, wave, do

25   something, get my attention, stand up. And if it's not

PIMA COUNTY SUPERIOR COURT

1   on when it needs to be on, because sometimes I forget to

2   turn it on after we've had a conference, I ask you to let

3   me know that too. For the folks right here close that

4   might hear, I ask you to direct your attention elsewhere

5   and try not to listen to what we're talking about, and

6   that affords some privacy to members that do come up.

7   Now, for those that haven't been called, first I

8   apologize to have you stand now.

9   This is a 15-count indictment. It's going to

10   take us a few minutes to go through it, but I believe

11   some will be excused. And if I excuse any of you from

12   the panel, you have to go back down to the jury

13   commissioner's office and tell them that you've been

14   excused from this jury.

15   For those whose names haven't been called, you

16   don't have to answer questions now, and that's the first

17   26. But make a mental note of any questions you would

18   make a yes answer to because as you are called forward,

19   the first thing I'll ask you is if you have a yes answer

20   to any of the questions that I've asked up to that point.

21   I want to quickly introduce the people who will

22   be participating in the trial.

23   Peter Shackter you've already met. He's our

24   bailiff. He works with the jury, getting you into the

25   courtroom and what have you, if you're selected to sit on

PIMA COUNTY SUPERIOR COURT

```
 1    this jury.  He'll take you to the jury room and handle
 2    exhibits and things like that for you during
 3    deliberations.

 4           Someone not in the courtroom who might
 5    substitute for Peter is Joyce Burbridge.  She's my
 6    judicial assistant, and she can substitute for Peter.
 7    And she would also be the one who, if you were to call
 8    the court and need to talk to somebody during the course
 9    of the trial, you would probably talk to.

10           Marty is our court clerk.  She keeps the
11    official records, handles the exhibits, and swears
12    witnesses and jurors as you recognize that she's already
13    done.

14           Right in front of me is Cheryl.  She's our court
15    reporter.  She takes down everything that is said so we
16    have a word-for-word record.  If I'm speaking too softly
17    and you see a pained expression on her face, let me know
18    because I'll need to speak up.  And I'll ask you to speak
19    up, too, as we go along.

20           My name is Ted Borek, and I'm the judge for
21    Division 24.

22           The State in this case is represented by Shawn
23    Jensvold.

24           Mr. Jensvold.

25           He's in the Pima County Attorney's Office.
```

PIMA COUNTY SUPERIOR COURT

```
 1              First question.  Does anybody know Mr. Jensvold?
 2    Does anybody have a regular either professional or
 3    personal relationship with anybody in the county
 4    attorney's office that's ongoing?
 5              Yes, sir, Mr. Alexander.
 6              PROSPECTIVE JUROR:  Yes, sir.  Tucson Police
 7    Department.
 8              THE COURT:  You're in the Tucson Police
 9    Department?
10              PROSPECTIVE JUROR:  Yes, I am.
11              THE COURT:  Okay.  What area are you in, sir?
12              PROSPECTIVE JUROR:  I work for bikes, but we
13    have cases that come before them occasionally.
14              THE COURT:  Okay.
15              PROSPECTIVE JUROR:  On a regular basis.
16              THE COURT:  So you don't know anything about
17    this case yet.  But just the fact that you are in the
18    Tucson Police Department and what have you and work with
19    the county attorney's office, would that cause you to
20    favor one side or the other in this case?
21              PROSPECTIVE JUROR:  No.
22              THE COURT:  Can you be fair and impartial in
23    determining this case and judging it only based on the
24    evidence presented in this case?
25              PROSPECTIVE JUROR:  I can.
```

PIMA COUNTY SUPERIOR COURT

```
1          MR. JENSVOLD:  There was a hand that went up in
2    the back.
3          THE COURT:  For the first 26, remember, if
4    there's a hand that went up, remember you have a yes
5    answer, and I'll get to that as we go on if you are
6    called forward.
7          The defendant in this case is represented by
8    James Lagattuta.
9          Mr. Lagattuta.
10         Does anybody know Mr. Lagattuta?
11         Apparently not.
12         Sir, would you like to introduce your client and
13   also your assistant, there?
14         MR. LAGATTUTA:  Ladies and gentlemen, my client
15   is James Coghill.
16         James, stand up, please.
17         THE COURT:  Anybody know Mr. Coghill?
18         Apparently not.
19         MR. LAGATTUTA:  And my legal assistant today is
20   Thomas Coghill.
21         THE COURT:  Anybody know Mr. Thomas Coghill?
22         Apparently not.
23         Thanks, please be seated.
24         I know that jury service is an inconvenience to
25   all of you to one extent or another.  It's very
```

PIMA COUNTY SUPERIOR COURT

1   important, of course, that you serve in the capacity.

2   You will be the deciders of the guilt or innocence of

3   Mr. Coghill. You will make the determination of the

4   facts. Some people say direct democracy at work, and

5   it's a privilege living in our country. And I hope that

6   certainly you will take it seriously. It's very

7   important to the whole process that we have a fair and

8   impartial jury.

9   I want to tell you a little bit about the

10 schedule for the case. We expect this case probably to

11 be to you Friday of this week, but it's going to be all

12 week and it may conceivably go into Monday or Tuesday of

13 next week, and that would depend on where we are. So it

14 could end on Friday, but it might go into next week. So

15 if you have plans for the weekend that take you out of

16 state next week or something like that, I want -- I want

17 to know about that.

18   We will normally begin at 10:30. I know this

19 has been a long day for you already. We usually go from

20 10:30 to 5. I try to end between 4:30 and 5. We'll take

21 an hour and a half lunch break between 12 and 1:30, and

22 then we'll take a short afternoon break also as we get

23 into dealing with the case and exhibits and witnesses and

24 things.

25   Now, I have to apply a standard that I can

PIMA COUNTY SUPERIOR COURT

1   excuse you from jury service only if a juror demonstrates

2   they're incapable of performing jury service due to a

3   mental or physical condition or because jury service

4   would substantially and materially affect either the

5   public interest or welfare in an adverse manner or would

6   cause undue or extreme physical or financial hardship

7   either to the juror or to someone under the juror's care.

8   An example of something that would be a basis

9   for me to excuse you would be if you don't understand the

10   English language. All our testimony and any exhibits and

11   what have you here will be in English. That's our

12   primary language. So if anybody fits that category, that

13   would be an example of why I'm able to excuse you.

14   So with this in mind, the standard that I have

15   to apply, is there anyone here who, based on the

16   anticipated length, daily schedule of the trial presents

17   such a problem, either personal, business, or health that

18   is significant enough for you to ask to be excused from

19   this jury?

20   First, Mr. Massey.

21   PROSPECTIVE JUROR: Yes, sir. It's my fifth

22   week, my second open heart surgery recovery, and a

23   six-day -- six-hour-a-day situation would be quite

24   fatiguing.

25   THE COURT: Sir, please go back down to the jury

PIMA COUNTY SUPERIOR COURT

```
1    commissioner.  I'm going to excuse you from this trial.
2    You can just let them know that, and they might keep you
3    for a shorter trial.  I appreciate you being here now.
4    And good luck on your recovery.
5            And, Mr. Escalante.
6            PROSPECTIVE JUROR:  Yes, sir, I work two jobs.
7    So a week-long thing would seriously alter my family --
8            THE COURT:  Okay, I appreciate knowing that.
9            Are you the sole source of income for your
10   family?
11           PROSPECTIVE JUROR:  Yes, sir.
12           THE COURT:  It would be a financial difficulty?
13           PROSPECTIVE JUROR:  Yes, sir.
14           THE COURT:  I'll come back to you.
15           Anybody else in the back row?
16           Front row, Ms. Levy.
17           PROSPECTIVE JUROR:  Yes, I have a psychiatrist
18   appointment on Monday regarding my -- mental -- more like
19   physical health being which was due to an accident.
20   Previously, on St. Patrick's Day, I cut my arm and I had
21   to carry through.
22           THE COURT:  That's next Monday, a week from
23   today?
24           PROSPECTIVE JUROR:  Yes.
25           THE COURT:  Thank you, ma'am.  I'll come back to
```

PIMA COUNTY SUPERIOR COURT

1   you.

2   Anybody else in the front row?

3   Okay, then I'll excuse both of you.

4   Mr. Escalante, we're not here to not have you have a job.

5   And Ms. Levy, with the medical appointment, just the same

6   as Mr. Massey, I'll excuse you and good luck with your

7   appointments.

8   So we'll replace first Juror No. 2, Mr. Massey.

9   THE CLERK: Terri Parcelluzzi.

10   THE COURT: If you're called forward, I have a

11   sheet that you need to give Peter, so if you could bring

12   that out.

13   And the seats open up, I hope others feel free

14   to take that.

15   We'll replace also Juror No. 6, Mr. Escalante.

16   THE CLERK: Angela Charette.

17   THE COURT: And replace next Juror No. 14,

18   Mr. Levy.

19   THE CLERK: Richard Johnson.

20   THE COURT: Front row here, Mr. Johnson.

21   All right. To the you three of you that just

22   joined us, any scheduling problem?

23   Okay, I see no hands raised. Thank you.

24   Ladies and gentlemen, the defendant's pled not

25   guilty to the charges in this case. I'm going to read

PIMA COUNTY SUPERIOR COURT

1   those to you. I understand that the incident in this

2   case took place in the area of 3356 East Benson Highway,

3   and I'm going to ask some follow-on questions after I

4   read the indictment to you.

5   It's, of course, in the case involving State of

6   Arizona vs. James Coghill, and Case No. is 20042573. As

7   I say, there are 15 counts here, so I'm going to read

8   them to you now.

9   Count One is sexual exploitation of a minor

10   under 15. On or about the 1st day of April, 2003, James

11   Coghill knowingly committed sexual exploitation of a

12   minor by receiving, possessing or exchanging any visual

13   depiction in which a minor, under 15 years of age, is

14   engaged in exploitive exhibition or other sexual conduct,

15   to wit: a video and/or movie showing an adult perhaps

16   female performing oral sex on a prepubescent girl and an

17   adult male engaged in penile slash vaginal intercourse

18   with a prepubescent female located on a CD -- on CD in a

19   file entitled, quotation, R at gold style hyphen

20   Lucy.mpg, end quotation, in violation of Arizona Revised

21   Statutes.

22   Count Two, sexual exploitation of a minor under

23   15. On or about the 1st day of April, 2003, James

24   Coghill knowingly committed sexual exploitation of a

25   minor by receiving, possessing, or exchanging any visual

PIMA COUNTY SUPERIOR COURT

```
 1   depiction in which a minor, under 15 years of age, is
 2   engaged in exploitive exhibition or other sexual conduct,
 3   to wit: a movie and/or video depicting a prepubescent
 4   female performing oral sex on an adult male, contained on
 5   CD file, quotation, R at gold style BabyJ 3yo girl eats
 6   c-u-m2.mpg, end quotation, in violation of Arizona
 7   Revised Statutes.
 8            Count Three, sexual exploitation of a minor
 9   under 15.  On or about the 1st day of April, 2003, James
10   Coghill knowingly committed sexual exploitation of a
11   minor by receiving, possessing, or exchanging any visual
12   depiction in which a minor, under 15 years of age, is
13   engaged in exploitive exhibition or other sexual conduct,
14   to wit: a movie and/or video depicting a prepubescent
15   girl masturbating and have a dildo inserted in her anus,
16   contained on CD on a file entitled, quotation, R at gold
17   underline i-l-i-k-e-i-t period mpg, in violation of
18   Arizona Revised Statutes.
19            Count Four, sexual exploitation of a minor under
20   15.  On or about the 1st day of April, 2003, James
21   Coghill knowingly committed sexual exploitation of a
22   minor by receiving, possessing or exchanging any visual
23   depiction in which a minor, under 15 years of age, is
24   engaged in exploitive exhibition or other sexual conduct,
25   to wit: a movie and/or video depicting an adult male
```

PIMA COUNTY SUPERIOR COURT

1 attempting to vaginally penetrate a prepubescent female

2 contained on CD file, quotation, Vicky complete.mpg, end

3 quotation, in violation of Arizona Revised Statutes.

4   Count Five -- this is the last time I'm going to

5 read the first line until I get to a count where there

6 might be any difference. But the first lines up to "to

7 wit:" are essentially the same as in all counts, so I

8 think you've gotten the idea what the charges are. Any

9 jurors who are selected to try the case will have a copy.

10 I'm not going to read that first part again. This is the

11 last time I'll read that to the end because it's

12 repetitive in all counts.

13   But as to Count Five, sexual exploitation of a

14 minor, and this part is consistent up until Count

15 Fifteen, it says: On or about the 1st day of April,

16 2003, James Coghill knowingly committed sexual

17 exploitation of a minor by receiving, possessing or

18 exchanging any visual depiction in which a minor, under

19 15 years of age, is engaged in exploitive exhibition or

20 sexual conduct, to wit: -- and then this will change from

21 this point on, and this is what I'm going to read -- a

22 movie and/or video depicting two prepubescent males

23 masturbating each other and an adult male contained on CD

24 on file, quotation, R at gold russian 2 preteen boys

25 sucking one teen boy paren 2.mpg, in violation of Arizona

PIMA COUNTY SUPERIOR COURT

```
1    Revised Statutes.

2          Count Six reads the same as previously to the to

3    wit.  To wit follows: a movie and/or video depicting a

4    prepubescent female performing oral sex on an adult male

5    contained on CD in file, quotation, Reel Kiddy M-o-v dash

6    Vicky Sucking, paren, New.mpg, end quotation, in

7    violation of Arizona Revised Statutes.

8          Count Seven, after the to wit: a movie and/or

9    video depicting an adult male ejaculating into the mouth

10   of a prepubescent female contained on CD file, quotation,

11   Vicky underline good underline daughter underline 2.mpg,

12   end quotation, in violation of Arizona Revised Statutes.

13         Count Eight, the same up to the to wit: a movie

14   and/or video depicting a prepubescent female masturbating

15   and performing oral sex on an adult male contained on CD

16   in file, quotation, R at gold style hyphen RCA3, paren,

17   1, end paren, paren, 1, end paren, period mpg, end

18   quotation, in violation of Arizona Revised Statutes.

19         Count Nine, sexual exploitation of a minor --

20   it's the same.  Sexual exploitation of a minor, and it

21   reads the same up to the to wit, which follows, to wit: a

22   movie and/or video depicting a prepubescent female

23   stripping, displaying her genitals, and performing oral

24   sex on an adult male contained on CD in file, quotation,

25   R at gold underline tvg013bound period mpg, end
```

PIMA COUNTY SUPERIOR COURT

1   quotation, in violation of Arizona Revised Statutes.

2   Count Ten, same -- sexual exploitation of a

3   minor, same up to the to wit which reads: a movie and/or

4   video depicting an adult male ejaculating into the mouth

5   of a partially clothed prepubescent female contained on

6   CD in file, quotation, BabyJ hyphen b-a-b-y-c-u-m period

7   mpg, end quotation, in violation of Arizona Revised

8   Statutes.

9   Count Eleven, sexual exploitation of a minor

10   under 15 same up to the to wit: a movie and/or video

11   depicting a bound prepubescent female vaginally, anally,

12   and digitally penetrated by an adult male contained on CD

13   in file, quotation, BabyJ hyphen Captive period avi, end

14   quotation, in violation of Arizona Revised Statutes.

15   Count Twelve, sexual exploitation of a minor

16   under 15 reads the same up to to wit: a movie and/or

17   video depicting a prepubescent female performing oral sex

18   on an adult male contained in -- on CD in file,

19   quotation, Baby Joe (sic) hyphen LO1 dash 01.avi, end

20   quotation, in violation of Arizona Revised Statutes.

21   Count Thirteen, same sexual exploitation of a

22   minor under 15 up to the to wit: a movie and/or video

23   depicting a prepubescent female performing oral sex on an

24   adult male contained in CD in file, quotation, BabyJ

25   hyphen Teddy.mpg, end quotation, in violation of Arizona

PIMA COUNTY SUPERIOR COURT

1   Revised Statutes.

2   Count Fourteen, sexual exploitation of a minor

3   under 15 the same up to to wit: a movie and/or video

4   depicting a prepubescent female taking off her underwear,

5   masturbating, and being vaginally penetrated by an adult

6   male contained on CD in file, quotation, R at gold BabyJ

7   period Compilation 776394eof0380a88af26e53b9de -- I'm

8   sorry, that's debe739083.mpg, end quotation, in violation

9   of Arizona Revised Statutes.

10   Count Fifteen, sexual exploitation of a minor

11 under 15 in the second degree. It says: On or about the

12 1st day of April, 2003, James Coghill knowingly committed

13 sexual exploitation of a minor in the second degree by

14 attempting to receive, possess, or exchange any visual

15 depiction in which a minor under 15 years of age is

16 engaged in exploitive exhibition or other sexual conduct,

17 to wit: videos and/or movies depicting multiple scenes of

18 prepubescent males and females engaged in various sexual

19 acts with each other, contained in, quotation, R at gold

20 style hyphen Open underline 111 dash Trade Only comma No

21 Exceptions exclamation, exclamation, exclamation point

22 period mpg, end quotation, in violation of Arizona

23 Revised Statutes.

24   The defendant, as I said, has pled not guilty to

25 the counts in this charge.

PIMA COUNTY SUPERIOR COURT

```
 1              The very first question that I'd like to ask
 2    after reading these is have any of you ever seen, heard,
 3    or read anything about this case or have you heard anyone
 4    express an opinion about it?
 5              And I see no hands.
 6              Have any of you or members of your family or
 7    close friends ever been involved in any way in a case
 8    such as this?
 9              A couple folks.  Let me go first, Mr. Salmen.
10              PROSPECTIVE JUROR:  Salmen.  May I approach the
11    bench, please?
12              THE COURT:  Sure.
13              Counsel approach, please.
14                (Bench conference.)
15              PROSPECTIVE JUROR:  I'm a convicted sex
16    offender.
17              THE COURT:  Okay.  I think that does it.  I'll
18    excuse you, unless there's any objection by counsel.
19              MR. LAGATTUTA:  I'm sorry, I didn't hear.
20              THE COURT:  He's a convicted sex offender.
21              Thank you, sir, for being here.
22              Why don't you all stay here for a minute.
23                (Open court.)
24              THE COURT:  I think Ms. O'Hara was next.
25                (Bench conference.)
```

PIMA COUNTY SUPERIOR COURT

```
1          THE COURT:  My daughter was sexually molested,
2     and I feel I cannot be fair and impartial.
3          THE COURT:  I'll excuse you.
4          I'm going to tell you, anybody I excuse, if you
5     have an objection to me doing that, tell me as we go
6     along.
7          Thanks for being here, ma'am.  I appreciate it.
8               (Open court.)
9          THE COURT:  And, then, Ms. Contreras, I think
10    you had your hand up also.  You can answer there or come
11    up.  Thank you.
12              (Bench conference.)
13         PROSPECTIVE JUROR:  I just want to say that when
14    I was a child, I was molested by a family member.  Now,
15    that gentleman, he's passed on now, so I haven't -- there
16    was never a case on it, but I also --
17         THE COURT:  Would you move over this way?  I'm
18    having a little hard time -- I understand you said as a
19    child you were molested?
20         PROSPECTIVE JUROR:  Yes, I was.
21         I also have a daughter, so -- in my opinion, I
22    think -- I wouldn't even give this guy a chance.
23         THE COURT:  You'd have a difficult time being --
24         PROSPECTIVE JUROR:  I would have a difficult
25    time.
```

PIMA COUNTY SUPERIOR COURT

```
 1            THE COURT:  If there's any questions, I would
 2    intend to excuse Ms. Contreras.
 3            Thank for being here.  Please go back
 4    downstairs.
 5                (Open court.)
 6            THE COURT:  Anybody else?  Yes, Ms. Buchanan.
 7                (Bench conference.)
 8            PROSPECTIVE JUROR:  My nine-year-old son was
 9    sexually molested.
10            THE COURT:  How long ago was that?
11            PROSPECTIVE JUROR:  This year, February.
12            THE COURT:  Would that affect you in this case
13    or cause you to favor one side or the other in this case?
14            PROSPECTIVE JUROR:  Yes.
15            THE COURT:  It would be difficult for you to be
16    fair?
17            PROSPECTIVE JUROR:  Yes.
18            THE COURT:  Thank, ma'am.  I'll excuse you.
19                (Open court.)
20            THE COURT:  Ms. Gonzales, would you like to come
21    up?
22    Thanks, ma'am.
23                (Bench conference.)
24            PROSPECTIVE JUROR:  I was sexually abused as a
25    child.
```

PIMA COUNTY SUPERIOR COURT

```
 1            THE COURT:  Sexual abused when you were a child?
 2            PROSPECTIVE JUROR:  I'm sorry?
 3            THE COURT:  I see you're even emotional right
 4   now.  Thank for being here, ma'am.  You're excused.
 5            I'm going to excuse Ms. Gonzales.
 6              (Open court.)
 7            THE COURT:  Anybody else?  Then -- and the
 8   question was, have you or any members of your family or
 9   close friends ever been involved in any way in a case
10   such as this?
11            I see no more hands.
12            Well -- well, if you're called up later, I'll
13   bring you up.  But thank you, sir.
14            You all can take a seat for a minute, please.
15            We're going to replace in order Juror No. 1,
16   Ms. Buchanan.
17            THE CLERK:  That would be Julie Penny.
18            THE COURT:  As your name is called forward,
19   please take a seat where Peter directs you.
20            And Juror No. 21, Ms. Gonzales.
21            THE CLERK:  That would be James Stenlund.
22            THE COURT:  And Juror No. 22, Ms. Contreras.
23            THE CLERK:  That would be Lora Davison.
24            THE COURT:  Ms. Davison, you'll be in the seat
25   there, and if you want to walk over there.
```

PIMA COUNTY SUPERIOR COURT

```
 1            And Mr. Stenlund will be in the first seat.

 2            And, Peter, you need to pick it up for

 3   Mr. Stenlund.

 4            And then the -- we'll replace Juror No. 24,

 5   Ms. O'Hara.

 6            THE CLERK:  Susan Ludwig.

 7            THE COURT:  And Juror No. 27, Ms. Peterson.

 8            THE CLERK:  Ms. Peterson would be Richard Hoy.

 9            THE COURT:  I said Peterson, but it was

10   Juror No. 26 -- all right, we have 26 back.

11            My questions to those of you that just joined

12   us, would you have answered yes to any of the questions

13   that I've asked so far, either knowledge of the people

14   here or nature of the case and what have you?

15            Okay, Ms. Ludwig?

16            PROSPECTIVE JUROR:  Can I come up?

17            THE COURT:  Sure.

18            Counsel.

19            I take it that but for Ms. Ludwig, nobody would

20   have answered anything so far?

21            (Bench conference.)

22            THE COURT:  This is Ms. Ludwig.

23            PROSPECTIVE JUROR:  Yes.

24            I was molested as a child.

25            THE COURT:  You don't think you can serve fair
```

PIMA COUNTY SUPERIOR COURT

1   and impartially?

2   PROSPECTIVE JUROR: No.

3   THE COURT: Thanks for being here, and please go

4   back down to the jury commissioner.

5   (Open court.)

6   THE COURT: Ms. Davison.

7   MR. LAGATTUTA: No. --

8   THE COURT: She was 24. Ms. Ludwig was 24.

9   (Bench conference.)

10   THE COURT: Ms. Davison.

11   PROSPECTIVE JUROR: I have a friend whose son

12   was sexually molested.

13   THE COURT: It would be difficult for you?

14   PROSPECTIVE JUROR: Yes, because I was her drive

15   to and from court, and I saw what it did to her.

16   THE COURT: Thank you, ma'am, for being here.

17   I'll excuse Ms. Davison.

18   (Open court.)

19   THE COURT: Anybody else up to now that's joined

20   us for any question so far would have answered yes to?

21   I don't see any hands, so we're going to replace

22   two more jurors.

23   Juror No. 22, Ms. Davison.

24   THE CLERK: Tammi John.

25   THE COURT: Ms. John, I'm going to ask you

PIMA COUNTY SUPERIOR COURT

1   before you walk in front of everybody in there, would you

2   have answered yes to any of the questions so far?

3   PROSPECTIVE JUROR: Yes.

4   THE COURT: Why don't you come on up here now,

5   then?

6   (Bench conference.)

7   PROSPECTIVE JUROR: Mine's actually a scheduling

8   one. I have a preschool son, and my husband is the sole

9   provider; and I don't have anybody to watch him, so he

10   has to take the day off.

11   THE COURT: It would be difficult for you to be

12   here?

13   PROSPECTIVE JUROR: Yeah.

14   THE COURT: Without objection I'll go ahead and

15   excuse you. Thanks for being here.

16   MR. JENSVOLD: Who was that?

17   THE COURT: She's No. 22, Ms. John.

18   MR. JENSVOLD: Okay.

19   THE COURT: Replace Juror No. 22.

20   (Open court.)

21   THE COURT: We'll replace -- I'm going to excuse

22   Ms. John and replace Juror No. 22.

23   THE CLERK: Karl Carr.

24   THE COURT: Mr. Carr, before you make that hike,

25   would you have answered yes to any questions?

PIMA COUNTY SUPERIOR COURT

```
 1            PROSPECTIVE JUROR:  No, sir.
 2            THE COURT:  Okay.  Thank you, sir.  Please have
 3       a seat.
 4            And we still have Juror No. 24, Ms. Ludwig, to
 5       be replaced.
 6            THE CLERK:  That would be Oscar Paredes.
 7            THE COURT:  Mr. Paredes, would you have answered
 8       yes to any questions so far?
 9            PROSPECTIVE JUROR:  Not so far.
10            THE COURT:  Okay.  Thank you, sir.
11            Next question is a little broader than the last
12       question, and that is, is there anything about the nature
13       of this case that would make it difficult for any of you
14       to serve as a fair and impartial juror?
15            Ms. Charette, I think it is?
16            PROSPECTIVE JUROR:  That would be private.
17            THE COURT:  Do you want to come up here?
18            PROSPECTIVE JUROR:  Uh-huh.
19            THE COURT:  Counsel, come on up.
20            (Bench conference.)
21            THE COURT:  Okay, Ms. Charette.
22            PROSPECTIVE JUROR:  There was an inappropriate
23       experience when I was a young child.
24            THE COURT:  Affect your ability --
25            PROSPECTIVE JUROR:  It would.
```

PIMA COUNTY SUPERIOR COURT

```
1          THE COURT:  -- ability to be fair and impartial?

2          PROSPECTIVE JUROR:  Yeah.

3          THE COURT:  Excuse you.  Thanks for being here.

4   Please go back down to the jury commissioner.  They might

5   have another jury.

6               (Open court.)

7          THE COURT:  Replace Juror No. 6, Ms. Charette.

8          THE CLERK:  Joanne Martin.

9          PROSPECTIVE JUROR:  I'm fine.

10         THE COURT:  Yes, Mr. Paredes, you have your hand

11  up, sir?

12         Just for the record, Ms. Martin, I understand

13  you would not have answered any of the questions so far?

14         PROSPECTIVE JUROR:  That's correct.

15         THE COURT:  And, Mr. Paredes?

16              (Bench conference.)

17         THE COURT:  Now, we need to make sure the

18  lawyers can hear.

19         PROSPECTIVE JUROR:  Okay.  Single parent,

20  raising two kids.  I don't believe I'd be unbiased in

21  this matter at all.

22         THE COURT:  Difficult to be fair?

23         PROSPECTIVE JUROR:  Right.

24         THE COURT:  I'll excuse you.  Thank you for

25  being here for now.
```

PIMA COUNTY SUPERIOR COURT

```
 1            PROSPECTIVE JUROR:  Thank you.

 2                 (Open court.)

 3            THE COURT:  We'll excuse Mr. Paredes and replace

 4      Juror No. 24.

 5            THE CLERK:  Pauline Malcom.

 6            THE COURT:  Ms. Malcom, would you have answered

 7      yes to any questions so far?

 8            PROSPECTIVE JUROR:  Yeah.

 9            THE COURT:  Do you want to talk to me up here?

10            PROSPECTIVE JUROR:  Yeah.

11            THE COURT:  Let me say as you're approaching, as

12      seats up open and you don't have a seat, please have a

13      seat.  And maybe the people that are, you know, on the

14      outside can move in a little bit so you don't have to

15      crawl over them.  And we appreciate that, and that will

16      open up some seats for folks.  Thank you.

17                 (Bench conference.)

18            PROSPECTIVE JUROR:  My nieces were molested by

19      their father, and I know I --

20            THE COURT:  Couldn't be fair?

21            PROSPECTIVE JUROR:  Yeah, I couldn't be fair.

22            THE COURT:  Niece molested, so I'll excuse you,

23      ma'am.

24                 (Open court.)

25            THE COURT:  Replace Ms. Malcom, Juror No. 24.
```

PIMA COUNTY SUPERIOR COURT

```
 1          THE CLERK:  Jennifer Day.

 2          THE COURT:  Ms. Day, would you have answered yes

 3    to any questions?

 4          PROSPECTIVE JUROR:  No.

 5          THE COURT:  Please have a seat.

 6          Okay.  Again, I'll ask this question:  Is there

 7    anything about the nature of this case that would make it

 8    difficult for any of you to serve as a fair and impartial

 9    juror?

10          And I see no more hands -- yes, sir, I'm sorry,

11    Mr. -- is it Stenlund?

12          PROSPECTIVE JUROR:  Yeah.

13          THE COURT:  Do you want to tell me from there or

14    come up?

15          Come on up.

16             (Bench conference.)

17          PROSPECTIVE JUROR:  A couple of things.  My

18    wife's pregnant, and I have some difficulties.  And I

19    don't think she's going to be able to work much longer,

20    so I'm really worried about taking this much time off of

21    work.

22          THE COURT:  Okay.

23          PROSPECTIVE JUROR:  And I'm expecting a

24    daughter, and so maybe more sensitive to the issues.

25          THE COURT:  You're both the situation with your
```

PIMA COUNTY SUPERIOR COURT

```
 1   wife and the care of your wife, as well as your concern
 2   about the nature of the case?
 3           PROSPECTIVE JUROR:  Right.
 4           THE COURT:  Do you think it would be difficult
 5   for you to be fair in this case?
 6           PROSPECTIVE JUROR:  I think so, yes.
 7           THE COURT:  Sir, I'll excuse you, thanks.
 8               (Open court.)
 9           THE COURT:  Replace Mr. Stenlund, Juror No. 21.
10           THE CLERK:  Jeffery Goss.
11           THE COURT:  Would you have answered yes,
12   Mr. Goss?
13           PROSPECTIVE JUROR:  Not yet.
14           THE COURT:  Okay.  Thanks.  Have a seat.
15           I'm going to read a list of witnesses that may
16   be called to testify in the case.  The fact that I'm
17   naming them doesn't mean necessarily for sure they're
18   going to be called, but they may be referred to in
19   reports or by another witness.  And so I'd like to know
20   whether you know or think you know any of the following
21   potential witnesses:  Detective Jeff Englander -- if you
22   do, please raise your hand as I go along -- Officer Jace
23   Judd, Detective William Knuth, Alan Kreitl, Brian McGraw,
24   Gerrard Moretz, M-o-r-e-t-z, Officer Brenda Schupbach,
25   Jacob Franks, Kathleen Bright-Birnbaum, it's B-r-i-g-h-t
```

```
 1    wife and the care of your wife, as well as your concern
 2    about the nature of the case?

 3              PROSPECTIVE JUROR:  Right.

 4              THE COURT:  Do you think it would be difficult

 5    for you to be fair in this case?

 6              PROSPECTIVE JUROR:  I think so, yes.

 7              THE COURT:  Sir, I'll excuse you, thanks.

 8                   (Open court.)

 9              THE COURT:  Replace Mr. Stenlund, Juror No. 21.

10              THE CLERK:  Jeffery Goss.

11              THE COURT:  Would you have answered yes,

12    Mr. Goss?

13              PROSPECTIVE JUROR:  Not yet.

14              THE COURT:  Okay.  Thanks.  Have a seat.

15              I'm going to read a list of witnesses that may

16    be called to testify in the case.  The fact that I'm

17    naming them doesn't mean necessarily for sure they're

18    going to be called, but they may be referred to in

19    reports or by another witness.  And so I'd like to know

20    whether you know or think you know any of the following

21    potential witnesses:  Detective Jeff Englander -- if you

22    do, please raise your hand as I go along -- Officer Jace

23    Judd, Detective William Knuth, Alan Kreitl, Brian McGraw,

24    Gerrard Moretz, M-o-r-e-t-z, Officer Brenda Schupbach,

25    Jacob Franks, Kathleen Bright-Birnbaum, it's B-r-i-g-h-t
```

PIMA COUNTY SUPERIOR COURT

```
1    hyphen B-i-r-n-b-a-u-m, Matt Gidney, and finally Scott

2    Greene.  Anybody know or think you know any of those

3    folks.

4             Have I overlooked any potential witnesses,

5    counsel?

6             MR. JENSVOLD:  I didn't catch it.  Did you

7    mention Jacob Franks?

8             THE COURT:  Yes.

9             MR. JENSVOLD:  Okay.

10            THE COURT:  Have any of you ever served as a

11   member of a grand jury, either federal or state or

12   county?

13            I see no hands.

14            Have any of you been called to testify as a

15   witness in a criminal case?

16            Of course, Mr. Alexander, sir, I'm going to ask

17   questions that will come up kind of repeatedly.  And I'll

18   give you an example for all of you, these will come up

19   again.  Can you make a determination based in this case

20   based only on the evidence that's presented in court here

21   on this case?

22            PROSPECTIVE JUROR:  Yes.

23            THE COURT:  And can you follow the law as I give

24   you in the instructions, disregarding your own notions

25   about what the law -- what you think the law ought to be?
```

PIMA COUNTY SUPERIOR COURT

```
1          PROSPECTIVE JUROR:  Yes.

2          THE COURT:  Okay.  Can you be fair and impartial

3    in this case?

4          PROSPECTIVE JUROR:  I can.

5          THE COURT:  Anybody else called as a witness in

6    a criminal case?

7          I see no other hands.

8          Have you or members of your family or friends

9    ever served as a law enforcement officer?  And I would

10   include in that people who are corrections business or

11   things of that nature.  And you already know about

12   Mr. Alexander, so I'll excuse you from answering that.

13         PROSPECTIVE JUROR NO. ONE:  Did you say friends?

14         THE COURT:  Close friends or family members.

15         Ms. Penny.

16         PROSPECTIVE JUROR:  Uh-huh.

17         THE COURT:  What's -- a little bit about the

18   describing relationship.

19         PROSPECTIVE JUROR:  Well, just, our kids are

20   friends on the same baseball team.  My husband coaches

21   with several police officers.  Not necessarily -- I think

22   a couple in Tucson and then some sheriffs.

23         THE COURT:  Would the fact that you have friends

24   that are police officers cause you to favor one side or

25   the other in this case?
```

PIMA COUNTY SUPERIOR COURT

```
1                PROSPECTIVE JUROR:  No.

2                THE COURT:  Can you be fair and impartial in

3       this case?

4                PROSPECTIVE JUROR:  Yes.

5                THE COURT:  Okay.  Thank you.  Anybody else, law

6       enforcement?

7                Yes, Mr. Theiss?

8                PROSPECTIVE JUROR:  Yeah, I have close friends

9       that's a Pima County Sheriff's Department.  I went to

10      school with him.  Grew up with him.

11               THE COURT:  Okay.  Do you know what kind of work

12      he does?

13               PROSPECTIVE JUROR:  He was a detective.  I don't

14      know what he's doing now.

15               THE COURT:  Okay.  Would -- would that -- the

16      fact that you have a friend in the police department

17      cause you to favor one side or the other in this case?

18               PROSPECTIVE JUROR:  No.

19               THE COURT:  Thank you, sir.

20               Mr. Loding, I think it is.

21               PROSPECTIVE JUROR:  Sheriff Dupnik.

22               THE COURT:  Sheriff Dupnik is a friend?

23               PROSPECTIVE JUROR:  Yes.

24               THE COURT:  This isn't a sheriff's office case I

25      don't think, but --
```

PIMA COUNTY SUPERIOR COURT

```
 1              MR. JENSVOLD:  It is, your Honor.

 2              THE COURT:  Oh, I'm sorry, it is.  Would that

 3    cause you to favor one side or the other in this case?

 4              PROSPECTIVE JUROR:  No.

 5              THE COURT:  You haven't talked to him about this

 6    case by chance?

 7              PROSPECTIVE JUROR:  No.

 8              THE COURT:  What -- describe your relationship

 9    with him a little bit.

10              PROSPECTIVE JUROR:  We work together at the

11    church.

12              THE COURT:  You work together at the church?

13              PROSPECTIVE JUROR:  Yeah.

14              THE COURT:  Will you follow the law as I give

15    you?

16              PROSPECTIVE JUROR:  Yes.

17              THE COURT:  And can you make a determination

18    here based only on the evidence in this case?

19              PROSPECTIVE JUROR:  Yes.

20              THE COURT:  Thank you.  Anybody else, back row?

21              Front row, come over here, Ms. Nichelson.

22              PROSPECTIVE JUROR:  I have a friend whose

23    significant other is on the border patrol.

24              THE COURT:  Border patrol.  Okay.  Do you ever

25    talk to that person about the kind of work he does?
```

PIMA COUNTY SUPERIOR COURT

```
1              PROSPECTIVE JUROR:  No.

2              THE COURT:  He or she, I don't know.

3              PROSPECTIVE JUROR:  No.

4              THE COURT:  Can you follow the law as I give you

5    in this case?

6              PROSPECTIVE JUROR:  Yeah.

7              THE COURT:  Can you be fair and impartial?

8              PROSPECTIVE JUROR:  Yes.

9              THE COURT:  Okay.  Saw another hand here.  I

10   think Mr. Smith.

11             PROSPECTIVE JUROR:  Yeah.  Similar, just --

12             THE COURT:  Friend?

13             PROSPECTIVE JUROR:  A neighbor and a friend, but

14   it wouldn't impede my --

15             THE COURT:  So you have a couple of

16   acquaintances in law enforcement, but that wouldn't

17   affect you in this case?

18             Thank you, sir.

19             Back row, over here, yes, Mr. Cardenas.

20             PROSPECTIVE JUROR:  I have a son-in-law that's a

21   policeman.

22             THE COURT:  Do you know what kind of work he

23   does?

24             PROSPECTIVE JUROR:  He worked at the U of A.

25             THE COURT:  U of A?
```

PIMA COUNTY SUPERIOR COURT

```
 1              PROSPECTIVE JUROR:  Yes.

 2              THE COURT:  The fact that he's a police officer

 3      cause you to favor one side or the other in this case?

 4              PROSPECTIVE JUROR:  No.

 5              THE COURT:  Okay.  Can you be fair and

 6      impartial?

 7              PROSPECTIVE JUROR:  Yes.

 8              THE COURT:  Thank you.

 9              Anybody else?  Yes, Ms. Villalobos.

10              PROSPECTIVE JUROR:  Yes, my husband was with the

11      Pima County Sheriff's Department 27 years, and he's with

12      the court system.

13              THE COURT:  He's in the court system now?

14              PROSPECTIVE JUROR:  Uh-huh.

15              THE COURT:  What court -- what court is he in?

16              PROSPECTIVE JUROR:  In bankruptcy.

17              THE COURT:  In bankruptcy court.  So that's the

18      federal court system.  Is there anything about the fact

19      that he's involved in that kind of a system cause you to

20      favor one side or the other in this case?

21              PROSPECTIVE JUROR:  No.

22              THE COURT:  Can you be fair and impartial?

23              PROSPECTIVE JUROR:  Yes.

24              THE COURT:  Thank you.

25              Anybody else?
```

PIMA COUNTY SUPERIOR COURT

```
 1          Counsel may follow up in this area a little bit
 2     more, but I'd like to know whether any of you or family
 3     members are -- had particular training in the area of
 4     computers -- I mean, have a degree in computers.  I know
 5     we all probably work with computers one way or the other,
 6     but have any of you had any special expertise or
 7     background or what have you in the area of computers?
 8          Yes, Mr. Smith.
 9          PROSPECTIVE JUROR:  Yeah, I taught computers at
10     a middle school, technology, software using Microsoft
11     Word, Power Point.
12          THE COURT:  Okay.  So do you have a degree in
13     computers?
14          PROSPECTIVE JUROR:  Don't have a degree, just do
15     it in staff development, training teachers or students.
16          THE COURT:  Somebody else?  Yes, sir, Mr. --
17          PROSPECTIVE JUROR:  I have 40 years' employment
18     with IBM.
19          THE COURT:  Mr. Hoy?  Friesenborg?  I got my
20     dis -- and I try to get it in the right spot.
21     Mr. Friesenborg, you work with IBM?
22          PROSPECTIVE JUROR:  Right.
23          THE COURT:  In the computer field?
24          PROSPECTIVE JUROR:  Right.
25          THE COURT:  Anybody else have special training
```

PIMA COUNTY SUPERIOR COURT

```
1    in that area?  A couple others.  Mr. Hoy.

2              PROSPECTIVE JUROR:  I'm an engineer by trade.

3              THE COURT:  Computer work.  Okay.

4              And then I think there was somebody else.

5    Mr. Carr.

6              PROSPECTIVE JUROR:  Yes.  I was a systems admin

7    for ABDS.

8              THE COURT:  I'm not sure about this, and counsel

9    may get to follow up on it.  But you may have some

10   testimony with regard to computers or how they work or,

11   you know, work on the internet and what have you.  Can

12   you lay aside your knowledge about that and determine the

13   facts in this case based only on the evidence that's

14   presented in this case?

15             I see nodding from everybody -- each of you that

16   I asked that question.

17             Counsel can maybe follow up on that because

18   they're more familiar with the nature of the case.

19             In deciding the facts of this case, the jury

20   will have to evaluate the testimony of witnesses.  Is

21   there anyone here who could not judge the testimony of

22   each witness by the same standard?

23             I don't see any hands.

24             Let me explain it a little bit more.  By this I

25   mean, is there anyone who is likely to give more or less
```

PIMA COUNTY SUPERIOR COURT

```
 1    weight to the testimony of, let's just say, a law

 2    enforcement officer, for example, than to the testimony

 3    of another witness simply because one person is employed

 4    as a law enforcement officer and another person is not?

 5              I don't see any hands.

 6              Is there anyone here who would be unable to

 7    follow the law as given in the instructions, disregarding

 8    your own notions or ideas about what the law is or what

 9    it ought to be?

10              And I don't see any hands.

11              If selected to sit on this case, would any of

12    you be unable or unwilling to render a verdict solely on

13    the evidence presented at this trial?

14              And I see no hands.

15              Now, the law requires the State to prove the

16    defendant guilty beyond a reasonable doubt.    The

17    defendant is presumed by law to be innocent, and this

18    means that the defendant is not required to prove

19    innocence or to produce any evidence.   If you were to

20    have to vote right now on whether or not Mr. Coghill was

21    guilty or not guilty, there could be only one answer, and

22    that answer is he's not guilty because there's been no

23    evidence that's presented upon which you make a

24    determination that would avoid the presumption and negate

25    the presumption.
```

PIMA COUNTY SUPERIOR COURT

```
 1            Also, in -- a defendant in a criminal case has a
 2     right not to testify at trial, and the exercise of that
 3     right cannot be considered by the jury in determining
 4     guilty or -- not guilty or innocence.  So I'd like to ask
 5     you, is there anyone here who doesn't understand the
 6     principles of law that I have just stated?
 7            (No response.)
 8            THE COURT:  Is there anyone who does not agree
 9     with these things or thinks they shouldn't be the law?
10            And I see no hands.
11            There is a rule that if you're selected to sit
12     on the jury -- as a matter of fact, even if you're not,
13     I'm going to tell you you can't discuss the case outside
14     this area.  You can't even discuss it amongst yourselves
15     if you're selected as a jury until you go into the
16     deliberation room and you've heard all of the evidence
17     and the argument of counsel and the law that I give you.
18            Also, there's a rule that precludes you from
19     listening to any media reports about it or doing any
20     research on your own.  In other words, you can't go to
21     the computer and check things out.  That would be
22     improper.  Is there anybody who would have any difficulty
23     at all following the instructions that I give you with
24     regard to not doing any research on your own, not
25     listening to any media reports, not discussing the case
```

PIMA COUNTY SUPERIOR COURT

1   with anyone until the trial is over?

2   Okay, I don't see anybody that indicates a

3   problem with that.

4   Do any of you happen to know another member on

5   the jury panel, those that are selected up here?

6   Yes, I see Ms. Richardson is raising her hand.

7   And you know --

8   PROSPECTIVE JUROR: Ms. Saucedo.

9   THE COURT: Ms. Saucedo. How do you know --

10   Ms. Richardson, how do you know Ms. Saucedo?

11   PROSPECTIVE JUROR: Our kids went to school in

12   elementary school.

13   THE COURT: School people together. And are

14   you -- do you work together other than at school?

15   PROSPECTIVE JUROR: We don't -- our kids aren't

16   together anymore. It was a few years ago.

17   THE COURT: Okay. Sometime back.

18   Let me just ask you, if you go to the jury room

19   and you're in there deliberating, would you be able to

20   consider the views of others but make your own

21   independent view and not be overly influenced by

22   Ms. Saucedo?

23   PROSPECTIVE JUROR: Yes.

24   THE COURT: Same question to you, Ms. Saucedo.

25   Would you be able to be fair in making a determination if

PIMA COUNTY SUPERIOR COURT

```
1    you were to sit, not be overly influenced about the views

2    of Ms. Richardson?

3              PROSPECTIVE JUROR:  Yes.

4              THE COURT:  You can do that?  Okay.  Thank you.

5              Anybody else know one another?  Yes, Ms. Day.

6              PROSPECTIVE JUROR:  Yeah, Mr. Smith was my

7    teacher.

8              PROSPECTIVE JUROR:  I was wondering.  I've been

9    trying to make that connection.

10             THE COURT:  Well, now you've heard the questions

11   I've asked.  If you're selected to sit on this, would you

12   be overly influenced by Mr. Smith having been your

13   teacher, or can you --

14             PROSPECTIVE JUROR:  No, I can.

15             THE COURT:  You can be fair?  Okay.

16             Mr. Smith, same thing.

17             PROSPECTIVE JUROR:  Yeah.

18             THE COURT:  Okay.  Sometimes the next couple of

19   questions that I ask, people also like to come up.  And

20   we've done that already now, so you know it's quite all

21   right to do that, and so please feel free to do that if

22   you like to.

23             Have any of you, close friends, or relatives of

24   yours ever been arrested, charged, or convicted of any

25   crime other than a minor traffic offense?
```

PIMA COUNTY SUPERIOR COURT

```
 1                 We'll go back here.  Mr. Loding.

 2             PROSPECTIVE JUROR:  My younger brother.

 3             THE COURT:  A brother.

 4             PROSPECTIVE JUROR:  He was arrested for theft.

 5             THE COURT:  Arrested for theft?  How long ago,

 6     sir?

 7             PROSPECTIVE JUROR:  That was 40 years ago.

 8             THE COURT:  Would that cause you to favor one

 9     side or the other in this case?

10             PROSPECTIVE JUROR:  (Shaking head.)

11             THE COURT:  Anything about that case affect you

12     in this case?

13             PROSPECTIVE JUROR:  (Shaking head.)

14             UNKNOWN PROSPECTIVE JUROR:  Would you repeat the

15     question?

16             THE COURT:  Sure.  Have you, a close friend, or

17     relative -- have you, a close relative or friend ever

18     been arrested, charged, or convicted of any crime other

19     than a minor traffic offense?

20             Come back over here.  Ms. Penny.

21             PROSPECTIVE JUROR:  Yes.  One of our good

22     friends is going to -- he was indicted.  I think it was

23     last year.

24             THE COURT:  Is he in trial now or in the

25     process?
```

PIMA COUNTY SUPERIOR COURT

```
 1          PROSPECTIVE JUROR:  I know he was in court
 2   yesterday.  They're going through the process, but it
 3   keeps --
 4          THE COURT:  Do you know the nature of the case?
 5          PROSPECTIVE JUROR:  Yeah.  And I think most
 6   people here do.
 7          THE COURT:  So is there anything -- if the case
 8   is going on and what have you, would that affect you in
 9   this case?
10          PROSPECTIVE JUROR:  No, no.
11          THE COURT:  Okay.  You have a friend that's
12   involved in another ongoing case?
13          PROSPECTIVE JUROR:  Yeah, federal.
14          THE COURT:  It's a federal case.
15          PROSPECTIVE JUROR:  Uh-huh.
16          THE COURT:  Okay.  And you're sure -- I just
17   want -- I want to come back on it.  It would not affect
18   you in any way in this case?
19          PROSPECTIVE JUROR:  No.
20          THE COURT:  I'm working with the back row to try
21   to keep order to my list.
22          Ms. Noriega.
23          PROSPECTIVE JUROR:  My son for drunk driving.
24          THE COURT:  Okay.  How long ago was that?
25          PROSPECTIVE JUROR:  He is in prison right now.
```

PIMA COUNTY SUPERIOR COURT

```
1            THE COURT:  He's in prison right now?  Okay.
2    And were you involved in his trial or anything or
3    however -- in any of the processing of his case?
4            PROSPECTIVE JUROR:  No.  I went to see -- I --
5    sitting, but --
6            THE COURT:  You were an observer of the trial?
7            PROSPECTIVE JUROR:  Yeah.
8            THE COURT:  You know, sometimes -- and the
9    reason I ask this question is sometimes people will have
10   a feeling based on how a relative or son or daughter or
11   anyone who was treated, either by law enforcement, maybe
12   they didn't like the lawyers, maybe they didn't like the
13   judge and thought the whole system is unfair.  Anything
14   like that causes you to spill over in this case in any
15   way?
16           PROSPECTIVE JUROR:  No.
17           THE COURT:  Can you be fair and impartial in
18   this case?
19           PROSPECTIVE JUROR:  Oh, yes.
20           THE COURT:  Sure, thank you.
21           Ms. Carillo.
22           PROSPECTIVE JUROR:  I have a nephew arrested for
23   robbery, and he's in jail right now.
24           THE COURT:  Okay.  Were you involved in his
25   trial?
```

PIMA COUNTY SUPERIOR COURT

```
1              PROSPECTIVE JUROR:  No.

2              THE COURT:  Or processing?  Was it here in

3    Arizona or someplace?

4              PROSPECTIVE JUROR:  Yes.

5              THE COURT:  Can you be fair and impartial in

6    this case?

7              PROSPECTIVE JUROR:  I can.

8              THE COURT:  Would the fact that you have -- you

9    know the relative that's --

10             PROSPECTIVE JUROR:  It won't affect me.

11             THE COURT:  It won't affect you?

12   Back row here.  Yes, Ms. Taylor.

13             PROSPECTIVE JUROR:  My cousin was charged with

14   DUI.

15             THE COURT:  Affect you in this case in any way?

16             PROSPECTIVE JUROR:  No.

17             THE COURT:  Okay.  Thank you.  Back row still.

18   Yes, Ms. Martin.

19             PROSPECTIVE JUROR:  My three children for

20   different offenses, minor in possession.

21             THE COURT:  Minor in possession?  How long ago

22   were those, ma'am?

23             PROSPECTIVE JUROR:  Less than two years.

24             THE COURT:  Here in Tucson?

25             PROSPECTIVE JUROR:  Uh-huh.
```

PIMA COUNTY SUPERIOR COURT

```
 1            THE COURT:  Again, you heard my question, and I
 2    mentioned it to Ms. Noriega about whether or not, you
 3    know, the way they were treated by any of the officials,
 4    one thing or another that would maybe spill over in this
 5    case, would that affect you in any way here?
 6            PROSPECTIVE JUROR:  I can remain objective.
 7            THE COURT:  Can you be fair and impartial?
 8            PROSPECTIVE JUROR:  Yes.
 9            THE COURT:  Anybody else in the back row?
10        Mr. Smith's row, middle row?
11        Yes, Mr. Johnson.
12            PROSPECTIVE JUROR:  Yes, my stepson was involved
13    in various breaking and enterings and minor possessions.
14            THE COURT:  How long ago?
15            PROSPECTIVE JUROR:  Two, three years ago.
16            THE COURT:  Here in Tucson?
17            PROSPECTIVE JUROR:  Yeah.
18            THE COURT:  Okay.  Sir, would that affect you in
19    this case in any way?
20            PROSPECTIVE JUROR:  No.
21            THE COURT:  Can you be fair and impartial here?
22            PROSPECTIVE JUROR:  Yes.
23            THE COURT:  Anybody else in the middle row
24    there?  I'm getting both sides.  We'll go, Ms. Coffey.
25            PROSPECTIVE JUROR:  My ex-husband took my
```

PIMA COUNTY SUPERIOR COURT

```
 1    children out of the state without my permission, and he
 2    was arrested.
 3              THE COURT:  Would that affect you in this case?
 4              PROSPECTIVE JUROR:  No.
 5              THE COURT:  And, then, Mr. Storie.
 6              PROSPECTIVE JUROR:  My son was arrested, never
 7    went to trial, but they were serious charges.  And he was
 8    held in juvie detention for an extended without matter,
 9    and it was dropped before he went to court.  But I have a
10    soft spot for the sheriff's department.
11              THE COURT:  The soft part, would you tend to
12    favor them over other witnesses?
13              PROSPECTIVE JUROR:  I think they behaved really
14    badly in my son's case, really badly.
15              THE COURT:  Only you can you can tell me -- how
16    long ago was that case?
17              PROSPECTIVE JUROR:  It was ten years ago.
18              THE COURT:  Ten years ago.  Okay.  And in this
19    case, if you think it would cause you to be unfair to one
20    side or the other -- I don't care which side.  I don't
21    want to know which side, only you can tell me.
22              PROSPECTIVE JUROR:  I think I would be skeptical
23    of testimony from the sheriff's department.
24              THE COURT:  Okay, sir.  Without objection I'm
25    going to excuse you.  Thanks for being here, and we'll
```

PIMA COUNTY SUPERIOR COURT

```
1    excuse Mr. Storie.

2              And replace Juror No. 13.

3              THE CLERK:  Linda Coleman.

4              THE COURT:  Ms. Coleman, we've asked a lot of

5    questions.  Would you have answered yes to any of them?

6              PROSPECTIVE JUROR:  No.

7              THE COURT:  Okay.  Please have a seat.  I've

8    lost track of time, and it's noon already, and I'm sorry.

9    We're going to go ahead and continue right where we are,

10   but I'm going to let you all go have lunch.  And let me

11   say things before everybody runs for the door.

12             First of all, I do need to have all of you to

13   come back.  If you've got a number and you've been called

14   up, look to the left and the right, get a friend, count

15   the seats in.  Somehow you have to come back to the same

16   seat you're in.  It's easy to some of you, but -- we're

17   on the 5th floor, and you go out there, there will be a

18   lot of jurors out there.

19             Now, I mentioned to you that I'll be giving

20   instructions not to talk about the case.  I know you

21   don't know much about it other than the charges, but

22   there could be witnesses out there and I just need you to

23   avoid discussion.

24             If you need to call somebody in the office or in

25   the home and say, "I'm in the process of being selected
```

PIMA COUNTY SUPERIOR COURT

```
 1    for a jury," a scheduling matter, "I don't know if I'm
 2    going to be selected yet," you can do that.  If you're
 3    wife's planned -- or husband has planned a trip that you
 4    didn't know about over the weekend, I'd rather have you
 5    come back and tell me that when you come back from lunch.
 6    So that kind of thing is okay, but nothing else about the
 7    case.
 8              I need you all back.  Peter will ask you to come
 9    in at 1:30.  So you just go out there, and I think he's
10    told you you have to take the elevators.  But if some of
11    you would like a little exercise, there are stairs on
12    each of the corners you can go to to walk down, and
13    you'll get outside if you go that way.  So we're in
14    recess now until 1:30.
15                   (Whereupon, the prospective jury panel was
16                   excused from the courtroom.)
17                   (Luncheon recess.)
18         THE COURT:  I think we're ready to continue.
19                   (Whereupon, the prospective jury panel
20                   entered the courtroom.)
21         THE COURT:  Please be seated.  Peter, we're
22    waiting for one juror, Ms. Noriega.  Can you go out and
23    see if you can locate him?
24              Okay.  Thank you.  We're here now with all
25    jurors, counsel, and the defendant.
```

```
 1              Please be seated.
 2              Continuing on with the voir dire.  Let me
 3     introduce Mr. Jonathan Mosher.
 4              Mr. Mosher.
 5              He's going to assist in the jury selection for a
 6     period of time here.  Mr. Jensvold had another thing that
 7     he had to step out to do.
 8              And so does anybody know Mr. Mosher?
 9              Apparently not.
10              Now, I was addressing questions with you in
11     the -- and the last question -- well, first of all,
12     Ms. Coleman, you came up to me I think afterwards, and
13     you indicated that you may have a problem scheduling?
14              PROSPECTIVE JUROR:  I just got my baby back from
15     CPS, and I have no day care or nothing yet.
16              THE COURT:  And so it would be real difficult
17     for you to be here?
18              PROSPECTIVE JUROR:  Unless I brought the baby
19     with me.
20              THE COURT:  I think I'll excuse you.  It's not
21     that I have anything against babies.
22              I'll excuse Ms. Coleman, and replace
23     Juror No. 15.
24              THE CLERK:  Mary Stubbins.
25              THE COURT:  Ms. Stubbins, before we walk you all
```

PIMA COUNTY SUPERIOR COURT

1   the way over there and what have you, would you have

2   answered yes to any of the questions?

3   PROSPECTIVE JUROR: Yes, sir.

4   Can I come up?

5   THE COURT: Sure.

6   Counsel, please.

7   (Bench conference.)

8   THE COURT: Okay, Ms. Stubbins.

9   PROSPECTIVE JUROR: I was raped as a child, and

10   I have trouble with it.

11   THE COURT: Don't say anything further. Thanks,

12   ma'am, for being here, and I appreciate your being here.

13   You're excused.

14   (Open court.)

15   THE COURT: Replace Ms. Stubbins, Juror No. 15.

16   We're going to excuse her.

17   THE CLERK: George Runger.

18   THE COURT: Mr. Runger, would you have answered

19   yes to any of the questions I asked previously?

20   PROSPECTIVE JUROR: No.

21   THE COURT: If you have a seat, please, up here,

22   and you can give Peter your notes there after

23   Ms. Stubbins gets done.

24   Okay, now back on track. The last question that

25   1 had asked is whether you, close friend or relative of

```
 1    yours or -- have ever been arrested, charged, or
 2    convicted of any crime other than a minor traffic
 3    offense.  And so for anybody who hasn't up to now
 4    answered that question before, if you haven't answered it
 5    up to now and it applies, please raise your hand.
 6          Mr. Alexander.
 7          PROSPECTIVE JUROR:  I have two cousins for many,
 8    many things in the books in Douglas.
 9          THE COURT:  You've -- do you think it will
10    affect you in this case in any way?
11          PROSPECTIVE JUROR:  No.
12          THE COURT:  Can you be fair and impartial in
13    this case?
14          PROSPECTIVE JUROR:  Yes.
15          THE COURT:  Thank you.
16          Anybody else?  Okay.  A couple more.  Yes,
17    Mr. Cardenas.
18          PROSPECTIVE JUROR:  May I approach the bench?
19          THE COURT:  Sure.  Sure, come on up.
20          Counsel.
21          (Bench conference.)
22          PROSPECTIVE JUROR:  I was convicted in 1980 of
23    DWI.
24          THE COURT:  1980?
25          PROSPECTIVE JUROR:  Right.
```

PIMA COUNTY SUPERIOR COURT

```
 1          THE COURT:  Civil rights been restored?

 2          PROSPECTIVE JUROR:  They never were taken away.

 3          THE COURT:  It was a minor?

 4          PROSPECTIVE JUROR:  They don't consider that a

 5     felony.

 6          THE COURT:  Does that affect you in this case in

 7     any way?

 8          PROSPECTIVE JUROR:  No.  I was -- by the way, I

 9     was fined $150, and I spent one day in jail.

10          THE COURT:  Okay.  And that was sometime ago,

11     and I'd just like to ask is whether you think --

12          PROSPECTIVE JUROR:  No, it wouldn't affect me.

13          THE COURT:  Thank you for sharing, sir.

14          PROSPECTIVE JUROR:  Okay.

15               (Open court.)

16          THE COURT:  I saw another hand coming across.  A

17     couple folks.  Yes, Ms. Villalobos.

18          PROSPECTIVE JUROR:  A son for violation of

19     probation.

20          THE COURT:  A son for violation of probation?

21     He was convicted and something and violated.  Would that

22     affect you in this case?

23          PROSPECTIVE JUROR:  No.

24          THE COURT:  How long ago was that?

25          PROSPECTIVE JUROR:  Just recently.
```

PIMA COUNTY SUPERIOR COURT

```
1              THE COURT:  Just recently as --
2              PROSPECTIVE JUROR:  A couple weeks.
3              THE COURT:  The nature of the charges had
4    nothing to do with what we're trying?
5              PROSPECTIVE JUROR:  No.
6              THE COURT:  Thank you.
7              Mr. Goss, I think you had your hand up, sir.
8              PROSPECTIVE JUROR:  Yes, sir.  I had a DUI.
9              THE COURT:  How long ago was that?
10             PROSPECTIVE JUROR:  Oh, 18 years ago.
11             THE COURT:  Okay.  Here in Arizona?
12             PROSPECTIVE JUROR:  Yes.
13             THE COURT:  Would that affect you in this case
14   in any way?
15             PROSPECTIVE JUROR:  No, sir.
16             THE COURT:  Okay.  Thank you.  I think Mr. -- is
17   it Carr?  I think you had your hand up.
18             PROSPECTIVE JUROR:  Yes, sir.  I also had a DUI
19   about five years ago in the City of Tucson.
20             THE COURT:  Affect you in this case in any way?
21             PROSPECTIVE JUROR:  No.
22             THE COURT:  Okay.  Keep on going along here.
23   Yes, Ms. Day, I think it is.
24             PROSPECTIVE JUROR:  My brother was arrested for
25   domestic violence and DUI.
```

PIMA COUNTY SUPERIOR COURT

```
1           THE COURT:  How long ago?

2           PROSPECTIVE JUROR:  Last year.

3           THE COURT:  Would that affect you in this case

4    in any way?

5           PROSPECTIVE JUROR:  No.

6           THE COURT:  Thank you.  Either one of those

7    situations?  Thank you.

8           And, then, Mr. Peterson.

9           PROSPECTIVE JUROR:  Yeah, my son was arrested

10   for a fight in a high school and then released.

11          THE COURT:  This was a high school situation?

12          PROSPECTIVE JUROR:  Yeah.

13          THE COURT:  Okay.  When the charges brought or

14   anything like that?

15          PROSPECTIVE JUROR:  No.

16          THE COURT:  Would that affect you in this case?

17          PROSPECTIVE JUROR:  No.

18          THE COURT:  Anybody else, then?

19             (No response.)

20          THE COURT:  Okay.  Have you, close friends or

21   relatives ever been the victim of a crime of any kind?

22   You, close relatives or friends victim of a crime?

23   Anything at all?  Traffic, or someone taking your car, or

24   burglaries?  We have some of those in this town.  And I

25   just -- I try to do that to help you kind of remember the
```

PIMA COUNTY SUPERIOR COURT

```
 1    things that might -- Ms. -- Ms. Penny.

 2             PROSPECTIVE JUROR:  Yes.  Last year my husband's

 3    wallet was stolen, and they took about $7,000 from our

 4    account, so -- and then my sister has been hit by drunk

 5    drivers.

 6             THE COURT:  Would the nature of those charges

 7    and what happened involving you affect you in this case?

 8             PROSPECTIVE JUROR:  No, no.

 9             THE COURT:  Would you be able to base this case

10    based only on the evidence presented here?

11             PROSPECTIVE JUROR:  Yes, sir.

12             THE COURT:  Going across, Mr. Theiss.

13             PROSPECTIVE JUROR:  Yeah, my brother's van was

14    stolen a couple of months ago.

15             THE COURT:  Okay.  Would that affect you in this

16    case in any way?

17             PROSPECTIVE JUROR:  No.

18             THE COURT:  Okay.  Going along the back row.

19    Ms. Perez.

20             PROSPECTIVE JUROR:  My daughter was -- well, she

21    was car-jacked in Phoenix.

22             THE COURT:  Would that affect you in this case

23    in any way?

24             PROSPECTIVE JUROR:  No.

25             THE COURT:  Ms. Taylor.
```

PIMA COUNTY SUPERIOR COURT

```
 1              PROSPECTIVE JUROR:  Burglaries, including one
 2    two years ago.
 3              THE COURT:  Of your home?
 4              PROSPECTIVE JUROR:  Of my grandmother's home.
 5              THE COURT:  Grandmother's home where you live.
 6    Would that affect you in this case?
 7              PROSPECTIVE JUROR:  No.
 8              THE COURT:  Anybody else back row?
 9              Middle row here?  Yes, Ms. Richardson?
10              PROSPECTIVE JUROR:  I had a truck stolen about
11    ten years ago.
12              THE COURT:  How long ago -- would that affect
13    you in this case?
14              PROSPECTIVE JUROR:  No.
15              THE COURT:  Okay.  Ms. Coffey.
16              PROSPECTIVE JUROR:  Murder.
17              THE COURT:  This was something that was in your
18    family?
19              PROSPECTIVE JUROR:  Well, she's like family.
20              THE COURT:  Like family.  And it was a close
21    friend yours?
22              PROSPECTIVE JUROR:  It was my daughter's best
23    friend.
24              THE COURT:  How long ago was that, ma'am?
25              PROSPECTIVE JUROR:  Two years.
```

PIMA COUNTY SUPERIOR COURT

```
1          THE COURT:  Here in Tucson?

2          PROSPECTIVE JUROR:  Yes, sir.

3          THE COURT:  I understand that you're emotional

4     about that.

5          PROSPECTIVE JUROR:  No, it's totally different.

6     It just upsets me to talk about it.

7          THE COURT:  And only you can -- can you be fair

8     and impartial in this case?

9          PROSPECTIVE JUROR:  Yes.

10         THE COURT:  And make a determination in this

11    case based only on this case?

12         PROSPECTIVE JUROR:  Yeah.  This is different

13    than that.

14         THE COURT:  Okay.  Thank you, ma'am.

15         Mr. Johnson.

16         PROSPECTIVE JUROR:  I was burglarized about 25

17    years ago in Colorado.

18         THE COURT:  Okay.  Would that affect you in this

19    case?

20         PROSPECTIVE JUROR:  No.

21         THE COURT:  Okay.  Thank you.  Did you even

22    remember it until I asked?

23         PROSPECTIVE JUROR:  I didn't, to tell you the

24    truth.

25         THE COURT:  Mr. Runger.
```

PIMA COUNTY SUPERIOR COURT

```
1          PROSPECTIVE JUROR:  About a year ago, all of the
2    windows in my truck were broken.
3          THE COURT:  Did they ever catch anybody or
4    anything?
5          PROSPECTIVE JUROR:  No.  I was in it at the
6    time.
7          THE COURT:  Would you hold that against the
8    police in they testify against the police?
9          PROSPECTIVE JUROR:  No.
10         THE COURT:  Would you hold it against anybody
11   else?
12         PROSPECTIVE JUROR:  No, just the guy.
13         THE COURT:  Can you make a determination in this
14   case based only on the evidence presented here?
15         PROSPECTIVE JUROR:  Yes.
16         THE COURT:  Okay.  Thank you.
17         Ms. Nichelson.
18         PROSPECTIVE JUROR:  My husband's car was stolen
19   about ten years ago.
20         THE COURT:  Would that affect you in this case
21   at all?
22         PROSPECTIVE JUROR:  No.
23         THE COURT:  Sure.  Mr. Alexander.
24         PROSPECTIVE JUROR:  Aggravated assault.
25   Wouldn't affect me.
```

PIMA COUNTY SUPERIOR COURT

```
1          THE COURT:  In line of duty?

2          PROSPECTIVE JUROR:  Uh-huh.

3          THE COURT:  Okay.  Thank you.

4          Ms. Fee.

5          PROSPECTIVE JUROR:  Attempted stealing of my

6    vehicle several times.

7          THE COURT:  You must have a nice car.

8          PROSPECTIVE JUROR:  (Nodding head.)

9          THE COURT:  Would that affect you in this case

10   in any way?

11         PROSPECTIVE JUROR:  No.

12         THE COURT:  Okay.  Thank you.

13         Anybody else as we go along the row there?

14         Ms. Day.

15         PROSPECTIVE JUROR:  My boyfriend was murdered.

16         THE COURT:  How long ago was that?

17         PROSPECTIVE JUROR:  Three years ago.

18         THE COURT:  Here in Tucson?

19         PROSPECTIVE JUROR:  Yes.

20         THE COURT:  Would that affect you in this case?

21         PROSPECTIVE JUROR:  Huh-uh.

22         THE COURT:  Okay.  Thank you.

23         Anybody else, then?

24         Thank you.

25         I've asked about all the questions I intend to
```

PIMA COUNTY SUPERIOR COURT

1   ask. The lawyers are going to get to ask some questions,
2   and I still need to hear from everybody with regard to
3   the sheet that you have. But sometimes by the time we
4   get close to the end of the questions, you will have
5   thought of an answer to a question that you wonder
6   whether you should have given. Something will be
7   reminded -- maybe over the lunch break you thought,
8   "Well, maybe I should have told them about this. I
9   didn't."
10   If there's anything like that that you heard
11   about so far that's on your mind that you think we should
12   know about with regard to whether you can be fair and
13   impartial, now is the time to tell us. Anything at all.
14   Answer to a prior question and what have you.
15   Okay, I see no hands.
16   We all have a sheet, and I'm going to -- I turn
17   my mike on. I'm sorry, again, it's one of those things.
18   On and off and all the rest of that.
19   And I'm going to go through the sheet and tell
20   you a little bit about myself and help the attorneys and
21   you all. And I'm using a prototype to get an explanation
22   about things that you might tell us about yourself.
23   On the sheet it asks about what -- what your
24   employment is or if you're retired. We'd like to have a
25   little bit of specificity on that. In other words, if

PIMA COUNTY SUPERIOR COURT

1   you're a teacher, if you say, "I'm a math teacher,"

2   "social science teacher," whatever it is, it will help.

3   If you teach computers or have a degree or something in a

4   particular area, that will help us. And the same thing

5   with your spouse.

6   My name is Ted Borek.

7   I was born in Pittsburgh, Pennsylvania, and my

8   family moved to Tucson, Arizona, in 1953. I live in the

9   north/central part of Tucson.

10   I have a bachelor of science degree from the

11   military academy, a juris doctorate degree from the

12   University of Arizona.

13   Married, coming up on 37 years, and we have two

14   adult children that live and work out of state.

15   I was in the service for a period of time. I

16   was an Army -- a lawyer in the Army for about 20 years.

17   I was in the U.S. Attorney's office for 10 years. I've

18   been on the bench now for a little over five -- well, a

19   little over six years.

20   My wife has been a teacher while I was in the

21   service, and she was also was a minister for a period of

22   time, and she's recently gotten her Ph.D. in theology,

23   and she's pursuing lecturing and things like that in that

24   area.

25   We get the morning paper, the New York Times.

PIMA COUNTY SUPERIOR COURT

1   We get Time magazine. I don't get to read them all,

2   but -- Smithsonian magazine. I think we still get the

3   Atlantic and New Yorker. I get a host of legal

4   publications that are publications, and I try to keep up

5   with those.

6   Marty and I are both hooked on 24, and so I

7   don't know, we've -- I enlist a program, and she tells me

8   about. That's the only thing I'm watching. The other

9   programs I seemed to have watched have gone off the air.

10   I try to get the Jim Lehrer Newshour in the evening time.

11   We enjoying traveling, bicycling, and I'm in a

12   book group and enjoy reading. I have been called for

13   jury service but not served as a juror in Pima County.

14   And I'm going to ask you all to stand because

15   you don't have a mike, and it will help Cheryl hear you

16   all. And so if you could stand, Ms. Penny, and tell us

17   about yourself.

18   PROSPECTIVE JUROR: My name is Julie Penny.

19   And I was born and raised here in Tucson, so I

20   guess I've lived here all my life. I did live in

21   Flagstaff for a little bit.

22   I did go to school for a little bit, which is

23   the NAU. I graduated with a degree in marketing.

24   I am married. I have two children, 10 and

25   almost 8 in two days.

PIMA COUNTY SUPERIOR COURT

1   And I'm a stay-at-home mom. I did work. I was

2   a -- I'm a licensed real estate agent here and also a

3   preschool teacher for a while. My husband works for Dex

4   Media, and he does sales.

5   We do get -- my grandma likes to give me some

6   magazines she gets, so I get Good Housekeeping and Ladies

7   Home Journal. We don't get a newspaper usually.

8   I like Sunday night TV. Desperate Housewives,

9   Grey's Anatomy and I do like to read. I do volunteer

10   work for my children's school and for church, and that

11   pretty much takes up my free time.

12   And I have never -- I've been called, but I was

13   in Flagstaff so I've never served and never gone through

14   this process before.

15   THE COURT: Okay. Thank you very much.

16   PROSPECTIVE JUROR: Thank you.

17   THE COURT: Ms. Parcelluzzi.

18   Even close to right?

19   PROSPECTIVE JUROR: No, you got it right.

20   Perfect.

21   THE COURT: Longest name on the list here.

22   PROSPECTIVE JUROR: Yeah, I know.

23   Okay, my name is Terri Parcelluzzi.

24   I was born in West Virginia -- Charleston, West

25   Virginia. Been here 13 years.

PIMA COUNTY SUPERIOR COURT

117

1   I graduated high school. I did one year
2   paralegal in college.

3   I am married. I have four children and one
4   grandchild.

5   I am a mail room supervisor in a collection
6   company. My husband is manager of the collection
7   company.

8   We don't get a newspaper. I get magazines like
9   People, Star, those kinds of things.

10   My favorite show is Desperate Housewives, Grey's
11   Anatomy.

12   I like to read. I cross-stitch, play games with
13   my kids, going to movies. I love to go to movies.

14   And I've gotten one jury summons but got excused
15   before I got here.

16   THE COURT: Thank you very much.

17   Mr. Theiss.

18   PROSPECTIVE JUROR: My name is Richard Theiss.

19   I was born and raised here in Tucson, so I've
20   lived here all my life.

21   I have no college education.

22   I'm single.

23   I own my own landscaping business.

24   I read the newspaper. I don't have a regular TV
25   show that I watch all the time.

PIMA COUNTY SUPERIOR COURT

```
 1          I enjoy camping, hunting, fishing.

 2          And I've never been on a jury before.

 3          THE COURT:  Thank you very much.

 4          And, Mr. Friesenborg.

 5          PROSPECTIVE JUROR:  Good pronunciation.

 6          THE COURT:  I always get it whether it's the i-e

 7  or the e-i.

 8          PROSPECTIVE JUROR:  It's pronounced the second

 9  one.

10          THE COURT:  Thank you.

11          PROSPECTIVE JUROR:  My name is Siebo

12  Friesenborg.

13          I've been here for about four years.  Live down

14  on Old Spanish Trail on the southeast side of Tucson.

15          Went to university.  Mechanical engineer.

16          Three children, one grandchild.  Anybody like to

17  see a couple hundred pictures, I'll crank up the

18  computer.

19          IBM system analyst.

20          Newspapers, magazines:  I get the Air and Space

21  Museum magazine and a couple other airplane magazines.

22          Regular TV show:  Military Channel.

23          Hobbies:  I do things with airplanes, but I like

24  to travel.

25          Prior jury experience:  zero.  None.
```

PIMA COUNTY SUPERIOR COURT

```
1          THE COURT:  Thank you very much.

2          Mr. Loding.

3          PROSPECTIVE JUROR:  My name is Chuck Loding.

4          I was born and raised in Chicago, Illinois.  I

5   moved to Tucson in 1976.  I live around TMC.

6          I've got an electrical communications degree

7   from DeVrie.

8          Married.  Have three adult children.

9          My wife and I are both retired from Tucson

10  Unified School District.

11         I get the Citizen, the Wallite, Reader's Digest,

12  National Geographic.  I watch maybe CSI, Military

13  Channel -- CSI and mostly lawyer series.

14         Hobby is golf.  Sometimes I fish.

15         And I was on jury on a criminal case and found

16  the victim (sic) not guilty.

17         THE COURT:  How long ago was the jury service?

18         PROSPECTIVE JUROR:  It was back in '78.

19         THE COURT:  Okay, was that here in Tucson?

20         PROSPECTIVE JUROR:  Tucson.

21         THE COURT:  Do you recall the nature of the

22  charges in the case?

23         PROSPECTIVE JUROR:  It was theft, possession of

24  stolen property.

25         THE COURT:  Okay.  Thank you very much.
```

PIMA COUNTY SUPERIOR COURT

```
 1              Ms. --

 2              PROSPECTIVE JUROR:  I am Joanne Martin.

 3              And I was born in Orlando, Florida, and I lived

 4    in Arizona since 1971.  I live on the northeast part of

 5    Tucson.

 6              I have a master's degree in public health from

 7    the University of Arizona.

 8              I've been happily married for 23 years.  Have

 9    three children; old children, as I say.  They're 17, 19

10    and 22 years old.

11              My occupation:  I'm an administrator at one of

12    the hospitals here in town.  My husband is self-employed

13    for a paint and body shop.

14              And we get the newspaper, but I don't read it.

15    Magazines I do read are Sunset, Homes and Garden.  And I

16    like to garden, hike Sabino Canyon.

17              And I had -- this is the third time I've been

18    called for jury duty but first time to get this far.

19              THE COURT:  Thank you very much.

20              And, Ms. Perez.

21              PROSPECTIVE JUROR:  I'm Patty Perez.

22              I was born in Prescott, Arizona.  I've lived in

23    Arizona for 48 years.  I live approximately on the west

24    side.

25              I have an associate's in business.
```

PIMA COUNTY SUPERIOR COURT

```
 1              I'm married and I have two children.

 2              I'm an administrative assistant at Pima

 3    Community College.  My husband is an engineer at

 4    Raytheon.

 5              I read the Tucson Citizen.  My favorite program

 6    is General Hospital.  I like to bike and I like to

 7    garden.

 8              And I have been on a case involving a weapon,

 9    and the verdict was guilty.

10              THE COURT:  Thank you very much.

11              Ms. Taylor.

12              PROSPECTIVE JUROR:  My name is Andrea Taylor.

13              I was born in Loring Air Force Base, Limestone,

14    Maine.  I've lived in Arizona for about 13 and a half

15    years.  I live with my grandmother who is near the

16    U of A.

17              I graduated from high school, and I got two to

18    three years of college experience.

19              I'm single.

20              I am a receptionist secretary for Chem-Dry of

21    Tucson.

22              If I do read a newspaper, it's probably the

23    Tucson Weekly.  And I don't really have a regular TV

24    show.  I read, I play video games.

25              And I've been summoned for jury duty once
```

1 before, but I just stood in the jury room all day.

2 THE COURT: Okay. Thank you.

3 Ms. Carrillo.

4 PROSPECTIVE JUROR: My name is Teresa Carrillo.

5 I was born in Morenci, Arizona, and I've lived

6 in Arizona all my life: 70 years. I live on the east

7 side of Tucson.

8 I went to school at St. Mary's Hospital, when

9 they had a school of nursing there. Got my RN.

10 And I'm married, 49 years. I have four

11 children. I'm retired now, but I worked for Hughes

12 Aircraft for 23 years as a occupational health nurse.

13 I read the Star. My favorite regular TV are the

14 Mexican soaps. I watch three of them. And bingo-holic.

15 I sing in the choir at church. My husband directs the

16 Spanish choir at church.

17 I've been on a criminal case. It was illegal

18 drugs, and the person was found guilty.

19 THE COURT: Thank you very much.

20 PROSPECTIVE JUROR: You're welcome.

21 THE COURT: Ms. --

22 PROSPECTIVE JUROR: My name is Irene Noriega.

23 And I have been in Tucson all my life. I live

24 on the south side.

25 I graduated from high school.

PIMA COUNTY SUPERIOR COURT

1   I've been married 48 years and have three adult

 2   sons.

 3   And their wives and I never worked; a housewife.

 4   My husband is painter.

 5   We get the Tucson Daily Citizen. And my

 6   favorite programs are Law and Order and Grey's Anatomy.

 7   My hobbies are my six grandchildren.

 8   And I've been twice, but never, you know, left

 9   the room.

10   THE COURT: Stayed downstairs before?

11   PROSPECTIVE JUROR: Yes, sir.

12   THE COURT: Mr. Smith.

13   PROSPECTIVE JUROR: My name is Ron Smith.

14   I was born and raised in Arizona, so about 41

15   years. Presently live over by Broadway and Craycroft

16   area, east side of town.

17   I have an associate's degree from Pima College

18   and the community college of the Air Force. And bachelor

19   degree from the University of Arizona and master's degree

20   from NAU.

21   I'm married for 18 years. I've got three kids:

22   13, 12, and 7.

23   Worked for 17 years as an educator at Flowing

24   Wells, and recently started my own nonprofit organization

25   to train teachers across the city. My wife is a labor

1   and delivery nurse at St. Joe's.

2   Read the morning paper. Don't get magazines. I

3   never read them, so I never order them. Found 24 this

4   years also. Missed last night, by the way. I have no

5   idea where they are. And we'll watch some TV news shows

6   as well.

7   Hobbies: You know, I've got a daughter in

8   basketball, soccer, and softball, so my hobbies are going

9   to all their games.

10   Prior jury experience has been pretty much in

11   the audience, and that's it.

12   THE COURT: Okay. Thank you.

13   Ms. Richardson.

14   PROSPECTIVE JUROR: My name is Lisa Richardson.

15   I was born in Tucson, and I've lived here all my

16   life except for three years in Seattle. I live on the

17   northeast side of town.

18   Graduated from high school.

19   I've been married for 18 years and have a son,

20   15, daughter, 13.

21   My husband's recently retired, and I'm a

22   stay-at-home mom.

23   I get the paper every day and read it. My

24   favorite TV show is 24 also. I like to hike and bike.

25   And I have no prior jury experience.

PIMA COUNTY SUPERIOR COURT

```
1              THE COURT:  Thank you very much.
2         Ms. Coffey.
3         PROSPECTIVE JUROR:  My name is Denise Coffey.
4         I was born in Michigan, raised in Illinois.
5    I've been in Arizona for about 18 years.  I -- right now
6    I live, like, central part of town so my son can walk
7    across the street to high school.  But I spend a lot of
8    time on the south side too because I work down there and
9    my parents are down there.
10        I have a BA from the U of -- a BA in English and
11   creative writing, and they're both from the U of A.
12        I am not married.  I have five children; four
13   adult children and the 16-year-old is the baby.  Have two
14   and a half grandchildren.  One is -- the third one is due
15   in June.
16        Right now I work in catering, and that's what I
17   do; in banquets and catering.  I freelance for different
18   catering companies.  I work at Embassy Suites, the Desert
19   Museum, just word of mouth work.  And I love it, so...
20        I like to read the -- I take -- I don't take --
21   whatever, the USA Today.  My parents take the morning
22   paper, so I read that also, and I'm a magazine junkie.  I
23   love all kinds of magazines.
24        I love to watch Law and Order.  I like the
25   Medical Channel because I was a CNA in Illinois, so I
```

PIMA COUNTY SUPERIOR COURT

1   like anything medical also. My favorite radio is KXZI,

2   community radio.

3   What I do for recreation? Don't have much time.

4   I like to -- if I have free time, I usually have enough

5   kids to call them up and say, "What do you want to do?",

6   so they have something for me to do. We go out and go to

7   shows and go eat.

8   I've been on one jury before. I think it's

9   criminal. It's a DUI, and he was guilty.

10   THE COURT: Okay. Thank you very much.

11   Mr. Johnson.

12   PROSPECTIVE JUROR: My name is Richard Johnson.

13   I was born and raised in a small town in Kansas.

14   Lived majority of my life in Denver, Colorado. Have been

15   here seven years. Was gone for about five. Before that

16   I was here about ten. I'm a retired IBM. I live, like,

17   central, like Country Club and Ft. Lowell.

18   Two years of college.

19   Married. Three kids -- three boys.

20   I am a computer operator here at Pima County.

21   My wife doesn't work.

22   I get the morning newspaper, sometimes I read it

23   and sometimes I don't.

24   I watch mostly sports on TV and I flip all over

25   the radio. I play tennis.

PIMA COUNTY SUPERIOR COURT

```
 1          I have no previous jury experience.  This is the
 2   first time.
 3          THE COURT:  Thank you, sir.
 4          Let's see, Mr. Runger.
 5          PROSPECTIVE JUROR:  My name is George Runger.
 6          I was born and raised in Tucson.  I've been here
 7   20 years.
 8          I'm currently three years into a mechanical
 9   engineering degree at the University of Arizona.
10          I am single.  No children.
11          I don't work during the school year.  I kind of
12   pick up this and that over the summer.  I'm not sure of
13   my plans for this summer.
14          Newspapers, I read the U of A paper because it's
15   free.  And regular TV show, anything on the History
16   Channel and occasional Cops.  And hobbies:  off-roading.
17   I used to do mountain biking.  Kind of hot out.
18          And no jury experience.
19          THE COURT:  Thank you.
20          Ms. Nichelson.
21          PROSPECTIVE JUROR:  My name is Tamara Nichelson.
22   I go by Tammy.
23          I was born and raised in Albuquerque, New
24   Mexico.  I've lived in Arizona six years.  I live in the
25   Rancho Sahuarita community.
```

PIMA COUNTY SUPERIOR COURT

```
1              I have a bachelor of arts and master's in
2    mechanical engineering.
3              I am married.  I don't have any children.
4              I am a systems engineer at Raytheon, and my
5    husband is a mechanical engineer out at Raytheon.
6              We don't get any magazines.  The only magazine
7    is Hot Rod, and I don't read it.  My favorite TV shows
8    are CSI and Charmed.  My hobbies include quilting,
9    soccer, weight-lifting and triathlons.
10             And I was summoned once but never served on a
11   jury.
12             THE COURT:  Okay.  Thank you.
13             Mr. Alexander.
14             PROSPECTIVE JUROR:  My name is Matt Alexander.
15             I was born in Phoenix, and I've lived here for
16   34 years.  I live on the east side of town.
17             I have an associate's in criminal justice and
18   about five more years of college after that.
19             I'm married.  Three children.
20             I work for the City of Tucson Police Department,
21   and my wife works for TUSD as a teacher.  I'm a bike
22   officer for them.
23             Let's see, I read the Arizona Daily Star, I read
24   Smithsonian, and some outdoor magazines.  I don't watch
25   TV very much.  The news is about it.  Cycling, SCUBA
```

PIMA COUNTY SUPERIOR COURT

```
 1   diving, sailing.
 2           I've been called for jury duty but never served.
 3           THE COURT:  Thank you very much.
 4           Ms. Fee.
 5           PROSPECTIVE JUROR:  My name is Amy Fee.
 6           I'm from Bloomington, Indiana.  Lived out here
 7   seven years.  Live near the Tucson Mall.
 8           I have a bachelor's in recreation, a bachelor of
 9   nursing.
10           Single.
11           Currently registered nurse at the VA Hospital.
12           Read the Tucson Citizen, watch the History
13   Channel and ABC soap operas.  Travel, photography.
14           And called to jury but never served.
15           THE COURT:  Thank you.  Thank you.
16           Mr. Cardenas.
17           PROSPECTIVE JUROR:  My name is Victor Cardenas.
18           I've lived in Arizona all my life.  I live on
19   the west side.
20           I graduated from high school.
21           Married and have four kids.
22           I'm retired, and I used to work with Learjet as
23   a mechanic.
24           I read the Citizen, and I watch the History
25   Channel, and I like to work on old cars.
```

PIMA COUNTY SUPERIOR COURT

```
 1                And I've had no jury experience.
 2                THE COURT:  Okay.  Thank you, sir.
 3                And then, Ms. Villalobos.
 4                PROSPECTIVE JUROR:  My name is Esmeralda
 5       Villalobos.
 6                I was born in Yuma, Arizona.  I've lived here in
 7       Tucson for 36 years.  I live on the northwest side.
 8                I went to Arizona College; degree of nursing.
 9                I am married, 36 years.  Three adult children.
10                I'm a nurse.  My husband is with the federal
11       court system.  I'm employed by Dr. Michael Bibberhoff
12       (ph.), and I am the office nurse.
13                I read the newspaper, and that's about it.  I
14       rarely watch TV.  I bike, I read, I travel.
15                And I've been called for jury duty but never
16       served.
17                THE COURT:  Thank you very much.
18                And, Mr. Carr.
19                PROSPECTIVE JUROR:  My name is Jeff Goss.
20                I was born in Japan.
21                THE COURT:  I skipped ahead.  I'm sorry.  I got
22       lost on my list again.
23                Mr. Goss.
24                PROSPECTIVE JUROR:  I was born in Japan.  I've
25       been here in Arizona since 1984.  I live on the southeast
```

1 side of town.

2   I do not have a college education. I spent a

3 year in school.

4   I'm married. I have two children, ages eight

5 and three.

6   My wife is a stay-at-home mom. I work for

7 Tucson Electrical Power in the distribution center. I

8 get to run the distribution system. So when the lights

9 go out, it's probably my fault.

10   Newspapers: read the Daily Star. Magazines: I

11 read Newsweek. As far as TV, radio shows, I like NCIS.

12 I like sports. I've an avid NASCAR fan. Hobbies: I

13 like to play golf.

14   And as far as jury, I was on a criminal case.

15 It was a DUI and he was convicted.

16   THE COURT: Okay. Thank you.

17   Now Mr. Carr.

18   PROSPECTIVE JUROR: My name is Karl Carr.

19   I live over on the east side and been in Arizona

20 since '72. I was born in Alabama and then raised mostly

21 in Montana.

22   I have a master's degree.

23   And I'm married. I have four children. Only

24 one is home. One is 15. The other three are grown and

25 gone.

```
 1            Currently I'm working for Alcoa (ph.)
 2   Manufacturing System as a tech.  And my wife is a teacher
 3   with Sunnyside School District.
 4            We don't take any newspapers or magazines.
 5   Generally, we'll read the Sunday paper and get the comics
 6   and things.  Due to my work hours and stuff, I don't
 7   really watch TV regularly.  My hobbies are working at the
 8   house or gardening, camping, and fishing.
 9            I've been called to jury duty twice before but
10   never served.
11            THE COURT:  Mr. Carr, what's your master's in?
12   What field?
13            PROSPECTIVE JUROR:  Counseling, psychology.
14            THE COURT:  Thank you.  Sir.
15            Ms. Saucedo.
16            PROSPECTIVE JUROR:  My name is Esperanza
17   Saucedo.
18            I was born in Tucson.  Been here all my life.
19   Live on the northeast side.
20            Graduated from high school.
21            Married.  I have five kids ranging from 21 down
22   to 7.
23            I took an early retirement from the TUSD at the
24   print shop, but I'm currently back over there, which --
25   working on -- as a sub.  But I was a press specialist and
```

PIMA COUNTY SUPERIOR COURT

```
 1    computers and graphics.

 2              Newspaper: Arizona Daily Star. Magazines:

 3    just At Home magazine. Favorite TV: Lifetime Channel,

 4    reality shows. Hobbies: five kids, you don't have any.

 5              I came to jury duty once but never served.

 6              THE COURT: Okay. Thank you very much.

 7              Ms. Day.

 8              PROSPECTIVE JUROR: My name is Jennifer Day.

 9              I was born here in Tucson. Lived in

10    North Carolina and moved back here, unfortunately. I

11    live on the west side of town.

12              I graduated high school and currently in college

13    for nursing.

14              I'm not married. No children.

15              I work at Northwest Hospital.

16            Don't really read. I like Lost, the TV show,

17    and General Hospital. My hobby is dancing. I take tons

18    of dance classes.

19              And this is my first jury.

20              THE COURT: Thank you very much.

21              Mr. Peterson.

22              PROSPECTIVE JUROR: My name is Reed Peterson.

23              I was born in Redondo Beach, California. I've

24    lived here in Arizona for about three and a half years.

25    I live up in the northwest area, up near Mountan View
```

PIMA COUNTY SUPERIOR COURT

```
 1    High School.
 2          I have a bachelor's in Japanese, a master's in
 3    Japanese literature at the University of Arizona, and a
 4    year away from finishing a Ph.D. in modern Japanese
 5    literature at the University of Arizona.
 6          I've been married for almost 21 years.  I have
 7    seven children.  Only one is a girl.
 8          Along with being a student, I teach some classes
 9    at the U of A:  Japanese language, history, literature,
10    culture.  Just about everything related to Japan.  My
11    wife is a stay-at-home mother -- also, I do translation.
12    My wife is a stay-at-home mother.  She also volunteers at
13    the elementary school.
14          Being a graduate student, I don't read or watch
15    much not related to that, though I do read a Japanese
16    newspaper.  And I try to watch the Three Stooges Slap
17    Happy Hour when I'm grading papers.  I like baseball,
18    reading, music, doing things with the kids.
19          And I don't have any prior jury experience.
20          THE COURT:  Okay.  Thank you very much.
21          And then, Mr. Hoy.
22          PROSPECTIVE JUROR:  Okay.  My name is Richard
23    Hoy.
24          I was born in New York state.  I've lived in
25    Arizona for the past six years.  I live on the east side
```

PIMA COUNTY SUPERIOR COURT

```
 1      of town.
 2              I have a bachelor's and master's degree in
 3      engineering.
 4              My wife and I are currently separated.  I have a
 5      five-year-old and a two-year-old at home.
 6              I'm an engineer at Raytheon, and she's a
 7      stay-at-home mom.
 8              We do not get the newspaper.  I read magazines,
 9      Newsweek, Business Week, Aviation Week, sometimes Time.
10              I don't generally watch TV, but my hobbies are
11      reading, playing games, and just started exercising.
12      Strongly encourage it.
13              And I don't have any prior jury experience.
14              THE COURT:  Thank you very much.
15              One last chance for you at all to ask me --
16      remembrance of my questions, and then counsel are going
17      to get to ask some questions.
18              Let me just -- sometimes one question, and that
19      is:  Does anyone here who feels you can't sit in judgment
20      in a case such as this?
21              Apparently not.
22              Mr. Mosher, your panel.
23              MR. MOSHER:  May we approach, your Honor?
24              THE COURT:  Sure.
25                  (Bench conference.)
```

```
 1              MR. MOSHER:  Just because it's Mr. Jensvold's

 2    case, and I have some hope of him returning, maybe

 3    defense counsel would be willing to ask the questions

 4    first.  I can proceed at this time if it's the Court's

 5    wish.

 6              THE COURT:  Do you mind?

 7              MR. LAGATTUTA:  It doesn't bother me.

 8              THE COURT:  Just because?

 9              (Open court.)

10              THE COURT:  Mr. Lagattuta, your panel first.

11              MR. LAGATTUTA:  Can I start from here?

12              THE COURT:  Yes, go ahead.  Your questions --

13    your voir dire.

14              MR. LAGATTUTA:  Okay.  This is a question

15    directed to the potential jurors here.  As you've been

16    sitting here this morning, gaining some information about

17    the case, the Judge some time ago read to you certain

18    counts that make up the indictment.  And contained in

19    each one of these counts is the allegation that on or

20    about a certain date and time, that my client knowingly

21    committed sexual exploitation of a minor by distributing,

22    transporting, exhibiting, receiving, selling, purchasing

23    or exchanging visual depiction of a minor engaged in

24    exploitive exhibition or other sexual conduct.  That's a

25    paraphrase of what the statute reads.
```

PIMA COUNTY SUPERIOR COURT

```
 1          Does anyone here, as a potential juror, have
 2     a -- what I want to call a preconceived notion about what
 3     that allegation means?  Anybody here?  I mean, you must
 4     have some thoughts?  You heard that there were going to
 5     be 15 charges of this particular crime.  Anybody have a
 6     notion of what this charge relates to?
 7               (No response.)
 8          MR. LAGATTUTA:  How about -- how about you,
 9     Mr. Johnson?
10          PROSPECTIVE JUROR:  Yeah.
11          MR. LAGATTUTA:  What do you think it means?
12     Don't be embarrassed because you're going to learn
13     through the process what it is.
14          PROSPECTIVE JUROR:  Porno.
15          MR. LAGATTUTA:  Porno what?
16          PROSPECTIVE JUROR:  Pornographic materials.
17          MR. LAGATTUTA:  Okay.  Is there anybody here on
18     the -- you mean a person possessing pornographic
19     material?
20          PROSPECTIVE JUROR:  Correct.
21          MR. LAGATTUTA:  Okay.  Is that the general idea
22     about what the panel believes these charges relate to?
23          PROSPECTIVE JUROR:  There's all kinds of verbs:
24     possessing, exchanging.  It's any of those things?
25          THE COURT:  That was Ms. Nichelson that
```

PIMA COUNTY SUPERIOR COURT

```
 1   where we found people for prostitution and then, at the
 2   same time, doing internet porn.
 3              MR. LAGATTUTA:  Okay.  Being that some of that
 4   experience you've had might relate, depending on what you
 5   hear from the witness stand --
 6              PROSPECTIVE JUROR:  Uh-huh.
 7              MR. LAGATTUTA:  -- to the evidence in this case,
 8   does that put you in any position to be fair -- more fair
 9   to one side than the other?
10              PROSPECTIVE JUROR:  No.
11              MR. LAGATTUTA:  Okay.  Who else raised their
12   hand?
13              THE COURT:  Ms. Fee raised her hand.  I'm sorry,
14   I saw Ms. Fee first.
15              MR. LAGATTUTA:  Okay, Ms. Fee.
16              PROSPECTIVE JUROR:  When I worked in the
17   hospital, we had a gentleman who was convicted of
18   sexually molesting a minor, and he parole violation -- he
19   had -- he had escaped parole, so we had to call law
20   enforcement to get him service time out.
21              MR. LAGATTUTA:  Okay.  But will that experience
22   itself have any affect on you one way or another in terms
23   of how fair you might be able to be as a juror in this
24   case?
25              PROSPECTIVE JUROR:  Uh-huh.
```

PIMA COUNTY SUPERIOR COURT

```
 1          MR. LAGATTUTA:  What do you think that might be?
 2          PROSPECTIVE JUROR:  I don't know if I could be
 3     fair.
 4          MR. LAGATTUTA:  Okay.
 5             (Bench conference.)
 6          MR. LAGATTUTA:  I don't know how you do this.
 7          THE COURT:  Let me -- go through all of them,
 8     and, you know, I would probably rather have you do voir
 9     dire, and then you come up and make your challenges.  I
10     don't know if --
11             (Open court.)
12          THE COURT:  I ask you to direct your attention,
13     but the court reporter has to hear what we're talking
14     about, and your voices are picking up, and so --
15             (Bench conference.)
16          THE COURT:  Why don't you go ahead and finish
17     your voir dire, and we'll see where we are.  And then we
18     can bring them back in.
19          MR. LAGATTUTA:  Okay.  All right.
20             (Open court.)
21          MR. LAGATTUTA:  Okay.  Who else?  Is it --
22          PROSPECTIVE JUROR:  Carrillo.
23          MR. LAGATTUTA:  Ms. Carrillo.
24          PROSPECTIVE JUROR:  Yes.  I was on the Victim's
25     Compensation Board for six years, and I reviewed many,
```

PIMA COUNTY SUPERIOR COURT

```
 1    many, many cases of pornography and child molestation.
 2    And I don't think I could be fair.
 3            MR. LAGATTUTA:  Okay.  When you say you
 4    reviewed --
 5            PROSPECTIVE JUROR:  Well, we would review the
 6    cases and then allow -- compensate the victims.
 7            MR. LAGATTUTA:  Oh, I see.
 8            PROSPECTIVE JUROR:  Victim's Compensation Board.
 9            MR. LAGATTUTA:  I'm familiar with that.  Okay.
10    And you think that that would affect your ability --
11            PROSPECTIVE JUROR:  Yes.
12            MR. LAGATTUTA:  -- to be a fair and impartial
13    juror?
14            PROSPECTIVE JUROR:  Yeah.
15            MR. LAGATTUTA:  Anybody else raise their hand?
16            The whole -- let's face it, the whole concept or
17    the whole, even, discussion, I think, of child
18    pornography is not an easy one to undertake particularly
19    because it's a crime and it's a way serious crime.
20            Is there anyone here, as a juror -- as a
21    potential juror, who's thinking that they may be exposed
22    to either language or evidence about this charge, do you
23    think that based on either the way you're brought up or
24    how you feel now or what you've been exposed to in your
25    life would be so uncomfortable with -- with actually
```

PIMA COUNTY SUPERIOR COURT

```
 1   having to deal hands-on with a discussion or presentation
 2   of this type of case, is there anyone who feels they may
 3   be just so uncomfortable with that aspect that they could
 4   not serve fair and impartially in the case?  Please raise
 5   your hand and don't be shy.
 6          If you want to talk about that --
 7          THE COURT:  Sure, you can come up.  You can all
 8   come up here.
 9          PROSPECTIVE JUROR:  Well, I can tell you right
10   now.
11          MR. LAGATTUTA:  Ms. Noriega?
12          PROSPECTIVE JUROR:  Yes.
13          MR. LAGATTUTA:  Go ahead.
14          PROSPECTIVE JUROR:  I'm very uncomfortable.  And
15   I have granddaughters and grandsons and, you know, I
16   just --
17          MR. LAGATTUTA:  So this would be -- this would
18   be a topic that should we get into a discussion about it,
19   it would be uncomfortable for to you serve fairly?
20          PROSPECTIVE JUROR:  Yes.
21          MR. LAGATTUTA:  Okay.  Anybody else?
22          PROSPECTIVE JUROR:  Truthfully, you know, I'm
23   saying that I really --
24          MR. LAGATTUTA:  Right.  And we appreciate that.
25          As I said, the rest of you, don't be
```

PIMA COUNTY SUPERIOR COURT

```
 1   where we found people for prostitution and then, at the
 2   same time, doing internet porn.
 3            MR. LAGATTUTA:  Okay.  Being that some of that
 4   experience you've had might relate, depending on what you
 5   hear from the witness stand --
 6            PROSPECTIVE JUROR:  Uh-huh.
 7            MR. LAGATTUTA:  -- to the evidence in this case,
 8   does that put you in any position to be fair -- more fair
 9   to one side than the other?
10            PROSPECTIVE JUROR:  No.
11            MR. LAGATTUTA:  Okay.  Who else raised their
12   hand?
13            THE COURT:  Ms. Fee raised her hand.  I'm sorry,
14   I saw Ms. Fee first.
15            MR. LAGATTUTA:  Okay, Ms. Fee.
16            PROSPECTIVE JUROR:  When I worked in the
17   hospital, we had a gentleman who was convicted of
18   sexually molesting a minor, and he parole violation -- he
19   had -- he had escaped parole, so we had to call law
20   enforcement to get him service time out.
21            MR. LAGATTUTA:  Okay.  But will that experience
22   itself have any affect on you one way or another in terms
23   of how fair you might be able to be as a juror in this
24   case?
25            PROSPECTIVE JUROR:  Uh-huh.
```

PIMA COUNTY SUPERIOR COURT

```
1    embarrassed.  This is something that each lawyer needs to
2    know.  And so does the Court because is it something,
3    just on its face, the subject of it, something that would
4    make you uncomfortable to the point that you wouldn't be
5    able to judge fairly, you'd be more comfortable as a
6    juror on a different type of case?
7              You are Ms. --
8              PROSPECTIVE JUROR:  Saucedo.
9              MR. LAGATTUTA:  Juror No. 23.  Yes.
10             PROSPECTIVE JUROR:  Well, I have five kids and
11   two daughters.  And just kind of disgusts me.
12             MR. LAGATTUTA:  So the part of being a part of a
13   case where you might be exposed to this evidence would
14   make you uncomfortable to the point where you could not
15   judge fairly; is that correct?
16             PROSPECTIVE JUROR:  Yes.
17             MR. LAGATTUTA:  Okay.  Anybody else?  The same
18   subject involves potentially -- evidence that you will
19   hear about that involves activity that involves children.
20   How many here have children under the age of 15?
21             And how many between 15 and, say, 25?
22             THE COURT:  We'll, just say for the record I'd
23   say about a third of the people raised their hand under
24   15, and 15 to 25 is less than that.
25             MR. LAGATTUTA:  Within that first group, the
```

PIMA COUNTY SUPERIOR COURT

```
 1    people that raised their hand and said they have

 2    children, say, under the age of 15, if, for example, you

 3    were to be introduced to some evidence in this case that

 4    involved some, as the statute refers to, sexual

 5    exploitation of a minor child that was in the range that

 6    your child was in, that fact alone, would any of you feel

 7    uncomfortable enough in receiving evidence like that that

 8    it would tend to make you unable to sit fairly as a juror

 9    in the case?

10              PROSPECTIVE JUROR:  Richardson.

11              MR. LAGATTUTA:  Ms. Richardson.

12              PROSPECTIVE JUROR:  Yeah.  I -- it bothers me.

13    It makes me just wonder if someone has that, then -- if

14    it's something that they would act out.

15              MR. LAGATTUTA:  Okay.  As a parent, then, you

16    have concerns that hearing evidence of this, you might

17    not be able to sit impartially because you have some

18    ideas about --

19              PROSPECTIVE JUROR:  Possibly.

20              MR. LAGATTUTA:  -- what the charge would be?

21              Ms. Richardson, and who else raised their hand?

22    And Mr. Goss.

23              PROSPECTIVE JUROR:  Yes, sir.

24              MR. LAGATTUTA:  Okay, sir.

25              PROSPECTIVE JUROR:  Yeah, I have children.  I
```

PIMA COUNTY SUPERIOR COURT

```
 1   want to be fair, but I don't know if I came down to it --
 2   it's one of those things where I can sit here now and say
 3   I can be fair, but once I get down to it, am I
 4   predisposed to be honest?  I don't know.
 5        MR. LAGATTUTA:  That's fair enough.  Say, for
 6   example, this was a case that involved the stealing of an
 7   automobile.  It had absolutely nothing to do with
 8   children in any way, shape, or form, would it be fair to
 9   say that for you to sit in judgment on a case like that
10   would be a much more comfortable position?
11        PROSPECTIVE JUROR:  I would definitely agree
12   with that.
13        MR. LAGATTUTA:  And would you say that because
14   at this point you want to be fair enough, because you're
15   just not sure whether or not --
16        PROSPECTIVE JUROR:  Right.  I don't know -- if
17   the time comes down to that, and if I go home at some
18   point in the future, would that have an affect?  I can't
19   honestly tell you no, it wouldn't.
20        MR. LAGATTUTA:  Okay.  Who else raised their
21   hand?
22        PROSPECTIVE JUROR:  I feel the same way.
23        MR. LAGATTUTA:  You're name is?
24        PROSPECTIVE JUROR:  Esperanza --
25        MR. LAGATTUTA:  Esperanza Saucedo.
```

PIMA COUNTY SUPERIOR COURT

1   We talked about this already before; right?
2   PROSPECTIVE JUROR: Yes.
3   MR. LAGATTUTA: Anybody else?
4   Okay. How about this: You're going to hear
5   testimony from several police officers in the case here,
6   and we have a police officer on the panel. Is there
7   anyone here that should they -- should they -- should
8   they hear information that suggests that a police
9   investigation was not as thorough as it should have been
10 or could have been, if they were to hear that information
11 alone and hear testimony from the witness stand on that
12 topic, is there anyone who feels that because of their
13 background or their relation with anybody else, that that
14 would be a concept that would make them uncomfortable to
15 sit fairly as a juror in the case? No?
16   PROSPECTIVE JUROR: I don't know. I don't
17 understand the question.
18   MR. LAGATTUTA: Okay. That's fair enough. And
19 that's Mr. Johnson.
20   Okay. My question is to you and for the rest of
21 the panel, is there anyone, because of their background
22 or the people they know or organizations they belong to
23 or such that if you were to -- were to hear evidence that
24 the police investigation in this case was either not
25 thorough enough or not done the right way or wasn't

PIMA COUNTY SUPERIOR COURT

```
 1    complete enough in receiving that type of evidence, is
 2    that -- given any of your background, is that the type of
 3    information, should you be convinced that that's true,
 4    would make you so uncomfortable that you wouldn't be able
 5    to judge fairly?  Is that any more clear?
 6              PROSPECTIVE JUROR:  Yeah, that's clear.
 7              MR. LAGATTUTA:  All right.  Mr. Alexander, what
 8    do you think?
 9              PROSPECTIVE JUROR:  Was it clear or what do I
10    think?
11              MR. LAGATTUTA:  What do you think?
12              PROSPECTIVE JUROR:  It wouldn't bother me.
13              MR. LAGATTUTA:  This would be, in your case, a
14    different agency than the one you worked for.
15              PROSPECTIVE JUROR:  Yes, sir.
16              MR. LAGATTUTA:  Would you be able to sit in
17    judgment fairly of another police agency?
18              PROSPECTIVE JUROR:  Uh-huh.
19              MR. LAGATTUTA:  In terms of as a person with
20    your training and just as a regular juror hearing the
21    evidence from the witness stand right here?
22              PROSPECTIVE JUROR:  Yeah.
23              MR. LAGATTUTA:  Okay.  All right.
24              Finally, I know we've gone through this a little
25    bit.  Aside from the people who have mentioned this is a
```

PIMA COUNTY SUPERIOR COURT

```
 1   profession, is there anybody else on the prospective jury
 2   panel that has any -- who they -- what they would be
 3   consider to be special skills in the use of computers?
 4              (No response.)
 5              MR. LAGATTUTA:  How about video games?  Who
 6   plays video games?  Okay.  And you are?
 7              PROSPECTIVE JUROR:  Terri Parcelluzzi.
 8              MR. LAGATTUTA:  Juror No. 2.  Which games do you
 9   play?
10              PROSPECTIVE JUROR:  Old ones, Pac Man and stuff
11   like that.
12              MR. LAGATTUTA:  How about Pong.  Too old for
13   you?
14              PROSPECTIVE JUROR:  Yeah, I play that.
15              MR. LAGATTUTA:  All right.  Are these things
16   that you do at home or do you go out to places?
17              PROSPECTIVE JUROR:  I do them at home.
18              MR. LAGATTUTA:  Okay.  Who else plays games?
19              PROSPECTIVE JUROR:  Runger.
20              MR. LAGATTUTA:  Okay.
21              PROSPECTIVE JUROR:  I play Battlefield 2,
22   Counter Strike Force.  The newer ones.
23              MR. LAGATTUTA:  Okay.  And you play these at
24   home?
25              PROSPECTIVE JUROR:  Yeah, at home.
```

PIMA COUNTY SUPERIOR COURT

```
1          MR. LAGATTUTA:  Do you collect these games or do
2    you just --
3          PROSPECTIVE JUROR:  No.
4          MR. LAGATTUTA:  -- play them when you can?
5          PROSPECTIVE JUROR:  Not really collect.  I play
6    the ones I like.
7          MR. LAGATTUTA:  Okay.  Anybody else raise your
8    hand back there?  Ms. Taylor.
9          PROSPECTIVE JUROR:  Final Fantasy, Zeldas, and
10   King of Hearts.
11         MR. LAGATTUTA:  Okay.  And how often do you play
12   those games?
13         PROSPECTIVE JUROR:  Probably once every three
14   days or so.
15         MR. LAGATTUTA:  Okay.
16         PROSPECTIVE JUROR:  Just when I'm bored, nothing
17   else to do.
18         MR. LAGATTUTA:  Pretty good at it?
19         PROSPECTIVE JUROR:  As long as I have a guide
20   next to me.
21         MR. LAGATTUTA:  Very good.  Who else raised
22   their hands?
23         Help me with your name.
24         PROSPECTIVE JUROR:  Richard Hoy.
25         MR. LAGATTUTA:  Richard Hoy.
```

PIMA COUNTY SUPERIOR COURT

```
1        PROSPECTIVE JUROR:  I play games like design-
2   your-own-study-type, thrill-the-world-type games by
3   myself when there's nothing better to do.
4        MR. LAGATTUTA:  Is that more of an educational
5   tool?  I'm not --
6        PROSPECTIVE JUROR:  I wouldn't degrade to that.
7        MR. LAGATTUTA:  So, this is somewhat fantasy,
8   somewhat fun?
9        PROSPECTIVE JUROR:  Yeah.
10       MR. LAGATTUTA:  Okay.  All right.  And --
11       PROSPECTIVE JUROR:  Goss.
12       MR. LAGATTUTA:  Mr. Goss.
13       PROSPECTIVE JUROR:  Mostly sports.  My son's
14  racing things, but mostly sports, golf, football,
15  baseball.
16       MR. LAGATTUTA:  How often do you do that?
17       PROSPECTIVE JUROR:  Well, it's more along his
18  lines.  But if I get a chance to play it, once a week for
19  an hour or so makes him happy.
20       MR. LAGATTUTA:  Okay.  All right.  And was there
21  anybody else over here that I missed?  I hope this is
22  understandable.
23       Given what you've been asked so far and the
24  information that you received from the Court so far, is
25  there anyone sitting here that has anything in either
```

PIMA COUNTY SUPERIOR COURT

```
1    their background or training or just the way -- just the
2    way they feel about the court system that wouldn't want
3    to have themselves seated as a juror in the case if they
4    were my client here?  And if there's a reason for that
5    that we just haven't covered, and you're willing to share
6    that with us, that's the question.
7              So one more time.  Do you want me to --
8              PROSPECTIVE JUROR:  Yeah, do it again.  Say it
9    one more time.
10             If I were --
11             MR. LAGATTUTA:  If you were the defendant --
12             PROSPECTIVE JUROR:  If I was sitting over there.
13             MR. LAGATTUTA:  If you were the defendant --
14             PROSPECTIVE JUROR:  Yes.
15             MR. LAGATTUTA:  -- would you want Richard
16   Johnson --
17             PROSPECTIVE JUROR:  Oh, yeah.
18             MR. LAGATTUTA:  -- to sit as a juror?
19             PROSPECTIVE JUROR:  Yeah.
20             MR. LAGATTUTA:  And that applies to everybody.
21   I mean, if you were the defendant in this case, would you
22   want someone of your fairness, ability to judge, ability
23   to make decisions about what happens here in the
24   courtroom, would you want someone with that like mind and
25   that like stability to sit as a juror in the case?  And
```

PIMA COUNTY SUPERIOR COURT

```
1    if everybody is in agreement with that, then thank you.

2            That's all the questions I have.

3            THE COURT:  Okay.  Thank you, Mr. Lagattuta.

4            Mr. Jensvold made it just in time to -- either

5    you or Mr. Mosher, you get one of you to --

6            MR. JENSVOLD:  If I could only clone myself.

7            THE COURT:  Normally, the State would ask their

8    questions in voir dire first.  But counsel had agreed,

9    because Mr. Jensvold had to step out, to switch that

10   order.

11           And so, Mr. Jensvold, your voir dire.

12           MR. JENSVOLD:  Thank you, your Honor.

13           Sorry I didn't hear all the questions, but has

14   anybody been involved in programming computers in any

15   aspect, whether simple to extremely complex programming?

16   See if I can decipher Mr. Mosher's handwriting.

17           Mr. Alexander?  Smith?

18           THE COURT:  Hoy.  Mr. Hoy.

19           MR. JENSVOLD:  Mr. Hoy.  Now I've got it.

20           Can you describe what you've done?

21           PROSPECTIVE JUROR:  Part of this job at Raytheon

22   I do occasional programming computers.

23           MR. JENSVOLD:  What kind, what languages?

24           PROSPECTIVE JUROR:  Fortran, C Plus Plus,

25   missile-simulation type.
```

PIMA COUNTY SUPERIOR COURT

```
 1            MR. JENSVOLD:  Okay.  Has anybody --
 2            THE COURT:  There was one other.  Ms. Nichelson.
 3            PROSPECTIVE JUROR:  I took --
 4            MR. JENSVOLD:  I missed it entirely.  I'm sorry.
 5            PROSPECTIVE JUROR:  I took a Fortran class in
 6    college ten years ago.
 7            MR. JENSVOLD:  Have you used it since then?
 8            PROSPECTIVE JUROR:  No.
 9            THE COURT:  Mr. Friesenborg?
10            PROSPECTIVE JUROR:  Yeah, I've done a lot of
11    programming for a long time.  Mostly data reduction.
12            MR. JENSVOLD:  And this is in your work with
13    IBM?
14            PROSPECTIVE JUROR:  Yeah.
15            MR. JENSVOLD:  Anybody else that I missed?
16            (No response.)
17            MR. JENSVOLD:  Okay.  And this is not meant to
18    get anybody in trouble, so has anybody ever used KaZaA or
19    Napster or any sort of -- any of those programs involving
20    file-sharing for music?
21            Mr. Peterson and Ms. Day.
22            Okay, Mr. Peterson, can you describe --
23            PROSPECTIVE JUROR:  Yeah, a few years ago when I
24    first heard of Napster, I tried it once trying to find a
25    song.  And then there was another one called Soul Seek.
```

PIMA COUNTY SUPERIOR COURT

```
1    I found a few songs.  Limited use a few years ago.

2         MR. JENSVOLD:  How about you, Ms. Day?

3         PROSPECTIVE JUROR:  Napster.

4         MR. JENSVOLD:  Does anybody --

5         THE COURT:  There were a couple other answers to

6    that question over here.

7         MR. JENSVOLD:  Everybody raise their hand a

8    little higher so I can see them.

9         And, Mr. Smith.

10        PROSPECTIVE JUROR:  Alexander.

11        MR. JENSVOLD:  Okay.  Mr. Alexander.

12        PROSPECTIVE JUROR:  KaZaA for music before they

13   started suing everybody.

14        MR. JENSVOLD:  And who else?  Mr. George.

15        PROSPECTIVE JUROR:  Yeah, Mr. Runger.  Yeah, I

16   used Raimster, Napster before they started to crack down

17   on it, to try out new music.

18        MR. JENSVOLD:  Okay.  Anybody else?  How about

19   anybody used iTunes now, which is obviously entirely

20   illegal?

21        Mr. Carr?

22        PROSPECTIVE JUROR:  I'm Mr. Goss.

23        MR. JENSVOLD:  You're Mr. Goss?

24        PROSPECTIVE JUROR:  Yes.

25        iTunes just for downloading to the iPod.
```

PIMA COUNTY SUPERIOR COURT

```
1              MR. JENSVOLD:  Now, this is -- I'm going to go
2     one by one here and ask you to briefly go through this.
3              Let's start with you, Ms. Penny.  Can you
4     describe your musical interests?
5              PROSPECTIVE JUROR:  I listen to all kinds.  I
6     listen to country, I listen to 93.7 because I've got kids
7     and we like dance music.
8              MR. JENSVOLD:  Okay.  Thank you.  And -- I'm
9     going to butcher your last name.
10             PROSPECTIVE JUROR:  It is Parcelluzzi.
11             MR. JENSVOLD:  Parcelluzzi.  What's your --
12             PROSPECTIVE JUROR:  I listen to everything but
13    opera and classical.
14             MR. JENSVOLD:  Okay.  And, Mr. Theiss.
15             PROSPECTIVE JUROR:  Pretty much everything
16    except for rap music.
17             MR. JENSVOLD:  Okay.  And, Mr. Friesenborg.
18             PROSPECTIVE JUROR:  Oldies.
19             MR. JENSVOLD:  Mr. Loding.
20             PROSPECTIVE JUROR:  Country-western, oldies,
21    '50s, '60s.
22             MR. JENSVOLD:  No Marilyn Manson or anything
23    like that?
24             Ms. Martin.
25             PROSPECTIVE JUROR:  Country, soft rock,
```

PIMA COUNTY SUPERIOR COURT

```
 1   definitely not hard rock.

 2           MR. JENSVOLD:  Okay.  Ms. Perez.

 3           PROSPECTIVE JUROR:  Mainly listen to 94.9.  It's

 4   the easy-listening channel station.

 5           MR. JENSVOLD:  Ms. Taylor.

 6           PROSPECTIVE JUROR:  New rock, hard rock, punk

 7   rock, grunge rock, pretty much anything.

 8           MR. JENSVOLD:  And, Ms. Carillo.

 9           PROSPECTIVE JUROR:  90.5 Spanish station, and

10   then I sing in the Spanish choir at church.

11           MR. JENSVOLD:  Ms. Noriega.

12           PROSPECTIVE JUROR:  1400, 1450.

13           MR. JENSVOLD:  Mr. Smith.

14           PROSPECTIVE JUROR:  Air One and K-LOVE,

15   contemporary Christian.

16           MR. JENSVOLD:  Okay.  Ms. Richardson.

17           PROSPECTIVE JUROR:  Mostly rock, KFMA.

18           MR. JENSVOLD:  And, Ms. Coffey.

19           PROSPECTIVE JUROR:  Mostly rock, '50 -- well,

20   '60s and '70s and classical and that's about it.  I like

21   to hear what's new coming, KXZI, but I don't do country.

22           MR. JENSVOLD:  Okay.  And, Mr. Johnson.

23           PROSPECTIVE JUROR:  I prefer jazz, but I listen

24   to everything.

25           MR. JENSVOLD:  What radio stations would you
```

PIMA COUNTY SUPERIOR COURT

```
1    listen to?

2            PROSPECTIVE JUROR:  The Point.  I listen to --

3            MR. JENSVOLD:  That's 104.1; right?

4            PROSPECTIVE JUROR:  I think that is.  I listen

5    to the rap station.  I listen to the hard rock station.

6    I don't know what the call letters are.

7            MR. JENSVOLD:  Mr. Runger.

8            PROSPECTIVE JUROR:  Used to be only rock, but

9    now kind of involved to jazz, classical, anything that

10   sounds good.

11           MR. JENSVOLD:  Ms. Nichelson.

12           PROSPECTIVE JUROR:  I listen -- I flip through

13   the channels on the radio.  Mostly country and I also do

14   dance music and hip-hop, and so it's just kind of

15   whatever.

16           MR. JENSVOLD:  Okay.  And, Mr. Alexander.

17           PROSPECTIVE JUROR:  I listen to just the mix of

18   the radio.

19           MR. JENSVOLD:  And, Ms. Fee.

20           PROSPECTIVE JUROR:  Technohouse, Scottish --

21   Irish music.

22           MR. JENSVOLD:  Mr. Cardenas.

23           PROSPECTIVE JUROR:  Mexican, 1600 on the dial,

24   1030.

25           MR. JENSVOLD:  And Ms. Villalobos.
```

PIMA COUNTY SUPERIOR COURT

1   PROSPECTIVE JUROR: I listen to 94.9, and I like
2   country music also.
3   MR. JENSVOLD: And Mr. Goss.
4   PROSPECTIVE JUROR: Mostly classic rock, KLPX.
5   MR. JENSVOLD: And, Mr. Carr.
6   PROSPECTIVE JUROR: Soft rock.
7   MR. JENSVOLD: Ms. Saucedo.
8   PROSPECTIVE JUROR: A little bit of everything,
9   93.7.
10   MR. JENSVOLD: And, Ms. Day.
11   PROSPECTIVE JUROR: Pretty much everything, but
12   I'm a country girl.
13   MR. JENSVOLD: Okay. And, Mr. Peterson.
14   PROSPECTIVE JUROR: Classical, neoclassical
15   metal, progressive, and with a little blues thrown in.
16   MR. JENSVOLD: Okay. You're not listening to
17   the radio, then, much are you?
18   PROSPECTIVE JUROR: Only when I get really
19   frustrated.
20   MR. JENSVOLD: And, Mr. Hoy.
21   PROSPECTIVE JUROR: Alternative rock. Radio
22   stations are The Z104 and BOB station.
23   MR. JENSVOLD: Thank you very much.
24   And this is obviously totally unrelated area to
25   what we were just talking about, but if -- if there's a

PIMA COUNTY SUPERIOR COURT

```
 1    witness in this case who -- and there will be a witness
 2    in this case who you will hear from that has been
 3    convicted of burglary and auto-theft-type crimes.  Is
 4    there anyone that has either been a victim of those kinds
 5    of crimes or, for any other reason, would just be so bent
 6    against that person that would be bent on disbelieving
 7    that person just because of those convictions?
 8              That's all I have.
 9              Thank you.
10              THE COURT:  Counsel approach, please.
11              Mr. Mosher, you probably need to come up, too.
12                   (Bench conference.)
13              THE COURT:  Challenge for cause by the State?
14    There were several people that defense is --
15              MR. LAGATTUTA:  Just, I went first.
16              MR. JENSVOLD:  No, I don't believe there's any
17    challenges for cause.
18              THE COURT:  Pass the panel?
19              MR. JENSVOLD:  Correct.
20              THE COURT:  Defense?
21              MR. LAGATTUTA:  I've got No. 9.
22              THE COURT:  Carrillo.
23              MR. LAGATTUTA:  Carrillo.
24              THE COURT:  There were several people that,
25    based on the charges -- based on the nature of the
```

PIMA COUNTY SUPERIOR COURT

```
 1    charges and what they had, find it difficult to be
 2    partial.  And I think he is -- Ms. Carrillo was one of
 3    those.
 4              MR. LAGATTUTA:  I will say that I believe these
 5    numbers, and collectively my reason is during the
 6    questioning each one of them admitted they couldn't be
 7    fair and impartial.
 8              No. 10.
 9              THE COURT:  9, 10.
10              MR. LAGATTUTA:  And 12.
11              THE COURT:  9, 10, and 12.
12              MR. LAGATTUTA:  12.  Also No. 18, No. 21, and
13    No. 23.  Each of them, during the questions I asked,
14    admitted that they felt that they could not be fair and
15    impartial.  I hope I got them all because I was walking
16    around.
17              THE COURT:  Yeah, I think you did.  The one I
18    might have follow up on was Mr. Goss because he was more
19    hesitant and what have you.  But --
20              MR. JENSVOLD:  Did he mention 12?  12.
21              THE COURT:  Yeah, 12.
22              10, 12, 18, 21 -- are you going to have any
23    follow up?
24              MR. MOSHER:  I defer to Mr. Jensvold.  It may be
25    necessary to pass the panel.  I don't think we got that
```

1 | far.

2 THE COURT: Well, I asked that question,

3 proclivity, and I asked it of all of those. But I make a

4 determination on excusing them, and I think they've all

5 said they would have some problems, and I think there is

6 a follow-up questions, and I probably ought to, in

7 fairness, ask.

8 I'll make a call on that, and then we'll bring

9 the others in and strike them. Okay.

10 Any other challenges?

11 MR. LAGATTUTA: No.

12 THE COURT: Other than them, would you pass the

13 panel?

14 MR. LAGATTUTA: Yes.

15 THE COURT: Now, if I strike some, we'll bring

16 them on and I'll ask the general questions. If there's

17 any follow up --

18 MR. LAGATTUTA: 9, 10, 12, 18, 21, 22.

19 (Open court.)

20 THE COURT: I have a follow-up question or two

21 for several of you. I'll make -- I'll make a mention of

22 all of you, and then I'm going to ask one question of all

23 of you. And it's Ms. Carrillo and Ms. Noriega and

24 Ms. Richardson and Ms. Fee and Mr. Goss and Ms. --

25 Ms. Saucedo, in the questioning today you exhibited some

PIMA COUNTY SUPERIOR COURT

```
 1    concern on fairness with regard to the nature of kinds of
 2    things that you might see or just the nature of the
 3    charges and what have you here.
 4              I'm going to ask you -- each of you to think
 5    about whether or not you can disregard that and follow
 6    the law in the instructions that I give you, regardless
 7    of your intention or whether your feelings are such that
 8    you don't think you could honestly be fair in this case?
 9              I guess we can start -- I'll start with you,
10    Ms. Carrillo.
11              PROSPECTIVE JUROR:  I don't think I could be
12    fair.
13              THE COURT:  Ma'am, I'm going to excuse you.  So
14    we'll excuse Juror No. 9.
15              And then, Ms. Noriega?
16              PROSPECTIVE JUROR:  I -- truthfully, I cannot.
17              THE COURT:  Okay.  Thank you, ma'am.  I'm going
18    to excuse Ms. Noriega.  If you all go back downstairs to
19    the jury commissioner's office.
20              Ms. Richardson.
21              PROSPECTIVE JUROR:  I don't think so.
22              THE COURT:  I appreciate your being here and
23    bearing with us through the questioning and what have
24    you, and I'll excuse you.  Go back downstairs.
25              And then I think, Ms. Fee, my last question is
```

PIMA COUNTY SUPERIOR COURT

```
1    with your statements earlier in questioning, you
2    indicated that you might not be able to be fair.  And I
3    just want to confirm that, or whether or not you can lay
4    your feelings aside and judge this based on just the
5    evidence?
6            PROSPECTIVE JUROR:  I don't think I can be fair.
7            THE COURT:  Thanks, ma'am.  You'll be excused,
8    Ms. Fee.
9            Juror No. 18, Mr. Goss, same kind of questions
10   to you, sir.
11           PROSPECTIVE JUROR:  To be honest, I can't give
12   you a definite answer yes or no.  I want to be, but I
13   can't honestly say that I -- that I could be.
14           THE COURT:  Okay.  I'm going to err on the side
15   of caution, sir.  And thanks for being here, and I'm
16   going to excuse you.
17           And then the final one is Ms. Saucedo.
18           PROSPECTIVE JUROR:  I don't think I can be fair.
19           THE COURT:  Okay.  Thank you.  We'll excuse
20   those jurors.  We're going to call jurors in their place
21   now, and I'll see whether you -- let's bring all of you
22   up and have you seated.
23           First replace Juror No. 9, Ms. Carrillo.
24           THE CLERK:  That would be Lois Morgan-Heisch.
25           THE COURT:  Replace Juror No. 10, Ms. Noriega.
```

PIMA COUNTY SUPERIOR COURT

```
 1              THE CLERK:  Sheila Smith.

 2              THE COURT:  And Juror No. 12.

 3              THE CLERK:  Rhome Winslow.

 4              THE COURT:  And Juror No. 18.

 5              THE CLERK:  Erica Bauer.

 6              THE COURT:  We might be a going a little too

 7   quickly.  And we have Ms. Morgan-Heisch right here, and

 8   Ms. Smith next, and then we have Mr. Winslow.

 9              PROSPECTIVE JUROR:  Yeah.

10              THE COURT:  Sir, you would be over here.

11              And for Ms. Gonzales, No. 21 -- I'm sorry, we

12   have Ms. Bauer for 18.

13              THE CLERK:  Ms. Bauer for 18.

14              THE COURT:  And then Juror No. 21, for Ms. Goss.

15              THE CLERK:  Lorenzo Guerra.

16              THE COURT:  And then for Juror No. 23,

17   Ms. Saucedo.

18              THE CLERK:  Would be Marcy Cropp.

19              THE COURT:  I know we've had a number of

20   questions.  For those jurors just joined us, we'll start

21   right in the back here and go around.

22              Would you have answered yes to any questions,

23   Ms. Morgan-Heisch?

24              PROSPECTIVE JUROR:  Unfortunately, yes.

25              THE COURT:  And which one would that be?  Or
```

1   which ones?

2   PROSPECTIVE JUROR: I had a daughter that was

3   molested when she was 13 -- a week after her 13th

4   birthday. The guy is still on the street.

5   THE COURT: Let me just -- you've had an

6   incident in your life. Do you think you can sit in this

7   case and be fair and impartial?

8   PROSPECTIVE JUROR: Definitely not.

9   THE COURT: Okay. Thanks, ma'am. I'll excuse

10   you.

11   We'll replace Ms. Morgan-Heisch with

12   Juror No. 9.

13   THE CLERK: Mary Barrett.

14   THE COURT: Ms. Barrett, would you have answered

15   yes to any questions?

16   PROSPECTIVE JUROR: No, I haven't.

17   THE COURT: Please have a seat.

18   And then, Ms. Smith, any yes answers from you?

19   PROSPECTIVE JUROR: Yes, sir. May I approach?

20   THE COURT: Sure. Counsel, please.

21   (Bench conference.)

22   THE COURT: We're here with Ms. Smith.

23   PROSPECTIVE JUROR: I have an uncle who tried to

24   molest me a number of times. There's no way in the world

25   I could be impartial.

PIMA COUNTY SUPERIOR COURT

```
 1              THE COURT:  Thanks for being here, ma'am.  Sorry
 2      for your situation.
 3                   (Open court.)
 4              THE COURT:  We'll replace Ms. Smith, No. 10.
 5              THE CLERK:  Willy Carlton.
 6              THE COURT:  Mr. Carlton, would you have answered
 7      yes to any questions, sir?
 8              PROSPECTIVE JUROR:  No.
 9              THE COURT:  Okay.  Thank you.
10              Let's see, over here.  Mr. Winslow, yes to any
11      questions?
12              PROSPECTIVE JUROR:  Yes.  I'm self-employed, so
13      this would have an affect on me.
14              THE COURT:  Are you sole employ or sole source
15      of your family?
16              PROSPECTIVE JUROR:  Sole income.
17              THE COURT:  Be difficult to be here for the rest
18      of this week?
19              PROSPECTIVE JUROR:  Yes.
20              THE COURT:  Replace Juror -- Mr. Winslow,
21      Juror No. 12.
22              THE CLERK:  Robert Brown.
23              THE COURT:  Mr. Brown, would you have answered
24      yes to any questions?
25              PROSPECTIVE JUROR:  No.
```

PIMA COUNTY SUPERIOR COURT

```
1          THE COURT:  Okay.  Please have a seat.
2          Then we're going over here -- I don't want to
3   miss anybody here.  Ms. Bauer, would you have answered
4   yes to any questions?
5          PROSPECTIVE JUROR:  Yes, I have.
6          THE COURT:  Would you tell us which ones?
7          PROSPECTIVE JUROR:  May I approach?
8          THE COURT:  Sure.
9              (Bench conference.)
10         PROSPECTIVE JUROR:  I had a boyfriend that was
11  sexually abused.  And as far as it goes to me, it's
12  probably he's guilty and I know I definitely cannot be
13  fair.
14         THE COURT:  Okay.  This was your boyfriend?
15         PROSPECTIVE JUROR:  He was sexually abused for
16  nine years of his life.  And I've got a two-year-old son
17  that --
18         THE COURT:  Thanks, ma'am.  I'm going to excuse
19  you for being here.
20             (Open court.)
21         THE COURT:  We'll replace Ms. Bauer,
22  Juror No. 18.
23         THE CLERK:  And that would be Janice Miller.
24         THE COURT:  Ms. Miller, would you have answered
25  yes to any questions?
```

PIMA COUNTY SUPERIOR COURT

```
 1          PROSPECTIVE JUROR:  The only one would be law

 2   enforcement, and that's my father is a retired agent FBI

 3   agent.

 4          THE COURT:  And you say "retired."  How long ago

 5   did he retire?

 6          PROSPECTIVE JUROR:  Thirty, forty years ago.

 7          THE COURT:  Okay.  Anything about that cause you

 8   to favor one side or the other in this case?

 9          PROSPECTIVE JUROR:  No.

10          THE COURT:  Okay.  Thanks.  Please have a seat.

11          And I think, Mr. Guerra, No. 21.

12          PROSPECTIVE JUROR:  Yes.

13          THE COURT:  Would you have answered yes to any

14   questions?

15          PROSPECTIVE JUROR:  Yes, I would.  May I

16   approach some?

17          THE COURT:  Sure.

18          (Bench conference.)

19          PROSPECTIVE JUROR:  I have a niece that was

20   molested at 11 years old.  I feel like I don't think I

21   could be impartial.

22          THE COURT:  How long ago was that?

23          PROSPECTIVE JUROR:  That was approximately

24   thirteen years ago.

25          THE COURT:  Thirteen years ago?
```

PIMA COUNTY SUPERIOR COURT

1   PROSPECTIVE JUROR: Yes.

2   THE COURT: Were you involved in a trial or

3   anything like that?

4   PROSPECTIVE JUROR: No. Just emotion about the

5   family involvement.

6   THE COURT: And so, frankly, you think you

7   couldn't lay that aside and be fair and impartial in this

8   case?

9   PROSPECTIVE JUROR: At this point in time, I

10   don't know that I can or I can't. I just --

11   THE COURT: Can you follow the law as I give it

12   to you in the instructions?

13   PROSPECTIVE JUROR: I could probably follow the

14   law. I don't know what my emotions would be at the time.

15   THE COURT: Okay. So I'll go ahead and excuse

16   you.

17   (Open court.)

18   THE COURT: We'll replace Mr. Guerra,

19   Juror No. 21.

20   THE CLERK: That would be Tim Stroud.

21   THE COURT: Sir, would you have answered yes to

22   any questions?

23   PROSPECTIVE JUROR: No.

24   THE COURT: Please have a seat.

25   And then I think we have one more person that's

PIMA COUNTY SUPERIOR COURT

```
 1    joined us, Ms. Cropp.

 2             PROSPECTIVE JUROR:  Yes.

 3             THE COURT:  Would you have answered any

 4    questions?

 5             PROSPECTIVE JUROR:  Yes.  Shawn and his family

 6    are close personal friends of ours.

 7             THE COURT:  You know the prosecutor?  How close

 8    is close?

 9             PROSPECTIVE JUROR:  My husband married he and

10    his wife.

11             THE COURT:  You mean he performed -- well, my

12    wife is a minister, and someone one time came up and

13    said, "Well, will you marry us?"  And she said, "What do

14    I do with my husband Ted?"

15             So you're in your church or something of that

16    nature?

17             PROSPECTIVE JUROR:  Uh-huh.

18             THE COURT:  Would that affect you in this case

19    or can you be fair and impartial?

20             PROSPECTIVE JUROR:  I think it would be

21    affected.

22             THE COURT:  Thanks, ma'am.  We'll excuse you.

23    You can go back downstairs.

24             We replace Juror No. 23, Ms. Cropp.

25             THE CLERK:  That would be Thomas Fallows.
```

PIMA COUNTY SUPERIOR COURT

```
 1          THE COURT:  Mr. Fallows, before you walk across
 2    there, would you have answered yes to any questions, sir?
 3          PROSPECTIVE JUROR:  No, sir.
 4          THE COURT:  Okay.  Now, to all of you --
 5          PROSPECTIVE JUROR:  Oh, I'm sorry.  Yes, I do
 6    have a brother that's a Utah Highway Patrol and a son
 7    that spent five years in the U.S. military police.
 8          THE COURT:  How long ago was the last one that
 9    was in either of those capacities?
10          PROSPECTIVE JUROR:  Five years ago.
11          THE COURT:  Okay.  Would that affect you in this
12    case?
13          PROSPECTIVE JUROR:  No, sir.
14          THE COURT:  Can you be fair and impartial in
15    this case?
16          PROSPECTIVE JUROR:  I can.
17          THE COURT:  Okay.  Please have a seat.
18          Let me just go back and ask all of you that have
19    joined us now particularly two questions that I ask
20    everybody that I want to be sure, and just tell me if the
21    answer is yes.
22          Can you follow the law as given in the
23    instructions that I give you?
24          Let me phrase that a different way so you would
25    answer it no.  Is there anybody who couldn't follow the
```

PIMA COUNTY SUPERIOR COURT

```
 1   law -- that's joined us -- in the instructions?
 2           Any of you that joined us would be unable to
 3   make a determination based only on the evidence presented
 4   in this case?
 5           Okay, and I see no hands to that.
 6           I'll ask one further question and that is this:
 7   And that is, you're likely to see some depictions of the
 8   acts that were described, and you're probably going to
 9   have to go back, and you may talk about some of that in
10   the mixed group back there, men and women on the jury.
11   Anybody find that so difficult that you simply wouldn't
12   be able to do it?
13           And I see no hands.
14           So I'm going to ask those of you who joined us
15   to please stand and tell us about yourself.  We'll start
16   first with Ms. Barrett.  I think the sheets are left.  I
17   hope they were.
18           PROSPECTIVE JUROR:  I haven't had a chance to
19   look it over.
20           My name is Mary Ann Barrett.
21           I was born in Cheyenne, Wyoming.  I've lived in
22   Arizona 13 years.  I live on the southeast side, Rita
23   Ranch area.
24           I have an associate's degree in medical
25   transcription.
```

PIMA COUNTY SUPERIOR COURT

1   I've been married 23 years, and I have three

2 children.

3   I'm currently a window clerk at the Vail Post

4 Office. My husband is a manager at Raytheon.

5   I don't get any newspapers or magazines. My

6 favorite TV show is Food Network. My radio program is

7 Air One.

8   I'm very involved in my daughter's high school

9 band program. I do that for my recreation.

10   And I've previously -- I've been called to jury

11 duty but never served.

12   THE COURT: Okay. Thank you very much.

13   Mr. Carlton.

14   PROSPECTIVE JUROR: My name is Willie Carlton.

15   I was born in Carmel, California. I've lived in

16 Arizona for about 14 and a half years. I live on the

17 southeast side of town.

18   I have an associate's degree in medical

19 technology from community college at the Air Force.

20   I'm married. I have no children.

21   I'm retired from the Air Force, also retired

22 from Pima County, Kino Community Hospital. My wife is

23 retired from the Air Force and currently is on

24 disability. She was an RN.

25   I read the Arizona Daily Star. I watch quite a

```
 1    bit of TV; mostly the three major networks.
 2               No current hobbies.  I used to play quite a bit
 3    of golf.  I haven't played in a couple year now.
 4               I've been called for jury duty but never served.
 5               THE COURT:  Thank you.
 6               And, Mr. Brown.
 7               PROSPECTIVE JUROR:  My name is Robert Brown.
 8               I was born in California, but I've lived in
 9    Arizona for nine years.  I live on the northeast side of
10    town.
11               I have a bachelor's degree in electrical
12    engineering from New Mexico State University.
13               I'm married and have one son who is 18 years
14    old.
15               My current occupation is I'm a manager at IBM
16    here in Tucson.
17               Newspapers:  I read the Daily Star occasionally.
18    Don't really read any magazines.  Television:  I watch
19    news programs basically.  That's it.  Sports radio,
20    listen to lots of different music, country, rock, things
21    like that.
22               Hobbies:  I play guitar, I work out pretty much
23    every day, and I hang out with my family.
24               And my previous jury experience, I've been on
25    two juries.  I think the last, probably five years.  This
```

PIMA COUNTY SUPERIOR COURT

```
 1    is my third one.

 2            THE COURT:  Do you recall the verdicts in those

 3    cases?

 4            PROSPECTIVE JUROR:  One was not guilty and one

 5    was guilty.

 6            THE COURT:  Nature of the charges?

 7            PROSPECTIVE JUROR:  First one was possession --

 8    marijuana possession.  Second one had to do with a

 9    civil -- it was more of a civil case.

10            THE COURT:  Okay.  Thank you, sir.

11            And we slip on over here to Ms. Miller.

12            PROSPECTIVE JUROR:  My name is Jan Miller.

13            I've been in Arizona for about 24 years.  I was

14    born in Hartford, Connecticut.  I live on the east side.

15            I went to high school.

16            I have -- I'm not married.  I have two kids; a

17    girl, 14, and a boy, 11 years old.

18            I work part-time at Kmart as a sale's associate.

19            I get the Sunday paper.  My favorite program is

20    Lost, but it's not a -- when it's not a repeat, and Cops.

21    And I like to read and do puzzles.

22            And I've been on a jury duty once; been called

23    four times in the past five years.

24            THE COURT:  You say you actually sat as a juror?

25            PROSPECTIVE JUROR:  Yes, I did.
```

PIMA COUNTY SUPERIOR COURT

```
1          THE COURT:  Do you remember the verdict?

2          PROSPECTIVE JUROR:  The verdict was not guilty

3     on DUI.

4          THE COURT:  Okay.  Thank you very much.

5          And, then, Mr. Stroud.

6          PROSPECTIVE JUROR:  My name is Tim Stroud.

7          I was born and raised in Tucson.  I live in

8     central Tucson.

9          I have a liberal arts degree.

10         I'm divorced with a 14-year-old daughter.

11         I'm a musician and a psychiatric technician.

12         I read Tucson Weekly and magazines about movies.

13    And the Sopranos.  And my hobbies are dancing, listening,

14    and playing music.

15         And I was here once before, but I didn't get

16    picked.

17         THE COURT:  Okay.  Thank you, sir.

18         And, then, Mr. Fallows.

19         PROSPECTIVE JUROR:  My name is Tom Fallows.

20         I have lived in Arizona for 22 years.  I was

21    born in San Francisco, California.  The -- I live up in

22    the Picture Rocks area.

23         I have a college degree in medicine.

24         And I've been married for 46 years, and I have

25    three children.
```

PIMA COUNTY SUPERIOR COURT

1   My occupation is that of medical profession,

2 physician's assistant. And my wife is employed as a

3 housewife. I am retired from the U.S. Air Force as a

4 Major.

5   And I like to read medical magazines, Jammin',

6 New England Journal of Medicine. My favorite TV

7 programs, I don't really have any.

8   My hobbies include music. I've sang tenor with

9 the Mormon Tabernacle Choir.

10   I have been called to be on a jury, but I never

11 served.

12   THE COURT: Okay. Thank you, sir, very much.

13   Will counsel approach now?

14   (Bench conference.)

15   THE COURT: Okay. I understand the State's

16 passed the panel?

17   MR. JENSVOLD: Yes.

18   THE COURT: Half an hour, to 3:30?

19   Pass the panel?

20   MR. LAGATTUTA: I do, your Honor, but I'm

21 wondering if you wouldn't mind, Mr. Brown here said he

22 was a manager of IBM.

23   THE COURT: Okay.

24   MR. LAGATTUTA: Could you ask him what that job

25 entails?

PIMA COUNTY SUPERIOR COURT

```
 1              THE COURT:  Sure.
 2              MR. LAGATTUTA:  And also the other gentleman who
 3    spoke -- not last one, but the previous one said he's --
 4              THE COURT:  Stroud?
 5              MR. LAGATTUTA:  Yeah.  -- a psychological
 6    tech -- a psych tech.  Maybe just ask him what that
 7    means.  I'm just not sure.
 8              THE COURT:  Okay.  Why don't you stand here
 9    while I do that.
10                   (Open court.)
11              THE COURT:  Mr. Brown, could you explain a
12    little bit more what your job is at IBM?
13              PROSPECTIVE JUROR:  Yeah, I manage a department
14    of people, 24 people currently.  And also I'm a program
15    delivery manager for two new products that we're trying
16    to deliver this year.
17              THE COURT:  And does that get real involved in
18    computers?
19              PROSPECTIVE JUROR:  It's based off of computers,
20    yes.  I'm not actually doing the technical work anymore,
21    but I kind of manage the day-to-day activities.
22              THE COURT:  More the human resources person?
23              PROSPECTIVE JUROR:  Well, no, just the tasks and
24    who's -- I assign the tasks, both technical work to be
25    done and keep an eye on days.
```

PIMA COUNTY SUPERIOR COURT

```
1          THE COURT:  Do you have any questions or follow

2     up, either counsel?

3          MR. JENSVOLD:  I don't.

4          MR. LAGATTUTA:  To get to that position how --

5     you worked your way up and sort of skills or training?

6          PROSPECTIVE JUROR:  Well, I used to program.  I

7     did computer programming, the C Fortran.  I used to work

8     in aerospace for both Lockheed Martin.  I took some

9     project manager training, tier one curriculum, took

10    project management.  Professional exam; passed that.  And

11    basically that's why I'm doing this.

12         THE COURT:  Bottom line:  Is there anything with

13    your experience or what have you that causes you to think

14    that you -- well, can you be fair and impartial in this

15    case?

16         PROSPECTIVE JUROR:  Yes, I believe so.

17         THE COURT:  And the technical things that we're

18    talking about here, if you hear testimony, can you

19    determine this case based only on the evidence presented

20    in this case?

21         PROSPECTIVE JUROR:  Yes.

22         THE COURT:  Okay.  Thank you.  And then another

23    question over here to Mr. Stroud.

24         Sir, if you could explain your -- your job just

25    a little bit more, please, sir?
```

PIMA COUNTY SUPERIOR COURT

```
 1              PROSPECTIVE JUROR:  I assist the psychiatrists
 2    and the nurses in delivering services to the patients.
 3              THE COURT:  Okay.  So you get into diagnosis and
 4    things of that kind of nature, or you're more --
 5              PROSPECTIVE JUROR:  I'm just -- I just help
 6    them.  But I think I'm probably more unbiased than most
 7    people would be because I -- they talk to me about their
 8    problems.
 9              (Bench conference.)
10              THE COURT:  Counsel, follow up either on
11    Mr. Jensvold?
12              MR. JENSVOLD:  I don't have any.
13              THE COURT:  Mr. Lagattuta?
14              MR. LAGATTUTA:  No, thank you.
15              THE COURT:  Okay.  Challenges?
16              MR. LAGATTUTA:  No.
17              MR. JENSVOLD:  No.
18              THE COURT:  Take to half past?  It's probably
19    going to be half an hour.
20              MR. JENSVOLD:  Do we want to make a record about
21    not doing any witnesses today?
22              THE COURT:  Let me deal with that after we get
23    the jury decided.  I think what we might do is do
24    openings, but we'll see where we are.  Give instructions.
25              (Open court.)
```

PIMA COUNTY SUPERIOR COURT

```
1         THE COURT:  Okay, folks, each you has been found
2    to be a fair and impartial juror, so don't take it
3    personally if you're not selected at this point.  We're
4    going to have 14 people selected because I like to have
5    two jurors because it's a -- you know, goes through the
6    week.  And people do get sick and things like that, so
7    we're going to do that.
8         So we're going to take a recess now.
9         Those that have not been called so far, I still
10   need you to come back.  You've seen how people have been
11   changed even sort of toward the end, and so -- and now at
12   this point it's possible that we may need some of you.
13        So what I'd like for you to do, this will
14   probably take until about 25 till or so.  It's ten after
15   3 right now, so we'll take that break.
16        When you come back, you all don't sit up here.
17   Everybody is going to sit behind the bar, back there, and
18   we'll call those of you that will be seated to hear the
19   case.
20        Now, don't talk about it.  I've said that to you
21   before.  You will hear me, if you're out here long
22   enough, hear me say over and over again.  If you need to
23   go out and get a stretch or something like that, this is
24   a good time to do that.  Just be back by 25 till, and
25   it's 10 after now.
```

```
 1        So we're in recess.

 2             (Pause.)

 3        THE COURT:  If you are a juror, I'm going to ask

 4   you to step out.  I hope you can get a seat out there.

 5             (Whereupon, the prospective jury panel was

 6             excused from the courtroom.)

 7        THE COURT:  Okay.  Thanks.  Make your strikes.

 8   And as soon as you're all ready we'll come back in.

 9        MR. LAGATTUTA:  What time?

10        THE COURT:  I told them to be back at 25 till.

11        If you need -- you know, if you need your --

12   give your strikes to Marty and, you know, take a quick

13   break if you need it.  And then --

14        MR. LAGATTUTA:  We need to run down to the

15   restroom.

16        THE COURT:  Do that and what have you.  And if

17   it takes a little longer, I understand.  We'll see where

18   we are at that point, how far we go today.

19             (Recess.)

20        THE COURT:  We are on the record.  With the time

21   we bring them in here, how long do you expect your

22   opening to be, Shawn?

23        MR. JENSVOLD:  Not very long, five minutes.

24        THE COURT:  Jim?

25        MR. LAGATTUTA:  Same.  Fifteen, maybe twenty.
```

PIMA COUNTY SUPERIOR COURT

```
 1            THE COURT:  Okay.  Well, if we bring them in and
 2    my instructions are going to take fifteen, so we could
 3    probably do openings tonight if you want to do that.  Or,
 4    you know, if you want to let them go and do them tomorrow
 5    morning, do you have any preference?
 6            MR. LAGATTUTA:  I prefer to do them tomorrow.
 7            MR. JENSVOLD:  I think I would too.
 8            MR. LAGATTUTA:  It's better if we give them a
 9    fresh start.
10            THE COURT:  Okay.  Are you satisfied with that?
11    You know how long it's going to take, so I don't want --
12    I don't want to dally, but then on the other hand I don't
13    want to push it, doing something that -- for either of
14    you.
15            MR. JENSVOLD:  Right.
16            THE COURT:  Are you happy going tomorrow?
17            MR. JENSVOLD:  That's fine.
18            THE COURT:  Okay.  Both of you?
19            MR. LAGATTUTA:  Yes.
20            THE COURT:  We'll bring them in, I'll do my
21    instructions, and then we'll release them until tomorrow.
22            THE CLERK:  Julie Penny, and then I have Siebo
23    Friesenborg, Charles Loding, Joeanne Martin, Patty Perez,
24    Andrea Taylor, Willy Carlton, Ronald Smith, Robert Brown,
25    Tamara Nichelson, Victor Cardenas, Karl Carr, Jennifer
```

PIMA COUNTY SUPERIOR COURT

184

1   Day, and Reed Peterson.

2   Is that what everybody was expecting?

3   MR. LAGATTUTA: That's it.

4   THE COURT: Okay. Then we'll bring the jurors

5   in, I'll give them instructions, and we'll take our break

6   for the evening.

7   Peter, you can bring the jurors.

8   (Whereupon, the prospective jury panel

9   entered the courtroom.)

10   THE COURT: Thanks. Please be seated.

11   Ladies and gentlemen, as your name is called

12   please come forward. Peter will help you. We're going

13   to again be seated in the back row here. We have seats

14   for eight of you in the back and six of you in the front

15   by the desk.

16   And so, Marty, if you'll call the names of

17   jurors selected, please.

18   THE CLERK: Julie Penny, Siebo Friesenborg,

19   Charles Loding, Joeanne Martin, Patty Perez, Andrea

20   Taylor, Willy Carlton, Ronald Smith, Robert Brown, Tamara

21   Nichelson, Victor Cardenas, Karl Carr, Jennifer Day, and

22   Reed Peterson.

23   THE COURT: Thank you very much, ladies and

24   gentlemen. Thanks for being with us for this process.

25   For those that weren't even questioned or anything, I do

1   hope that you understand it was very important for the

2   process as a whole that you were here. We appreciate

3   your time and attention. You all can go back down to the

4   jury commissioner. My guess is they'll release you, but

5   I can't be sure about that because I don't know what's

6   going on in other courts. But thank you for your time

7   here, and you all are excused.

8   Now, as those jurors are departing I'm going to

9   ask you all to stand once again. We're going to

10   administer an oath, and that's done at this time.

11   (The jury panel was sworn.)

12   THE COURT: Please be seated. Thank you.

13   Let me tell you what we're going to do. I have

14   some instructions here. You have copies of those

15   instructions, and you can just sit back and listen to me

16   read the instructions to you, or you can follow along.

17   You'll have a copy of those instructions during the

18   period of time of the jurors.

19   I'm going to read the instructions to you and

20   let you have a recess tonight. We'll come back tomorrow

21   morning and do the parts that start the trial after the

22   instructions. I know it's been a long day for you. I

23   know you were here pretty early, and everyone agreed

24   that's the best way to proceed.

25   But I do need to read these to you, and so again

```
1    you can just sit back and listen to me read them or
2    follow along.
3            Ladies and gentlemen, now that you have been
4    sworn I will briefly tell you about your duties as jurors
5    and give you preliminary instructions.  At the end of the
6    trial I will give you more detailed instructions, and
7    those instructions will control your deliberations.
8            It will be your duty to decide the facts.  You
9    must decide the facts only from the evidence presented in
10   court.  You must not speculate or guess about any fact.
11   You must not be influenced by sympathy or prejudice.  You
12   will hear the evidence, decide the facts, and then apply
13   the law that I will give you to those facts.  That is how
14   you will reach your verdict.  In doing so you must follow
15   the law whether you agree with it or not.
16           Now, you must not take anything that I may say
17   or do during the trial as indicating any opinion about
18   the facts.  You and you alone are the judges of the
19   facts.
20           The law does not require a defendant to prove
21   innocence.  Every defendant is presumed by law to be
22   innocent.  The State has the burden of proving the
23   defendant guilty beyond a reasonable doubt.  This means
24   the State must prove each element of any charge beyond a
25   reasonable doubt.  In civil cases it is only necessary to
```

PIMA COUNTY SUPERIOR COURT

1   prove that a fact is more likely true than not or that

2   its truth is highly probable. In criminal cases such as

3   this, the State's proof must be more powerful than that.

4   It must be beyond a reasonable doubt.

5   Proof beyond a reasonable doubt is proof that

6   leaves you firmly convinced of the defendant's guilt.

7   There are few things in this world that we know with

8   absolute certainty, and in criminal trials the law does

9   not require proof that overcomes every doubt. If, based

10   on your consideration of the evidence, you are firmly

11   convinced that the defendant is guilty of the crime

12   charged, you must find the defendant guilty. If, on the

13   other hand, you think that there is a real possibility

14   that the defendant is not guilty, you must give the

15   defendant the benefit of the doubt and find the defendant

16   not guilty.

17   You will decide what the facts are from the

18   evidence presented here in court. That evidence will

19   consist of testimony of witnesses, any documents and

20   other things received into evidence as exhibits, and any

21   facts stipulated or agreed to by the parties or which you

22   are instructed to accept.

23   You will decide the credibility and weight to be

24   given to any evidence presented in the case whether it be

25   direct evidence or circumstantial evidence.

PIMA COUNTY SUPERIOR COURT

```
 1          Now, direct evidence is the physical exhibit or
 2     the testimony of a witness who saw, heard, touched,
 3     smelled, or otherwise actually perceived an event.
 4     Circumstantial evidence is the proof of a fact from which
 5     the existence of another fact may be inferred.  For
 6     example, if you see the sidewalk is wet, you may find
 7     that it rained.  However, other evidence, such as a
 8     turned on garden hose, may explain the water on the
 9     sidewalk.  Therefore, before you decide whether a fact
10     has been proven by circumstantial evidence, you must
11     consider all of the evidence in light of reason, common
12     sense, and experience.
13          You must determine the weight to be given to all
14     of the evidence without regard to whether it is direct or
15     circumstantial.
16          Admission of evidence in court is governed by
17     rules of law.  I will apply those rules and resolve any
18     issues that arises during the trial concerning the
19     admission of evidence.  If an objection to a question is
20     sustained, you must disregard the question and you must
21     not guess what the answer to the question might have
22     been.  If an exhibit is offered in evidence and an
23     objection to it is sustained, you must not consider that
24     testimony -- excuse me, you must not consider that
25     exhibit as evidence.  If testimony is ordered stricken
```

PIMA COUNTY SUPERIOR COURT

1 from the record, you must not consider that testimony for

2 any purpose.

3   Do not concern yourselves with the reasons for

4 the ruling of admission of evidence and do not regard

5 those rulings as any indication from me of the

6 credibility or weight you should give to evidence that

7 has been admitted.

8   In deciding the facts of the case, you should

9 consider what testimony to accept and what to reject.

10 You may accept everything that a witness says, or part of

11 it, or none of it.

12   In evaluating testimony, you should use the

13 tests for accuracy and truthfulness that people use in

14 determining matters of importance in everyday life,

15 including such factors as the witness' ability to see or

16 hear or know the things the witness testified to, the

17 quality of the witness' memory, the witness' manner while

18 testifying, whether the witness has any motive, bias, or

19 prejudice, whether the witness is contradicted by

20 anything the witness said or wrote before trial, or by

21 other evidence and the reasonableness of the witness'

22 testimony when considered in light of the other evidence.

23 Consider all of the evidence in light of reason, common

24 sense, and experience.

25   A witness qualified as an expert by education or

PIMA COUNTY SUPERIOR COURT

1   experience may state opinions on matters in that witness'
2   field of expertise and may also state reasons for those
3   opinions. Expert opinion testimony should be judged just
4   as any other testimony. You are not bound by it. You
5   may accept it or reject it, in whole or in part, and you
6   should give it as much credibility and weight as you
7   think it deserves considering the witness' qualifications
8   and experiences, the reasons given for the opinions, and
9   all the other evidence in the case.
10   As I mentioned earlier, it is your job to decide
11 from the evidence what the facts are, and here are six
12 rules on what is and what is not evidence.
13   One, evidence to be considered. You are to
14 determine the facts only from the testimony of witnesses
15 and from exhibits received in evidence.
16   Two, lawyers' statement. Ordinarily, statements
17 or argument made by the lawyers in the case are not
18 evidence. Their purpose is to help you understand the
19 evidence and law. However, if the lawyers for the
20 parties agree or stipulate that some particular fact is
21 true, you should accept it as the truth.
22   Three, questions to a witness. By itself a
23 question is not evidence. A question can only be used to
24 give meaning to a witness' answer.
25   Four, objections to questions. If a lawyer

PIMA COUNTY SUPERIOR COURT

1   objects to a question and I do not allow the witness to

2   answer, you must not try to guess what the answer might

3   have been. You must also not try to guess the reason why

4   the lawyer objected in the first place.

5   Five, rejected evidence. At times during the

6   trial, testimony or exhibits will be offered as evidence

7   but I might not allow them to become evidence. Since

8   they never become evidence, you must not consider them.

9   Six, stricken evidence. At times I may order

10   some evidence to being stricken from the record. Then it

11   is no longer evidence and you must not consider it for

12   any purpose.

13   At the end of the trial you will have to make

14   your decisions based on what you recall of the evidence.

15   You will not be given a written transcript of any

16   testimony. You should pay close attention to the

17   testimony as it is given.

18   Now, you have been provided with notepads and

19   pencils. I encourage you to take notes during the trial

20   if you wish to do so. Do not let note-taking distract

21   you so that you miss hearing or seeing other evidence.

22   You may take your notes and notebooks with you when you

23   leave the courtroom or for recesses; however, you must

24   not discuss your observations with other jurors during

25   recess. You may use your notes and notebooks during your

PIMA COUNTY SUPERIOR COURT

1   deliberations at the end of the trial. Until then, keep

2   your notes to yourself. If you do not want to take your

3   notes and notebooks with you during the trial, you should

4   just leave them on your seat.

5   Whether you take notes or not, you should rely

6   on your own memory of what was said and not be overly

7   influenced by the notes of other jurors. After you have

8   rendered your verdict, the bailiff will collect your

9   notes and destroy them.

10   Do not be influenced at all by my taking notes

11   at times. What I write down may have nothing to do with

12   what you will be concerned with during the trial.

13   There may or may not be news media coverage of

14   the trial. What the news media covers is up to them. If

15   there is media coverage, you must avoid it during the

16   trial. If do encounter something about the case in the

17   news media during the trial, end your exposure to it

18   immediately and report it to me as soon as you can.

19   There are a number of important rules governing

20   your conduct as jurors. They are largely dos and don'ts

21   that I will call the "admonition."

22   First, do wear your juror badges at all times in

23   and around the courthouse so that everyone will know that

24   you are on a jury.

25   Second, do not read any news stories or articles

PIMA COUNTY SUPERIOR COURT

1 or listen to any radio or television reports about the

2 case or about anyone who has anything to do with it.

3 Third, do not do any research or make any

4 investigation about the case on your own. Do not view or

5 visit the locations where the events of the case took

6 place. Do not consult a dictionary, internet, or any

7 other reference material about the case.

8 Four, although it is entirely natural to want to

9 talk or visit with the people that you see during the

10 trial, do not talk to anyone about the case or about

11 anyone who has anything to do with it. Do not let anyone

12 talk to you about these matters until the trial has ended

13 and you have been discharged as jurors. Until then you

14 may tell people you are on a jury, and you may tell them

15 the estimated schedule for the trial. But do not tell

16 them anything else except to say you can't talk about it

17 until the case is over.

18 If someone should try to talk to you about the

19 case, stop them or walk away. If you should overhear

20 others talking about the case, stop them or walk away.

21 If anything like this happens, report it to me or any

22 member of my staff as soon as you can.

23 Fifth, to avoid even the appearance of improper

24 conduct, do not talk to any of the parties, the lawyers,

25 or the witnesses about anything until the case is over

PIMA COUNTY SUPERIOR COURT

even if it has nothing to do with the case. This rule is
an effort to assure the parties of the absolute fairness
they are entitled to expect from you as jurors.

If the attorneys, parties, and witnesses do not
greet you outside of court or avoid riding in the same
elevator, they are not being rude. They are carefully
avoiding even an appearance of impropriety.

Six, do not form final opinions about any fact
or about the outcome of the case until you have heard and
considered all of the evidence, the closing arguments,
and the rest of the instructions I will give you on the
law. Keep an open mind during the trial. Form your
final opinions only after you have had an opportunity to
discuss this case with each other in the jury room at the
end of the trial.

Now, before each recess I will not repeat the
entire I have just given you. I will probably refer to
it by saying, "Please remember the admonition," or
something like that. However, even if I forget to make
reference to it, remember that the admonition still
applies at all times during the trial.

If at any time during the trial you have
difficulty hearing or seeing something that you should be
hearing or seeing, or if you get into personal distress
for any reason, raise your hand and let me know. If you

PIMA COUNTY SUPERIOR COURT

1   have any questions about parking, restaurants, or other

2   personal matters relating to jury service, feel free to

3   ask one of the court staff. But remember, the admonition

4   applies to the court staff as it does to everyone else,

5   and so do not try to discuss the case with the court

6   staff.

7   If you have a question about the case for a

8   witness or for me, write it down but do not sign it.

9   Hand the question to the bailiff. If your question is

10   for a witness who is about to leave the witness stand,

11   please signal the bailiff or me before the witness leaves

12   the stand. The lawyers and I usually will discuss any

13   question you ask, and the Rules of Evidence or other

14   rules of law may prevent some questions from being asked.

15   If the rules permit the question and an answer

16   is available, an answer will be given at the earliest

17   opportunity. Now, when we do not ask a question, that is

18   no reflection on the person asking it and you should

19   attach no significance to the failure to ask a question.

20   I will apply the same legal standards to your questions

21   as I do to the questions asked by the lawyers. If a

22   particular question is not asked, please do not try to

23   guess why or what the answer might have been.

24   Trial is expected to last through Friday of this

25   week. And as I mentioned earlier, there is some

PIMA COUNTY SUPERIOR COURT

```
 1   possibility it could go into Monday or Tuesday of next
 2   week.  We will all do our best to move the case along,
 3   but delays often occur.  These won't be anyone's fault,
 4   and so don't hold them against the parties.  Delays
 5   usually occur because the attorneys and I often need to
 6   resolve certain legal matters before these matters may be
 7   presented to you in court, or because I have to address
 8   emergency matters in other cases.
 9            Usual hours of trial will be from 10:30 a.m. to
10   5 p.m.  We will recess about noon and usually begin again
11   at 1:30 p.m.  We will take a short recess in
12   mid-afternoon and occasionally stretch breaks in place.
13   Unless a different starting time is announced prior to
14   recessing for the evening, you may assume a starting time
15   of 10:30 a.m. for the next day.
16            At the beginning of the day, please assemble in
17   the jury room for the division.  Now, do not come back
18   into the courtroom until you are called in by the
19   bailiff.
20            Criminal trials generally proceed in the
21   following order:
22            First, the prosecuting attorney will make an
23   opening statement giving a preview of the case.  The
24   defendant's attorney may make an opening statement
25   outlining the defense case immediately after the
```

PIMA COUNTY SUPERIOR COURT

1   prosecutor's statement, or the attorney may postpone that

2   opening statement until after the State's case has been

3   presented. What is said in opening statements is not

4   evidence, nor is it an argument. The purpose of an

5   opening statement is to help you prepare for anticipated

6   evidence.

7   Second, the State will present its evidence.

8   After the State finishes the presentation of its

9   evidence, the defendant may present evidence. If the

10   defendant does produce evidence, the State may present

11   additional or rebuttal evidence.

12   With each witness there is a direct examination,

13   a cross-examination by opposing side, and finally

14   redirect examination. This usually ends the testimony of

15   that witness.

16   Third, the attorneys will make closing arguments

17   and tell you what they think the evidence shows and how

18   they think you should decide the case. The State has the

19   right to open and close the argument since the State has

20   the burden of proof. Just as in opening statements, what

21   is said in closing arguments is not evidence.

22   Now, fourth, after all the evidence is in, I

23   will read and give you copies of the final instructions;

24   the rules of you law you must follow in reaching the

25   verdict.

PIMA COUNTY SUPERIOR COURT

```
 1          Fifth, you will deliberate in the jury room
 2   about the evidence and rules of law and decide upon a
 3   verdict.  Once you agree upon a verdict, it will be read
 4   in court with you and the parties present.
 5          Finally, you will be discharged and released
 6   from the admonition.
 7          Now, a charge against the defendant is not
 8   evidence, and you must not think that the defendant is
 9   guilty just because of the charge.  The defendant has
10   pled not guilty, and the plea of not guilty means the
11   State must prove every part of any charge beyond a
12   reasonable doubt.
13          In this case the State has charged the defendant
14   as follows -- and at this point you have a copy of the
15   indictment, and I read that to you this morning.  I had
16   one typo in that that I wish that you would take a look
17   at that now and correct this typo with me, and that is
18   under Count Ten, on the third page, on the third line
19   from the bottom of that count, we had the word "mount"
20   which was "mouth."  So if you just see the third word
21   from the end there, you'll see "into the mouth of a" --
22   at the very end of that, and that word is "mouth," and
23   that was just simply a typo.
24          And then I'm not going to reread this, but
25   continuing on in the instructions after the indictment,
```

PIMA COUNTY SUPERIOR COURT

1   the crime of sexual exploitation of a minor under the age

2   of 15 requires proof of the following:

3   One. The defendant knowingly possessed,

4   received, or exchanged any visual depiction in which an

5   actual minor is engaged in exploitive exhibition or other

6   sexual conduct;

7   Two. The actual minor depicted in any

8   visual depiction was under the age of 15 at the time.

9   The crime of attempted sexual exploitation of a

10   minor under 15 requires proof of one of the following:

11   One. The defendant intentionally engaged

12   in conduct which would have been a crime if the

13   circumstances relating to the crime were as the defendant

14   believed them to be; or,

15   Two. The defendant intentionally committed

16   any act which was a step in a course of conduct which the

17   defendant planned would end or believed would end in the

18   commission of a crime; or,

19   Three. The defendant engaged in conduct

20   intended to aid another person to commit a crime, in a

21   manner in which would make the defendant an accomplice,

22   had the crime been committed or attempted by the other

23   person.

24   Visual depiction includes each visual image that

25   is contained in an undeveloped film, videotape, or

PIMA COUNTY SUPERIOR COURT

photograph or data stored in any form and that is capable
of conversion into a visual image.

"Exploitive exhibition" means the actual or
simulated exhibition of the genitals or pubic or rectal
areas of any person for the purpose of sexual stimulation
of the viewer.

"Sexual conduct" means actual or simulated:

One. Sexual intercourse including genital/
genital, oral/genital, anal/genital, or oral/anal,
whether between persons of the same or opposite sex; or,

Two. Penetration of the vagina or rectum
by an object; or,

Three. Masturbation, for the purpose of
sexual stimulation of the viewer.

"Minor" means a person or persons who are under
18 years of age at the time a visual depiction was
created, adapted, or modified.

And "knowingly" means with respect to conduct or
to a circumstance described by a statute defining an
offense that a person is aware of or believes that his
conduct is of that nature or that -- or that the
circumstance exists. It does not require knowledge of
the unlawfulness of the act or omission.

"Computer" means an electronic device that
performs logic, arithmetic, or memory functions by the

PIMA COUNTY SUPERIOR COURT

1 manipulations of electronic or magnetic impulses and

2 includes all input, output, processing, storage,

3 software, or communication facilities that are connected

4 or related to such a device in such a system or network.

5   "Computer system" means a set of related,

6 connected, or unconnected computer equipment, devices,

7 and software including storage, media, and peripheral

8 devices.

9   "Network" includes a complex of interconnected

10 computer or communication systems of any type.

11   "Producing" means financing, directing,

12 manufacturing, issuing, publishing, or advertising for

13 pecuniary gain.

14   "Simulated" means any depicting of the genital

15 or rectal area that gives the appearance of sexual

16 conduct or incipient sexual conduct.

17   Counsel have any additions or corrections to the

18 instructions?

19   MR. JENSVOLD: No.

20   MR. LAGATTUTA: No.

21   THE COURT: I have one other that I want to tell

22 you about, and that is the rule of exclusion of witnesses

23 has been employed by the parties. And I have a thing

24 that I usually read from that and tell you about it, and

25 I think I lost my sticky that shows where it is.

1   The rule of exclusion is in effect and will be
2   observed by all witnesses until the trial is over and the
3   result announced. And what this means is that witnesses
4   will remain outside the courtroom during the entire trial
5   except when one is called to the witness stand. They
6   will wait in the area directed by the bailiff unless
7   other arrangements have been made with the attorneys who
8   have called them.
9   Now, this rule forbids witnesses from telling
10   anyone but the lawyers what they will testify about or
11   what they have testified to. If witnesses do not -- do
12   talk to the lawyers about their testimony, other
13   witnesses and jurors should avoid being present or
14   overhearing.
15   The lawyers know and are directed to look out
16   for their witnesses and to remind them of their
17   obligation from time to time as that might be necessary.
18   The parties and the lawyers should keep a careful lookout
19   to make sure that any witnesses don't inadvertently enter
20   the courtroom. State has the right to have a case agent
21   here, and so that person may be in the courtroom and
22   testify. And we'll keep a lookout, so that there are
23   exceptions that the lawyers know about.
24   Now, with that we'll recess for the evening, and
25   when you come back tomorrow we'll start with the opening

PIMA COUNTY SUPERIOR COURT

1   statements of counsel.

2   I'd like for you, when you leave, to go with

3   Peter. There's a new way in and out of the courtroom.

4   I'd like for you to take your books with you so they can

5   be stored in the jury room. There a step here. Don't go

6   right quite yet. And Peter will take you back to the

7   room. Tomorrow he'll arrange for you to get into the

8   room. You can get in. I hope he'll have it open for you

9   early.

10   Can't talk about the case. The admonition still

11   applies. I keep reminding you of that, and we'll see you

12   tomorrow morning at 10:30. I'll tell you, I start a

13   calendar, and I want you to know as the days go on, I

14   start a calendar and start seeing people at about 8:30.

15   And that goes on, and we usually are able to start

16   tomorrow -- I don't have a long calendar. Sometimes we

17   spill over and don't start right at 10:30, and that's

18   because I've got a whole lot of other matters that come

19   on between the 8:30 time and 10:30. But tomorrow the

20   calendar is short, and we should be able to start right

21   at 10:30, and so please be here to begin.

22   We'll see you tomorrow.

23   (Whereupon, the jury was excused from the

24   courtroom.)

25   THE COURT: Before you all take off, I just want

```
1    to say one thing, and that is I spent my lunch hour
2    reading through some of the 404 (B), 404 (C) evidence and
3    stuff like that.  And one of the things -- I know that I
4    made my ruling and what have you, but it would be very
5    helpful for me if the State has a theory on admission of
6    any of these things that you look to say what that theory
7    might be so I can look at that and compare with the 404
8    (B) and 404 (C).  I'm not sure that 404 (C) applies, but
9    there's case law, and I've looked at some cases.
10            I pulled out some cases.  You may find these of
11   interest to look at one way or the other, and I'll just
12   give you the citations to them if you want to take a look
13   at them.
14            There's Grainge, G-r-a-i-n-g-e, at -- I'll give
15   you the Pacific cite.
16            MR. LAGATTUTA:  Could you spell that again?
17            THE COURT:  G-r-a-i-n-g-e.  It's at 918 P.2d.
18   1073.  I looked at Feld, F-e-l-d, vs. Gurtz.  It's at 66
19   P.3d. 1268.  I've looked at Beck, at -- I'm sorry, it's
20   726 P.2d. 227.  I've looked a little bit at a Idaho case.
21   It's called Hoots.  It's at 961 P.2d. 1195.  And there's
22   a California case by the name of Couls, C-o-u-l-s.  And
23   that is at -- it's a Westlaw cite.  And a couple of
24   these, I'll be honest with you, are red-flagged.  So they
25   may have some interesting legal discussion in them, but
```

PIMA COUNTY SUPERIOR COURT

1   you couldn't cite for authority. But this is a 2003
 2   Westlaw, 1908428. They may or may not apply. I just,
 3   you know, did some research.
 4   So if you want to look at the citations here,
 5   and I have the cases here, and before there's a final
 6   ruling on those things -- I have ruled, but I want to
 7   know the theories on both sides before I admit any of the
 8   evidence.
 9   So thank you, and we'll see you tomorrow.
10   MR. LAGATTUTA: Thank you.
11   (Proceedings closed.)
12
13
14
15
16
17
18
19
20
21
22
23
24
25

PIMA COUNTY SUPERIOR COURT

```
 1    STATE OF ARIZONA    )
                          )      ss.
 2    COUNTY OF PIMA      )

 3

 4

 5

 6

 7

 8           I, CHERYL L. AUSTIN, Certified Reporter #50029,

 9    Official Reporter for the Superior Court, in and for the

10    County of Pima, do hereby certify that I took the

11    shorthand notes in the foregoing matter; that the same

12    was transcribed under my direction; that the preceding

13    pages of typewritten matter are a true, accurate and

14    complete transcript of all the matters adduced, to the

15    best of my skill and ability.

16

17

18    _____

19

20           CHERYL L. AUSTIN,   CR #50029, RMR-CRR
             Official Reporter
21           Pima County Superior Court

22

23

24    DATED:   JUNE 25, 2006

25
```

PIMA COUNTY SUPERIOR COURT

Day One

March 28, 2006

Page 34–18: Defendant said he had lived there two months because I arrived in late February and it was early April. I was not advised of Miranda when this statement was made and was speaking generally.

Page 36–13: Judge admits he doesn't know how contraband files got on the computer.

Page 37–10: The fact there could have been more counts than the 15 charged points to selective prosecution.

Page 39-8: There was no pornography of any kind on this computer. The porn folder where I told Englander adult pornography would be located is empty. (See second printout of Volume C, Page 1, Supplemental Disclosure – February 1, 2005)

Page 39–24: Jensvold states Jake was looking at adult pornography on my computer.

Page 42–10: Judge admits to knowing Jake downloaded adult pornography.

Page 44–16: Jensvold states the complete hard drives had been disclosed. They hadn't been. Only data compressed images were disclosed defense expert could do nothing with.

Page 57–11: Judge to jury estimates length of trial.

Page 61- 9 to 76-23: Judge reads charges to jury. There is no mention of dangerous crimes against children. Judge abbreviates the reading of the charges to the jury Judge states on or about April 1, 2003, yet the dates contraband disks were created on March 6, 2003, also duplicitous charging.

Jury Selection

Robert Brown, works for IBM. Served on two prior juries.

Julie Penny, friends who are police, Page 80, friend indicted current in trial, Page 91, 92, mother in federal court, husband's wallet stolen, Page 103, three children, one grandchild.

Siebo Friesenborg, worked at IBM, Page 85, three children, schoolteacher, brother arrested for theft, Page 91.

Charles Loding, friend of Pima County Sheriff Deputy, works with him at church, Page 80.

Willy Carlton, married, no children.

Joeanne Martin, public health degree, hospital administrator, three children.

Patty Perez, two children, previous juror.

Andrea Taylor, home burglary, Page 106.

Ronald Smith, three children, teacher, wife – delivery nurse, pro dad, Page 120, 121.

Tamara Nichelson, husband's car stolen, Page 80, system engineer for Raytheon.

Victor Cardenas

Karl Carr, four children, wife is a teacher, system administrator for ABDS, Page 86, DUI conviction, Page 103.

Jennifer Day, nursing student, DUI, brother convicted for domestic violence, Page 103, boyfriend murdered, Page 109-21.

Reed Peterson, teacher, Page 159, Pro dad, seven children.

No Record of Pre-Emptive Strikes

Page 134-23-25: Jury left with impression that if any of the possible verbs applied defendant was guilty.

Page 151-20: Prosecutor states ITunes is illegal. It's not.

Page 182: Jury's oath not in record.

Page 183: Jury instructed, "The State must prove each element of any charge beyond a reasonable doubt." This would include DCAC.

Page 196-3. The defendant engaged in conduct intended to aid another person to commit a crime, in a manner in which would make the defendant an accomplice, had the crime been committed or attempted by the other person."

This statement being true makes Jake, by law, a co-defendant of the crime he has already confessed to.

ARS 13-3559. Reporting suspected visual depictions of sexual exploitation of a minor; immunity

A. Any communication service provider, remote computing service, system administrator, computer repair technician or other person who discovers suspected visual depictions of sexual exploitation of a minor on a computer, computer system or network or in any other storage medium may report that discovery to a law enforcement officer.

B. A person who on discovery in good faith reports the discovery of suspected visual depictions of sexual exploitation of a minor is immune from civil liability.

C. It is an affirmative defense to a prosecution for a violation of section 13-3553 that on discovery a person in good faith reports the discovery of unsolicited suspected visual depictions involving the sexual exploitation of a minor.

Page 199-1-8: Rule of Exclusion invoked in courtroom. Yet Englander was allowed to sit in throughout trial as case manager. All totaled, this man delivered the only evidence presented to the grand jury, was responsible for serving the search warrant and collecting evidence, was the person who conducted computer forensics report and is now, after he left employment with the Pima County Sheriff's Department, appointed as case manager of the trial where he can sit with the prosecutor, who admits to a lack of knowledge of computers, who can then coach him with his questioning throughout the trial. This is simply too much power for a single man to have.

Day Two

1   IN THE SUPERIOR COURT OF THE STATE OF ARIZONA

2   IN AND FOR THE COUNTY OF PIMA

3

4   THE STATE OF ARIZONA,   )

           Plaintiff,   )

5   )

   vs.   )   CR-20042573

6   )

)   2 CA-CR 2006-0215

7   JAMES PRENTISS COGHILL,   )

)

8   Defendant.   )

)

9

10 BEFORE: THE HONORABLE TED B. BOREK

           Judge of the Superior Court

11   Division 24   DEFENSE

12

13   APPEARANCES: SHAWN JENSVOLD

             Deputy County Attorney

14   on behalf of the State;

15   JAMES LAGATTUTA

          on behalf of the Defendant.

16

17

18   REPORTER'S TRANSCRIPT ON APPEAL

19   JURY TRIAL DAY TWO

20   —————————————————————

21   TUCSON, ARIZONA

22   MARCH 29, 2006

23   SEP19'06 PDA am10:15

24   Reported By: CHERYL L. AUSTIN, OFFICIAL

25   RMR, CRR, Certified Reporter #50029

PIMA COUNTY SUPERIOR COURT

211

PIMA COUNTY SUPERIOR COURT

```
 1                  P R O C E E D I N G S
 2          THE COURT:  Peter, you can bring the jury.
 3              (Whereupon, the jury panel entered the
 4              courtroom.)
 5          THE COURT:  Please be seated.  As you get in
 6   or -- it looks like everybody lined up to come in, in
 7   order.  Thank you very much.  Please be seated.
 8              We're here with jurors, counsel, and defendant.
 9   And please be seated.
10              Let me apologize.  I had a calendar that was
11   short in a number of cases but long with one case.  I had
12   11 defendants sitting where you are earlier this morning,
13   and it turned out that I had a longer proceeding with
14   many of them.  And so the lawyers were here ready to go
15   today, and I wasn't because I had those other things.
16   And I apologize to you, but don't hold them against the
17   parties.
18              We are ready to begin now with the opening
19   statements of counsel.
20          Mr. Jensvold.
21          MR. JENSVOLD:  Thank you, your Honor.
22
23      OPENING STATEMENT ON BEHALF OF THE STATE
24          Ladies and gentlemen, the dates, the most
25   significant of which I have, I have written on the board
```

PIMA COUNTY SUPERIOR COURT

```
 1   touch.
 2           Now, you're going to hear that Mr. Franks went
 3   to prison shortly after they met, at some point during
 4   2000.  And then the dates indicated 2001 to 2002 and then
 5   2002 to 2003, those are a little vague.  I'm not sure how
 6   well those will be defined.  But during those periods,
 7   somewhere in there is where Mr. Franks moved in with the
 8   defendant in his RV, which the defendant had at his
 9   parents' house in Moon Valley, the Moon Valley area of
10   Phoenix.  And it's during that time when Mr. Franks is
11   going to tell you that he first found out that the
12   defendant possessed child pornography.
13           And Mr. Franks will tell you that there are
14   reasons why he didn't tell anyone about that.  You know,
15   No. 1, the defendant was sort of taking him in.
16   Mr. Franks wasn't exactly the most consistently employed
17   person in the world, and he had to go from place to
18   place.  So he was giving him a place to stay and, you
19   know, he considered him a friend, so he didn't say
20   anything about it.
21           Now, again, that question mark after the January
22   of 2003 is important because that may be -- you'll see
23   what the evidence -- whatever the evidence shows about
24   that end date, you'll find out during the trial.
25           But February of 2003 is important because that's
```

PIMA COUNTY SUPERIOR COURT

1 when the defendant took his RV down here to Tucson. And
2 we know it was February of 2003 because the defendant
3 tells Detective Englander on April 1st of 2003, your
4 bottom date down there, that he had been there for about
5 two months in Tucson. The defendant was working for
6 Hamilton Aerospace. He was an aircraft mechanic by
7 trade.
8   And it's in February of 2003, somewhere, you
9 know, the defendant and Mr. Franks were communicating by
10 e-mail. And Mr. Franks is again sort of out of
11 employment, between employment, however you want to put
12 it, and looking for a place to stay. And so again the
13 defendant says okay. He goes up and he picks up Jacob
14 Franks in Phoenix where Mr. Franks was living on around
15 March 25th. Now, I'll get back to March 4th and March
16 6th in just a minute.
17   And we know, it's about March 25th, maybe March
18 24th, one of those two days most likely because the
19 defendant and Mr. Franks both tell sheriff's department
20 deputies/detectives that Mr. Franks had been there about
21 a week since April 1st of 2003.
22   Interestingly, Mr. Coghill, the defendant, sort
23 of tells a couple of different versions of that time
24 frame when the deputies first arrived to Mr. Coghill's RV
25 after speaking with Mr. Franks. He tells them that

1   Mr. Franks had been there for about two months. But then
2   later on, a couple hours later when he's talking to
3   Detective Englander, he says that he went to pick him up
4   last week.
5   And then again, further point during the
6   interview with Detective Englander, Detective Englander
7   asked him a question about, "So who's been using the
8   computer over the last couple of weeks?" And the
9   defendant says, "Well, I've been barely able to get on
10   the computer other than just to do e-mail the last two
11   weeks because Jacob has been here." So you will evaluate
12   that on your own at the end, but that's where we're
13   getting the March 25th date, and you'll hear about
14   March 25th.
15   You will hear about it also, and I'll get back
16   to -- there's Dirty in quotation marks. We'll get to
17   that in just a second.
18   March 27th -- so March 26th is important.
19   You'll find out because you're going to hear a bunch of
20   computer testimony and see potentially documents, and
21   it's going to be pretty technical. And Detective
22   Englander, who is now Mr. Englander -- he's a computer
23   consultant for a company called Spinelli Corporation, but
24   at the time of this case he was working for the sheriff's
25   department as a detective -- he's going to tell you how

PIMA COUNTY SUPERIOR COURT

1   all his experience in dealing with these kinds of cases,
 2   his background in computers -- and I won't do that now,
 3   I'll let him do that. He'll do it much better than I
 4   could. But what he's going to tell you specifically
 5   about March 26th is when he analyzed the hard drives that
 6   were taken from the defendant's RV out of the computer,
 7   there were two of them, a master drive and a slave drive,
 8   he's going to tell you that there was a record of KaZaA
 9   activity.

10   Specifically, there's going to be this My
11   Documents KaZaA light folder. Something like that.
12   You're going to see a record of basically usage on KaZaA.
13   And the March 26th is going to be important because
14   during those times, from about midnight -- I wrote those
15   times specifically. You will evaluate those based on the
16   evidence. Between about 12:43 a.m. to 3:42 a.m. there
17   were a number of pornography files downloaded. And some
18   of those you may see during this case. And those --
19   those files that you may see during this case are going
20   to contrast substantially with the charged files in this
21   case which you heard about already.

22   And then from about 3:11 to 4:13, there's some
23   times in there where music is being downloaded. And then
24   again between -- various times between about 1137 and
25   2024, that's 8:24 p.m. -- so between 11 a.m. and 8 p.m.

PIMA COUNTY SUPERIOR COURT

1   there's more music downloaded, and you can see the

2   records of it from KaZaA.

3   What Mr. Franks is going to tell you is that all

4   of that activity on March 26th is most likely his. And

5   we'll talk about that during the closing arguments

6   specifically as to what that means.

7   March 27th through the 30th is similar in nature

8   to March 26th except there don't appear to be any

9   pornography files downloaded during that period. It's

10   mostly music. And again, Mr. Franks is going to tell you

11   whether that looks like that's his activity or not.

12   Finally, March 31st, that's the day before --

13   the day before April 1st is when -- April 1st is when the

14   defendant had set up this job interview for Mr. Franks at

15   Hamilton Aerospace. Now, March 31st, there will be some

16   more music and stuff downloaded from around 11 a.m. to

17   2 p.m., and then there's -- there's a break. And

18   Mr. Franks is going to tell you that he was out using the

19   defendant's, with his permission, his MoPed. And he was

20   supposed to be out looking for a job.

21   Well, he ends up going to downtown Tucson, he

22   says, on Broadway somewhere. And he's crossing in the

23   crosswalk, and a car hits him, and so the defendant's

24   MoPed is basically totaled. Mr. Franks is taken to Kino

25   Hospital for some minor injuries, but -- which he's given

PIMA COUNTY SUPERIOR COURT

1 prescriptions, Ibuprofen, and stuff for. Well, needless

 2 to say when Jacob gets back to the defendant's RV, the

 3 defendant is not real happy. He's not real happy that

 4 his MoPed is destroyed despite the fact that Mr. Franks

 5 says it's not his fault. That sort of starts an argument

 6 between the two.

 7   The defendant's not happy, thinks that Jacob is

 8 just basically messing around, not taking him seriously.

 9 That was his -- that was going to be Mr. Franks' mode of

10 transportation to get down to Hamilton if he were to get

11 the job. And so this goes on. This argument goes on,

12 and it spills over into the next day, which is April 1st

13 of 2003.

14   During that morning Mr. Franks actually gets

15 ready to go to this interview. He shaves, he puts on a

16 shirt. Now, you're not going to see the shirt I don't

17 think, but that caused further tension between the two

18 because the defendant said you can't go out in a shirt

19 like that. Evidently it looked like a fairly oversized

20 and unprofessional shirt from what you could tell. That

21 caused more arguments. The defendant tells Mr. Franks to

22 put on a white shirt to go to this interview. They start

23 arguing about that.

24   Eventually just gets to the point where the

25 defendant's fed up, and he said, "Why don't I just take

1   you back to Phoenix?", and Mr. Franks says, "Fine." And
2   Mr. Franks at some point leaves the RV, walks down to a
3   Circle K, and he's angry. And he thinks about calling
4   the police to turn in Mr. Franks (sic) for child
5   pornography. He doesn't do it. He thinks about it, then
6   he goes back to the RV and asks the defendant one more
7   time, "Are you going to take me down to the interview or
8   not?" And the defendant says no, so at that point
9   Mr. Franks leaves, calls the police, and that starts
10   basically this case in motion.
11   Deputies arrive to the Circle K to talk to
12   Mr. Franks. Then, based on what Mr. Franks tells them,
13   they go to the defendant's RV. The defendant invites
14   them in, and they see spindles and spindles, several
15   spindles of CDs. Some of them labeled "KP." And you're
16   going to see some of those CDs in this case, the CDs and
17   the files on them. "KP." They ask -- the deputies ask
18   the defendant what "KP" means. He said, "I don't know.
19   You know, I think" -- "I think Jacob was downloading some
20   porn. They must be his." Now, what Mr. Franks is going
21   to tell you is he didn't label any of those CDs labeled
22   "KP."
23   You're going to hear from a handwriting analyst
24   as well. What Mr. Franks will admit to is on March 25th,
25   that's where Dirty is in quotation marks there, on

PIMA COUNTY SUPERIOR COURT

```
 1    March 25th he was going to use the computer.  And the
 2    defendant had some child pornography in there, and Jacob
 3    wanted to burn something onto a CD.  And Mr. Franks is
 4    going to tell you that the defendant told him to write
 5    "Dirty" on it.  And you're going to see that CD, and
 6    you're going to hear some testimony about handwriting
 7    analysis based on that word "Dirty" on that CD.  And
 8    you'll -- the handwriting testimony will be about some of
 9    the other CDs labeled "KP" as well.
10              So deputies get a search warrant, and they take
11    the hard drive, and the case is basically started from
12    there.
13              Now, I just want to warn you.  You've been told
14    this by the Judge already.  You're going to see some of
15    these images.  They're going to be movie files.  And
16    we're not playing these for you to make you uncomfortable
17    or anything worse than that.  I mean, we're doing it
18    because we have a case to prove.  We have to prove the
19    elements of each offense.  I mean, if this were a DUI, we
20    would have to bring in, you know, the blood evidence.
21    Obviously this is much more difficult to deal with, but
22    that's the reason why we're showing it.  I just want to
23    prepare you for that.
24              But based on all of this testimony, it's going
25    to be clear -- let me go back to March 4th and March 6th.
```

PIMA COUNTY SUPERIOR COURT

```
1    I almost forgot.
2            Why the State is going to ask you to find the
3    defendant guilty on all these counts is based on a lot of
4    what Detective Englander is going to tell about the
5    dates.  But specifically, some of what he's going to tell
6    you is on March 4th and on March 6th.  Some of these CDs
7    labeled "KP" with child pornography on them, the ones
8    that will -- I will propose to you will be significantly
9    different from those files downloaded on March 26th.
10   Those files were created, some of the CDs were burned
11   around that time, and you can contrast that with the
12   dates in which Mr. Franks was there.
13           Based on all of that, the State's going to ask
14   you during closing arguments to find the defendant guilty
15   of all 15 counts.  Thank you.
16           THE COURT:  Thank you, Mr. Jensvold.
17           Mr. Lagattuta.
18           MR. LAGATTUTA:  Thank you, your Honor.
19
20       OPENING STATEMENT ON BEHALF OF THE DEFENDANT
21           MR. LAGATTUTA:  Ladies and gentlemen, as I sat
22   there and listened to the State present its opening
23   statement to you, I couldn't help but wonder if all of
24   the information that they have given to you so far,
25   particularly with the dates here on the board, here, will
```

PIMA COUNTY SUPERIOR COURT

1 amount to proof to you beyond a reasonable doubt that my
2 client committed these horrible crimes. And this is the
3 simple assessment that you have to make in listening to
4 the evidence in the case.
5   Now, from our perspective here, the perspective
6 of being accused, we can look at these dates and we can
7 hear the prosecutor speak and make promises to you, but
8 he will deliver evidence to you. But from what our
9 perspective has been for the last couple of years, I
10 suggest to you that what this case will be to you is an
11 incredible, almost unbelievable story as to how on one
12 date, on April 1st, 2003, within a period of about an
13 hour and a half, an investigation done by the sheriff's
14 department will transform my client from an otherwise
15 hardworking, law-abiding citizen, a good friend and a
16 good neighbor to all, transform him into an accused
17 felon. Accused and later indicted on some of the most
18 horrible charges you can ever think of because of one
19 simple thing. Jacob Franks, who was a convicted felon,
20 who has been to prison several times, tells the police
21 one story. Tells them one story and they believe it
22 hook, line, and sinker.
23   And it is that story and that story alone that
24 is the basis for all of these charges. It is the basis
25 for the accusations made in the case. And it will be the

PIMA COUNTY SUPERIOR COURT

1 story that you will have to examine bit by bit as this
2 case unfolds.
3   So who is Jacob Franks? What is his story? Why
4 would the police believe his story? What implications
5 are there in believing his story over the story of my
6 client? These are the three separate areas that I
7 suggest to you the evidence in the case will focus on.
8   Now, as we hear from the witnesses in the case
9 and Mr. Franks himself, you will learn that Jacob Franks
10 is a young man, a convicted felon. At the time during
11 the course of time that he knew my client or my client
12 knew him, had not much of a family. Very rarely did he
13 have a place to stay, which is why on several occasions
14 my client would offer him a place to stay in his motor
15 home. Very little family support. You will hear that
16 both his aunt kicked him out of her house in Phoenix,
17 couldn't live with his father. By his own words, they
18 were sick of him, too.
19   He admits to being a car thief, a drug addict,
20 and someone who, in his own words, always seems to find
21 someone to take him in. That will be the evidence I
22 believe you can hear -- you will hear and you will
23 consider and have to consider in understanding the story
24 of Jacob Franks.
25   Well, why, you ask then, would somebody like

PIMA COUNTY SUPERIOR COURT

that in any way, shape, or form be involved with James

Coghill, who, by all aspects, is the complete opposite?

Always been employed, never broken the law, solid

citizen. How can the two of them even have a

relationship? That's one of the real ironies of the case

and one that is not something I can stand before you and

give you the short answer to.

And I've asked Jim Coghill about that, and the

police officers may have asked him about that. By his

own testimony or by his own words, I should say, Jim

describes himself as an altruist. What does that mean?

That means quite simply that he is a person that gets

some reward in life by helping others rather than helping

himself. Does that sound odd? In this case it sounds

very odd, particularly when you line up the

characteristics these individuals possess right next to

each other.

It is somewhat ironic because you will hear

throughout the course of their relationship the only

thing that Jim ever tried to do was help Jacob out.

That's all he ever tried to do. And in the end, when

Jacob had absolutely nothing left to lose, when he was at

a point where he had no place further to go, no money, no

time, and he was about to be at the end of his rope, he

turns on what literally was the only friend that he

PIMA COUNTY SUPERIOR COURT

1   really ever had in his life. Why, you ask yourself. I
 2   can't answer that either. That will be the testimony
 3   that you have to evaluate. And you will hear it from the
 4   witness stand as the case progresses.
 5   Now, there are a lot of other questions you'll
 6   have to answer, too. For example, you look at the dates
 7   that the prosecutor has put on the board here. The only
 8   real important date is April 1st, 2003. That's when the
 9   investigation began, and this investigation lasted about
10   maybe an hour and a half. Maybe an hour and a half.
11   That's all the time that the police took to take,
12   evaluate, investigate, and accuse Mr. Coghill of
13   committing these crimes.
14   And sometime in the morning hours of the day or
15   mid-morning hours of the day, the events that
16   Mr. Jensvold described happened probably exactly the way
17   he said they did in that Jim and Jacob got into an
18   argument about how Jacob would actually dress or prepare
19   himself to go to an interview. It seems so trivial.
20   It's almost incomprehensible probably to the rest of us,
21   but at some point Jake became so upset that Jim now
22   wouldn't help him that one step forward that he goes down
23   and he makes a phone call to the police and he says: I
24   want you to meet me at such and such a place, a Circle K.
25   I have some information to give you.

PIMA COUNTY SUPERIOR COURT

```
 1          And so he goes down and he meets with the
 2    police, and he says:  I need to tell you this.  He says:
 3    I've been staying with this friend of mine for some time,
 4    and, yeah, he's a good guy.  No, he doesn't do anything
 5    wrong, but I've got to tell you this.  He's got some
 6    child pornography in his trailer.  And you know what,
 7    I'll tell you exactly where it is.  So Jacob tells the
 8    police.  He says:  It's in a stack of discs which is in
 9    the trailer -- by the way, it's not a trailer.  It's a
10    motor home, and you'll see pictures of the motor home.
11    It's not very big.  In fact, the living space in it is
12    shorter -- or probably much smaller than the box that the
13    12 of you are sitting in.
14          And Jacob says:  If you go in there and look in
15    this one pile, you will find amidst hundreds of other
16    discs some child pornography discs.  And the police say:
17    Well, you know, Jacob, it sounds a little bit like you
18    might be making this up.  You just told us you got into
19    an argument with your friend.  How do we know that
20    this -- this really is true?  And he says:  Well -- he
21    says:  I'll tell you, there's going to be one in there.
22    I know it's child pornography because I made it myself.
23    You made it yourself?  He said:  Yeah, you know, at some
24    point within the last couple of days there was some child
25    pornography floating around, or it was on the computer,
```

PIMA COUNTY SUPERIOR COURT

and Mr. Coghill, Jim Coghill, my roommate, he made me make this disc. Jacob Franks said: He made me make this disc.

Police officers don't say: Did he force you with a gun? Did he force you with a knife?

He made me make this disc. And not only that, I wrote the word "Dirty" on top. He made me write that on there. You will find this. I created it. He says: I put it in -- put it in the stack. There it is. You'll find it. And you'll find some other things in there, and they'll be labeled a certain way, but those aren't mine. Those are Jim's. And away we go.

So the police officers take this information hand in hand, and they go down and they greet Jim at the trailer, and they ask him if they could come in. He says: Fine, what can I help you with? He thinks there's a problem with Jake; Jake, having previously gone out and wrecked his MoPed.

Said: No, we just want to talk to you about some stuff. And they come in the trailer and look around, and they say: You've got a lot of discs in here. And in fact, you'll see hundreds of discs. CD discs. Hundreds. Uncountable.

What about some of those over there? They point to, you know, a stack of these discs, and they ask Jim to

PIMA COUNTY SUPERIOR COURT

go through them and look through them. And as he goes

through the stack, sure enough, mixed in, in this whole

group of hundreds of CDs, are some discs labeled "KP."

And the police say: Jim Coghill, what does this

stand for? And he says: I don't know. I don't know.

These are not mine. I don't know. I've had someone

living with me here off and on over the years. I don't

know. We both have complete access to the computer.

These are not mine. I don't know. And that's the end of

the investigation.

Police come back. They get a search warrant.

Police seize the computer. They seize the discs. They

come in, they take some fingerprints, specifically they

take fingerprints on these discs that are labeled "KP."

They never compare them. For months and months never

compare them to Jim Coghill. Fingerprints are readily

available. It just falls through the cracks. There is

some indication that these discs have been initialed,

written in a certain way. You'll see the letters on

there. They don't take a handwriting sample of Jim,

compare it to this, which would be a clue that he may

have been involved in this.

But the investigation ends on the strength of

the words of Jacob Franks. And that's it. And, by the

way, the important thing to remember when we're talking

1   of occasions, a couple of occasions looked over his

2   shoulder and said he saw Jim doing it. That is the

3   entirety of the strength of that evidence.

4   The computer, I suggest to you, will show a

5   number of different things. Pay careful attention to

6   what all the witnesses have to say in the case about the

7   computer evidence. And at the end of the case, having

8   analyzed both the situation as it occurred and the

9   evidence in the investigation as it was presented, you

10   will, I think, have to put yourself in a position to

11   judge whether or not an individual, Jacob Franks, who

12   comes before you with the record that he does, you will

13   have to be in a position to judge whether his word will

14   carry the strength of proof beyond a reasonable doubt.

15   And given the word of Jim Coghill and his

16   motivation, his background and his character placed

17   against Jacob Franks, will, I think, be the -- will be

18   the measuring point by which you can evaluate the

19   evidence. At the close of all this, ladies and

20   gentlemen, we're going to ask you to take this two-year

21   investigation, this two-year case, this two-year

22   nightmare for Mr. Coghill and put it to rest. We are

23   going to ask you to come back and find on each and every

24   one of these counts that he is not guilty.

25   Thank you.

PIMA COUNTY SUPERIOR COURT

```
1          THE COURT:  Thank you.  Mr. Lagattuta.

2          Your first witness.

3          MR. JENSVOLD:  Your Honor, do you want to start

4   now or should we --

5          THE COURT:  About the only thing we get is the

6   name and maybe to begin with -- why don't I give you a

7   head start on lunch and come back at 25 after 1.

8          MR. JENSVOLD:  Okay.

9          THE COURT:  Take -- and try to do that at least.

10  You can leave your books here.  No one else is going to

11  be using the courtroom.  And get back by 25 after.  We'll

12  be in recess till 1:25.

13          (Luncheon recess.)

14          MR. JENSVOLD:  Your Honor?

15          THE COURT:  Yes.

16          MR. JENSVOLD:  Do we want to take up that matter

17  before -- I don't think it will matter.  I'm going to

18  bring Deputy Schupbach on first.  The ruling won't affect

19  that.

20          But before Mr. Franks testifies, I'd like to get

21  the ruling on some of my motions in limine --

22          THE COURT:  Okay.

23          MR. JENSVOLD:  -- settled, if that's okay.

24          THE COURT:  I think to this point said that you

25  can't use the material.  But I looked at a number of
```

PIMA COUNTY SUPERIOR COURT

1	cases here and what have you, and it seems like some
2	things are just so intertwixably -- inextricably
3	intertwined. And you both talked in your opening
4	statements about these number of tapes and CDs or
5	whatever they have, discs that were picked up. I don't
6	think you can possibly not say what some of them are,
7	quite honestly, at this point.
8	But I don't know whether it goes further than
9	that, to have some connections of some specific tapes to
10	how they're downloaded computerwise, so I'm still in the
11	position of having to defer finally. I have to be more
12	specific on precisely what issue you are trying to raise
13	under 404 (B) or 404 (C) issue, or exactly what -- what
14	you have -- specific evidence you would intend to admit
15	on what specific issue, Mr. Jensvold.
16	MR. JENSVOLD: Okay. I think from the State's
17	perspective, the only -- the only thing that actually --
18	that actually goes to the level of being another act is
19	the other child pornography files that were found. All
20	of the other adult porn, that's legal from the State's
21	perspective. That's not another act to begin with. And
22	also rebuttal evidence, especially since the defense
23	attorney -- Mr. Lagattuta made several remarks about
24	Mr. Coghill's character, how solid it was and how, you
25	know, solid citizen, never been in trouble. I mean,

PIMA COUNTY SUPERIOR COURT

obviously it's a different issue as to whether someone is
downloading this kind of material or not. I think it's
relevant.

I guess the best analogy I can come up with: If
we are in a heroin possession case, and someone is saying
that somebody else did it, and yet the defendant himself
had, you know, got -- had prescribed medication for
Oxycodone, which is, you know, very well -- very closely
related to heroin, why wouldn't that come in? It's
legal, but it's relevant. It also goes to opportunity.

I think under 404 (B), you know, these other
things, these adult videos that were found in the living
space, sort of bedroom so to speak, where Mr. Coghill was
sleeping, evidence indicates those were not Mr. Franks.

THE COURT: Is this adult pornography or child
pornography?

MR. JENSVOLD: The tapes are adult pornography.

THE COURT: Pardon me?

MR. JENSVOLD: Adult pornography. And during
the interview with Detective Englander he says he and
Jake both downloaded adult pornography off the computer,
so two different situations there.

THE COURT: You know, it's really -- it's --
this is -- well, let me hear from you, Mr. Lagattuta.
We've done it already, and I don't know whether

PIMA COUNTY SUPERIOR COURT

1 Mr. Jensvold gave you a copy of the cases, or make a
2 comment on the cases I found yesterday.
3   MR. LAGATTUTA: Well, your Honor, there's really
4 two issues here. First of all, I understand what the
5 Court's saying. The Court is saying: Mr. Jensvold, tell
6 me why you want to use this information. Under 404 (B)
7 as a motive, plot, or -- describe requirements for -- or
8 reasons for using that rule. And I don't think we can
9 identify it because if we're talking about this adult
10 pornography, there isn't anything about that that -- that
11 has anything to do with child pornography. I mean,
12 just -- just because --
13   THE COURT: Then you shouldn't have any reason
14 to be concerned.
15   MR. LAGATTUTA: I think it's prejudicial. I
16 think it's prejudicial. And I think the Court does, too.
17 And I think not only that, but if it was going to be used
18 as 404 (B) evidence, we should have gotten notice of it
19 so we could prepare to defend against it.
20   For example, Mr. Jensvold says there's a couple
21 of adult movies that were seized in the bedroom area, and
22 the evidence tends to point to the fact that they don't
23 belong to Mr. Franks. Well, what is that evidence of?
24 And had we been on notice that these movies were either
25 going to be shown or mentioned or played, we might even

PIMA COUNTY SUPERIOR COURT

1   have investigated them. We might have requested to

2   actually see them. I don't think they've been viewed by

3   anybody, much less if we had the opportunity to explore

4   whether or not these are going to actually be used as

5   indicators of guilt in the case.

6   THE COURT: The problem I have right now is

7   there's -- the vast amount of the material. And I don't

8   know what different aspects go to or exactly where it was

9   found or exactly what you're offering. If you come in

10   and say there were other things found and some of them

11   had titles that indicated they were adult pornography or

12   not, or child pornography found in the bedroom -- I think

13   if there's child pornography found in the bedroom, that

14   certainly goes -- would be indicative of knowledge. And

15   so I can understand that under 404 (B), you know -- it's

16   just you didn't charge them all. You would be able to

17   have that kind of evidence, and that's where I'm leaning.

18   You know, I don't think you would have to have

19   notice for sexual conduct cases under 404 (C), and I

20   don't think that that's been provided or whether it has

21   on that kind of issue. But you're entitled, and there's

22   a whole series of things I have to make a ruling on if

23   you're intending, under 404 (C), to admit documents that

24   show a predilection to commit the sexual offense. And no

25   one has raised any of that kind of issue.

PIMA COUNTY SUPERIOR COURT

```
 1          We're in an unusual situation here because the
 2    State's coming forward, and I want to be sure I can admit
 3    this stuff, and you haven't even filed a motion in
 4    limine.  The defense has not filed and said you didn't
 5    want to have the stuff in.  I think some of the stuff
 6    goes to knowledge.  I can understand, just as
 7    Mr. Jensvold -- and the cases support if you have a
 8    person who is charged with marijuana possession and
 9    they've got other kinds of drugs that have been involved
10    with, that does tend to show knowledge of that kind of a
11    thing.  And this really, as you've pointed out, is very
12    much who you believe on the knowledge aspect.
13          So I'm just -- at this point in time where we
14    are, you can -- you can ask your question.
15          And if you object, I'll rule at that point, and
16    I know what evidence I've got up to that point, and I'm
17    going to know whether I admit or not.  I understand your
18    objections on -- well, you'll have to raise your
19    objection and come up, and we'll see where we are at that
20    point.
21          So I'm not saying you can't ask any question
22    right now, just ask it in such a way that the defense has
23    an opportunity to object and we can hear exactly what it
24    is you're going to at that point.
25          MR. JENSVOLD:  Okay.
```

PIMA COUNTY SUPERIOR COURT

1   THE COURT: That's the best I can do now. You
 2 all both know so much more about the specific kinds of
 3 things on this, and I have to hear the evidence before I
 4 know, you know, how it fits and how it's relevant and
 5 what the reason for the question is that the State's
 6 asking.
 7   MR. LAGATTUTA: Just so you know, your Honor,
 8 for the record, as far as our interest in not exploring
 9 or having the State be able to bring up evidence of adult
10 pornography or whether it was in the motor home or
11 anything else, just about the exact time that I was
12 drafting that as a motion in limine, I received --
13 Mr. Jensvold, which addressed the issue, which I want to
14 let you know -- you made a comment. We didn't bring that
15 up. That having been raised, I thought it would be -- be
16 the right forum to discuss it in.
17   THE COURT: Well, that's fine. No one cited a
18 case to me, you know -- well, Mr. Jensvold did today. I
19 did all the research on the cases, and so no one has come
20 in and said -- so the 404 (B) stuff comes up as
21 evidentiary, and I just rule up here. I appreciate the
22 heads up knowing where we are on the things, but I have
23 to see where we are at that point.
24   And if there's evidence of -- evidence that
25 demonstrates the defendant's knowledge with this kind of

1   material, which I can certainly see that possession of

2   noncharged child pornography would demonstrate knowledge

3   of the possession of that and use of that, that really

4   would go to the issue of the defendant's knowledge and

5   knowing possession of child pornography.

6   And if there are documents that weren't charged

7   that were in a different kind of form and different

8   place, again, I can see that that would be relevant and

9   admissible.

10   MR. JENSVOLD: Your Honor, State would also

11   contend it goes to opportunity as well based on the

12   number of them and dates and so forth. Some of that

13   evidence you haven't seen yet.

14   THE COURT: Well, you've got dates here, and two

15   people that are there, and really difficult thing to know

16   from what I heard from both of you which one of those two

17   people had opportunity and knowledge of those things, who

18   put them there. And, you know, whether -- the big thing

19   here is which one of the two people did it. And what I

20   am looking for is if there's any of the evidence that

21   supports the State's position that it's this defendant

22   that did it. And that's -- that's -- you know, I don't

23   know who had what room, what thing or another. That's

24   why I have to hear more and see what you've got.

25   So we'll bring the jury and go from there. I'll

PIMA COUNTY SUPERIOR COURT

1	hear the objection and we'll rule on it at the time.
2	Who is your first witness, Mr. Jensvold?
3	MR. JENSVOLD: Deputy Schupbach,
4	S-c-h-u-p-b-a-c-h.
5	THE COURT: Why don't you bring her in so that
6	she can -- while Peter is bringing the jury.
7	MR. JENSVOLD: Okay.
8	THE COURT: Ma'am, hold just a minute and give
9	the clerk your name. We'll swear you in when the jury
10	comes back.
11	(Whereupon, the jury panel entered the
12	courtroom.)
13	THE COURT: Thank you, please be seated.
14	We're here with jurors, defendant, and counsel.
15	And we have the first witness, and you can be
16	sworn, please.
17	(The witness was sworn.)
18	
19	DEPUTY BRENDA SCHUPBACH,
20	called as a witness herein, having been first duly sworn,
21	was examined and testified as follows:
22	
23	DIRECT EXAMINATION
24	BY MR. JENSVOLD:
25	Q Would you please introduce yourself to the jury?

PIMA COUNTY SUPERIOR COURT

1   A   My name is Deputy Brenda Schupbach. I'm a
2 deputy sheriff, Pima County. I'm been employed as such
3 for the last seven and a half years.
4   Q   And, deputy, were you on duty on April 1st of
5 2003 at about 7:30 in the morning?
6   A   Yes, I was.
7   Q   And did you receive any calls at that time?
8   A   Yes. I was dispatched as a backup officer on a
9 suspicious activity call.
10   Q   And where did you go?
11   A   I met the reportee at the Circle K at Benson
12 Highway and Country Club.
13   Q   And who was the reportee?
14   A   He was identified as Jacob Franks.
15   Q   What was Mr. Franks' demeanor when you talked to
16 him?
17   A   He seemed irritated or angry to me when he was
18 speaking to me about his friend, Mr. Coghill.
19   Q   Was he upset?
20   A   Yes. I would say he was.
21   Q   And what did he tell you initially?
22   A   Initially, he told me that he was angry and that
23 he wanted to report that his friend, James Coghill, was
24 in possession of child pornography.
25   Q   And then without going into detail, you got

PIMA COUNTY SUPERIOR COURT

```
 1    details about that?

 2         A    Yes, I did.

 3         Q    And how long did you talk to Mr. Franks?

 4         A    I would say I talked to him for five to ten

 5    minutes until Deputy Judd, the other deputy, arrived.

 6    And then Deputy Judd and I went to Mr. Coghill's

 7    residence.

 8         Q    And how far away was it from the Circle K to

 9    Mr. Coghill's residence?

10         A    Not even a three- or four-minute drive.

11         Q    And when you -- what kind of place was it when

12    you went to Mr. Coghill's?

13         A    It was a recreational vehicle park.

14         Q    How many RV's were there?

15         A    Maybe 12.  It's just one driveway, and then

16    there's RV's parked on either side of the drive.

17         Q    And did you meet Mr. Coghill?

18         A    Yes, I did.

19         Q    And is Mr. Coghill in the room today?

20         A    I believe he is.  I can't remember what he looks

21    like though, honestly.  It's been so long.

22         Q    Okay.  Was this location within Pima County?

23         A    Yes.

24         Q    And so did you speak to Mr. Coghill?

25         A    Yes, I did.
```

PIMA COUNTY SUPERIOR COURT

     1   Q   Okay.   Where did you talk to him, specifically?

     2   A   Well, we were outside his RV and we asked him if

     3   we could go inside to speak to him.   He invited us in, so

     4   inside his RV.

     5   Q   And did you ask Mr. Coghill about Mr. Franks'

     6   property?

     7   A   Yes, I did.

     8   Q   And what was his response?

     9   A   We did not want to have to have Mr. Franks go

    10   back to Mr. Coghill's, so I asked if Mr. Franks had any

    11   property here.   There was a stack of clothing by the

    12   door, and Mr. Coghill indicated that that was Mr. Franks'

    13   property.

    14   Q   And was there anything else that belonged to

    15   Mr. Franks, according to Mr. Coghill, at that time?

    16   A   At that time, no.

    17   Q   Now, did you ask Mr. Coghill about some specific

    18   CDs?

    19   A   Yes.

    20   Q   What did you ask him?

    21   A   Actually, I think it was Deputy Judd that

    22   specifically asked about the compact discs that were

    23   stacked next to the computer.

    24   Q   Were you present for the conversation?

    25   A   I was present during the conversation, yes.

PIMA COUNTY SUPERIOR COURT

1   Q   Do you remember what the question was and what
2   the response was?
3   A   The question was -- we told Mr. Coghill we were
4   there because of the allegation that he may be in
5   possession of child pornography; specifically, the child
6   pornography may be on compact discs or CDs, and there was
7   a stack of spindles of CDs next to the computer. And we
8   asked: Are those your compact discs? Or: Are those the
9   compact discs?
10   Q   And what did Mr. Coghill say?
11   A   He said, yes, those were the compact discs in
12   his RV. And we specifically asked about one compact disc
13   which was marked with the initials "KP."
14   Q   Was that visible to you without having
15   Mr. Coghill go through the stacks of CDs?
16   A   Yes, that one was visible.
17   Q   Was it on a spindle?
18   A   Yes, it was.
19   Q   And what was asked about that CD?
20   A   We asked if he knew -- if Mr. Coghill knew what
21   was on that compact disc.
22   Q   And what did he say?
23   A   He told us that he believed that was
24   Mr. Franks'. But it was -- also had the word
25   "photographs" written on that compact disc, and

PIMA COUNTY SUPERIOR COURT

1   Mr. Coghill said he believes he put some of his

2   photographs on the empty space on that compact disc.

3   Q   And how long were you there, speaking with

4   Mr. Coghill?

5   A   I don't know. I'd have to check the radio log.

6   It was maybe a half hour or more. We then called

7   detectives and stood by until they arrived.

8   Q   And they took over the investigation after they

9   arrived?

10   A   Yes.

11   Q   And have you had any other involvement in this

12 case since then?

13   A   No.

14   Q   Oh, I'm sorry, did you provide information to

15 detectives about -- information for a potential search

16 warrant?

17   A   Yes, I did. I provided them with the

18 information which Mr. Franks had given me reference these

19 spindles and computer information.

20   MR. JENSVOLD: That's all I have, then. Thank

21 you.

22   THE COURT: Cross.

23   MR. LAGATTUTA: Thank you, your Honor.

24 ///

25 ///

PIMA COUNTY SUPERIOR COURT

```
 1                    CROSS EXAMINATION
 2   BY MR. LAGATTUTA:
 3        Q    Deputy Schupbach -- it's deputy; right?
 4        A    Yes, deputy.
 5        Q    This incident occurred -- that we're talking
 6   about -- April 1st, 2003; right?
 7        A    Yes.
 8        Q    So it's been just about three years ago; is that
 9   correct?
10        A    Yes.  It has.
11        Q    Now, when you say you got this call, you were
12   the first one to have contact with Jacob Franks; is that
13   right?
14        A    Yes, I was.
15        Q    Okay.  And describe for the jury -- what did he
16   look like at the time you saw him?
17        A    As I recall -- it's been three years, but I
18   recall he was thin, a Caucasian male, younger.  He was
19   angry, and he was on foot.  And as I drove up, he came
20   walking up to my car.
21        Q    Okay.  You mentioned the word "irritated" also
22   in your report.  Does that apply, do you think?
23        A    Yes, angry, irritated, yes.
24        Q    How about desperate?
25             MR. JENSVOLD:  Objection; speculation.
```

PIMA COUNTY SUPERIOR COURT

```
 1            THE COURT:  Overruled.
 2    BY MR. LAGATTUTA:
 3        Q    Is that appropriate?
 4            THE COURT:  Overruled.
 5            THE WITNESS:  He just seemed angry to me,
 6    irritated.
 7    BY MR. LAGATTUTA:
 8        Q    All right.  So when he approached you, although
 9    the other deputies arrived shortly after, you were the
10    first one to meet him; right?
11        A    Yes, I was.
12        Q    When you talked to him, were you -- you were
13    dressed in full uniform?
14        A    Yes, I was.
15        Q    And did you talk inside or outside of your car?
16        A    Outside of my car.
17        Q    Okay.  Were the first things out of his mouth
18    that he had knowledge of Jim Coghill having child
19    pornography in his trailer?
20        A    Yes.
21        Q    Is that the first thing that he told you?
22        A    As I recall.  I'd have to look at the radio
23    history, but I believe that was part of what the
24    suspicious activity that was dispatched was; that a
25    friend of his was in possession of child pornography.
```

PIMA COUNTY SUPERIOR COURT

1   Q   Okay. And so I assume that -- so when you meet
2 up with Jacob, you're armed with that knowledge already
3 from receiving information from the call that you're
4 going to go talk with somebody who has information about
5 another person possessing child pornography; is that
6 correct?
7   A   Yes. But when I was dispatched they did not
8 know the name of the reportee, Mr. Franks. It was just
9 at that time an anonymous male.
10   Q   Okay. Right. But once you begin to talk to
11 Mr. Franks, then, you're aware that he is the reportee
12 and that he is the one that has called the police to
13 inform them that Mr. Coghill has child pornography?
14   A   Yes, yes.
15   Q   So I assume you want to ask enough questions to
16 really get to the bottom of the information that
17 Mr. Franks has to give you; right?
18   A   Right. I want to get the basic questions: who,
19 what, where.
20   Q   Well, let's start with the basic questions.
21   Did he admit to you that the motor home that you
22 were going to go over and search was a place that he had
23 spent any time in himself?
24   A   Yes. He told me he had resided with Mr. Coghill
25 for one week is what he told me.

PIMA COUNTY SUPERIOR COURT

```
 1      Q    That's it?  Just one week?

 2      A    One week.  That he had resided there for one

 3 week.

 4      Q    When you asked that, do you remember -- did you

 5 put that in any parameters, like just one week down here

 6 in Tucson, or one week for your entire life?  Do you

 7 recall how you did that?

 8      A    I asked him how long he had known Mr. Coghill,

 9 and he said he had known Mr. Coghill for four to five

10 years.

11      Q    Right.

12      A    And I asked him how long he had lived with

13 Mr. Coghill, and he said he had lived with Mr. Coghill in

14 Tucson one week.

15      Q    Did you ask him if he had any of his possessions

16 in Mr. Coghill's trailer?

17      A    No, I did not.

18      Q    You must have noticed that while he was talking

19 with you, he had literally no possessions with him; is

20 that correct?

21      A    Correct.  Just him at the Circle K.

22      Q    Did it occur to you that this was a situation

23 where the two of them lived together and, for example,

24 shared possessions?

25      A    I don't know.  But I do know that I asked
```

PIMA COUNTY SUPERIOR COURT

1	Mr. Coghill about the possessions when I was there to get
2	it clarified, what all was there that needed to leave so
3	Mr. Franks would not have to go back.
4	Q Okay. All right. Now, did Mr. Franks tell you
5	at that time anything about his personal background?
6	A About Mr. Franks' or Mr. Coghill's?
7	Q Mr. Franks'.
8	A He told me that he was from Phoenix.
9	Q Okay.
10	A He told me that he was supposed to go to a job
11	interview that day.
12	Q Right.
13	A That Mr. Coghill was going to take him to that
14	job interview. He indicated that he had wrecked
15	Mr. Coghill's motorized scooter the day prior.
16	Q Uh-huh.
17	A And that Mr. Coghill now wanted him to pack up
18	all his belongings and that he was going to take him back
19	to Phoenix.
20	Q Okay. Did he tell you that he had been
21	previously convicted of a felony?
22	A No, he did not.
23	Q Did you do anything when you were taking a
24	statement to kind of even do a preliminary background
25	check on Mr. Franks as you did a statement?

PIMA COUNTY SUPERIOR COURT

1   A   I just took his picture identification card and

2 copied its information down for my notes.

3   Q   And what -- is that like a photo ID? It's not a

4 driver's license?

5   A   I don't know if he had a driver's license or a

6 photo ID, but it would have been an Arizona picture

7 identification or driver's license card.

8   Q   Okay. Would that have been something, for

9 example, that you could have used at that time to check

10 with the police department to see, for example, if he had

11 any wants or warrants or anything like that?

12   MR. JENSVOLD: Objection; relevance.

13   THE COURT: Overruled.

14 BY MR. LAGATTUTA:

15   Q   Is that something that you could have used?

16   A   I could have, and I don't know if we checked

17 Mr. Franks to see if he had any warrants or not. We were

18 just trying to get the information at that time.

19   Q   Okay. All right. He didn't give you any --

20 Mr. Franks didn't give you any specific information at

21 that time about him having knowledge that Mr. Coghill

22 viewed these discs, did he?

23   A   We asked him how he knew there was child

24 pornography on those compact discs, and Mr. Franks told

25 me that he couldn't help but see them when Mr. Coghill

```
 1    was on the computer.  The RV is one room, like a kitchen/
 2    living room area, and then a separate bedroom.
 3    Mr. Franks told me that he was staying in the living room
 4    portion of the RV, and that's where the computer was.
 5         Q    Okay.  Did he give you a time frame as to when
 6    that would have occurred?
 7         A    He -- I asked him -- I asked Mr. Franks:  How
 8    long have you known that Mr. Coghill has had child
 9    pornography?  And he told me that he's known for about
10    two years that Mr. Coghill has been in possession of
11    pornography.
12         Q    So you didn't narrow that down to any more
13    specific time frame?
14         A    He told me he had seen images in the RV in the
15    living room.  And since he had been there a week, I
16    assumed that during that week he stayed with Mr. Coghill
17    is when he was referring to seeing the images on the
18    computer in the RV.
19         Q    You assumed that.  Okay.  When you went over to
20    the RV, Mr. Coghill was there by himself?
21         A    Yes.
22         Q    Okay.  And approximately what time was this?
23         A    It would have been probably around quarter to 8
24    or 8:00 in the morning.
25         Q    Okay.  And at that time you were assisted by
```

PIMA COUNTY SUPERIOR COURT

1   which other officer?

2   A   Deputy Judd and I responded.

3   Q   Okay. And Mr. Coghill let you into the motor

4   home without any problem?

5   A   We asked if we could talk to him, and we asked

6   if it would be okay to step inside to talk to him. And

7   he said yes; he invited us in.

8   Q   And I think I recall from when I interviewed

9   you, when you came into the motor home you kind of came

10 in and moved yourself more toward the back of the motor

11 home and Deputy Judd positioned himself more toward the

12 front; is that right?

13   A   When we first walked in, you walk up some steps

14 and there's just a little aisleway between like a sofa

15 and a desk.

16   Q   Right.

17   A   It's a very cramped space. I remember seeing

18 the computer off to my right and -- where the driver's

19 seats would be off to my right, and then I moved toward

20 the kitchen area, yes.

21   Q   Okay. So Deputy Judd would have been physically

22 between you and where Mr. Coghill would have been

23 standing at the time you both were in the motor home;

24 right?

25   A   I can't recall where Mr. Coghill was standing at

```
 1   that time.  It's just one little area.
 2        Q    Okay.  When you went over with -- is it Deputy
 3   Judd?
 4        A    Yes, Deputy Judd.
 5        Q    -- to do the examination of the motor home at
 6   that time, at that time was Jacob Franks a suspect in the
 7   case?
 8        A    No.
 9        Q    No.  And in your mind, was he ever a suspect?
10        A    No.
11        Q    No.  And that's because he had given you
12   information about someone else, and you later acted upon
13   that information; right?
14        A    Yes.  To investigate, yes.
15        Q    All right.  How long do you think the two of you
16   were inside the motor home, you and Officer Judd?
17        A    I'm not sure.  Maybe 20 minutes.  Half hour.  We
18   spoke to him, he showed us some items inside the --
19   inside the vehicle, and then we contacted supervisors and
20   detectives.  So I don't know exactly how long we actually
21   were inside.
22        Q    Okay.  You got some information.  Was it from
23   Jacob Franks that led you to believe that his possessions
24   might be stored more toward the front of the motor home?
25   Is that what your testimony is?
```

PIMA COUNTY SUPERIOR COURT

1   A   There was a stack of clothing by the front door

2   in a chair, and we asked about that stack of clothing and

3   items.   And Mr. Coghill told us that that was

4   Mr. Franks'.

5   Q   Okay.   And when you questioned Mr. Coghill about

6   the CDs that were inside the RV that were alleged to have

7   contained child pornography, his response was that they

8   weren't his; is that correct?

9   A   The question about the CDs?   He said some of

10 them were Mr. Franks'.

11   Q   Right.   Okay.   Describe for me the stack of CDs

12 on a spindle, if you will?

13   A   They were spindles, just pieces of wood or

14 plastic; I can't remember what they were made of.   And

15 they had stacks of compact discs on them, so the discs

16 aren't in any cases.   They were just -- the holes in the

17 middle of the CDs is what the spindle went through, and

18 they were stacked on top of each other.

19   MR. LAGATTUTA: Your Honor, could I have this

20 photograph marked for use as an exhibit?

21   THE COURT: Sure.

22   MR. JENSVOLD: It may have been marked already

23 in my stack if you want to check.

24   THE COURT: What exhibit no?

25   THE CLERK: No. K.

PIMA COUNTY SUPERIOR COURT

```
 1          THE COURT:  Defense -- be K.

 2          MR. LAGATTUTA:  May I approach?

 3          THE COURT:  Sure.  Any time.

 4   BY MR. LAGATTUTA:

 5          Q    I'm going to show you, deputy, what's been

 6   marked as Defense Exhibit K.  Have you taken a look at

 7   that?

 8          A    Yes.

 9          Q    Okay.  First of all, does that photograph

10   refresh your recollection a little bit, refresh your

11   memory a little bit about what the inside of the motor

12   home looked like?

13          A    Yes.

14          Q    Now, when you described it, you came into the

15   motor home, you came up to the stairs and you look over

16   to the right, and that's where you saw the spindle of

17   CDs; is that right?

18          A    Yes, and the computer.

19          Q    And when you're looking at the picture, does

20   that picture also depict the way it's taken?  Looking

21   down the hallway you can see if a person were to walk in

22   the door, the computer would be on the right, and the

23   spindles of CDs would be on the right?

24          A    Yes.  As this is taken it's almost in the

25   doorway of the motor home looking to the right.
```

PIMA COUNTY SUPERIOR COURT

1   Q   Okay.

2   A   Toward the front of the RV.

3   Q   Now, looking at the two stacks of CDs by the

4   computer -- oh, one of them I think is sitting on top of

5   what would be a scanner or another piece of equipment?

6   A   Okay.

7   Q   Okay. Are those -- now, describe it to me what

8   you're looking at.

9   A   I'm looking at two spindles or stacks of CDs on

10 the scanner next to the computer, and then there's four

11 stacks of spindles on the carpeted area next to it.

12 Q   Okay. The two spindles to the right, how many

13 discs does it look like are in those?

14 A   I don't know. I didn't count them.

15 Q   Okay. Would you say that that stack of CDs is

16 as tall as that water pitcher sitting in front of you?

17 A   I really don't know. I -- it looks like maybe

18 it would be six inches. I'm not sure. However high the

19 scanner is, it looks to be that high.

20 Q   There are actually -- we're talking about the

21 two stacks of CDs right there; correct?

22 A   Yes.

23 Q   One is taller than the other?

24 A   Yes, yes.

25 Q   How tall is the small one?

PIMA COUNTY SUPERIOR COURT

```
1      A    The small one, maybe six -- six inches, maybe.
2      Q    And the other one is at least twice as big as
3 that?
4      A    Yes.
5      Q    Okay.  The bigger within is more like 12 --
6      A    Yes.
7      Q    -- inches tall?
8      A    Okay.
9      Q    And are those CDs contained inside of anything?
10 It looks like a plastic holder, doesn't it?
11     A    Just a little cover that would go over the top
12 of it to keep the dust off your stack.
13     Q    Ever heard the reference of cake box in
14 reference to storage of CDs?
15     A    I'm not a computer person, really.
16     Q    But they are actually covered up by something
17 that would be somewhat of a storage unit?
18     A    Yes, a piece of plastic that would go over it.
19     Q    Is that plastic completely see-through or not?
20     A    Yes, I can see through.
21     Q    And it's clear plastic or somewhat sort of
22 opaque?
23     A    I can see through it.  I don't know.
24     Q    Well, when you came into the motor home, did
25 either you or Deputy Judd see through that plastic onto
```

PIMA COUNTY SUPERIOR COURT

1   those stacks of discs? Could you actually see right

2   through them from where you were?

3   A   You could see that they were discs, yes.

4   Q   Could you see, for example, the labels on the

5   discs? Labels being the markings on the top of the discs

6   as they're laying down in the stack formation?

7   A   I didn't go through the CDs when we were inside

8   the RV, so I was more back toward the living -- the

9   kitchen area.

10   Q   Okay. Okay. But my question is when you

11   entered the motor home, for example, and you looked over

12   and you saw these spindles --

13   A   Yes.

14   Q   -- which are stacks of CDs --

15   A   Yes.

16   Q   -- by nature of the way they were stacked and in

17   their containers, were you able to look through the

18   containers and see the labels on top of the discs?

19   A   I did not look at the CD spindle cases, so, no,

20   I just saw what they were and did not investigate

21   further.

22   Q   Okay. Did you ask Mr. Coghill to open up one of

23   those spindles and kind of look through it?

24   A   I did not. Deputy Judd may have. I don't know.

25   Q   Did you see him do that?

PIMA COUNTY SUPERIOR COURT

```
 1        A    I saw Mr. -- I saw Deputy Judd looking at some
 2    of the compact discs.
 3        Q    And how is it that -- looking mean-looking at
 4    them while they were in his possession?
 5        A    Deputy Judd asked him, he said:  There's a lot
 6    of compact discs here.  Tell me how they're separated.
 7    And Mr. Coghill said some of them are Star Wars compact
 8    discs and some of them are some other science fiction
 9    show.
10        Q    Right.
11        A    So I don't know.  I just remember hearing them
12    talking about that and about what was in each stack of
13    spindles.
14        Q    Okay.
15        A    And then I remember Deputy Judd asking
16    specifically about a compact disc marked with the
17    initials "KP."
18        Q    Okay.  And at that point did Deputy Judd, did he
19    have that compact disc in his hands?
20        A    I don't know.
21        Q    Do you know if Mr. Coghill had it in his hands?
22        A    I don't know.
23        Q    Did you ever see either one of them holding the
24    CDs that were marked "KP"?
25        A    I don't remember anybody showing me the CD
```

PIMA COUNTY SUPERIOR COURT

1   marked "KP."   I remember hearing them talk about it.

2   Q   Talk about it.   Okay.   But I'm -- did you see

3   where they actually came from, physically?

4   A   I just saw all these stacks as you showed me.

5   Q   Right.

6   A   And I did not see where any particular compact

7   disc came from.

8   Q   Okay.   Okay.   Now, with respect to the disc

9   that's marked "KP," is it your testimony that while you

10   were there you saw just one of those discs marked that

11   way or more than one?

12   A   I remember there was one disc in particular, but

13   I did not go through all the stacks and I did not look at

14   all the compact discs.

15   Q   Okay.   All right.   Just as a -- to your best

16   recollection, how many discs -- actual CD discs were

17   present in the area just where Deputy Judd was standing,

18   within his immediate area?

19   A   I don't know.   I didn't count them.

20   Q   Over two or three hundred?

21   A   I really don't know.

22   Q   Okay.   So we know at least the one stack is at

23   least six inches, the other one is taller than that?

24   A   Yes.

25   Q   And there's how many other stacks other than

1 that?

2   A   There are four other stacks that I can see in

3 this picture.

4   Q   Okay. All right. So after you had this

5 questioning with Mr. Coghill about these discs, what was

6 the next thing that you and Deputy Judd did?

7   A   We asked him if he would be willing to speak to

8 detectives.

9   Q   Okay. And he said yes?

10   A   He said yes.

11   Q   Okay. And then what happened?

12   A   And so we called the supervisors, advised them

13 of the situation, and told them he was willing to talk to

14 detectives. And we were told that detectives were going

15 to come out to our location.

16   Q   Okay. So what did you do then?

17   A   I stood by and waited for the detectives so we

18 could brief them. They also wanted information to obtain

19 a search warrant.

20   Q   So at this point Mr. Coghill is under arrest?

21   A   No, he's not.

22   Q   Is he free to go?

23   A   I had no reason to keep him. He said he wanted

24 to talk to detectives, so I assumed he was going to stay

25 there and wait for the detectives.

PIMA COUNTY SUPERIOR COURT

1 Q Okay. You assumed also, then, that also -- at

2 that point he's at the very minimum a suspect in this

3 case; right?

4 A I would say suspect. We had suspicions, but we

5 didn't have reasonable cause to arrest him or probable

6 cause to arrest him. We didn't place him in handcuffs or

7 anything.

8 Q Okay. All right. How long was he there and

9 waiting for the detectives to arrive?

10 A Probably took 20 minutes for detectives to

11 arrive.

12 Q Okay. And at that point was there anymore

13 search of the motor home completed?

14 A After the search warrant was obtained, yes.

15 Q And were you involved in that search?

16 A No.

17 Q Okay. Were you involved in any other

18 conversations with Jacob Franks?

19 A No.

20 Q Did you go back and meet with him after you had

21 been to the motor home?

22 A Deputy Judd went back and picked him up and

23 transported him to the sheriff's department headquarters

24 so he could talk to detectives there.

25 Q Okay. And you weren't involved in that at all?

PIMA COUNTY SUPERIOR COURT

```
 1        A    Not that I recall, no.

 2        Q    Okay.  Do you recall any time when you and

 3   Deputy Judd were in Jim Coghill's motor home -- did you

 4   guys ever put on the rubber gloves as if you were going

 5   to conduct a search?

 6        A    Deputy Judd did put on rubber gloves in case he

 7   was going to touch any items.

 8        Q    Did you see him actually handling any of the CD

 9   discs?

10        A    I can't recall seeing him handle individual

11   discs.  I remember him pointing toward stacks, wanting to

12   know what was in each stack, trying to narrow it down

13   because there were quite a few compact discs there.

14        Q    Okay.  Did Jacob Franks, at the time prior to

15   you going over to Jim Coghill's residence, inform you

16   that he had access to Jim's computer?

17        A    It's in the living room where Mr. Franks said he

18   was staying.

19        Q    But did he tell you that he had access to Jim's

20   computer and also had a hobby of burning CDs?  Did he

21   tell you that?

22        A    He just told me that the computer was in the

23   same area where he was staying.

24        Q    Did you question him about whether or not he had

25   access to the computer?
```

PIMA COUNTY SUPERIOR COURT

```
1        A    I did not.
2        Q    Did you question him about how he believed these
3   computer discs containing child pornography were created?
4        A    I did ask him about that.
5        Q    Okay.  And did he tell you that they were
6   created on Jim's computer?
7        A    He told me that they were burned from the
8   internet onto the discs there in the recreational
9   vehicle.
10       Q    And you didn't inquire of him any time frame in
11  which this could have happened?
12       A    I did not because he told me he lived there for
13  a week.
14       Q    Right.
15       A    With Mr. Coghill.
16       Q    And your assumption was it happened during that
17  week?
18       A    Yes.
19       MR. LAGATTUTA:  That's all the questions I have,
20  your Honor.
21       THE COURT:  Redirect?
22       MR. JENSVOLD:  Thank you, your Honor.
23  ///
24  ///
25  ///
```

PIMA COUNTY SUPERIOR COURT

BY MR. JENSVOLD:

Q   You said that you didn't have enough information
to arrest Mr. Coghill. I assume that's because you
didn't even know what these images were at the time?

A   Correct. We didn't know what the compact disc
contained, and we just called the detectives to conduct
further investigation.

Q   And did you find out where Mr. Coghill was
sleeping in the RV?

A   There is a bedroom past the kitchen, which
contained some of Mr. Coghill's belongings. He took us
back in there and showed us some photo albums and other
VCR tapes.

Q   Did he ever indicate that any of the belongings
in that particular area of the RV belonged to Mr. Franks?

A   No, he did not.

Q   Was your purpose in talking to Mr. Franks at the
Circle K to conduct a forensic interview?

A   No, it was just to gather enough information to,
you know -- he wanted to report the suspicious activity.
I wanted to know what was suspicious, what he had seen,
what he knew, just the basics; enough to know if there
really was child pornography in the recreational vehicle.

Q   And to your knowledge, was somebody else going

PIMA COUNTY SUPERIOR COURT

```
1    to perform that forensic interview of Mr. Franks?

2        A    Yes.

3            MR. JENSVOLD:  That's all I have.  Thank you.

4            THE COURT:  Jurors get to ask questions if you

5    have any.  I'd like for you to write them out.  There are

6    white sheets or Peter should have some extra.  Jurors

7    have any questions?

8            You'll get used to this as we go along.  I'm

9    going to release her, so if you want to ask a question of

10   Officer Schupbach, now would be the time to do that.

11           MR. LAGATTUTA:  Your Honor, excuse me.

12           THE COURT:  Do you want to approach?

13           MR. LAGATTUTA:  I apologize, I had one other

14   question that I wanted to ask, and I wonder if I can do

15   that.

16           THE COURT:  You can go ahead and ask yours, and

17   then if you have follow-up then we'll do juror questions.

18

19                   RECROSS-EXAMINATION

20   BY MR. LAGATTUTA:

21       Q    I'm sorry, Deputy Schupbach, I was looking

22   through your report.  In the conversations that you had

23   with Jacob prior to going over to Mr. Coghill's place,

24   did he say to you that -- that he -- that he had always

25   told Jim, meaning Jim Coghill, that Jim had better not
```

PIMA COUNTY SUPERIOR COURT

```
 1   make him mad, and then he said he was just mad enough now
 2   that he wanted to report this to the police?
 3        A    Yes, I do recall him telling me that.
 4             MR. LAGATTUTA:  Okay.  Thank you very much.
 5             THE COURT:  Cross on that?
 6             MR. JENSVOLD:  No, your Honor.
 7             THE COURT:  Or redirect?
 8             Now juror questions.
 9             No questions?  Okay.
10             Thank you very much, officer or deputy, and
11   you're excused.
12             MR. JENSVOLD:  Your Honor, can we approach for
13   just a second?
14             THE COURT:  Sure.
15             (Bench conference.)
16             MR. JENSVOLD:  This is just a potential
17   scheduling issue.  Mr. Franks is going to take a while,
18   but I have Mr. Kreitl, the handwriting person, coming
19   down today from Phoenix, and I don't want to drag him
20   down tomorrow.  Would it be okay to lay foundation
21   through Jacob for the handwriting purpose, and then do
22   Mr. Kreitl?  I scheduled him for 3:00.  I can go as far
23   as we need to, but then can we do Mr. Kreitl's testimony
24   between that time?
25             THE COURT:  Any problem?
```

PIMA COUNTY SUPERIOR COURT

```
 1          MR. LAGATTUTA:  No, but I didn't quite
 2   understand it.
 3          THE COURT:  He's going to go so far as to lay
 4   the foundation, and then bring the expert and things --
 5          MR. LAGATTUTA:  And then bring him back?
 6          MR. JENSVOLD:  I can go because Mr. Kreitl is
 7   not supposed to be here until 3:00.
 8          THE COURT:  That will be a good time to take a
 9   break.  But you won't expect to finish with him?
10          MR. JENSVOLD:  Mr. Franks?  I'm sure we'll get
11   to the point it's cross.
12          THE COURT:  But you will get far enough to --
13          MR. JENSVOLD:  Yeah.
14          THE COURT:  -- to relate to the handwriting
15   expert's testimony?
16          MR. JENSVOLD:  Yes.
17          MR. LAGATTUTA:  I don't have any problem with
18   that.
19          THE COURT:  Okay.  We do have a question.  What
20   I do with these is I number them.  I'll let you see them,
21   and if there's any objection -- do tell them that you'll
22   answer the question in due course if there's --
23          MR. JENSVOLD:  There's other witnesses can
24   answer that question.
25          THE COURT:  We have no witness here.  I'll tell
```

PIMA COUNTY SUPERIOR COURT

```
 1   them that it will be answered in due course.  You all
 2   know about it.
 3            (Open court.)
 4            THE COURT:  The question that's been asked here,
 5   I think I tell you in the instructions in due course that
 6   counsel know about it, and they'll try to get it answered
 7   in due course with a witness that can answer it.
 8            And, with that, your next witness, Mr. Jensvold.
 9            MR. JENSVOLD:  Jacob Franks.
10            THE COURT:  Just come on over here, and you need
11   to give your name to the clerk, and he'll swear you in.
12            (The witness was sworn.)
13            THE COURT:  Your witness, Mr. Jensvold.
14            MR. JENSVOLD:  Thank you, your Honor.
15
16                 JACOB FRANKS,
17   called as a witness herein, having been first duly sworn,
18   was examined and testified as follows:
19
20                 DIRECT EXAMINATION
21   BY MR. JENSVOLD:
22       Q   Would you please state your name and spell your
23   last name for the record?
24       A   Jacob Robert Franks, F-r-a-n-k-s.
25       Q   And, Mr. Franks, where do you live now?
```

PIMA COUNTY SUPERIOR COURT

```
1        A    In Awatukee.

2        Q    And who do you live with?

3        A    My girlfriend.

4        Q    And how long have you -- how long -- how long

5   have you had this particular girlfriend?

6        A    Since February.

7        Q    Now, Mr. Franks, we discussed this, that you had

8   a criminal past; is that right?

9        A    Yeah.

10       Q    You had some criminal convictions?

11       A    Yeah.

12       Q    What are those?

13       A    Those are a burglary charge from when I was like

14  21, 20.

15       Q    Okay.  And then you had a couple more similar

16  convictions around the same time -- later on, but the

17  other two that were close in time to each other?

18       A    No.  I was drinking one night, and I ended up in

19  somebody's unlocked vehicle.  That's what happened.

20       Q    But you had three felony convictions; is that

21  right?

22       A    I think so.

23       Q    And when was the -- and you've been to prison

24  two different times?

25       A    Technically, yes.
```

PIMA COUNTY SUPERIOR COURT

```
 1        Q    What was the most recent?

 2        A    2003.

 3        Q    And how long were you in there?

 4        A    Like two and a half.

 5        Q    Two and a half years?

 6        A    Yes.

 7        Q    And you're on parole right now?

 8        A    Yes.

 9        Q    Okay.  For how long?

10        A    Till September.

11        Q    And your parole officer is in Phoenix; correct?

12        A    Yes.

13        Q    And are you employed right now?

14        A    In between jobs.  I lost my Social Security

15   card, and I have -- I had to reapply for a new one.

16        Q    And you're looking for employment now?

17        A    Yes.

18        Q    And, I guess, did you have a job recently

19   that --

20        A    Yes, I did.

21        Q    Okay.  And your past sort of caught up with you

22   for that job?

23        A    Well, before that I was laying carpeting.

24        Q    But what was the other job that you had?

25        A    Oh, loan specialist.
```

PIMA COUNTY SUPERIOR COURT

```
 1        Q    And then your past prevented you from continuing
 2   on?
 3        A    Unfortunately, yes.
 4        Q    All right.  Can you -- do you know Mr. Jim
 5   Coghill?
 6        A    Yes, I do.
 7        Q    And is Mr. Coghill in the courtroom today?
 8        A    Yes, he is.
 9        Q    And can you point him out, for the record?
10        A    He's right there in the gray.
11        Q    The third --
12        A    He's on the far left.
13             MR. JENSVOLD:  Your Honor, may the record
14   reflect the witness identified --
15             THE COURT:  Yes.
16   BY MR. JENSVOLD:
17        Q    And when did you first meet with Mr. Coghill?
18        A    November of '99 we had this training class for
19   Direct Marketing Services that we both worked at and we
20   met there.
21        Q    So what did that work involve?
22        A    Telemarketing, working for Nextel, taking
23   inbound calls, customer service, phone work.
24        Q    And how did your relationship with Mr. Coghill
25   start?
```

PIMA COUNTY SUPERIOR COURT

```
 1        A    We needed some programs for his computer, like
 2   for -- to write web pages.  And he wanted me to help him
 3   get that program, so I invited him over one day a long
 4   time ago.
 5        Q    And where were you living?
 6        A    North Phoenix.
 7        Q    And did you guys have some other things in
 8   common?
 9        A    Computers, basically at first, you know.
10        Q    What about later?
11        A    We worked together.
12        Q    Okay.  Was there something -- was there a
13   Buddhist interest between the two of you?
14        A    Maybe later.  Not -- not -- not originally.
15        Q    How much later?
16        A    Maybe the last year that we hung out.
17        Q    Can you -- so when did that start?  The last
18   year before this whole incident happened?
19        A    I would say so.
20        Q    Can you describe the interest between the two of
21   you and how -- relate your interest in Buddhism.
22        A    He knows quite a lot about that stuff, so he was
23   just kind of teaching me.
24        Q    How close of friends were you would you say you
25   were in the beginning and then later on?
```

PIMA COUNTY SUPERIOR COURT

```
 1       A    I would say we weren't quite close until maybe
 2    after September 11th, when the planes hit.  And then we
 3    kind of hung out.  We lived with each other for a little
 4    while.
 5       Q    And when did that happen?  When were you living
 6    with Mr. Coghill?
 7       A    Like October of '01 -- 2001.  It was off and on
 8    a couple months here and there.
 9       Q    When was the first time that you lived with
10    Mr. Coghill?
11       A    I think October, 2001.
12       Q    And how long were you there at that time?
13       A    I don't know.  A few months, I'm not sure on
14    dates.  I honestly don't remember.
15       Q    And then did you live with him again?
16       A    Yeah.
17       Q    When was that, do you remember?
18       A    Actually, I think I lived with him twice because
19    he got me rehired at DMS back in 2002, and I lived with
20    him for like maybe three or four months.  And then I
21    ended up moving into a townhome that summer of 2002,
22    which is I think August.  So, yeah, I'd say August it
23    was.
24       Q    Okay.  So August is when you moved back in with
25    him?
```

PIMA COUNTY SUPERIOR COURT

1   A   Like the summer of 2002 I pretty much stayed

2 with him, is what I'm saying, because I think it was in

3 August of '02 I ended up moving.

4   Q   But it wasn't continuous, then, from October of

5 2001 --

6   A   No, no, no, no.

7   Q   And then -- so -- sorry, we can't talk over each

8 other.

9   A   Okay.

10   Q   You started August 2002 the second time around?

11   A   Yes.

12   Q   And how long did that last, if you remember?

13   A   No, I didn't start August. I'm sorry, it was --

14 I would say May or June.

15   Q   That's when it started?

16   A   Yeah.

17   Q   And then it ended in August?

18   A   Yeah.

19   Q   And those were both in Phoenix?

20   A   Yeah.

21   Q   Where, specifically, was it in Phoenix?

22   A   715 West Moon Valley Drive.

23   Q   What kind of place was it?

24   A   It was a house, but we stayed in the motor home

25 that was next to it.

PIMA COUNTY SUPERIOR COURT

```
 1        Q    So after August of 2002, did you ever live with
 2   Mr. Coghill again in Phoenix?
 3        A    Yeah.  Well, I think I did.  Yeah, like January
 4   of '03 I -- I believe, for a couple of months.  And then
 5   my grandfather passed January of '03, and I went and
 6   stayed at my grandfather's house.
 7        Q    Okay.  Were you living with Mr. Coghill when he
 8   moved to Tucson?
 9        A    No.  No, I was not.  He had gotten a job at
10   Hamilton Aerospace where he -- because in Pima County, he
11   travels a lot, so he ended up working down in Tucson.  So
12   he took his motor home down there, and I didn't see him
13   for a few months.  I thought he was somewhere else.
14        Q    Do you know how long -- you said you were living
15   there January of '03, so -- hold on.  Got to wait for me
16   to finish.
17             How long before Mr. Coghill moved to Tucson were
18   you living with him in Phoenix?
19        A    Three months, maybe.  No.  I don't know when he
20   got the job down there.  I think it was February,
21   perhaps, or March.  I think he was only down there for
22   like a month or two before he came back up to Phoenix
23   from Tucson after he was already established down there.
24   See what I'm saying?
25        Q    Right.  So if he -- I'm just -- if he was down
```

PIMA COUNTY SUPERIOR COURT

1   there in February, in Tucson, of 2003 --

2   A   Should have been.

3   Q   Okay. -- then how long before that did you move

4   out of the motor home?

5   A   January.

6   Q   Okay. So you say around a month?

7   A   Yeah, my grandfather died. We all went over

8   there because we had to take care of things. Funeral

9   arrangements and stuff.

10   Q   So when he moved down to Tucson, did you keep in

11   touch with him?

12   A   Not often, but by phone occasionally or by

13   e-mail perhaps.

14   Q   And then eventually did you come down to Tucson?

15   A   Yeah. He came up to visit from Tucson, and he

16   said he could give me a job down there. So I went down

17   there with him.

18   Q   And were you sort of -- were you looking for a

19   place to stay again?

20   A   I had somewhere to stay, but it was like we were

21   sharing a studio apartment with two other people so it

22   was kind of cramped. So I decided to go for a little

23   while.

24   Q   And do you remember what day of the week that

25   might have been?

PIMA COUNTY SUPERIOR COURT

277

```
 1        A    It could have been a Tuesday.  It could have
 2   been a Thursday.  I'm not sure, so -- it could have been
 3   a Friday.
 4        Q    You don't remember?
 5        A    Honestly, I think it might have been a Friday.
 6        Q    Okay.
 7        A    This was a few years ago, so --
 8        Q    And so what was -- what was -- what were the
 9   circumstances behind you going down there besides he said
10   he was going to give you a job -- or get you a job down
11   there?
12        A    What were the other circumstances?
13        Q    He was basically -- was his sole purpose in
14   coming up there to pick you up and bring you back down
15   for the job interview?
16        A    I'm not sure what you're saying, sir.
17        Q    Was he up there to visit other people besides
18   yourself?
19        A    He might have went up to visit his parents.
20        Q    Okay.
21        A    I think he did.
22        Q    But was it prearranged by e-mail or phone or
23   whatever that he was coming?
24        A    Yeah, he said he was coming back -- coming back
25   up to Phoenix.  And I said, "Well, give me a call when
```

PIMA COUNTY SUPERIOR COURT

```
 1    you get up here," kind of thing.  It wasn't nothing
 2    arranged.
 3         Q    And what kind of job were you going to get --
 4    were you going to interview for, anyway?
 5         A    I believe either a -- like a clerk-type job at
 6    Hamilton Aerospace, pushing paperwork, perhaps.
 7         Q    And do you remember how long you were down there
 8    until this incident?
 9         A    A week.
10         Q    Do you remember exactly how many days or --
11         A    No.
12         Q    Now, you didn't go to the interview, did you?
13         A    No.
14         Q    Can you explain to the jury what happened?
15         A    The night before the interview, I took his GoPed
16    out, and I ended up getting hit by a car.  I was down by
17    Benson Highway and Alvernon, and I road up to 4th Avenue
18    and Broadway.  So I totaled his GoPed.  It got destroyed,
19    right?  So I had to explain that to him:  Why did I
20    destroy his $400 GoPed that he spent so much money on?
21    So I was kind of worried about that.
22              And I think they took me in the ambulance to
23    Kino, which everybody is lined up.  It's a crappy
24    hospital anyway.  I didn't have any money.  They gave me
25    a prescription for Vicodin.  I hitch-hiked partially the
```

PIMA COUNTY SUPERIOR COURT

1   way back because I don't know Tucson. I'm from Phoenix.

2   Q   Let me stop you there. Can you describe for the

3   jury what a GoPed is?

4   A   A GoPed is like a motorized skateboard. It's a

5   skateboard like a lawn mower engine and oil and gas. You

6   have to have a mixture. And a little thing of

7   handlebars, and you can -- the accelerator is right

8   there, and the brake on the other side.

9   Q   How far was it between where you are staying and

10   4th and Broadway?

11   A   I'm guessing ten miles at least.

12   Q   Did you have to stop at a gas station along the

13   way?

14   A   No, you get good miles per gallon on those.

15   Q   What happened to it? You hitch-hiked back?

16   A   I still had it. It wasn't completely -- it was

17   broke, but it wasn't like in pieces.

18   Q   Okay. So you took it with you?

19   A   Yeah. I had to. It wasn't mine.

20   Q   Okay. So you took it with you to the hospital,

21   and then you brought it back?

22   A   Yeah. They had me lock it up outside because it

23   had gasoline in it. They didn't want it in the hospital.

24   Q   Now, Mr. Coghill wasn't real happy about this?

25   A   Oh, no.

PIMA COUNTY SUPERIOR COURT

```
1      Q    What happened?

2      A    Yeah, he was quite pissed.  He said that was my

3    way to get back and forth to work.  And he just wanted to

4    send me home or send me back to Phoenix and never talk to

5    me again.  He was pretty irate with me.

6      Q    Do you know what time you got back to the RV?

7      A    That day that I got hit by a car?

8      Q    Yes.

9      A    That was the day before.  I would say 5,

10   5:30 p.m.

11     Q    And was -- was Mr. Coghill there when you got

12   back?

13     A    No, he wasn't back yet.  He probably came back,

14   I'd say, 45 minutes later, and he had some groceries and

15   stuff.  And I just, you know, straight up told him what

16   happened, you know, right away.  And he was as mad like

17   he was -- it didn't seem -- like the next day he was mad.

18   He was irate for -- he wasn't yelling and screaming

19   erratically or anything, but he was pretty ticked.

20     Q    And were you looking for a job that day when you

21   were out on the MoPed?

22     ˆA    Yeah, getting applications here and there.

23   There's a Waffle House on every corner in Tucson, so I

24   was --

25     Q    But was it your understanding you were only
```

PIMA COUNTY SUPERIOR COURT

1 supposed to go a short distance with that GoPed?

2   A   I don't know if there was an arranged,

3 specified -- as long as you have gas in it and you can

4 get back.

5   Q   Did he give you any instructions about keeping

6 off the roadways with it or anything like that?

7   A   Wear your helmet and use the light thing -- the

8 Mag lights. He had attached Mag lights to it, two

9 flashlights. He said use those at night. It works

10 surprisingly well.

11   Q   Okay. Mr. Franks, what's your sleeping schedule

12 like? What was it then when living with Mr. Coghill in

13 Tucson?

14   A   Then? In Tucson? Probably -- probably didn't

15 get as much sleep as I should have.

16   Q   I mean, are you an early to bed, early to rise

17 kind of person?

18   A   Not necessarily, no.

19   Q   What's your normal routine?

20   A   Then or now?

21   Q   How about then, the time that you were in

22 Tucson.

23   A   I'd stay up all night, probably, or fall asleep

24 at 2, 3, 4 in the morning, sleep till, I don't know, 1, 2

25 in the afternoon perhaps.

PIMA COUNTY SUPERIOR COURT

1   Q   What would you be doing during those early

2   morning hours?

3   A   Sitting in the motor home in the middle of

4   nowhere in Tucson. He had high-speed internet on his

5   computer, and I would pirate music. That's what I did.

6   Q   Did he have a TV or anything in there?

7   A   He had a TV, but there was nothing good to watch

8   down there. He had digital cable, but I'm not much of a

9   TV person.

10 Q   Where was the TV?

11 A   Sometimes he kept it up front, and sometimes he

12 would take it in the back room when he was watching

13 whatever he was watching back there.

14 Q   Now, you say you were pirating music. How did

15 you do that?

16 A   I don't know, I downloaded it from pure, pure

17 programs. That's about it. I wouldn't sell them or

18 nothing. I would just have them for personal use.

19 Q   Do you remember what program you were using?

20 A   KaZaA was one of them back then.

21 Q   What are your musical interests, if you can

22 describe those to the jury.

23   Let's go back then, first.

24 A   Then? Musical interests: Posse, Twisted,

25 Psychopathic Records.

PIMA COUNTY SUPERIOR COURT

```
 1        Q    And can you describe, some of the jurors might
 2   not be familiar with those bands, what kind of music is
 3   that?
 4        A    They're underground hip hop we'll say, but kind
 5   of dark.
 6        Q    Were there any other particular bands that you
 7   were listening to?
 8        A    Oh, Evanescence.
 9        Q    What kind of music is Evanescence?
10        A    It's hard to say.  There was a lot of different
11   genres that they -- I don't know what they are.  Now or
12   then?
13        Q    Well, back then.
14        A    Same as they are now.  They haven't put nothing
15   out since, really -- I don't know.  First time I heard it
16   I thought it was Lincoln Park with a woman singer.
17   That's what it sounded like to me.
18        Q    Now, were you listening to another band called
19   Disturbed?
20        A    Probably.
21        Q    How about Rare Bird?
22        A    Rare Bird?  Yeah, yeah, that's old school music.
23        Q    Did you mention Q Strange?
24        A    Yeah, some white dude who raps, like from
25   Providence, Rhode Island.
```

PIMA COUNTY SUPERIOR COURT

1   Q   How about Dr. Octagon?

2   A   Dr. Octagon, yeah he's pretty good.

3   Q   What kind of music is that?

4   A   It's like underground hip hop, I would say.

5 Kind of weird.

6   Q   30 Seconds to Mars?

7   A   30 Seconds to Mars.

8   Have you heard the actor Jader Leo?

9   Q   Just, if you can, I'm not supposed to answer

10 your questions.

11   A   Rock music. I'm sorry, rock music.

12   Q   That's okay. How about Queens of the Stone Age?

13   A   Rock music, all.

14   Q   All these artists are the ones you're listening

15 to?

16   A   Yeah. I was downloading everything because

17 that's what I do. I just like music. That's what I

18 would do. I started searching for stuff, and then next

19 thing I know I'm searching for all kinds of other stuff.

20   Q   Have you ever heard of Alan Watts?

21   A   Alan Watts? How do you spell his last name?

22   Q   W-a-t-t-s.

23   A   Not like that, no. I don't think so.

24   Q   Now, were you downloading anything else besides

25 music while you were there with Mr. Coghill in Tucson?

PIMA COUNTY SUPERIOR COURT

```
1        A    Music related?

2        Q    Nonmusic related, anything else?

3        A    Probably actual movies, like actual cinema

4   movies that come out in the theater; might have been

5   something on there.

6        Q    Okay.  Did you watch any -- did you download any

7   pornography while you were there, adult pornography?

8        A    Actual pornography that's legal?  Yeah.  I

9   believe so.

10       Q    And do you remember if that was around the same

11  time some of those early morning hours when you were

12  downloading music?

13       A    Probably.

14       Q    Would you recognize any of the titles of the

15  movies?

16       A    If I saw them probably I would.

17            THE WITNESS:  Excuse me, your Honor, you don't

18  mind if -- I have a sore throat.

19            THE COURT:  Mr. Jensvold, do you all need some

20  minutes here?

21            MR. JENSVOLD:  I'm not sure.  Maybe one more

22  minute.

23            THE COURT:  Go ahead if you need to talk with

24  Mr. Lagattuta for a minute, and we have a second in here.

25            If you all want water and want to stretch, don't
```

PIMA COUNTY SUPERIOR COURT

```
 1   hesitate.

 2                (Pause.)

 3           THE COURT:  Ready?

 4           Continue then, Mr. Jensvold.

 5           Give the jurors a second.  They're pouring some

 6   water.

 7           Okay, go ahead.

 8   BY MR. JENSVOLD:

 9       Q   Mr. Franks, I want to show you what's been

10   marked as State's Exhibit 12E.  Have you ever seen this

11   document before?

12       A   Have I ever seen 12E before?

13       Q   And we talked yesterday.  I asked if you had

14   seen Detective Englander's forensic report --

15       A   No.

16       Q   -- and you said no.

17           Now, I'd like you to turn -- there are page

18   numbers down there on the bottom that have been

19   handwritten in.

20       A   Okay.

21       Q   Turn to page 46.  And if you could kind of

22   glance through pages 46 through, say, 50.  There are

23   various descriptions.  Don't make -- don't make any

24   comments about them, just look at them yourself and see

25   if that appears to be something you would recognize as
```

PIMA COUNTY SUPERIOR COURT

1 something that you were viewing.

2   A   That one, no. I don't think so.

3   Q   Take a look at pages 47 through 50 also.

4   A   Okay. (Witness complied.) Maybe the ones on

5 47, I think so. 48, no. Maybe the middle one on 49.

6 Maybe. No, not 50.

7   Q   Now, are you sure about that based on -- again,

8 you're not -- obviously you're not looking at the movies

9 themselves at this point. You're looking at written

10 descriptions?

11   A   Uh-huh.

12   Q   Are you confident? You said no, you certainly

13 weren't watching --

14   A   The ones that I said no to, I'm confident. Now,

15 just because of a date with the files on them, somebody

16 else could have been cueing those up and downloading, and

17 they could have happened to be finished at that time.

18   Q   Okay. Can you explain more to the jury how

19 KaZaA works and how these times show up?

20   A   It's a peer-to-peer program. I don't know it

21 even works anymore. It was like Napster. Everybody

22 heard about that on the news. And like you would connect

23 with other people's computers to share files, movies,

24 music videos, pornography, software. It's about it.

25 Media.

PIMA COUNTY SUPERIOR COURT

```
 1           MR. LAGATTUTA:  No, but I didn't quite
 2  understand it.
 3           THE COURT:  He's going to go so far as to lay
 4  the foundation, and then bring the expert and things --
 5           MR. LAGATTUTA:  And then bring him back?
 6           MR. JENSVOLD:  I can go because Mr. Kreitl is
 7  not supposed to be here until 3:00.
 8           THE COURT:  That will be a good time to take a
 9  break.  But you won't expect to finish with him?
10           MR. JENSVOLD:  Mr. Franks?  I'm sure we'll get
11  to the point it's cross.
12           THE COURT:  But you will get far enough to --
13           MR. JENSVOLD:  Yeah.
14           THE COURT:  -- to relate to the handwriting
15  expert's testimony?
16           MR. JENSVOLD:  Yes.
17           MR. LAGATTUTA:  I don't have any problem with
18  that.
19           THE COURT:  Okay.  We do have a question.  What
20  I do with these is I number them.  I'll let you see them,
21  and if there's any objection -- do tell them that you'll
22  answer the question in due course if there's --
23           MR. JENSVOLD:  There's other witnesses can
24  answer that question.
25           THE COURT:  We have no witness here.  I'll tell
```

PIMA COUNTY SUPERIOR COURT

```
 1        Q    So what do you know with the times and which
 2   things show up?
 3        A    Whenever the file is complete, that's what the
 4   date is going to be on.  Like when it was modified last,
 5   do you know what I'm saying?
 6        Q    And these things might take various times to
 7   finish downloading?
 8        A    It depends on who you're connected with.  You
 9   could be connected up with some guy on a dial-up modem
10   who's going to be taking three days to download something
11   if he's going to sit there.
12        Q    But then it might take faster if you're on high
13   speed?
14        A    Yeah.  It depends on who you're with on the
15   other end, if they're on high speed.
16        Q    So I guess the slowest link is going to
17   determine the length of the download?
18        A    Yeah.  Sometimes they get messed up or canceled,
19   or the people get offline so they don't have the file.
20   So it's sitting in a cue, waiting for them to get back
21   on.  Do you know what I mean.
22        Q    Now, let's go back to page 1 of 12E.
23        A    1.  Okay.
24        Q    Now, does -- look through like pages 1, 2, and
25   3.  Are some of those bands that you mentioned earlier?
```

PIMA COUNTY SUPERIOR COURT

```
 1    Are those indicated?

 2         A    Yeah.  Yeah, yeah, I downloaded the music.

 3         Q    All right.  So do you see there files for Mp3

 4    for Twisted and Evanescence and some of those other

 5    bands?

 6         A    Yeah.

 7         Q    Now, look at that first one on the first page of

 8    12E.  Is that Alan Watts?  It says "Journey from India."

 9         A    You know what I think that might be?  A lecture.

10    That's a Buddhist audio book lecture.

11         Q    Do you remember that?

12         A    He might have -- I think he downloaded that

13    because he would download stuff like that, and like

14    Joseph Campbell and stuff and then play it.

15         Q    And there's a date on that Alan Watts file.

16    What's that?

17         A    Friday, March 21st.

18         Q    And then that Evanescence file below, what's the

19    date on that?

20         A    Wednesday, March 26th.

21         Q    Now, this is kind of a personal question, but

22    did you have -- in viewing pornography, do you have a

23    particular hair color preference in women at that time?

24         A    Probably red heads.  I like brunettes and black

25    hair.
```

PIMA COUNTY SUPERIOR COURT

```
 1       Q    Now, I want to skip sort of ahead a little bit.
 2       A    Yes, sir.
 3       Q    You did an interview -- a taped interview after
 4  you had called the police and everything; is that right?
 5       A    Oh, yeah.
 6       Q    Let me go ahead and get that from you now.
 7  Thanks.
 8            Okay, how long -- where did you go to do that
 9  interview?
10       A    Pima County Sheriff's office, I guess.  I don't
11  know where it's at.  I think it's on Alvernon or
12  something.  Is it Alvernon, that street that goes
13  diagonal?
14       Q    I can't answer your questions, Mr. Franks.
15            THE COURT:  You've got to let him ask the
16  questions and respond to his questions.
17            THE WITNESS:  I apologize.  I don't know where
18  it's at.
19  BY MR. JENSVOLD:
20       Q    But you went there.
21            Now, let's go back.  You called the police from
22  where?
23       A    Circle K.
24       Q    Now, let me go back prior to that.  You had the
25  argument with him over the -- over the -- the GoPed and
```

PIMA COUNTY SUPERIOR COURT

```
 1    all that stuff --
 2         A    Uh-huh.
 3         Q    -- the night before?
 4              What happened in the morning?
 5         A    I was going to go -- I was going to go to the
 6    interview, and he was upset about the shirt that I chose
 7    to wear, and he wanted me to wear a different shirt.
 8         Q    What kind of shirt did you have on?
 9         A    Big red shirt.  Probably wasn't the best choice.
10    He was probably right.  But we ended up getting into an
11    argument over it, and he wanted to send me back to
12    Phoenix and not go to the interview.
13         Q    What did he want to you wear?
14         A    A white button-up shirt.  It was better for the
15    interview anyway.
16         Q    Did you put the white shirt on?
17         A    I think I did put it on, but I don't know for
18    how long.
19         Q    Did you take it back off again?
20         A    Yeah.
21         Q    Did he get upset with you -- what did he say to
22    you about the shirt besides you should wear, the white
23    one?
24         A    Nothing else.
25         Q    Did he tell you -- did he get discouraged about
```

PIMA COUNTY SUPERIOR COURT

```
 1    you being there at all?
 2         A    What do you mean?
 3         Q    I mean, was he -- during that time, was he kind
 4    of fed up with you?
 5         A    Yeah.  Correct.
 6         Q    Did he say anything to -- along that line?
 7         A    Yeah:  I'm going to take you back to Phoenix and
 8    drop you off on the nearest street corner and be done
 9    with you.
10         Q    What did you do after that?
11         A    I just left without saying a word to him.
12         Q    And then where did you go?
13         A    Just walked around, kind of back behind like --
14    back behind where the -- what is it?  The mobile home
15    park that he was living at, kind of back behind here.
16    And thinking:  What I should do?  What's going to happen?
17         Q    What were you thinking about specifically?
18         A    Well, I knew -- I knew that he had files for a
19    little while, like -- he was letting me live with him and
20    stuff.  He wasn't really charging me for rent, so I
21    didn't want to say nothing about it because I wasn't
22    sure, because I didn't know.  I knew it was bad -- like I
23    never told on nobody because of my past and stuff.  I
24    learned you're not supposed to do stuff like that.  But I
25    just got fed up with it, and I said I've got to do the
```

PIMA COUNTY SUPERIOR COURT

```
1    right thing.
2        Q    Now, when you were pondering this, did you go
3    back into the RV?
4        A    No.  No I was walking around in the area,
5    wondering:  What I should do?  What should I do?  So I
6    decided -- it took me a while to gain the courage to do
7    it.  Probably took about 15, 20 minutes, and I said:
8    Screw it, I'm going to go do it.  And I called.
9        Q    Okay.  Right before then, did you have a
10   discussion about him taking you back up to Phoenix?
11       A    It wasn't really a discussion.  I didn't want to
12   go back.  I wanted to go to the interview and get that
13   job.
14       Q    Did you ask him about that again?
15       A    Yeah, but he was pissed.
16       Q    What did he say?
17       A    He said no.
18       Q    And then -- and that's the point at which you
19   went and made the phone call?
20       A    Possibly 20 minutes afterwards from that time.
21       Q    So what happened in those 20 minutes?
22       A    I was walking around, thinking by myself.  I got
23   the heck out because I didn't want to -- I don't know, I
24   was irritated.
25       Q    And so why did you finally make a phone call?
```

PIMA COUNTY SUPERIOR COURT

1   A   I should have done it a long time ago. It was

2   the right thing to do.

3   Q   How long had you known that he had these kinds

4   of files?

5   A   Probably a couple years, honestly. Probably

6   since -- probably since '01.

7   Q   How did you first find out that he had those?

8   A   Well, when he has discs that are labeled the way

9   they were, like kiddy porn, kind of obvious. You know

10   what I mean? When you find discs that say kiddy porn on

11   them.

12   Q   Were some of them marked "KP"?

13   A   Some of them were, yeah.

14   Q   Would you ever see them?

15   A   Sometimes I would. Because when you're in the

16   motor home, it's kind of close quarters. I slept like

17   right where the computer area was. Sometimes I would

18   wake up and see something, and, oh, God. And I would

19   roll my head just look the other way.

20   Q   Did you ever ask him about yes was watching that

21   stuff?

22   A   Yeah.

23   MR. LAGATTUTA: Objection; foundation as to

24   place and time.

25   THE COURT: Sustained.

PIMA COUNTY SUPERIOR COURT

```
 1            MR. JENSVOLD:  Okay.  Your Honor, may we
 2    approach?
 3            THE COURT:  Sure.
 4                (Bench conference.)
 5            MR. JENSVOLD:  I guess he's already said that.
 6            THE COURT:  Sustained on foundation.  He said
 7    it's sometime in the last two years.  We don't know
 8    whether we're talking about in Tucson or in Phoenix.
 9            MR. JENSVOLD:  Okay.  I just want to make sure
10    what the foundation --
11            THE COURT:  You can ask.
12            MR. LAGATTUTA:  And the other part of the
13    objection, not only foundation but obscure time he's
14    giving us.
15            THE COURT:  Same objection, so you have to pin
16    it down more.
17            MR. JENSVOLD:  Okay.
18                (Open court.)
19            THE COURT:  Okay.  Sustained objection on
20    foundation.
21            Go ahead, Mr. Jensvold.
22    BY MR. JENSVOLD:
23        Q   Okay.  Mr. Franks, where were you, if you
24    remember, the very first time that you saw some of these?
25        A   Actual -- actual movies playing?
```

PIMA COUNTY SUPERIOR COURT

```
 1        Q    Yes.
 2        A    Probably sometime in '01, like after like
 3   October when he had the computer in the house -- wait,
 4   did he have it in the house?  Honestly, I don't know
 5   if -- he either had it in the house or the basement, or
 6   he had it in the -- I believe it was in the house the
 7   first time I ever stumbled across anything like that that
 8   he had.
 9        Q    Okay.  You think you were in the house and not
10   the RV?
11        A    No, I was -- I'm pretty sure I was in the house.
12        Q    Were you ever in the RV when you saw him
13   watching that?
14        A    Uh-huh.
15        Q    Is that a yes?
16        A    Yes.
17        Q    You have to say yes for the court reporter?
18        A    I'm sorry.
19        Q    Now, if you were in the RV, what time period
20   would that have been?
21        A    Early in the morning because that's when I would
22   be asleep.
23        Q    I meant time period as far as month and year?
24        A    Oh, the -- I'm trying the more recent one.
25        Q    In Phoenix.
```

PIMA COUNTY SUPERIOR COURT

```
 1       A     Yeah.  Yeah, up in Phoenix and down in Tucson.

 2       Q     But you knew about them in Phoenix?

 3             MR. LAGATTUTA:  Objection; leading.

 4             THE COURT:  Overruled.

 5             THE WITNESS:  Yeah.

 6    BY MR. JENSVOLD:

 7       Q     And so you said earlier you think the first time

 8    that you were living in the motor home was October of

 9    2001?

10       A     Uh-huh.

11       Q     That's about when that started?

12       A     Yeah, because I don't think he had it before.

13       Q     Did he have -- when did he first get internet

14    access hooked up to the RV in Phoenix?

15       A     Probably when he actually got the motor home

16    because they probably took it in the house, and he just

17    took a wire from his room in the house, co-ax cable, and

18    just ran it to the motor home.  It wasn't wireless or

19    nothing.

20       Q     Did he have it in October of 2001 when you moved

21    in there with him?

22       A     Yeah.

23       Q     Now, do you remember if you saw any of those

24    files during that first time period you lived with him

25    starting in October of 2001?
```

PIMA COUNTY SUPERIOR COURT

```
 1          MR. LAGATTUTA:  Objection; foundation.

 2          THE COURT:  October of '01, no, overruled.

 3          MR. LAGATTUTA:  I'm sorry, your Honor, my

 4    question -- the question refers to those files or some

 5    files.  I'm not sure exactly what counsel is referring

 6    to.

 7          THE COURT:  I'll sustain on that aspect.

 8          Go ahead.

 9    BY MR. JENSVOLD:

10      Q    Okay.  Do you remember seeing any child

11    pornography viewed by Mr. Coghill in that first period of

12    time when you were living with him in the RV?

13      A    Yeah.  I'm pretty sure.  It's not like I sat

14    there behind him and watched or -- but, like, you see

15    something that you just knew wasn't right, it was your

16    intuition and didn't need to keep looking over that way.

17      Q    And do you remember the first time that you

18    asked him about that?

19          MR. LAGATTUTA:  Objection; foundation as to date

20    and time.

21          THE COURT:  Overruled.

22          THE WITNESS:  No.  I don't remember the actual

23    first time.  Probably toward the ending of our friendship

24    or whatever happened, toward the end, back in '03.

25    ///
```

BY MR. JENSVOLD:

    Q   Okay.

    A   Probably when I learned to speak up and speak out and not worry about what anybody thought of me or anything like that. Said what was on my mind.

    Q   Okay. Had you ever told Mr. Coghill while you were in Phoenix living with him that he better not make you mad or you'll turn him in?

    A   No, I never said anything like that to him, ever.

    Q   You didn't say that to -- you didn't tell Deputy Schupbach that that's something you would have told him earlier?

    A   Not that I can recall, honestly. You know, I don't remember that.

    Q   But did you ever -- what, if anything, did you say to him about the child pornography files?

    MR. LAGATTUTA: Objection as to place and time, foundation.

    THE COURT: Counsel approach.

    (Bench conference.)

    THE COURT: You've got to be specific in time and place. I know it's hard.

    MR. JENSVOLD: Your Honor, he's given a statement before saying he made the statement. I don't

1   think he was ever exactly clear exactly when he did.

2   MR. LAGATTUTA: Your Honor, we're jumping all

3   over the place here. We're going from topic to topic.

4   THE COURT: Did he have a prior statement you

5   can use to refresh his recollection?

6   MR. JENSVOLD: I don't know if it's very good

7   with the time and date.

8   MR. LAGATTUTA: My problem is I can't

9   cross-examine if I don't know when it took place.

10   THE COURT: Well, I've sustained the objection

11   so far.

12   We'll take a recess.

13   (Open court.)

14   THE COURT: We're right at 3:00, so we'll take a

15   15-minute recess at this point.

16   Remember the admonition not to talk about the

17   case. You can leave your books. No one else is going to

18   come in between now and the time we ask you back.

19   (Whereupon, the jury was excused from the

20   courtroom.)

21   (A recess was taken.)

22   THE COURT: Okay. We're here defendant and

23   counsel, ready for the jurors.

24   Peter.

25   You were talking about a witness out of order?

PIMA COUNTY SUPERIOR COURT

```
 1          MR. JENSVOLD:  I think I'm going to ask
 2   Mr. Franks some specific questions about handwriting, and
 3   then I'll bring Mr. Kreitl on after that.
 4          THE COURT:  And then we'll just interrupt the
 5   direct on Mr. Franks, do Mr. Kreitl, and then bring
 6   Mr. Franks back?
 7          MR. JENSVOLD:  Right.
 8          THE COURT:  Okay.
 9              (Whereupon, the jury panel entered the
10              courtroom.)
11          THE COURT:  Thank you.  Please be seated.
12          We are here with the jurors, counsel, and the
13   defendant.
14          And Mr. Franks is on the stand.  We're
15   continuing with direct examination.
16          Mr. Jensvold.
17   BY MR. JENSVOLD:
18      Q   Okay.  Mr. Franks -- I'm sorry.
19          Mr. Franks, I want to go into a new area right
20   now, and then we'll come back later.
21          Did you do a handwriting sample after you called
22   the police and were interviewed by the sheriff's
23   department?
24      A   Yes.
25      Q   When did you do that and where?
```

PIMA COUNTY SUPERIOR COURT

```
1        A    They came up to Phoenix after I got in trouble
2    for that burglary thing out at the Pima County Jail, and
3    I had a visitor.  And I never got visitors, so I was
4    like:  Hmm.  So it was a handwriting guy, so I sat there
5    for two hours doing handwriting samples.
6        Q    Did you know what it was for?
7        A    Yeah.
8        Q    And were you writing your normal handwriting
9    when you made the sample?
10       A    Yeah.
11       Q    And, Mr. Franks, I want to show you what's been
12   marked as State's Exhibit 21.  Have you ever seen that
13   envelope before?
14       A    No.
15            MR. JENSVOLD:  Your Honor, I want to just go on
16   the record.  I showed this exhibit, the outside package
17   of it, to Mr. Kreitl, who is the DPS analyst.  He said he
18   identified it and he identified his handwriting on it.
19   So for chain of custody, I was going to have to
20   Mr. Franks open it to see.
21            THE COURT:  Subject's been identified and that
22   will be fine.  Actually, why don't you take the scissors
23   here and open it up, Mr. Jensvold.  Cut open the envelope
24   of 21.
25   ///
```

PIMA COUNTY SUPERIOR COURT

```
 1   BY MR. JENSVOLD:

 2       Q    So, Mr. Franks, could you take a look at this

 3   handwriting sample?  Do you recognize what's inside?

 4       A    That's me.  That's my handwriting.

 5       Q    It's several pages long?

 6       A    Yeah.  Yeah, I remember this.

 7       Q    Is that your handwriting?

 8       A    Yeah, going through this was horrible because it

 9   took forever.  But, yeah, I remember this.

10       Q    And do you remember the exact month in which

11   that happened up in Phoenix?

12       A    Could have been -- how about October 15th, 2003.

13       Q    Is that date on the document?

14       A    There you go.

15       Q    Thank you, Mr. Franks.

16            MR. LAGATTUTA:  What year was that?  I'm sorry,

17   your Honor.

18            THE WITNESS:  2003.

19            MR. LAGATTUTA:  2003.

20            THE WITNESS:  Yes.

21   BY MR. JENSVOLD:

22       Q    And you, at some point during your stay in

23   Tucson, labeled a CD; is that right?

24       A    Yes.

25       Q    Did you label a CD and did you call it "Dirty"?
```

PIMA COUNTY SUPERIOR COURT

1   A   Yes.

2   Q   How did that come about?

3   A   Because where all my files were being downloaded

4   to, he had some files that had some names that would be

5   probably considered child porn or something that was

6   describing it. So I was like: Dude, you've got all

7   these files that are mixing with my files. And he said:

8   Well, burn them onto a CD. So I said: All right. What

9   do you want me to label it? And he said: Label it

10   "Dirty."

11   Q   And you handed it to him?

12   A   Yeah, deleted all the crap off the computer.

13   Q   And do you remember like from the time that you

14   got down there how long after you got down there did that

15   happen, if you remember?

16   A   A few days. Maybe that weekend. I don't know.

17   Q   You don't really remember?

18   A   I don't remember the dates and times on this

19   particular thing.

20   Q   But it was in Tucson?

21   A   Yeah, it was in Tucson, definitely.

22   Q   And do you know if you labeled any other CDs

23   while you were down there?

24   A   Maybe CDs I burnt for myself.

25   Q   I mean, do you remember specifically which ones?

PIMA COUNTY SUPERIOR COURT

1   A   I didn't label anything for him after that or

2   before that.

3   Q   Except for that one?

4   A   Just that one.

5   MR. JENSVOLD: Your Honor, this is State's

6   Exhibit 16. I'm going to make the same kind of record.

7   Detective Gidney will testify about chain of custody

8   about this particular bag and the contents of it. I'm

9   going to open it in order to show Mr. Franks one of the

10   CDs.

11   THE COURT: Okay.

12   MR. JENSVOLD: Actually, your Honor, I don't

13   have gloves, so I'm going to ask you if you have some.

14   THE COURT: There you go.

15   MR. JENSVOLD: Thank you.

16   Actually, they're in a case that's got the cake

17   box that Mr. Lagattuta was talking about.

18   BY MR. JENSVOLD:

19   Q   Mr. Franks, I just want to show you, this is a

20   CD spindle that has a plastic cover on the outside.

21   There are CDs, I don't know how many, within it. The top

22   one, do you recognize that?

23   A   Yeah.

24   Q   What is it?

25   A   It says the word "Dirty."

PIMA COUNTY SUPERIOR COURT

```
1    Q    Is that your handwriting?

2    A    It look like my quick jotting down, yeah.

3    Q    Does that look like the one you described

4    earlier?

5    A    Uh-huh.

6    Q    Is that yes?

7    A    I believe so, yeah.

8    Q    And for the record, the -- this is State's

9    Exhibit --

10   A    Was there another one labeled "Dirty" or is

11   there another one labeled "Dirty"?

12   Q    I'm sorry, Mr. Franks, I can't answer your

13   questions.

14        THE COURT:  State's Exhibit 16?

15        MR. JENSVOLD:  This is State's Exhibit 16.  And

16   the CD on the top has a 3A sticker on it as well.  And

17   for the record, I did not remove the plastic case and did

18   not touch the CDs inside.

19        Your Honor, I'm going to make the same record

20   for State's Exhibit 20.  It's labeled E5.  It's another

21   bag titled, "Spindle with multiple CD-ROMS."

22   Detective Gidney will establish chain of custody for this

23   at a later time.

24        THE COURT:  We have new gloves here or at least

25   a different version.
```

PIMA COUNTY SUPERIOR COURT

```
 1          MR. JENSVOLD:  Okay.  There's a plastic cover on
 2     this one as well.  And there's a shorter stack than in
 3     State's Exhibit 16 but same type of thing.  It's a
 4     plastic spindle with a plastic cover on the outside.
 5     BY MR. JENSVOLD:
 6          Q    Now, Mr. Franks, I want to show you the top CD
 7     here.  It's the one that you can see the front of.  Do
 8     you see that?
 9          A    Yeah, it looks like my quick jotting down.
10          Q    What does that appear to say?
11          A    Star Trek 5.
12          Q    Do you remember writing this on this particular
13     CD?
14          A    Yeah.  I don't know when.  Probably up in
15     Phoenix.
16          Q    But you're not positive or are you positive?
17          A    I'm -- I'm not positive.
18          Q    But you say that's your handwriting?
19          A    That's my handwriting.
20          MR. JENSVOLD:  Your Honor, at this time I would
21     like to bring in Mr. Kreitl.
22          THE COURT:  Okay.  Counsel agreed that we're
23     going to have another person come in who is an
24     out-of-town witness, and interrupt direct at this point
25     in time to take that witness.  And then, Mr. Franks,
```

PIMA COUNTY SUPERIOR COURT

```
1    we'll bring you back to continue your direct examination
2    here after both parties have had their time to
3    interview -- or to take the testimony of this next
4    witness.  So --
5            MR. LAGATTUTA:  I'm sorry, I just -- can I just
6    have one moment with counsel while you're doing this?
7            THE COURT:  Sir, you're subject to recall.  You
8    can step back out.
9            THE WITNESS:  Sure.
10           THE COURT:  Mr. Jensvold, give us the name of
11   the next witness so we can -- Peter, would you get
12   Mr. Kreitl, please.
13               (Pause.)
14           THE COURT:  Sir, you can be come over here and
15   be sworn, and then come over here and take the stand.
16               (The witness was sworn.)
17
18               ALAN KREITL,
19   called as a witness herein, having been first duly sworn,
20   was examined and testified as follows:
21
22               DIRECT EXAMINATION
23   BY MR. JENSVOLD:
24       Q    Would you please introduce yourself to the jury?
25       A    My name is Alan Kreitl, K-r-e-i-t-l.
```

PIMA COUNTY SUPERIOR COURT

1   Q   And who do you work for?

2   THE COURT: Wait a minute, we can't have the

3 witness in the courtroom. So, sir, if you could step out

4 until --

5   MR. FRANKS: Sorry.

6   THE COURT: Thank you.

7   Okay. I'm sorry for the interruption.

8   Go ahead.

9 BY MR. JENSVOLD:

10   Q   And who do you work for, Mr. Kreitl?

11   A   I'm a forensic document examiner with the

12 Arizona Department of Public Safety in Phoenix.

13   Q   And how long have you been in that position?

14   A   I've been with DPS since 1993, and as a document

15 examiner since the beginning of 1998.

16   Q   What did you do with DPS before becoming a

17 document examiner?

18   A   I hired on with DPS right out of college, and my

19 first position there was as a drug analyst in the

20 controlled substances unit; and transferred to the

21 questioned document unit in January of 1998.

22   Q   Okay. What training and education do you have

23 to be able to do the handwriting analysis?

24   A   I have a bachelor of science in forensic science

25 from Michigan State University. The training specific

PIMA COUNTY SUPERIOR COURT

1   for questioned document is a two-year, kind of on-the-job
2   apprenticeship with the senior analyst at the lab, the
3   majority of time spent working cases with that
4   individual. Also, training includes two weeks with the
5   secret service back in Quantico, Georgia, and a one-week
6   stint with the FBI in Quantico, and various training from
7   time to time. I try to attend two conferences a year.
8   Q   Are there journals and stuff that you need to
9   keep as well?
10   A   Oh, yeah, the majority of the training is
11   reading textbooks, articles, and just getting practical
12   experience with your primary trainer.
13   Q   Prior to this case, about how many times do you
14   think you can estimate that you analyzed documents for
15   forensic purposes?
16   A   Wow. I believe in the course of the training,
17   thousands of documents. I probably traditionally do
18   about 15 to 20 cases a month. So prior to this case I
19   had looked at thousands of documents. A majority of our
20   casework is handwriting comparisons.
21   Q   And does that include paper as well as other
22   forms -- forms of materials that handwriting is on?
23   A   Yeah. The other types of examinations we do are
24   counterfeit documents, ink comparisons, altered
25   documents. But, yes, the majority of our casework is

PIMA COUNTY SUPERIOR COURT

1   handwriting documents typically on paper. In some cases
2   we'll get handwriting on bathroom walls or chalkboards.
3   In this case, the handwriting happened to be on CDs.
4   Q   Now, are there specific forms that police
5   officers use for handwriting samples of a known
6   individual?
7   A   Yes, there two types of known handwriting. You
8   can get a source of business writing, which is someone's
9   driver's license application or job application or
10   something like that. Other types of known writing are
11   exemplars. You sit an individual down and have them fill
12   out a specific form. We have a 20-page form that we will
13   give to law enforcement personnel if it's requested.
14   Just a very -- your name, writing the alphabet, different
15   forms. It's usually about 20 pages.
16   Q   Are there any other instructions that the person
17   is trained -- the person giving the sample to the
18   individual, are there, oh, questions that they're
19   supposed to ask them or instructions be given?
20   A   Yes. We include with a handwriting exemplar
21   form a one-page sheet of instructions what to do, what
22   not to do, kind of -- don't let the suspect look at the
23   document that you're comparing it to and things like
24   that.
25   Q   Now, when you're going to compare two

PIMA COUNTY SUPERIOR COURT

1 handwriting samples, what are the steps that you

2 typically go through?

3   A   First thing I do is look at the questioned item

4 and determine whether or not, if it's a photocopy, good

5 enough quality to examine. Is the writing a limited

6 amount? Is it unique? Things like that. So we go

7 through and look at the questioned writing and pinpoint

8 what features we feel are significant, and go to the

9 known body and look for those characteristics. And then

10 kind of do a side-by-side comparison, looking for

11 similarities and differences, and kind of associate with

12 what the significance of similarities and differences are

13 and rendering an opinion.

14   Q   Okay. Are there different levels of opinions

15 that you can render?

16   A   Yeah. Yes, we basically -- in handwriting

17 comparisons there's essentially a nine-step scale.

18 Basically, you have inconclusive. We will conclusively

19 identify someone as the writer of a body of writing or

20 conclusively eliminate them. And then we have what we

21 call "qualified opinions." Indications somebody wrote,

22 probably wrote, and then highly probably. And the

23 reasons for those qualifications to be numerous things.

24   Sometimes we have bad photocopy qualities which

25 limit your opinion. Limited amount of unknown writing or

PIMA COUNTY SUPERIOR COURT

1   even the nature of the writing can be -- very blocked

 2   printing, which is not identifiable, those are -- you can

 3   have a limited known of the writing which is common from

 4   time to time.

 5   Q   And you did some analysis in this particular

 6   case; is that correct?

 7   A   Yes, I did.

 8   Q   Okay. What specifically did you analyze?

 9   A   The evidence that was submitted in this case

10   were some CD-ROMS.

11   Q   Actually, Mr. Kreitl, just for court purposes, I

12   have a copy of your report here.

13   A   Okay.

14   Q   I want to hand you what's been marked as State's

15   Exhibit 9. Do you recognize that?

16   A   Yes, I do.

17   Q   What is it?

18   A   This is the copy the scientific examination

19   report I issued in this case.

20   Q   Okay. Now, you have, with you some other --

21   your -- do you have notes and stuff that you took as your

22   basis with you?

23   A   Yeah, I do.

24   Q   Now, what specifically did you analyze in this

25   case?

PIMA COUNTY SUPERIOR COURT

1   A   In this case, we were given a total of 162 CDs,

2   29 of which had writing on the fronts of them. And of

3   those 29 we were given a body of known writing from an

4   individual by the name of Jacob Franks, and I was asked

5   to compare the writing on the CDs to the known writing of

6   Mr. Franks.

7   Q   What were the evidence numbers on these

8   particular items?

9   A   The CDs were broken up into Items JE-2 and JE-3,

10 and then from there, there were sub items. So the ones

11 that had writing were like JE-2 F through JE-2 M and JE-3

12 A through U. And the known writing in this case was

13 JE-15.

14   Q   Now, this is State's Exhibit 21. It's already

15 been identified and opened. Could you please open that

16 and take a look at that exhibit and see if you recognize

17 it?

18   A   Yes. This is the known writing specimen that

19 was provided, item JE-15.

20   Q   And that's for Mr. Jacob Franks?

21   A   Yes.

22   Q   And what does that writing sample consist of?

23   A   This is the form that we -- you know, that we

24 will give law enforcement personnel to use if they don't

25 have their own. It's basically just a personal history

PIMA COUNTY SUPERIOR COURT

1   form: your name, birth place, Social Security number,

2   and then just different forms of the letters. We give

3   samples: write dates, numbers, and then there's, you

4   know, spaces provided for any type of writing. If you

5   have a questioned check, we'll give you check forms. If

6   you have like a bank robbery note, we'll give a piece of

7   paper and duplicate the bank robbery note. So it's just

8   a variety of different types of words and phrases that we

9   use, trying to get -- try to incorporate all sorts of

10   letter formations and cover the whole alphabet.

11   Q   Does that sample appear to be in the same

12   condition as it was when you analyzed it?

13   A   Yes, it does.

14   Q   And what did you -- what conclusions did you

15   draw from your comparison from the handwriting sample to

16   the CDs?

17   A   There was one item that was labeled JE-3 A,

18   which was a CD that had a hand-printed word "Dirty" on

19   it. Conclusion on that one, it was probable that was

20   written by Jacob Franks. And the reason for the

21   qualified opinion there, it was just a very limited

22   amount of questioned writing which did not lend itself to

23   be conclusively identified.

24   The other items in the case contained various

25   words. Most of them had the initials "KP" on them. The

PIMA COUNTY SUPERIOR COURT

317

1 differences noted between that and the known writing of

2 Jacob Franks, I feel there was no evidence suggesting he

3 wrote any of those.

4 Q Why is that?

5 A Just -- there are fundamental differences in the

6 letters and the way the -- even though the initial "KP"

7 is a very limited amount of writing, the letter

8 formations were consistently formed one way on the CDs

9 and consistently formed in a different manner on the

10 provided known writing.

11 Q Can you be more specific?

12 A Well, sure. In the P -- well, just the K --

13 Q I'm sorry, if it will help you can flip that

14 page over, if it will help to draw it out.

15 A Actually, the case words on the CDs were written

16 with two strokes: a downward stroke on the K. If you

17 want I can try to demonstrate. My handwriting is pretty

18 bad, so -- on the CDs, the Ks were formed like this

19 (indicating), and the Ps were formed with a downward

20 stroke and then kind of like this (indicating).

21 And the known writing, the Ks were actually a

22 three-stroke, and the known writing it was formed like

23 that (indicating). Even though you're dealing with two

24 characters, both of them were formed consistently

25 different. So that led me to believe that those were not

PIMA COUNTY SUPERIOR COURT

1   written by Mr. Franks. There were other -- other CDs had

2   other writing on them. Again, those contained letter

3   formations that were also different.

4   Q   Did you draw any conclusions regarding whether

5   the CDs marked "KP" were written by the same person?

6   A   An issue -- that's not reflected in my report,

7   but one of the things we do when evaluating the

8   questioned writing is to see how many writers we're

9   dealing with. All the writing on "KP" all seemed

10   consistent, so just kind of went under the premise

11   dealing with only one writer on that. So if you're

12   asking if I felt they were all written by one writer,

13   yes.

14   Q   But where would you qualify that in your scale

15   of opinions?

16   A   Probable. If I'm going to go through and have

17   to nitpick every KP on every CD, it's certainly capable

18   two writers can write KP the same way. But given this

19   evidence, they were all consistent so I didn't feel there

20   were multiple writers on the CDs that involved KP and

21   some other writing. I believe some of the other CDs had

22   the word "Voyager" written on them.

23   Q   And any of them -- which ones had "Voyager"

24   written on them, do you know?

25   A   I have copies of all of them, the item numbers.

PIMA COUNTY SUPERIOR COURT

```
 1    One of the items labeled 2 H had the word "Voyager";
 2    2 J -- actually, I don't know what specific item numbers
 3    there were, but those were some CDs that were also
 4    submitted.
 5         Q    Do those, based on your notes -- I'm sorry, just
 6    describe for the jury what you're looking at, if you
 7    could, Mr. Kreitl.
 8         A    Our protocol states any item that we're going to
 9    examine in our unit, we photocopy or photograph or scan
10    in.  In this case I photocopied everything, and we keep
11    two copies of everything in our notes.  Our protocol is
12    we keep photocopies of every piece of evidence we
13    examine.  We keep that just without any notations on it.
14         Then I actually have in my notes some pages of
15    some notations just pinpointing out the differences I
16    noted and then on one of the items in red just the
17    similarities.  A lot of these were reflecting the KP.
18    Just make notations of what the differences are between
19    the writing on the questioned and the writing on the
20    known.
21         Q    And, I'm sorry, I just want to be specific.  The
22    word "Voyager" appears on Items No. 2 H and 2 J?
23         A    Yeah, that's what they're labeled.  They are
24    JE-2 would be J and K and then L and M have the word
25    "Voyager" written on them.
```

PIMA COUNTY SUPERIOR COURT

1   Q   Okay. So --

2   A   And in that case, the E formation was formed in

3   a completely different way than the E's in the provided

4   writing specimen.

5   Q   I just want to make sure I have my items right.

6   2 H, 2 J, K, L, and M had Voyager on it?

7   A   Actually, 2 G and 2 F, 2 H and I, J and K and L

8   and M only were handwritten words on those were the word

9   "Voyager," so --

10   Q   And --

11   A   So 2 G through 2 M all have the word "Voyager"

12 written on them.

13   Q   And do you have any opinion about whether that

14 was written by the same person?

15   A   Written by the same person?

16   Q   The words -- all of those that had the word

17 "Voyager," were any of those different from --

18   A   No. No. Those all look like they were written

19 by one writer.

20   Q   So the only item number that you identified as

21 probably written by Mr. Franks was JE-3 A?

22   A   Yes, that's correct.

23   Q   And, can you describe --

24   THE COURT: I'm sorry, I missed the -- the only

25 item number by Mr. Franks number was what?

PIMA COUNTY SUPERIOR COURT

```
1          MR. JENSVOLD:  JE-3 A.
2          THE COURT:  Thank you.
3  BY MR. JENSVOLD:
4      Q   And can you describe what specifically within
5  the word "Dirty" looks similar to the writing sample?
6      A   Sure.  Again, we're dealing with five
7  handwritten characters here.  But there were features
8  within those five letters in the known writing of the way
9  the D was formed.  Again, it's kind of -- the Ds are
10 formed where it comes down here, and then it wraps around
11 in this -- this staff is actually incorporated in the
12 letter of the D.
13         The T in "Dirty" comes here, and there's a drag
14 stroke and goes back up.  So essentially it's one stroke.
15         And then the R, it kind of tails off.
16         Another thing pretty significant, if you note
17 the baseline of the letters, you kind of form an arc.
18 And all of those features were consistent among the
19 questioned writing and in the known writing of
20 Mr. Franks.
21     Q   Was that arc present in the word "Voyager" in
22 any of those you talked about earlier?
23     A   That specific feature, no.
24         MR. JENSVOLD:  Your Honor, at this time the
25 State would move for the admission of State's Exhibit 9
```

PIMA COUNTY SUPERIOR COURT

```
 1   and 21.
 2              THE COURT:  Any objection?
 3              State's 9 is -- 9 is the -- just -- you said 9
 4   and 21.  9 is --
 5              MR. JENSVOLD:  9 is Mr. Kreitl's report.
 6              THE COURT:  And 21 is?
 7              MR. JENSVOLD:  Is Mr. Frank's writing exemplar.
 8              THE COURT:  Any objection to those two?
 9              MR. LAGATTUTA:  No objection, your Honor.
10              THE COURT:  Okay.  We'll admit 9 and 21.
11   BY MR. JENSVOLD:
12        Q    I'm sorry, just one last question.
13              When did you -- when did you perform your
14   analysis?
15        A    The report was issued on December 11th of 2003.
16   I began my examination a few days prior to that.
17        Q    And were you ever given a handwriting sample
18   Mr. James Coghill to analyze?
19        A    No, I was not.
20              MR. JENSVOLD:  That's all I have.  Thank you.
21              THE COURT:  Cross.
22
23                      CROSS EXAMINATION
24   BY MR. LAGATTUTA:
25        Q    Is it Officer Kreitl or --
```

PIMA COUNTY SUPERIOR COURT

1   A   Just Alan.

2   Q   Well, then, Mr. Kreitl, you've been involved in

3   the examination of handwriting comparison for a total of

4   how many years?

5   A   A little over eight.

6   Q   And approximately how many times now you've

7   testified in court?

8   A   As a document examiner, probably around 25.

9   Q   Okay.

10   A   As a drug analyst, probably 50 to 60.

11   Q   As a document analyst, have you testified mostly

12 in the capacity of working for the government?

13   A   Yes. Actually, I worked at DPS my whole career.

14   Q   Okay. You would agree with me sometimes that,

15 you know, in certain cases there's a dispute among

16 document examiners; is that correct?

17   A   There has been, unfortunately.

18   Q   Yeah. And so my question is, you know, how good

19 are you? Do you have an accuracy rating yourself?

20   A   We don't have an accuracy rating. I would like

21 to think that based on all the checks and balances at the

22 laboratory, meaning we go through an extensive training

23 program, all of our cases getting reviewed by another

24 document examiner, I'd like to say my results are

25 accurate.

PIMA COUNTY SUPERIOR COURT

1   Q   Probably?

2   A   I don't know a --

3   Q   Are they probably accurate or highly accurate?

4   A   I would say highly accurate. We have to go

5 through proficiency testing on an annual basis, and I've

6 never erred on a proficiency examination.

7   Q   Okay. How was it that you received this

8 assignment to perform --

9   A   Well, we get cases from all law enforcement

10 throughout the State of Arizona. And federal agencies.

11 In this case, this was a Pima County Sheriff's office

12 case.

13   Q   Did it come from Detective Englander?

14   A   Yes, it did.

15   Q   And would he be the one that you reported your

16 results back to?

17   A   Yes.

18   Q   And if you would have had, say, the need for

19 additional handwriting samples or additional information,

20 he would be the one that you would have gone to?

21   A   Yes. If I felt that was needed, yes.

22   Q   Okay. But when you were given this assignment,

23 were you given a particular directive as to what to

24 accomplish?

25   A   Only to compare the questioned writing on the

PIMA COUNTY SUPERIOR COURT

```
 1    CDs and the known writing of Mr. Franks.
 2         Q    Okay.  And what else did Detective Englander
 3    pass along to you by way of examination prior to your --
 4    prior to your exam?
 5         A    What do you mean "exam"?  What do you mean -- I
 6    don't specifically remember talking to him.  Actually, I
 7    just noticed in going through my case file today there
 8    was a little kind of attachment to the request form that
 9    came in this case.
10         Q    And what does the attachment say?
11         A    Well, it's a paragraph.  Did you want me to read
12    the whole thing.
13         Q    How about if you let me look at it?
14         A    Sure.
15              MR. LAGATTUTA:  That all right?
16              THE COURT:  Sure.
17    BY MR. LAGATTUTA:
18         Q    Okay.
19         A    This is the formal request.  And in this case it
20    says:  Please compare known writing with the questioned
21    items in this case.
22         Q    Okay.  Well, the -- so you did have a little bit
23    of information about what the case was about before you
24    started your analysis; right?
25         A    Yes.  In this case I did.
```

PIMA COUNTY SUPERIOR COURT

1   Q   Well, in this case you were given several discs.

2   And the one I want to focus on is the one that's been

3   referred to as item JE-3 A, the "Dirty" disc; right?

4   A   Yes.

5   Q   So you get a little package and a little

6   assignment, and it's got a handwriting sample of Jacob

7   Franks in it; right?

8   A   Yes.

9   Q   And it's got the "Dirty" disc in it; right?   The

10 disc labeled "Dirty"?

11   A   Yes.

12   Q   And there's information that you also received

13 that tells you that Jacob Franks has admitted to writing

14 the word "Dirty" on that disc?

15   A   Yeah, I noticed that today when I was going

16 through the file.

17   Q   Okay. So you take -- you take the sample, you

18 take his handwriting sample, you take the information

19 that he's already admitted it -- just so you know, he

20 admitted it in court just a few minutes ago that he had

21 written it.

22   A   Okay.

23   Q   And he admitted it previously, and you perform

24 your examination; right?

25   A   Yes.

PIMA COUNTY SUPERIOR COURT

1 very small limiting factor such as you have a photocopy

2 versus the original. Probable, in my opinion, is more

3 kind of a percentage of confidence.

4   Q   Well, in this case, you have a disc that's not a

5 photocopy. It's actually something written on something?

6   A   Uh-huh.

7   Q   You have the actual disc itself?

8   A   Yes.

9   Q   You have the actual handwritten sample?

10   A   Uh-huh.

11   Q   And the best that you can come up with is

12 probable?

13   A   Yes.

14   Q   Okay.

15   A   And that's because of the limited amount of

16 writing.

17   If you were to give me a day or so, you know, I

18 could probably duplicate that writing.

19   Q   When you say "limited amount of writing," do you

20 mean the limited amount of writing in the questioned

21 sample --

22   A   No.

23   Q   Let me finish. -- or the limited amount of

24 writing on the disc?

25   A   The limited amount of writing on the disc.

PIMA COUNTY SUPERIOR COURT

         Q   Well, you were also shown -- well, okay, if
there was limited writing on the disc, which you
apparently list in your report, why didn't you go back to
Detective Englander and say: You know, it's only
probable. If you can get me a little bit more writing,
maybe I can do a little better?
         A   How was he going to get me more questioned
writing? The questioned item in this case was a CD
labeled "Dirty."
         Q   Right.
         A   So if he could get me volumes and volumes of
known writing, it's not going to change my opinion. The
limitation in this handwriting comparison was the five
letters on the disc.
         Q   But you're forgetting something. What Detective
Englander submitted to you was a writing that he had
already -- the writer of it already admitted to him he
had written it. So he could have gathered more written
samples that had been admitted to by Mr. Franks and
submitted them to you; right?
         MR. JENSVOLD: Objection; speculation.
         THE COURT: Sustained.
BY MR. LAGATTUTA:
         Q   The fact of the matter is once you came to the
conclusion it was probable, you didn't request any more

PIMA COUNTY SUPERIOR COURT

```
 1    follow-up work; right?  Or any more follow-up information
 2    from Detective Englander; is that correct?
 3         A    No, I did not.
 4         Q    Okay.  When you said that there is no evidence
 5    to suggest that items JE-3 B through JE-3 U were written
 6    by Jacob Franks -- now, just so everybody knows, these
 7    are the items JE-3 B through JE-3 U, these are the items
 8    marked "KP"; is that correct?
 9         A    Yes.
10         Q    Okay.  The writing -- the initials "KP" is a
11    smaller amount, a more limited amount of writing than the
12    word "Dirty"?
13         A    Yes.
14         Q    But when you say there is no evidence to
15    suggest, is that no, period?  It's possible?  What are
16    the levels of no that go along with this?
17         A    Well, it's certainly not a conclusive
18    elimination.
19         Q    It's not a conclusive elimination?
20         A    I'm just saying based on the evidence we have, I
21    suppose you could rephrase it and say it's probably not
22    written by him.  I typically don't like to use that
23    phrase.  It seems a little cheesy.
24         Q    But could you use it in this case?
25         A    I could.  Yes.
```

PIMA COUNTY SUPERIOR COURT

1   Q   You feel confident that there was enough of the
2   questioned writing to enable you to make this finding
3   that there's probably no evidence to suggest --
4   A   The reason for my opinion on that is that even
5   given the limited amount, there were two pretty
6   significant differences in handwriting. In order to
7   identify somebody, you need to have a lot of similarities
8   and an absence of differences. In order to determine two
9   bodies of writing were written by two individuals, you
10   basically only need one significant difference. And in
11   this case, since there are two differences even with the
12   two characters of KP, in this case it was pretty obvious
13   to me that it wasn't written by him.
14   Q   Okay. All right. When I look at your
15   scientific examination report --
16   A   Uh-huh.
17   Q   You have that in front of you.
18   -- it lists your agency, lists the file number,
19   it lists the officer, Officer Englander, who I'm assuming
20   is the one that you would have communicated with on this
21   case; right?
22   A   Yes.
23   Q   It lists the day, December -- December 11th,
24   2003, then it lists names. And the first name listed is
25   James Coghill?

PIMA COUNTY SUPERIOR COURT

```
 1       A    Actually, it's misspelled.  It's Goghill, but,
 2    yes.
 3       Q    And then Jacob Franks is listed underneath him;
 4    right?
 5       A    Yes.
 6       Q    And in the information package that you
 7    received, that you have in your file there, you had
 8    information that the two of these individuals were
 9    roommates; right?
10       A    I believe that's what it stated.  Yes.
11       Q    Okay.  And you were given the writing sample
12    from Jacob Franks and asked to make the comparison on the
13    discs labeled "KP" against his handwriting; correct?
14       A    Yes.
15       Q    Okay.  Were you ever at any point given a
16    handwritten sample of Mr. Coghill to compare it against
17    those discs labeled "KP" to make any kind of
18    determination as to whether it was even possible that he
19    had been the writer on those discs?
20            MR. JENSVOLD:  Objection; asked and answered.
21            THE COURT:  Overruled.
22            THE WITNESS:  No, I was never provided any known
23    writing of Mr. Coghill.
24    BY MR. LAGATTUTA:
25       Q    Did that strike you as odd given both of their
```

PIMA COUNTY SUPERIOR COURT

```
 1    names are on the report sheet?

 2            MR. JENSVOLD:  Objection; speculation.

 3            THE COURT:  Overruled.

 4            THE WITNESS:  Actually, that's not really that

 5    uncommon.  Sometimes there will be multiple suspects

 6    listed on a report.  What their involvement is in the

 7    case I have no -- I'm not privy too.

 8    BY MR. LAGATTUTA:

 9        Q    Right.

10        A    So I don't know.

11        Q    It would have been up to Detective Englander to

12    let you know any more information about who was involved

13    and how in the case?

14        A    Yes.  We only do the examinations requested by

15    law enforcement.  I don't really feel it's my duty to pry

16    and give the officers, you know, suggestions on how to

17    run their investigation.

18        Q    Okay.  Well, without prying, then, you sent this

19    report back to Detective Englander on approximately what

20    date?

21        A    Well, the report was typed on the 11th, takes a

22    couple days to get reviewed, probably got to him

23    somewhere within a couple of weeks or so, somewhere in

24    the month of December of 2003.

25            MR. LAGATTUTA:  Okay.  That's all the questions
```

PIMA COUNTY SUPERIOR COURT

```
 1    I have.
 2              THE COURT:  Redirect?
 3              MR. JENSVOLD:  Thank you, your Honor.
 4
 5                   REDIRECT EXAMINATION
 6    BY MR. JENSVOLD:
 7         Q    In that paragraph that you were given along with
 8    the analysis, was there anything in that paragraph
 9    telling you what your analysis should reflect?
10         A    No.
11         Q    Have you ever seen that in an officer's
12    paragraph such as this, along with a handwriting sample?
13         A    No.
14         Q    What would you have done if you saw it?
15         A    If I were to see some officer saying this is
16    what my results should be?  Since I've never encountered
17    that, I think that would be a little odd.  My thought is
18    if he already knows what it is, then why are you sending
19    it to me?
20         Q    And someone else checked your conclusions in
21    this case?
22         A    Yes.  All of our cases are technically reviewed.
23         Q    Somebody else with DPS is a handwriting analyst?
24         A    Yes.
25         Q    In your opinion that it's the same writer that
```

PIMA COUNTY SUPERIOR COURT

```
 1   wrote "KP" and then the "Voyager," does the fact that the
 2   number of times it's repeated add to your confidence?
 3       A   Yes.
 4       Q   If it were just one time the KP appeared --
 5   maybe two, just two times, would that lower your
 6   confidence?
 7       A   I don't know if it would lower my confidence.
 8   In assessing the questioned writing elements, it was all
 9   consistent.  They were all formed the same way.  I can't
10   tell you for sure they were all written by one writer,
11   but I didn't see any differences to lead me down that
12   path.
13       Q   If you know, are there problems associated with
14   getting a known handwriting sample from someone who's
15   already been suspect of a particular offense?
16           MR. LAGATTUTA:  Objection; foundation, calls for
17   speculation.
18           THE COURT:  Sustained.
19   BY MR. JENSVOLD:
20       Q   Are there ways for individuals to fake
21   handwriting samples if they've been asked to give one?
22       A   Yes.  In some instances we will get request
23   specimens where the writing does not appear to be
24   naturally executed or, I guess you could say, disguised.
25   Lots of times people will write very slowly or with very
```

PIMA COUNTY SUPERIOR COURT

```
1    heavy pressure or write very small or sometimes use their
2    offhand.  It's usually pretty obvious.  In my experience
3    it's very unusual that someone is ambidextrous.
4        Q   In your opinion, State's Exhibit 21, Mr. Franks'
5    handwriting, does that exhibit any of those things you
6    talked about?
7        A   No, it appeared to be naturally executed.
8            MR. JENSVOLD:  That's all I have.  Thank you.
9            THE COURT:  Well, I'm going to ask one question.
10   What's "forensic" mean?
11           THE WITNESS:  Forensic?  Well, I guess the
12   general term is forensic is kind of a science and how it
13   applies to the law.
14           THE COURT:  Thank you.  Jurors have any
15   questions?
16           Counsel.
17           (Bench conference.)
18           THE COURT:  I'll mark this as 2.
19           MR. JENSVOLD:  He's already answered that, and I
20   don't think he can't answer either one.
21           THE COURT:  Let me take a look at them, too.
22           MR. LAGATTUTA:  That's really not a question. I
23   don't know what that is.
24           THE COURT:  Let me look at them.
25           And No. 2, there are three questions.  The one
```

PIMA COUNTY SUPERIOR COURT

```
 1    is why the witness sample taken from Coghill -- that's
 2    something for somebody else to address, and so it's not a
 3    question for him.  Both of you agree I shouldn't ask that
 4    question, so I'm not going to ask it.  I think that's
 5    right.
 6            MR. LAGATTUTA:  Well, I think you can ask it.
 7    He's going to tell you that it wasn't his job.
 8            THE COURT:  You don't have any objection?
 9            MR. JENSVOLD:  I object to it.  It calls for
10    speculation and foundation.  He doesn't have the
11    foundation.
12            THE COURT:  Well, I'll ask him if he knows.
13            Are there any known samples of Mr. Coghill?
14            MR. JENSVOLD:  He's already answered that.
15            MR. LAGATTUTA:  Well, not exactly.  He answered
16    that he was submitted something.  Maybe there's somebody
17    else down the line that did some comparison, but you
18    might not --
19            THE COURT:  I'll rephrase a couple of these
20    questions and ask whether or not.
21            This other one is how origin -- two different, I
22    think it is just a matter of -- of what he actually
23    compared.  And I think it would be useful for him to
24    clarify what KP he compared.
25            MR. JENSVOLD:  I think that may be asking a
```

PIMA COUNTY SUPERIOR COURT

```
 1   foundation question as to -- obviously, we haven't given
 2   them any of the CDs.
 3              THE COURT:  But I think it's fair for him to say
 4   it's the KPs that he compared.  That's what I think we're
 5   trying to get.
 6                   (Open court.)
 7              THE COURT:  Sir, a couple of questions here.
 8              If you know, do you have any knowledge as to why
 9   there were no samples taken from the defendant,
10   Mr. Coghill?
11              THE WITNESS:  I have no idea.
12              THE COURT:  And did you evaluate any samples
13   that were identified as coming from Mr. Coghill with any
14   of the unknown samples?
15              THE WITNESS:  No.  I was never provided of any
16   known writing of Mr. Coghill.
17              THE COURT:  You indicated that you did look --
18   look at a couple of different -- you looked at KP.   And
19   I'd just like to know what you compared or what you
20   looked at as far as the KP.  I think there's also a D-i-r
21   slash sample, but I'm not sure, so -- but as to the KPs,
22   what did you actually compare?
23              THE WITNESS:  On several of the discs, -- 13 of
24   the CDs that were examined simply contained the initials
25   KP.  And much like I drew up on the board, the top two
```

PIMA COUNTY SUPERIOR COURT

```
 1   KPs is how they were formed on the questioned --
 2            THE COURT:  I think you answered -- so the KP
 3   you compared were on CDs submitted to you?
 4            THE WITNESS:  Yes, yes.
 5            THE COURT:  Okay.  Now, was there a D-i-r or
 6   something else you compared?
 7            THE WITNESS:  You mean the handwritten -- oh,
 8   yeah, one of the CDs had the word "Dirty," D-i-r-t-y, on
 9   it.  And that was the only CD that I could associate with
10   Mr. Franks.
11            THE COURT:  There was something else that was
12   mentioned and it was Voyager.  Did you looking at
13   something identified as Voyager and having that --
14            THE WITNESS:  Yes.  There were some CDs with the
15   word "Voyager" written on them.
16            THE COURT:  And how many CDs had the word
17   "Voyager" on them?
18            THE WITNESS:  Eight CDs simply had the word
19   "Voyager" written on them.
20            THE COURT:  Follow-up, counsel?
21   First, Mr. Jensvold.
22            MR. JENSVOLD:  No, your Honor.
23            THE COURT:  Mr. Lagattuta.
24            MR. LAGATTUTA:  No, your Honor.  Thank you.
25            THE COURT:  With that, any other juror
```

PIMA COUNTY SUPERIOR COURT

```
1    questions?  I'm going to excuse Mr. Kreitl.  Did you have

2    a question?  No?  Okay.  Hand up?

3            Sir, thank you for your time and your testimony.

4    Why don't you hand me those exhibits.  I'll give them

5    back to the clerk, and you're excused.

6            We're going to bring back -- Peter, if would you

7    bring back Mr. Franks, please.

8            (Pause.)

9            THE COURT:  Okay.  We're back here with

10   Mr. Franks, and we're going to continue now the direct

11   examination of Mr. Franks.

12           Mr. Jensvold.

13

14               DIRECT EXAMINATION (Resumed)

15   BY MR. JENSVOLD:

16       Q    Mr. Franks, I want to go back then, again, to

17   your issue of when and where you would have seen some of

18   these files --

19           MR. LAGATTUTA:  Objection, your Honor, as to --

20           MR. JENSVOLD:  -- with child pornography.

21           THE COURT:  Let's have a question and have him

22   answer.  So go ahead and ask your question, Mr. Jensvold.

23   BY MR. JENSVOLD:

24       Q    I was just setting -- since we're back on the

25   record.
```

```
 1              Mr. Franks, I want to show you what's been
 2     marked as State's Exhibit 2.  Can you look through that
 3     and see if that appears to be something you recognize?
 4          A     Looks like a transcript of the initial interview
 5     with Detective Englander.
 6          Q     Okay.  There are some other detectives listed
 7     there?
 8          A     Moretz, I can't pronounce some of these, Knuth,
 9     and that's about it.
10          Q     And look through there.  Do the answers appear
11     to be your answers?
12          A     Yes.
13          Q     If you could do me a favor and turn to page 7.
14     And if you could start -- yeah, just read through pages 7
15     to 9 to yourself, please, and let me know when you've
16     glanced through it.  You don't have to read every word.
17          A     (Witness complied.)  Okay.
18          Q     And if you could turn back to page 5 and just
19     read the bottom answer there to yourself also.
20          A     (Witness complied.)
21          Q     Okay.  And after reading that, does that help to
22     refresh your memory as to when you might have seen the
23     child pornography files?
24          A     As far as the initial time I've ever seen him
25     looking at anything like that, this -- this whole
```

PIMA COUNTY SUPERIOR COURT

```
 1   conversation right here, the dialogue was sometime
 2   afterwards.  Do you know what I mean?
 3        Q    Can you be more specific?
 4        A    Like I would say a year or two after.  The
 5   dialogue right here at the very bottom of this page.
 6        Q    Are you referring to page 5?
 7        A    Yeah.  The dialogue right there was probably
 8   from like 2003.
 9        Q    Okay.  So does that help refresh your memory
10   when you first saw the child pornography files?
11        A    The actual -- I saw a disc.  I didn't actually
12   see the file.  I put --
13        Q    I'm sorry.  I keep saying "files."  You saw
14   images displayed on a computer screen?
15        A    Like, by accident.  Because probably the same
16   time I said 2001.
17        Q    And does this -- after reading all that, does
18   that help you to refresh your recollection as to when and
19   where you might have said something to Mr. Coghill about
20   those files?
21        A    Oh, I'd probably say sometime in Phoenix, and
22   maybe 2003 -- 2002/2003.  End of 2002, beginning of '03.
23   I'm not sure the exact date because I don't write a
24   journal or have a diary.  Do you know what I mean?  So I
25   don't really know.
```

PIMA COUNTY SUPERIOR COURT

```
 1        Q    Okay.  After reading this, did it help to
 2   refresh your memory what you said to Mr. Coghill?
 3        A    Yeah, that sounds right.
 4        Q    What did you say?
 5        A    I said:  If you weren't my friend, I would turn
 6   you in.
 7             But I don't remember when I said that or if I
 8   was drinking when I said it or whatever.  I have no idea.
 9        Q    What -- did you also say something to him about
10   what you thought about the child pornography?
11        A    That I didn't like it.
12        Q    Is there a specific word that you used in your
13   interview?
14             MR. LAGATTUTA:  Your Honor, I'm going --
15             THE WITNESS:  Disgusting.
16             MR. LAGATTUTA:  Improper use of the document to
17   refresh his memory.
18             THE COURT:  Overruled.
19   BY MR. JENSVOLD:
20        Q    Look at that bottom part of page 5 again, if you
21   could, Mr. Franks.
22        A    Uh-huh.  Yeah, I see that.
23        Q    Does that refresh your memory as to how you
24   described what you thought about child pornography?
25        A    Yes.
```

PIMA COUNTY SUPERIOR COURT

```
1      Q    What was that?

2      A    That is disgusting, I told him.

3      Q    Did you ever watch any pornography, period,

4    whether adult or child pornography, by -- in the presence

5    of Mr. Coghill?

6           MR. LAGATTUTA:  Objection; compound question.

7           THE COURT:  Sustained.  You can re-ask it.

8    BY MR. JENSVOLD:

9      Q    Okay.  Mr. Franks, when you were watching adult

10   pornography in the RV -- we'll talk about Tucson.  While

11   you were in Tucson, while you were watching adult

12   pornography, did you do that while Mr. Franks was in the

13   same vicinity?

14     A    I'm Mr. Franks.

15     Q    You're Mr. Franks.  Sorry.  Mr. Coghill was in

16   the same vicinity?

17     A    No, he was in the back in his little -- the

18   motor home was split off.  There was a curtain.  He had a

19   bedroom and the bed back there.  He had the curtain

20   closed.  He would be back there doing whatever he was

21   doing, and I would be up there doing whatever I was

22   doing.  There was a curtain, so I don't know he was ever

23   in the room unless I was like:  Hey, look at this really

24   quick.  But --

25     Q    Was it your tendency to watch pornography --
```

PIMA COUNTY SUPERIOR COURT

```
 1    adult pornography by yourself?
 2        A    More, yeah, absolutely, because I don't want to
 3    sit there and watch it with some dude.  That's just me.
 4        Q    And did you ever ask Mr. Coghill why he watched
 5    child pornography?
 6             MR. LAGATTUTA:  Objection; asked and answered.
 7             THE COURT:  Overruled.
 8             THE WITNESS:  Yes.
 9    BY MR. JENSVOLD:
10        Q    And what did he say?
11        A    What did he say?  Go ahead and repeat the
12    question one more time.
13        Q    About why he watches child pornography?
14        A    Why he watches, yes, yes, yes.
15        Q    What did he say?
16             MR. LAGATTUTA:  Objection, foundation as to
17    place and time.
18             THE COURT:  Sustained.
19    BY MR. JENSVOLD:
20        Q    Do you remember about when and where you might
21    have asked him that question?
22        A    Phoenix, more than likely.
23        Q    Do you remember which time period?
24        A    2002 sometime, maybe 2003.
25        Q    Do you remember what he said?
```

PIMA COUNTY SUPERIOR COURT

```
 1        A    Yes.

 2        Q    What was that?

 3        A    That he was molested as a child and stuff like

 4   that.  Aroused him, basically, in a nutshell.  It wasn't

 5   verbatim or whatever, but, you know, that was the gist of

 6   it.

 7        Q    Now, were you able to recognize some of the file

 8   names that were associated with child pornography?

 9             MR. LAGATTUTA:  Objection; foundation.  Place,

10   .time.

11             THE COURT:  Rephrase the question, please.

12   BY MR. JENSVOLD:

13        Q    Okay.  Mr. Franks, if you remember, was there

14   ever a time when you were on the computer in

15   Mr. Coghill's RV that you clicked on files and that

16   turned out to be child pornography?

17        A    I clicked on folders, yeah, and I seen it there

18   and just ignored it.  Pretended like it wasn't there

19   because it wasn't my computer.  To be sitting there,

20   messing with his files, do you know what I mean?

21        Q    Do you know when and where you would have done

22   that?

23        A    Random periods between 2001 and 2003.  I don't

24   know.  That's the best answer I can give you.

25        Q    Do you remember telling Detective Moretz that
```

PIMA COUNTY SUPERIOR COURT

1 you remember clicking on particular files that had

2 particular file names?

3   A   In the interview, yes.

4   Q   Okay. Do you remember what those file names

5 were?

6   A   No.

7   Q   Do you remember anything about them?

8   A   No.

9   MR. JENSVOLD: I apologize. I had the wrong

10 page number written down here.

11 BY MR. JENSVOLD:

12   Q   Mr. Franks, did you ever tell anyone else after

13 you found out that Mr. Coghill had child pornography?

14 Did you ever tell anyone else about it?

15   A   I believe my little brother and my dad or

16 something.

17   Q   Do you remember when you might have done that?

18   A   No. I don't know when.

19   Q   Do you know if it was before you came to Tucson?

20   A   Yeah. Yeah.

21   Q   And why would you have told them about it?

22   A   Just talking shit. Talking shit about him or

23 something. I don't know.

24   Q   You don't remember specifically?

25   A   No. Sorry.

PIMA COUNTY SUPERIOR COURT

```
 1        Q    Do you remember telling a girlfriend that you
 2   had at that time about it?
 3        A    No, I don't think so.  Maybe.
 4        Q    Did you have a girlfriend named Shannon Hudson?
 5        A    No, she wasn't my girlfriend; she was a friend.
 6        Q    Do you ever remember telling her about?
 7        A    Oh, I tell Shannon everything.  Okay, so, yeah.
 8        Q    Okay.  Mr. Franks, have you ever personally
 9   downloaded child pornography?
10        A    No, sir, I have not.
11             MR. JENSVOLD:  That's all I have.  Thank you.
12             THE COURT:  Cross.
13             MR. LAGATTUTA:  Thank you.
14
15                    CROSS EXAMINATION
16   BY MR. LAGATTUTA:
17        Q    Mr. Franks, do you mind if I call you Jacob?
18        A    Certainly.
19        Q    Now, we met once before, haven't we?
20        A    Correct.
21        Q    And the last time I saw you, you were in prison;
22   right?
23        A    Correct.
24        Q    And that was in December, last year; right?
25        A    Yes.
```

PIMA COUNTY SUPERIOR COURT

1   Q   When did you get out?

2   A   January.

3   Q   Mr. Jensvold asked you when he first started how

4   many felony convictions you had. I'm going to ask you

5   the same thing because I'm a little unclear about your

6   response. You have three of them, don't you, or at

7   least -- three or at least four, maybe?

8   A   Three, I believe. Yeah, it is three.

9   Q   Okay. And what -- and when did you get the

10 first one?

11   MR. JENSVOLD: Objection; asked and answered.

12   THE COURT: Overruled.

13 BY MR. LAGATTUTA:

14   Q   You can answer that?

15   A   Let's see, 1999.

16   Q   And that was for what? Burglary?

17   A   Theft of a vehicle.

18   Q   Theft of a vehicle?

19   A   Yes.

20   Q   And in 1999, then you were placed on probation;

21 right?

22   A   Yes.

23   Q   For how long?

24   A   Three years.

25   Q   Okay. And how well did you do on that?

PIMA COUNTY SUPERIOR COURT

1   A   Not well.

2   MR. JENSVOLD: Objection; relevance.

3   THE COURT: Sustained.

4   BY MR. LAGATTUTA:

5   Q   You violated the probation with your second

6   felony; is that correct?

7   A   No.

8   Q   Well, was your probation revoked?

9   MR. JENSVOLD: Objection; relevance.

10   THE COURT: Sustained.

11   MR. LAGATTUTA: Your Honor, may I approach the

12   bench?

13   THE COURT: Sure.

14   (Bench conference.)

15   MR. LAGATTUTA: I've got two big problems. One,

16   he's been asked about his felony background by the State,

17   and he's given very disjointed answers, okay. My notes

18   say that he admits to having been to prison even

19   technically twice. I need to clear this up. In the past

20   I requested from the State get me full documented

21   printouts of his prison record so we could be accurate

22   about it. The best that I have is a handwritten sheet

23   that Shawn showed me the other day that I am going to

24   have to introduce. I want to be able to get a straight,

25   factual answer about them. And the terms of not only his

1 prison sentence but his probation term are very relevant

2 to the events in the case. I don't know why the

3 objection is sustained.

4   MR. JENSVOLD: I don't see the relevance. The

5 609 purposes have been exceeded, especially since a lot

6 of this -- the second and third ones go after the time of

7 this incident.

8   MR. LAGATTUTA: But he opened the door to it.

9 He asked him about being convicted, when it happened. It

10 happened in '99. There's probation granted. I don't

11 want the jury to be under the impression he was in prison

12 the whole time or -- just needs to explain the times and

13 dates.

14   MR. JENSVOLD: Relevance still applies. 609

15 still applies if you open the door.

16   THE COURT: Well, he's already admitted the

17 felony conviction, and that's the conviction I see that's

18 relevant now. If there's another matter that's relevant

19 as far as timing is concerned, as far as being in prison,

20 I'll allow you to go into that. Prison time is relevant

21 to what we're talking about here.

22   MR. LAGATTUTA: Okay.

23   THE COURT: But the reason for probation

24 violation -- just, you can get other and tie it into

25 something that's relevant.

PIMA COUNTY SUPERIOR COURT

```
1        MR. LAGATTUTA:  Okay.  And also this background
2   and credibility has already been brought out by the
3   State.
4        MR. JENSVOLD:  Felony convictions do their job.
5        THE COURT:  It does.  And the basis of it, if
6   there's inconsistent statements or things like that, you
7   can certainly go into that.  And so that's fine.  But he
8   has admitted three felonies clear up to the types of
9   three felonies, but I don't think we need to get into the
10  reasons for every other issue that he might have been
11  violated for.  Felonies, but then nothing beyond that.
12  Now, something as to timing, when he was in jail that
13  relates when he was with the defendant --
14       MR. LAGATTUTA:  Okay.  Very good.
15            (Open court.)
16       THE COURT:  Go ahead, Mr. Lagattuta.
17       MR. LAGATTUTA:  Thank you, your Honor.
18  BY MR. LAGATTUTA:
19       Q    Just so we get this cleared up, Jake, and I can
20  move on to more important things, the three felony
21  convictions that you had covered what period of time?
22       A    1999 to 2003.
23       Q    Okay.  I don't want the jury to think you were
24  in prison that whole time.
25       A    No, no, no, no.
```

PIMA COUNTY SUPERIOR COURT

```
 1        Q    So in 1999, you were sentenced for how long?
 2        A    I had sentenced -- all right, I violated the
 3   probation.  They gave me a year, and I had like a year in
 4   prison.  I had like seven months county jail back time,
 5   so I did three or four months in prison in 2001.  And
 6   then the other time was in 2003.  I was sentenced to
 7   three years and I did about two and a half of those three
 8   years.
 9        Q    What about this time?
10        A    That was the last time.  That was the last one.
11        Q    So you've been out since January; is that
12   correct?
13        A    Yes.
14        Q    And you told us that at this point you're in
15   between jobs; right?
16        A    Yeah.
17        Q    Did you tell us earlier that you had a job as a
18   loan specialist?
19        A    I had it but I did not pass their background
20   check.
21        Q    What is a loan specialist?
22        A    Basically, a telemarketer who calls and sees if
23   you want to consolidate your student loans.
24        Q    And prior to that you said you were laying some
25   carpet?
```

PIMA COUNTY SUPERIOR COURT

```
 1        A     Yeah.

 2        Q     Okay.

 3        A     Carpet, vinyl, tile, wood.

 4        Q     Okay.  And you're living up in the Phoenix area

 5  right now?

 6        A     Correct.

 7        Q     Okay.  How did you get down here to go to court?

 8              MR. JENSVOLD:  Objection; relevance.

 9              THE COURT:  Sustained.

10  BY MR. LAGATTUTA:

11        Q     Did the State provide any transportation for you

12  to come down here to go to court today?

13              MR. JENSVOLD:  Objection; relevance.

14              THE COURT:  Sustained.

15  BY MR. LAGATTUTA:

16        Q     Where are you staying down here, Jake?

17        A     In a hotel somewhere.

18        Q     Did the State provide you with any compensation

19  for staying in that hotel to come down here to testify?

20              MR. JENSVOLD:  Objection; relevance.

21              THE COURT:  Overruled.

22              THE WITNESS:  Yeah.

23  BY MR. LAGATTUTA:

24        Q     They are?

25        A     Yeah.
```

PIMA COUNTY SUPERIOR COURT

```
 1        Q    Okay.  How about meals?  Is the State giving you

 2   money to buy meals while you're down here?

 3        A    Yeah.

 4        Q    How much?

 5        A    $21 a day.

 6        Q    Okay.  $21 a day.

 7             When are you planning on going back?

 8        A    Going back?

 9        Q    To Phoenix.

10        A    When I'm not needed here anymore.

11        Q    How many days have you been paid for to testify?

12        A    This is the second day.

13        Q    Were you paid in advance?

14        A    No.

15             MR. JENSVOLD:  Objection; relevance.

16             THE COURT:  Overruled.

17   BY MR. LAGATTUTA:

18        Q    All right.  You told us in answer to the

19   prosecutor's question that you were on parole at this

20   point; is that right?

21        A    Uh-huh.

22        Q    Isn't that called community service or

23   supervision?

24        A    Uh-huh.

25        Q    "Uh-huh," does that mean yes?
```

PIMA COUNTY SUPERIOR COURT

```
1       A    Uh-huh, yeah.

2       Q    Are you drug tested also?

3       A    Yes.

4       Q    How often?

5       A    Whenever a color comes up; usually about once a

6  month.

7       Q    When was the last time you were tested for

8  drugs?

9       A    Last month.

10      Q    When?

11      A    Last month.

12      Q    How did you do?

13      A    Fine.

14      Q    I want to take you back to the interview that

15 you gave back in April of '03, which I believe you have a

16 copy of right there.  Okay.

17           THE COURT:  That's Exhibit No. -- what's the

18 number, if you can see.

19           MR. JENSVOLD:  It's 2, I believe.

20           THE COURT:  2.  Thank you.  Plaintiff's 2.

21 BY MR. LAGATTUTA:

22      Q    Okay.  Now, just to make this easier for you,

23 these are your words, and I'm going to ask you if you

24 recall making these statements.  So I won't try to put

25 any words past you that you haven't said, all right?
```

PIMA COUNTY SUPERIOR COURT

```
 1              And really at page 3, at the bottom, the
 2     officers say to you:  When did you come in contact with
 3     him down here in Tucson?
 4              Do you see that?  Do you recall that question at
 5     all?
 6          A    Yes.
 7          Q    When the officer says to you, "When did you come
 8     in contact with him?," they're talking about Jim Coghill?
 9          A    Yes.
10          Q    And you say:  Okay, well, up in Phoenix my
11     grandfather had passed away.  I was staying with my aunt.
12     My aunt is all whacked out on methamphetamine, so she
13     didn't want me living there.
14          A    Yeah.
15          Q    You said that; right?
16          A    Yeah.
17          Q    And then you said that:  She burnt all my
18     clothes, like my belongings, so I have two duffel bags to
19     my name.  So I got a hold of Jim via e-mail.  I told him
20     the situation, what I was facing; basically, I didn't
21     have anywhere to live.  I was living on the streets up
22     there.
23              Those are your words; right?
24          A    Yeah.
25          Q    Okay.  So that was your situation when you
```

PIMA COUNTY SUPERIOR COURT

1   contacted Jim Coghill prior to coming to Tucson; correct?

2   A   Okay.

3   Q   All right. And the next question, sort of a

4   mumbled question, but you respond by saying --

5   MR. JENSVOLD: Objection, your Honor. This is

6   kind of narrative from the -- it's not questions. He's

7   going through the statement.

8   MR. LAGATTUTA: These are leading, direct,

9   pointed questions. I'm asking him if he made these

10   statements.

11   THE COURT: Will counsel approach for a minute,

12   please?

13   (Bench conference.)

14   THE COURT: I think the thing I'm concerned

15   about is there are so many statements in the record that

16   don't have anything at all to do as far as any kind of

17   relevant material, and so that's what I'm trying to get

18   at. So if it's -- I mean, if we're going through every

19   part of the statement --

20   MR. LAGATTUTA: Oh, not at all. And honestly,

21   your Honor, the reason why I'm doing this is because in

22   his previous testimony he was all over the place, and the

23   testimony turned out to be three times longer than it

24   should have. These four or five sections where he asked

25   direct questions and answers that are directly related to

PIMA COUNTY SUPERIOR COURT

```
 1    his background, his situation, and, you know, where he
 2    was at the time of these events.  I'm not going through
 3    the whole thing.
 4              MR. JENSVOLD:  And, your Honor, quite frankly
 5    the way --
 6              MR. LAGATTUTA:  Same thing.
 7              MR. JENSVOLD:  -- he asked, it's hearsay because
 8    he's -- if he's going to impeach him with a prior
 9    testimony, that's fine; the questions he answered.  But
10    going through verbatim answers through the interview is
11    improper impeachment.
12              THE COURT:  Here's the thing:  You can ask
13    questions with regard to his bias and things like that.
14    That's certainly relevant as to why he might have a
15    reason to, you know, be misstating or anything that has
16    to do with truth and veracity, but -- so in that area or
17    something that's relevant to time or something or
18    whatever is relevant to the case.  But just to continue
19    to go over every little thing about him I think needs to
20    narrow.
21              MR. LAGATTUTA:  I'll narrow it down, your Honor.
22              But the other form that was employed by the
23    prosecutor is to say:  Hey, read this.  Look at it a
24    while.  Now I'm going to ask you to repeat what you said.
25              I'm asking him direct, leading questions in
```

PIMA COUNTY SUPERIOR COURT

```
1    response, and I will be quick.

2              THE COURT:  Okay.  I'll overrule the objection

3    for now, but make sure it's in the area of relevancy.

4              (Open court.)

5              THE COURT:  Okay.  Go ahead, Mr. Lagattuta.

6    BY MR. LAGATTUTA:

7         Q    I'm sorry, Jacob.  I'm trying to, by reading

8    through your past statements, get some answers to what

9    kind of situation you were in when you came to down to

10   Tucson, okay?

11             Didn't -- when you contacted Jim Coghill here,

12   didn't he tell you he was down here in Tucson and he's

13   been working at Hamilton Aerospace, and he may be able to

14   hook you up with a job?  Isn't that what happened?

15        A    There was mention of that, yes.

16        Q    In fact, that was the whole purpose for him

17   coming up there to get you out of the situation you were

18   in Phoenix, to bring you down to Tucson to help you get a

19   job; right?

20        A    Pretty much.

21        Q    Okay.  And so once you got down to Tucson, okay,

22   he was already working at Hamilton Aerospace; is that

23   correct?

24        A    Right.

25        Q    So he would go to work all day; is that correct?
```

PIMA COUNTY SUPERIOR COURT

```
 1        A    Yeah.

 2        Q    And at that point you were like just looking for

 3   jobs; right?

 4        A    Yes.

 5        Q    Okay.  And that was during the time when the

 6   GoPed accident occurred; correct?

 7        A    Yeah.

 8        Q    During that time period down here in Tucson, in

 9   addition to you going out and looking for your own jobs,

10   Jim had also helped line you up with a job, didn't he?

11        A    Yeah.

12        Q    That's what this whole thing about the job

13   interview was all about, and about whether you were

14   dressed properly or not for the job interview; right?

15        A    Yeah.

16        Q    Because he had either spoken with somebody that

17   he worked with in the plant or done something positively

18   to help you get on board and work at the same place;

19   right?

20        A    Yeah.

21        Q    And in fact, there was going to be some

22   arrangement, whether it be the GoPed or something else,

23   as to how you would even get back and forth to work?

24        A    It wasn't discussed prior to.

25        Q    Okay.  But you would agree with me, wouldn't
```

PIMA COUNTY SUPERIOR COURT

```
 1    you, that by him helping you get a job with the place
 2    that he worked at, there might be a way for you guys to
 3    work out transportation back and forth to the same place?
 4         A    Yeah.
 5         Q    Okay.  Okay.  So the whole thing came down to a
 6    big disagreement that you had over how you should go and
 7    present yourself at this interview; right?
 8         A    That --
 9         Q    The big argument you had.
10         A    That and the car hitting me when I was on his
11    GoPed.
12         Q    Okay.  Okay, just to be fair to you, there was
13    something else that you talked about in here.
14              You got hit by the GoPed -- I'm sorry, you were
15    on the GoPed and you got hit and you got injured and you
16    got -- you got prescribed some medication; right?  I
17    think it was some Vicodin or something?
18         A    Yeah.
19         Q    Okay.  And when you got back to the trailer, you
20    told Jim about it.  You told him that you needed to
21    borrow some money from him to buy the Vicodin or the
22    medication because you had been injured in this GoPed
23    accident; right?
24         A    Yeah.
25         Q    And he said to you:  Well, I don't know, Jake,
```

PIMA COUNTY SUPERIOR COURT

```
1    about loaning you money to help you get better after
2    you've been in an accident where you wrecked my GoPed,
3    and he didn't want to give you the money?
4        A    Right.
5        Q    So you thought that was kind of unfair of him,
6    didn't you?
7        A    Not necessarily.
8        Q    That was one of those other things that kind of
9    led to this big disagreement; right?
10       A    No.
11       Q    No?  So that was a trivial matter?
12       A    Yeah, because I asked my mom -- or I called my
13   mother and I ended up getting it filled when I got back
14   to Phoenix anyway, so --
15       Q    All right.  But just so that you know I don't
16   leave anything out that you talked about with the police,
17   you did tell them that as a result of this accident you
18   needed some money for some medication and Jim wouldn't
19   loan it over to you; right?
20       A    I casually asked him.
21       Q    Right.  Okay.  And the fact that he didn't give
22   it to you made you a little upset?
23       A    Not really.  I was in pain.
24       Q    Right.
25       A    But I could see his point, do you know what I
```

PIMA COUNTY SUPERIOR COURT

```
 1   mean?

 2        Q    Right.  Okay.

 3        A    Yeah.

 4        Q    And the point would be what?

 5        A    I wrecked his GoPed; he's upset with me.  I'm

 6   not going to give you no money.

 7        Q    Okay.  All right.

 8             And then -- and was it after that that you got

 9   in this big discussion about, you know, what you should

10   wear?

11        A    That was the next morning.

12        Q    That was the next morning?

13        A    Yeah.

14        Q    And you said to us a little bit earlier under

15   examination by the State here that, you know, he was

16   telling you to put on this other shirt, and he was

17   probably right; is that correct?

18             MR. JENSVOLD:  Objection; asked and answered.

19             THE COURT:  Overruled.

20             THE WITNESS:  So, yeah, because it was more of a

21   professional shirt.

22   BY MR. LAGATTUTA:

23        Q    So looking back on it now, you think that maybe

24   the way you were dressed, the choice that you made might

25   have been a wrong one?
```

PIMA COUNTY SUPERIOR COURT

          A   My shirt was like oversized.

          Q   All right. Up until that point, when was the
last time that you had had a full-time job?

          A   Up until that point? Direct Marketing Services
in 2002, at the end -- last half of 2002.

          Q   Okay. So this is April of --

          A   No, this is not April at all. It was still
March.

          Q   When you first arrived in Tucson?

          A   Oh, yeah. It was the end of March.

          Q   Exactly. The end of March. Well, I'm talking
about the day that you had the argument and the GoPed.
That was the end of March?

          A   That day was actually April 1st day.

          Q   Right. Exactly. It was. And it was 2003?

          A   No. Oh, yeah, it was. My bad. It was.

          Q   So prior -- my question is, prior to March of
2003, when Jim came up to Phoenix to bring you down to
help you out with a job in Tucson, when was the last time
you had a full-time job?

          A   November of 2002.

          Q   November of 2002. And what was that job?

          A   I was working for Nextel via Direct Marketing
Services.

          Q   What did you do?

1   A   I -- when people would call the Nextel 800
2   number to order the phone and get them activated, I would
3   answer the phone and get --
4   Q   How long does that job last?
5   A   The second time? Three or four months.
6   Q   So in -- so are you telling me that in November
7   of 2002 --
8   A   I didn't work there after November of 2002.
9   Q   You didn't work after that?
10   A   No.
11   Q   You worked in the couple months preceding
12   November 2002?
13   A   No, I worked in November 2002. But any time
14   after that I did not work until -- until I got back --
15   no, actually -- yeah.
16   Q   This job that you talked about at Nextel, that
17   you worked at around the time of November of 2002, Jim
18   helped you get that job, didn't he?
19   A   Yeah, he pulled some strings and -- for the job.
20   Q   Okay. And you said "pulled some strings,"
21   meaning he helped?
22   A   He knew the human resources lady and got me back
23   in.
24   Q   Okay. Were you living with him in the motor
25   home any time during 2002?

PIMA COUNTY SUPERIOR COURT

```
 1        A    Yeah.  That was probably the time I moved back
 2   in.  And I said:  Hey, can you get the job back at
 3   Nextel?  And he said:  Yeah, I can try.  And that's
 4   probably what happened.  That is what happened, actually.
 5        Q    Okay.  So -- all right.  Well, you had work at
 6   Nextel previously then?
 7        A    That's how I met him to begin with.
 8        Q    Okay.  And how long did that last?
 9        A    That time?  Three or four months.  I can't stand
10   call center work for too long.  It's quite stressful.
11        Q    So you left the job on your own?
12        A    Yeah, stopped showing up.
13        Q    Okay.  And then you're out of work for a while
14   until you called Jim up and said:  Can you get me back on
15   board, maybe.  Is that right?
16        A    Yeah.
17        Q    And he helped you get back on board at the same
18   job?
19        A    Yeah.
20        Q    Put you back into the trailer and lived there
21   for awhile -- motor home?
22        A    Up until August.  From June to August, I think.
23   Or maybe -- yeah, it was about August.  Yeah.  August he
24   was like:  You need to move out today.  He would just do
25   something like that, and I'd have to find somewhere.  It
```

PIMA COUNTY SUPERIOR COURT

1   was like a challenge, I guess.

2   MR. LAGATTUTA: Okay. Your Honor, I have a

3   number of different questions in a different area, and I

4   wonder if this wouldn't be a good time to stop.

5   THE COURT: It's probably an excellent time.

6   It's about five -- well, between five and ten to 4 (sic).

7   So with that we will take the evening recess.

8   Remember not to talk about the case. I hate to

9   hesitate to tell you I have a short calendar tomorrow. I

10   do, but we still should be able to start at 10:30.

11   And so don't talk about the case. Remember the

12   admonition. If you'll take your books back with Peter

13   and keep them in the jury room, we'll be in recess till

14   tomorrow at 10:30.

15   Mr. Franks, you're subject to recall. You have

16   to be here tomorrow at 10:30.

17   (Whereupon, the jury was excused from the

18   courtroom.)

19   THE COURT: Let's see, the defendant slipped

20   out -- oh, he's back in here.

21   Jurors left.

22   I just want to check how are we are doing

23   witnesswise with you, Mr. Jensvold.

24   MR. JENSVOLD: Your Honor, we're a little behind

25   from what I expected, but --

```
 1          THE COURT:  Are you going to go most of the day?
 2          MR. JENSVOLD:  I have four witnesses who should
 3     be -- frankly, I may not even call all of them.  I'll
 4     call at least two of them:  Deputy Judd and Detective
 5     Gidney.  They should be very short.  Detective Englander
 6     is going to be quite a while.
 7          THE COURT:  Just bottom-line estimate.  Through
 8     most of tomorrow?  There's no chance that you'd be done
 9     tomorrow?  Little chance?
10          MR. JENSVOLD:  I don't think we're going to be
11     finished tomorrow, especially if Mr. Lagattuta is going
12     to call Scott Greene.
13          THE COURT:  I'm just trying to check when we
14     need to look at instructions.  There's not too much
15     there.
16          MR. LAGATTUTA:  Well, here's one thing:  I'm
17     trying to check with and I asked Shawn this earlier, we
18     were going to call Scott Greene.  I have to reserve time
19     for him.  I -- when we started this, I told him tomorrow
20     morning, which I think at this point is out of the
21     question.  Can I tell him tomorrow at 3:00, or is that
22     still --
23          MR. JENSVOLD:  I think that's wishful thinking.
24          MR. LAGATTUTA:  Okay.
25          THE COURT:  I'm trying to sort out scheduling.
```

PIMA COUNTY SUPERIOR COURT

```
 1    And if you go through and then tomorrow, and then you can
 2    bring your witness on -- let's see, tomorrow would be
 3    Thursday -- Friday morning, does that work out?
 4            MR. LAGATTUTA:  It would be easier for me
 5    probably to just go ahead and tell him that, Friday
 6    morning.
 7            By the way, we start at 10:30 on Friday?
 8            THE COURT:  Same thing.  Still have --
 9            MR. LAGATTUTA:  Still have a calendar?
10            THE COURT:  Yeah.  Friday's calendar is worse
11    than tomorrow.  I really only have a couple cases, three
12    things on the calendar.  Friday is busier.
13            MR. LAGATTUTA:  We'll try to make arrangements
14    for him to be here Friday in the morning.
15            THE COURT:  And if you end early tomorrow,
16    that's great.  And if not -- just best guess, do you
17    think you might end tomorrow, then, if you get through
18    this?
19            MR. LAGATTUTA:  I think there will be plenty to
20    do tomorrow.
21            MR. JENSVOLD:  Yeah.  There's plenty to do.  And
22    I'll evaluate two of my shorter witnesses to see if I
23    need them at all.  They're not --
24            THE COURT:  That's your call.  I'm not trying to
25    push you.  I'm just trying to help each of you
```

PIMA COUNTY SUPERIOR COURT

```
 1    understand, and you'll have at least one witness and
 2    maybe more and --
 3              MR. LAGATTUTA:  Yes.
 4              THE COURT:  And so earliest would probably be
 5    going to the jury is Friday afternoon the way we're
 6    looking at things.
 7              MR. LAGATTUTA:  I think that's more realistic
 8    than when we started.
 9              THE COURT:  Okay.
10              MR. JENSVOLD:  Your Honor, I wanted to bring up
11    the subject again about my motion in limine.  I'm still
12    not certain whether the foundation has been laid or what
13    we can get into and what we can't.
14              THE COURT:  You know, I have to say, there's so
15    many things here.  I don't know what's going to connect
16    up as far as any kind of testimony.  You've got certain
17    things.  There's a suggestion out there that certain
18    things belong.  I have to hear the question and know
19    where you are before I can rule.
20              MR. JENSVOLD:  Okay.  It's basically going to
21    come through Detective Englander primarily, so --
22              THE COURT:  Well --
23              MR. JENSVOLD:  I'll just ask to approach again.
24              THE COURT:  Just do -- I just can't -- you know,
25    there's so much that's developed each day, and I know
```

PIMA COUNTY SUPERIOR COURT

```
 1   where we are and whether things -- I just have to know
 2   what your reason for relevance on it is, or what your
 3   basis for 404 (B) would be.  I think I have a better
 4   knowledge, and so we have to see whether or not the
 5   evidence you offer would fit into whether the proper
 6   exceptions under 404.
 7            MR. JENSVOLD:  Knowledge and opportunity are the
 8   State's primary --
 9            THE COURT:  Okay.
10            MR. JENSVOLD:  And, your Honor, based on -- I've
11   got a copy of a transcript of the defendant's --
12   Mr. Coghill's interview.  And I was intending to play the
13   tape and stop it at a particular point.  I made a copy of
14   it.  I gave it to Mr. Lagattuta.  He indicated his
15   objections, which are sort of blocked off in blue
16   ball-point pen of what he would object to.
17            THE COURT:  You're going to have an admission or
18   have the defendant's statement that was given, and again
19   this is the first time learning that you intended to use
20   that.  But that's going to come through, and you're going
21   to have a copy of what you're going to play on the tape
22   for the jury as far as --
23            MR. JENSVOLD:  I have the tape.  And my
24   suggestion was to stop it at a particular point.  Mr. --
25   again, some of this is going to depend on the Court's
```

PIMA COUNTY SUPERIOR COURT

```
 1   ruling.  I didn't think there was any reason it wouldn't
 2   come in, to be quite honest.
 3            THE COURT:  Well, if you want me to look at it
 4   tonight.
 5            MR. LAGATTUTA:  Yes.
 6            THE COURT:  Look at it to see, you know, then --
 7   I can look at it and try to make an evaluation based on
 8   something specific.  That I can deal with if you want me
 9   to lack at that tonight.
10            MR. LAGATTUTA:  I would like that.  And I can
11   tell you the areas I marked off in the blue would be
12   objectionable under these things that we've been talking
13   about, about the State's request to introduce this
14   evidence under this 404 (B) theory.  That's what it's
15   related to.
16            THE COURT:  Okay.
17            MR. LAGATTUTA:  It's not objectionable because
18   of any other rights violation.  I think you understand
19   that when you read it.
20            THE COURT:  All I need is specificity so I can
21   really rule on something, so I know I'm ruling on
22   something and not ruling on something too nebulous to
23   be --
24            MR. LAGATTUTA:  Well, okay.  Then, just so you
25   know, the basis for my objection to the parts I've
```

PIMA COUNTY SUPERIOR COURT

```
 1   outlined is, No. 1, they're irrelevant.  And, No. 2, that
 2   they're -- the comments are just far too prejudicial;
 3   they don't have any probative value.  No. 3, if they were
 4   actually created or offered under a 404 (B) theory of
 5   plan or motive or something, that should have been
 6   disclosed to us.  So that's another notice problem.  We
 7   could have prepared to defend against that rather than
 8   coming in here and have to deal with that right now.
 9           THE COURT:  Are you using that under 404 -- I
10   think it's 404 (C).  Is that an issue that you're using
11   no notice on that -- the 404 (C)?
12           MR. LAGATTUTA:  Right.
13           MR. JENSVOLD:  And, your Honor, honestly the
14   statements in here deal strictly with adult pornography.
15   And it's the State's position that doesn't even fall
16   under 404 (B) because it's not a prior bad act.  It's
17   legal.  Same analogy.  I don't want to repeat myself.
18           THE COURT:  And the question is what the
19   defendant said about adult pornography based on his
20   statement to the detective.
21           MR. JENSVOLD:  Correct.  And I can lay the
22   foundation, you know, at least pretty peremptorily now
23   that he talked about a specific folder, My Documents
24   folder, title Porn.  Both of those were corroborated as
25   part of the hard drive.  And the hard drive there was My
```

PIMA COUNTY SUPERIOR COURT

```
1    Documents.  There was a folder titled Porn underneath My
2    Documents.
3              THE COURT:  I'll look at it understanding your
4    objections based on prejudicial outweighing and also lack
5    of notice.
6              MR. LAGATTUTA:  Thank you, your Honor.
7              Final thought.  Most of the time I've
8    encountered the 404 (B) evidence, it doesn't really have
9    to rise -- a bad act doesn't have to rise to the level of
10   criminal activity.  But other courts have held other bad
11   acts in and of themselves are not crimes but can be
12   considered too prejudicial just because of the nature of
13   what they are.
14             THE COURT:  Okay.  Thank you.
15             MR. JENSVOLD:  And, again, your Honor, I would
16   add that this is, in a sense, rebuttal evidence as well
17   because the only defense in this case is really that
18   Mr. Jacob Franks is the owner of all the pornography.
19             THE COURT:  Okay.  Got it.  Thanks.
20             (Proceedings closed.)
21
22
23
24
25
```

PIMA COUNTY SUPERIOR COURT

```
 1

 2    STATE OF ARIZONA    )
                          )    ss.
 3    COUNTY OF PIMA      )

 4

 5

 6

 7

 8            I, CHERYL L. AUSTIN, Certified Reporter #50029,

 9    Official Reporter for the Superior Court, in and for the

10    County of Pima, do hereby certify that I took the

11    shorthand notes in the foregoing matter; that the same

12    was transcribed under my direction; that the preceding

13    pages of typewritten matter are a true, accurate and

14    complete transcript of all the matters adduced, to the

15    best of my skill and ability.

16

17

18            _____

19
              CHERYL L. AUSTIN,   CR #50029, RMR-CRR
20            Official Reporter
              Pima County Superior Court
21

22

23    DATED:   JUNE 25, 2006

24

25
```

PIMA COUNTY SUPERIOR COURT

Opening Statements

Day 2, March 29, 2006

Page 211-8: Defendant met Jake in 1998 not 1999.

Page 211-18: Both defendant and Jake interested in Buddhism.

Page 212-12: Jake knew defendant-possessed contraband in Phoenix at his parents' house.

Page 212-25: Defendant moved motor home in February, 2003.

Page 213-5: Testimony not given under oath. Defendant arrived in Tucson shortly before February 28, 2003 when his cable and high speed Internet were installed. I was not read Miranda and was speaking generally.

Page 213-10: When was Jake ever working? One month at DMS and two months at Synergy Solutions.

Page 214-3: Unsworn testimony. No Miranda. The tape of this conversation, when played to completion, reveals no Miranda and that Jake had been living in Tucson almost two weeks.

Page 214-8: This statement is true as to the timeframe.

Page 215-10: Not true. It's not the My Documents, Kazaa Light folder. What the prosecutor is referring to is in c:\\programfiles\Kazaa\mysharefiles.

Page 215-16: On March 26, 2003, between 12:43 AM to 3:42 AM, pornography was downloaded by Jake. It was adult pornography.

Page 217-1: The prescription was for Vicodin, a narcotic, not Ibuprofen.

Page 218-1: Jake actually left without saying a word.

Page 218-5: Jake returns to the motor home.

Page 218-19: Defendant said he didn't know what was on the KP disks and assumed that since they weren't his, they must be Jake's.

Page 219-3: Defendant had never heard of or seen "dirty" disk prior to disclosure.

Page 219-21: Prosecutor states they are showing the files to the jury "because it's much more difficult to deal with."

Page 227-13: They take fingerprints from KP disks, but don't compare them to anyone.

Page 232-4: Nobody said anything about tapes.

Page 232-9: What tapes is the judge talking about?

Page 242-11: Defendant stated that was all his clothing.

Page 243-11: Defendant stated some of the CD's belonged to Jake.

Page 243-16: Deputy Schupbach contradicts this statement at Page 262-20. Perjury.

Page 244-6: Schupbach and Judd remained with defendant 1.5 hours until Detective Englander arrived.

Page 247-24: Jake was there more than a week.

SCHUPBACH

Page 250-25: Jake tells Deputy Schupbach he couldn't help but see files being played by defendant. No record of viewing.

Page 258-20: Schupbach states prior to this, she was there to conduct an investigation concerning CD's on a spindle on Page 247-16. She claimed she saw a CD marked KP on Page 247-11, then she says she "did not look at the CD spindle cases", yet she is there to conduct an investigation concerning CD's on a spindle. Perjury.

Page 259-15: Perjury concerning KP disks again.

378

Page 261-21: Defendant was not under arrest.

Page 262-10: Defendant waited 1.5 hours for Detective Englander to arrive. He had to call in sick to work.

Page 263-24: Schupbach didn't question Jake as to whether or not he used defendant's computer.

Page 264-12: Schupbach didn't question Jake about when CD's were created.

Page 267-3: Schupbach confirms Jake's statement about seeking revenge.

Page 272-18: It was September 1998.

JAKE

Page 273-1: His brother's computer that he was using was broken.

Page 274-1: This contradicts Jake's prison interview where he states he was in prison during September 11, 2001.

Page 274-11: Jake was living with defendant in early September 2001.

Page 276-9: Jake lived with defendant till a few days prior to February 28, 2003 when he moved to Tucson.

Page 276-13: A few months puts us deep into April or May, 2003. If defendant is to be held to pinpoint accuracy in regard to dates, Jake should be held to the same standards. He doesn't pass muster.

Page 276-19: Jake states he doesn't know when defendant left for Tucson.

Page 277-15: Jake states defendant came up to visit from Tucson. Then on Page 361-15, Jake states he contacted me about his situation. Perjury.

Page 279-9: Jake states he was visiting Defendant in Tucson for a week. Then on Page 279-11, he is unable to tell exactly how many days he was with Defendant in Tucson. Perjury.

Page 281-18: Jake states Defendant didn't yell and scream at him when he learned his goped was destroyed.

Page 281-22: Jake had no applications with him when he returned home.

Page 282-2: Jake was instructed not to leave a four-block radius because Defendant knew he had little experience with the goped and was concerned for his safety.

Page 282-23: Jake states he would stay up all night on Defendant's computer.

Page 283-5: Jake would use Defendant's computer to pirate music.

Page 285-16: Jake states, "and then the next thing I know for all kinds of other stuff". What other stuff is he talking about?

Page 285-23: Jake knows who Allan Watts and Joseph Campbell are because Defendant played recordings of them for him in Phoenix and discussed them at length with him.

Page 286-8: Jake admits to downloading adult pornography.

Page 293-7: Defendant told Franks he would take him back to his friend Shannon.

Page 293-4: Jake's statement contradicts his prison interview and his later testimony on _____, 2007.

Page 295-8: Jake states there were disks labeled kiddy porn. No such items are in evidence.

Page 295-15: Jake states he would wake up and observe Defendant viewing files. Statement is contradicted by police computer forensics report, no evidence of viewing.

Page 300-9: Contradicts Deputy Schupbach's testimony and her own police report on Page 60-3.

Page 304-12: For someone who remembers dates so poorly, it is surprising Jake remembers this date so accurately.

Page 305-3: Jake makes the assumption files in his area are contraband.

Page 306-1: Jake states he didn't label any other disk than the "dirty" disk. Then what about the disk "Star Trek 5" he admits to labeling on Page 312-11. Perjury.

Page 306-25: Top disk on spindle is "dirty" disk just like the lab report index, not KP as Deputy Schupbach stated on Page 36-16. Evidence tampering.

ARS 13-2407 Tampering with public record; classification.
A.   A person commits tampering with a public record if, with the intent to defraud or deceive, such person knowingly:
1.   Makes or completes a written instrument, knowing that it has been falsely made, which purports to be a public record or true copy thereof or alters or makes a false entry in a written instrument which is public record or a true copy of a public record; or
2.   Presents or uses a written instrument which is or purports to be public record, knowingly that it has been falsely made, with intent that it be taken as genuine; or
3.   Records, register or files in a governmental office or agency a written statement which has been falsely made, completed or altered or in which a false entry has been made or which contains a false statement or false information, or
4.   Destroys, mutilates, conceals, removes or otherwise impairs the availability of any public record; or
5.   Refuses to deliver a public record in such persons possession upon proper request of a public servant entitled to receive such record for examination or other purposes.

B.   In this section" public records" means all official books, papers, written instruments or records created, issued, received or kept by others for the information of government.

C.   Tampering with a public record is a class 6 felony.

Page 308-11: Jake has no interest in Star Trek or science fiction. He has labeled one of my disks. Proof labeling was communal effort. Statement contradicts testimony on Page 306-1. Perjury.

Page 308-14: Jake can't remember when he labeled the Star Trek 5 disk. Speculation.

Page 309-18: Mr. Kreitl brought in after Jake's direct examination not permitting immediate rebuttal of Jake's testimony by cross-examination. Should not have been allowed.

Page 314-18: Kreitl states his report is a "scientific examination" of handwriting submitted to him. Handwriting analysis is not a science, it is an art. If it were not so, it would not rely on a "qualified opinion" as stated by Mr. Kreitl on Page 316-21.

Page 316-21: The "qualified opinion" is that the "dirty" disk was written by Jake, yet there was not enough questioned writing to lend a conclusive identification. If this is true, then the same conditions apply to the KP disks because they have even less questioned writing on them.

Page 318-17: Kreitl states, "It is certainly capable two writers can write KP the same way."

Page 321-23: Kreitl is being asked to compare cursive handwriting to printing. It's not possible to do that because they are two totally different modes of writing and are therefore dissimilar.

Page 322-19: Kreitl was never given a handwriting sample of Defendant to analyze.

Page 328-2: Kreitl is basing his report on an opinion, not on any facts in evidence.

Page 330-17: Kreitl admits his report cannot be a "conclusive elimination" of Jacob Franks.

Page 332-4: Again, comparing handwriting to printing.

Page 332-22: Again, no handwriting sample of Defendant.

Page 335-22: It is possible to fake a handwriting sample.

Page 336-9: Judge doesn't know what the word "forensic" means.

Page 338-3: This question was already answered. The juror is not paying attention.

Page 338-15: Kreitl never given handwriting sample of Defendant.

JAKE

Page 342-15: Jake is lying. No record of viewing in police computer forensics report.

Page 344-9: Prosecutor doesn't even know who he is talking to.

Page 346-3: Never was said. Never happened.

Page 347-6: Jake can't remember file names he quoted and are in reports he gave to police.

Page 349-15: Jake stole a car as a juvenile, was on probation for that crime when Defendant met him in 1998. He violated probation and was sent to the Estrella Jail. Juvenile offenses don't show up on adult criminal records. This is why the first entry of his record is for a probation violation because he was already under probation for auto theft when Defendant met him.

Page 350-22: Defense counsel in sidebar states prosecutor has not been forthcoming about the dates of Jake's imprisonment.

Page 353-2: Jake reveals he received one year for violating his probation. Jake can't have been over the age of 18 because his adult criminal record would have indicated the nature and date of this offense that it doesn't. The first recorded if and as an adult is his probation violation for car theft which is the event we are talking about here. Because the probation violation is the first record on his adult criminal report he obviously had to have committed the car theft as a minor. When I met Jake he was 18 yoa. Born 08/24/80 as indicated on the states writs of habeas corpus, for his release to testify at my trial.

Page 349-24 Jake states he spent three years on probation. Therefore the timeline looks like this:

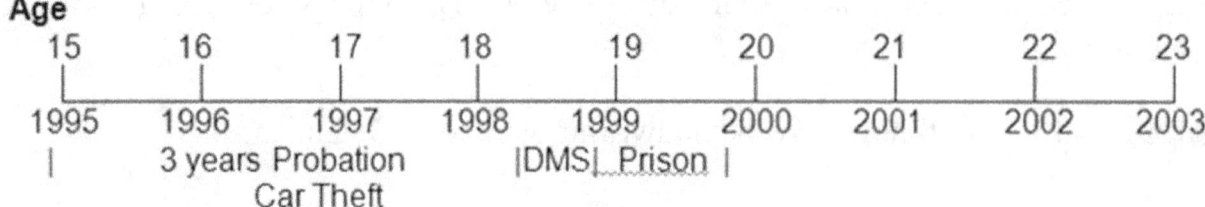

Age
| 15 | 16 | 17 | 18 | 19 | 20 | 21 | 22 | 23 |
| 1995 | 1996 | 1997 | 1998 | 1999 | 2000 | 2001 | 2002 | 2003 |

3 years Probation
Car Theft

|DMS| Prison |

Page 356-15: The court is limiting defense counsel in questioning.

Page 361-11: Jake's statement contradicts direct testimony given on Page 231-12. Perjury.

Page 363-24: Prescription was for the narcotic Vicodin.

Page 365-11. Vicodin argument took place on morning of April 1, 2003.

Page 366-16. Jake doesn't remember the year this event took place.

Page 367-5: He spent one month working there and quit the same day Defendant did.

Page 373-23: Prosecutor wants tape stopped at a particular point to hide Defendant's statement Jake had lived with him two weeks in Tucson and that statements had been obtained without Miranda.

U.S. v. Hurst, 228 F.3d 751 (6th CIR 2000)
Interrogation triggers the need to give Miranda warnings.

U.S. v. Butler
Because of the inherently coercive nature of custodial interrogations, a person must be advised of his Miranda rights, prior to questioning.

U.S. v. Allee, 299 F.3d 996 (8th CIR 2002)
Inquiry into defendant's silence following Miranda warnings constitutes trial error. (This would also apply to right to counsel.)

U.S. v. Bonner, 302 F.3d 776 (7th CIR 2002)
A defendant's right to silence, coupled with her right not to have any reference to her silence made at trial, exists even before defendant receives Miranda warnings.

Jocks v. Tavernier, 316 F.3d 128 (2003)
The appropriate remedy for violations of Miranda rights is exclusion of the evidence at trial.

U.S. v. Swint, 15 F.3d 286, 290 (3rd CIR 1994)
Confession involuntary because defendant thought statements were off the record "proffer" and officers did not clearly inform defendant's statements were on the record.

Sanna v. Dipalo, 265 F.3d 1 (1st CIR 2001)
When a person in police custody requests the presence of an attorney the authorities must cease interrogation.

Miranda v. AZ. No. 759 Argued Feb. 28 – Mar. 1, 1966 decided June 13, 1966
GO> 384 U.S. 436
When the accused is interrogated in a room cut off from the world or placed in a stressful condition the testimony gathered is inadmissible regardless of whether the accused was informed of his rights.

Page 375-3: The state had not disclosed the tape prior to trial in accordance with Rule 15.1 (b)(5). It is therefore inadmissible.

Page 376-17: Prosecutor states in sidebar, "Because the only defense in this case is really that Mr. Franks is the owner of all the pornography." Does this mean that if Defendant owned even one piece of adult pornography, he's guilty? Prosecution is misguided.

Day Three

3

4

5   STATE OF ARIZONA,

6   Plaintiff,

7   vs.   Case No. CR2004-2573
                                      2 CA-CR 2006-0215
8   JAMES COGHILL,

9   Defendant.
     _____

10

11   Tucson, Arizona
                                      MARCH 30, 2006
12

13

14   BEFORE: THE HON. TED B. BOREK, JUDGE
                Division 24
15

16   APPEARANCES: SEP25'86 POR PM 2:22

17   Shawn Jensvold, Esq.,
             appearing for the State;
18
             James Lagattuta, Esq.,
19   appearing for the Defendant.

20

21   JURY TRIAL DAY THREE

22
                  KRISTINE B. VALDEZ, RPR
23   CERTIFIED COURT REPORTER #50182
                  Pima County Superior Court
24   Tucson, Arizona 85701

25

                  SUPERIOR COURT, PIMA COUNTY

1   I N D E X

2

14

15

16

17

18

19

20

21

22

23

24

25

SUPERIOR COURT, PIMA COUNTY

         THE COURT: We are here with counsel, the

defendant -- counsel for both sides and the defendant.

I just wanted to tell you that I read over the

statement that was made by Mr. Coghill to Detective

Englander, and I'm still undecided on it. I want to

also say that the State gave me several cases this

morning, I'm not sure whether they gave them to you

also, Mr. Lagattuta.

         The one that I find most relevant here, and

perhaps helpful is the Utah case, the Miller case

dealing with some -- a similar issue. The other cases

don't really deal with sexual exploitation kind of

case, but they are certainly relevant with regard to

404(b). This is what I intend to do, when are you

going to call Detective Englander?

         MR. JENSVOLD: Anticipating today, Your

Honor, this afternoon would be my guess.

         THE COURT: This is what I want to do, I

want to talk to him before -- outside the presence of

the jury before he testifies and I intend to ask

questions that are going to be related to whether or

not the evidence that he would intend to present, what

he knows, would somehow connect up in such a way that

the issues of knowledge, intent and opportunity, you

know, would -- would -- would be enhanced or would be

                  SUPERIOR COURT, PIMA COUNTY

                                                      388

1   addressed by any of the -- any of the adult

2   pornography things that are found. I simply don't

3   know that. I don't know where things were found. I

4   don't know where things were marked. I don't know how

5   things got off the internet or could have gotten off

6   the internet. There are certainly things I think

7   could connect them up, but I don't know that right

8   now. And so I have to talk to him first.

9   And so we'll do him outside the presence of

10   the jury. You all, of course, will have the

11   opportunity to talk to him. So I'd like to plan that

12   in such a way that since we have continuing testimony

13   this morning, I rather not have a short testimony and

14   then take a break to do that, but I rather plan to do

15   it either at the end of the lunch hour -- I expect it

16   to take not more than ten minutes before the lunch

17   hour begins or, you know, at the end of the lunch

18   hour, 1:30.

19   MR. JENSVOLD: I have -- obviously Mr.

20   Franks is going continue, I don't know how long that

21   will take. I had Deputy Judd to testify at 11:30

22   assuming we get that far. I don't know whether we

23   will or not. And then I was going to put either

24   Detective Englander or Detective Gidney on the stand.

25   If you want to go ahead with Englander after Judd.

SUPERIOR COURT, PIMA COUNTY

1   THE COURT: It's -- you can call him any

2 time. I want to have a few minutes with him before.

3 I think we can probably plan to do that at the end of

4 the lunch hour. That will give -- Mr. Lagattuta -- to

5 look at the case that you have, so that's kind of what

6 I plan right now as far as the ruling on the admission

7 here and that would come through Englander anyhow, so

8 I'll talk to him before he testifies.

9   MR. JENSVOLD: I did want to bring up

10 something. This is -- this is State's argument that

11 Mr. Lagattuta opened the door to this by referring to

12 Mr. Franks' drug use during his opening and -- and

13 also the fact that Mr. Coghill is an altruistic

14 person, that was the sole basis of him taking Mr.

15 Franks in -- Mr. Franks said in his interview about

16 another reason for Mr. Coghill coming up to Phoenix to

17 get him and to bring him back down to Tucson was

18 because Mr. Franks could provide both of them and Mr.

19 Coghill with drugs.

20   THE COURT: Well --

21   MR. JENSVOLD: Obviously that's going to

22 come from Mr. Franks and no one else.

23   THE COURT: Well, now we're really getting

24 the -- the drug situation is something that -- this is

25 the first I heard of a drug situation and issue that

1   certainly --

2   MR. LAGATTUTA: Certainly didn't bring it

3   out through him, Your Honor.

4   THE COURT: Okay.

5   MR. JENSVOLD: He did mention -- he did

6   mention Mr. Franks was a drug user in his opening

7   statement.

8   THE COURT: Well, that's Franks, not the

9   defendant. And so, you know, I'm not sure how that's

10   going to relate here and the defense is portraying his

11   client as than upstanding citizen, what have you. It

12   may relate, but I don't know where you're going with

13   that. I don't know who you're expecting to deal up

14   with -- with drugs. We got Franks that's on the stand

15   so --

16   MR. JENSVOLD: Only Mr. Franks would be the

17   only witness, the only reason -- obviously wouldn't

18   have gone there at all, but I think Mr. Lagattuta did

19   open the door by basically portraying his client's

20   good character during his opening statement, whether

21   that's going to come into evidence or not will remain

22   to be seen.

23   THE COURT: Better keep Franks available for

24   cross at -- for, you know, subsequent time because,

25   you know, I don't see that in the evidence right now.

SUPERIOR COURT, PIMA COUNTY

1 I know it's in an opening statement, but I think the

2 drug area, getting into that with regard to the

3 defendant here, the kind of case we have, is far

4 afield at this point.

5   MR. JENSVOLD: Well, Your Honor, I guess I'm

6 not sure why -- 404(b) applies, both defendant and

7 State's witnesses, so I guess -- I guess my argument

8 is that, you know, it did, you know, bring up

9 something that's leaving the jury with an impression

10 based on Mr. Franks is a false one.

11   MR. LAGATTUTA: Your Honor, I don't think

12 there's been any -- any testimony about -- about that.

13 I don't think there's been any opening of the door. I

14 think if I want to characterize my client one way in

15 the opening, the State -- that doesn't just open the

16 door to the prosecution being able to introduce any

17 other -- any anything they want if they think the

18 opposite side of that.

19   THE COURT: Let me look at something here

20 for just a minute, please. Well, I don't think the

21 defense can raise, you know, the absolute stellar

22 character of the defendant and then not have allowed

23 that to be open to impeachment. So I just have to

24 hear, you know, to what degree impeachment will come,

25 right? We don't right now -- we have the opening

1   statement, we don't have any evidence, hold anybody --

2   you want to have -- impeach that kind of testimony

3   available in the case, that testimony is brought out.

4   I don't think up to now that we have that testimony on

5   the record.

6   MR. JENSVOLD: Well, Your Honor, I mean

7   obviously the problem that the prosecution has when

8   defense counsel brings up things that are during

9   opening statement may or may not come into evidence,

10   it's still left with the jury. Obviously I can argue

11   it at the end, but still without something to counter

12   it, it leaves the jury with a false impression based

13   on testimony that could be proffered there. Mr.

14   Franks --

15   MR. LAGATTUTA: I disagree. It sounds

16   almost like the State is asking you to do one of two

17   things or both; to say that they should be able to

18   introduce some -- some evidence and impeach the

19   character of the defendant who hasn't even -- well, we

20   haven't even begun our case. Number two, bring this

21   in as some other means of -- of -- I don't know,

22   describing his culpability in this case. Neither one

23   of them match up.

24   THE COURT: I'm going -- you can't get into

25   any drug involvement with regard to the defendant at

SUPERIOR COURT, PIMA COUNTY

393

1   this point in time. And now -- I'm not saying that

2   you -- keep Franks available and if other evidence

3   comes out at some other time, otherwise, it's argument

4   and, you know -- and if the -- if the defense

5   overbuilt his case on a issue during opening

6   statement, you'll have a chance to rebut that. But

7   right now, we don't have anything that really does

8   anything more then he -- he didn't -- he did in

9   opening his case. We don't have any evidence of it.

10   I've got to hear the evidence until I completely rule.

11   I'm cautious to get into any drug use by the defendant

12   in a case that deals with sexual exploitation.

13   So, with that, jurors ready? Okay, thank

14   you.

15   MR. JENSVOLD: Your Honor, Detective

16   Englander is here. He was going to sit in for part --

17   he would prefer to sit at the back right now unless

18   you want him up at the table.

19   THE COURT: Well, let's see. The rule has

20   been invoked.

21   MR. JENSVOLD: He is my case agent.

22   THE COURT: He is your case agent. Okay.

23   Then if he's your case agent, certainly can.

24   MR. JENSVOLD: Is it okay if he sits back

25   here, not at the case table until --

```
 1          THE COURT:  I don't mind that.  If he wants

 2    to sit in the back, that's fine.

 3          MR. JENSVOLD:  Okay.

 4          THE COURT:  He is here as your case agent.

 5          MR. JENSVOLD:  Okay, thank you.

 6          THE COURT:  Mr. Coghill, he's to be talking

 7    to you and so I don't want the reporter to have to

 8    pick up any kind of comments.  I understand your role

 9    and position really you're there but other than to

10    assist at his discretion or agreement of counsel.  So

11    not to be on the record.

12          (The following proceedings were held in open

13    court, in the presence of the jurors:)

14          THE COURT:  Sir, just retake the stand up

15    here.

16          Morning, please be seated.  We're here with

17    jurors, counsel and the defendant and we're continuing

18    with cross-examination of Mr. Franks who is on the

19    stand.  Mr. Lagattuta?

20          MR. LAGATTUTA:  Thank you, Your Honor.

21          Your Honor, if I can approach the witness?

22          THE COURT:  Sure.

23

24

25                    JACOB FRANKS,
```

SUPERIOR COURT, PIMA COUNTY

1 having been duly sworn, was examined and testified as

2 follows:

3   CROSS EXAMINATION

4 BY MR. LAGATTUTA:

5   Q.   I have what has been marked as Defendant's

6 Exhibit B and I want to show this to Mr. Franks.

7   Can you tell us what that document

8 describes, Mr. Franks?

9   A.   My conviction history.

10   Q.   Okay. On all right. And does it look

11 accurate to you the document that was provided to me

12 by the State?

13   A.   Yeah, yeah, it is pretty accurate.

14   Q.   Okay. Do you need to look at it anymore?

15   A.   No, I'm fine.

16   MR. LAGATTUTA: Your Honor, I would move for

17 admission of Defendant's Exhibit B which has been

18 described as it's a representation from the State of

19 what the defendant's actual prior convictions are.

20   THE COURT: Any objection?

21   MR. JENSVOLD: Objection, relevance and

22 foundation.

23   THE COURT: Would Counsel approach, please.

24   (The following proceedings took place at the

25 bench between Court and Counsel, out of the hearing of

SUPERIOR COURT, PIMA COUNTY

1   the jurors:)

2   MR. LAGATTUTA: Foundation, the State gave

3   it.

4   THE COURT: Well, but he's already testified

5   to it, so it's cumulative. If he's testified

6   inaccurately or you want to go over it's -- right now

7   we're being representative, so there is any question

8   about the three offenses, the times?

9   MR. LAGATTUTA: Your Honor, I went

10   meticulously through my notes the last couple days

11   when the State offered to bring out how many

12   convictions he had, he was a little unclear because

13   the actual time was it's uncertain he was -- how many

14   times he was in prison. This is just to clear it up.

15   This is a record given to me by the State. There's no

16   mistake about it. This is the official document.

17   It's relevant, it's just as if I drew it out on the

18   black board

19   THE COURT: Mr. Jensvold?

20   MR. JENSVOLD: The document is hearsay, it

21   shouldn't come in. He can ask him impeachment

22   questions about the dates and let him testify, but

23   booting the document is -- looks like it's an official

24   D.O.C. record when it's not.

25   MR. LAGATTUTA: Your Honor, well then, I

                    SUPERIOR COURT, PIMA COUNTY

1   need to make a record. I requested very early on in

2   the discovery phase we be given a certified Penpak,

3   certified record, that's what I got from the State.

4   I'm willing to accept it, that's what it is, I didn't

5   make this up, it came from them.

6   MR. JENSVOLD: This is not the same as

7   proving a prior conviction for a defendant.

8   THE COURT: Then, I'm going to not admit,

9   you can ask him each time whether this is accurate,

10 just lead him through each one. Let's get on with

11 this, taken a lot of time with it.

12   MR. LAGATTUTA: This is the problem, the

13 foundation of the document.

14   THE COURT: He admitted these are accurate,

15 just ask him, isn't it true -- were you convicted on

16 this offense at this time, this is what it is. You

17 know, all you get is the conviction, and -- and what

18 he was convicted of, burglary in the third degree on

19 -- and you were sentenced on 12/02, isn't that true

20 here in the Superior Court.

21   (The following proceedings were held in open

22 court, in the presence of the jurors:)

23   THE COURT: I'm going to not admit the

24 document but you can continue to use it for further

25 questions.

SUPERIOR COURT, PIMA COUNTY

1   MR. LAGATTUTA: Okay.

2   BY MR. LAGATTUTA:

3   Q.   Mr. Franks, promise this is the last time I

4   will ask you this, I just want to get those dates and

5   convictions straight. Maricopa County Superior Court,

6   burglary, third degree?

7   A.   What date?

8   Q.   CR-03020195?

9   MR. JENSVOLD: Objection.

10   THE COURT: Counsel, let's just -- just ask

11   him whether or not he was convicted on that date of

12   that particular offense, either going to admit it or

13   deny it.

14   BY MR. LAGATTUTA:

15   Q.   Sentencing date 12/2/03?

16   A.   Yeah.

17   Q.   Maricopa County Superior Court, burglary,

18   third degree, sentencing date 12/2/03?

19   A.   Yeah.

20   Q.   Maricopa County Superior Court, burglary,

21   two counts, sentencing 4/6/99?

22   A.   Yep.

23   MR. LAGATTUTA: That's all the questions I

24   have, Your Honor.

25   THE COURT: Okay. Anything -- are you done

SUPERIOR COURT, PIMA COUNTY

1   with the witness?

2   MR. LAGATTUTA: I'm done with the State's

3   witness, Your Honor.

4   THE COURT: Thanks. The State, redirect?

5

6   REDIRECT EXAMINATION

7   BY MR. JENSVOLD:

8   Q. Well, Mr. Franks, now, I think there was an

9   error in that last question. I'm going to show you

10 Defense Exhibit B. Look closely at the third part

11 there. Does that -- what's the sentencing date there?

12   A. Sentence to one year, Arizona Department of

13 Corrections.

14   Q. What's the date?

15   A. That was the day that I was actually

16 sentenced, okay 3/14/01 was when I was sentenced to

17 that year, the other date was probation, see what I'm

18 saying?

19   Q. What is -- what does it say the 1/18/99 date

20 is?

21   A. That's the date I had committed the offense

22 for this.

23   Q. So you were sentenced to one year to the

24 Department of Corrections on March 14th of 2001?

25   A. Uh-huh, yes.

                    SUPERIOR COURT, PIMA COUNTY

1   Q.   Is that the same offense that you talked

2   about yesterday where you had seven months back

3   credit --

4   A.   Yeah.

5   Q.   -- by Pima County Jail?

6   A.   Yes.

7   Q.   So you ended up serving about three months

8   or four months or something after -- in prison after

9   getting out, after being transferred from jail to

10 prison?

11   A.   Approximately from the sentencing date, the

12 14th until July 4th, 2001 when -- when they let me out

13 of there, so roughly three and a half months.

14   Q.   All right.   Now going back -- this is going

15 to go back to the argument between you and Mr. Coghill

16 on April 1st of 2003.   Do you recall an issue about

17 you possibly giving your first paycheck to Mr.

18 Coghill?

19   A.   During what time?

20   Q.   The argument about the job interview, that

21 Go-ped, all that stuff?

22   A.   Yeah, yeah.

23   Q.   Can you describe to the -- what that issue

24 was with your first paycheck?

25   A.   I was going to pay him back for the

1   destruction of his Go-pad with money that I would have

2   received from working at Hamilton.

3   Q.   Something that Mr. Coghill asked you to do?

4   A.   I'm not sure if -- I believe I brought it up

5   before he brought it up.

6   Q.   It was something -- was it something you

7   were going to agree to?

8   A.   Yes.

9   Q.   When you were living with Mr. Coghill in the

10   RV, Tucson and Phoenix, was anyone else ever living

11   there with you and Mr. Coghill?

12   A.   No one actually was officially living there,

13   every now and then my little brother would stay the

14   night, but that was about it. He just came over to

15   hang out with me pretty much.

16   Q.   How old is your little brother?

17   A.   At the time, I don't know, he's 22 now, so I

18   guess just have to go back a few years, probably 18,

19   19, 17, I'm not sure.

20   Q.   How many times would you guess he stayed the

21   night?

22   A.   Roughly four, five times.

23   Q.   Was he ever in the RV with you down in

24   Tucson?

25   A.   No, no.

1   Q.   In your various conversations with Mr.

2   Coghill, did he ever tell you anybody else had been

3   living there with him besides you?

4   A.   No.

5   Q.   What do you know about the Nero software

6   program?

7   A.   It's -- it's a software program that enables

8   you to burn CD's.

9   Q.   Did you know how to use that program?

10   A.   Yes.

11   Q.   And did Mr. Coghill know how to use that

12   program?

13   A.   Yes.

14   Q.   Have you ever seen Mr. Coghill use that

15   program?

16   A.   Yes.

17   Q.   Now, maybe we can since -- between the two

18   of us, we possibly confused things about these dates

19   when you were living up there.

20   You said yesterday during direct that you

21   had you remember living with Mr. Coghill in Phoenix in

22   the RV during the summer of 2002?

23   A.   Yes.

24   Q.   You said something about a townhouse that

25   you moved into in August of 2002?

1   A.   Yes.

2   Q.   Where was that townhouse?

3   A.   Off of North Phoenix, off of 29th Street

4   inbetween Greenway and Bell. I'm not sure what road,

5   between Paradise Lane, I believe. I don't remember

6   the name of them.

7   Q.   How long were you at that townhouse?

8   A.   I lived there until November when I because

9   -- I met this lady, this lady who had a couple kids,

10 whatever, she needed help with rent. She had an extra

11 room, so I ended up being her roommate, and it didn't

12 work out after November because she was getting

13 evicted anyway.

14   Q.   And then where did you go in November of

15 2002?

16   A.   I kind of lived out of my friend's car for

17 awhile. We went up to Flagstaff for a little bit,

18 came back to town, basically just lived out of his car

19 until -- I'm not sure, few months.

20   Q.   And then did you move back in with Mr.

21 Coghill in the RV some time after that?

22   A.   I believe it was either December or January.

23   Q.   Okay. Do you remember the specific day that

24 your grandfather passed away?

25   A.   January, I want to say January 20th, 2003.

```
 1   I believe that is the -- is right -- week before my
 2   cousin Nickie's birthday.
 3        Q.   Let me show you what is marked as State's
 4   Exhibit Two.  You had this document with you
 5   yesterday.  This is your interview transcript?
 6        A.   Uh-huh.
 7             THE COURT:  That's Plaintiff Two?
 8             MR. JENSVOLD:  Plaintiffs Two, yes, sir.
 9   BY MR. JENSVOLD:
10        Q.   Mr. Franks, can you turn to page 27 and look
11   at lines -- it's hard to tell, it must be 13 through
12   17, part of it is faded off at the left edge?
13        A.   Yes.
14        Q.   Is that what did you tell Detective Moretz
15   or Detective Englander in this case when your
16   grandfather died?
17        A.   January 20th.
18        Q.   And was that also the date that you moved
19   out of the RV?
20        A.   Yes.
21        Q.   Then the next time that you were ever in the
22   RV was at the end of March in Tucson?
23        A.   Yes.
24        Q.   I just wanted to show you some photographs,
25   Mr. Franks.  These are State's Exhibit 1K, 1GG, 1HH,
```

SUPERIOR COURT, PIMA COUNTY

1 1II, 1JJ, and 1KK. Let's start with 1K. Do you

2 recognize what is in that photograph?

3   A.   Yes.

4   Q.   Can you describe to the jury what it is?

5   A.   Computer with the scanner. There's a

6 printer, a CD rom drive, speakers, a zip drive, bunch

7 of CD spindles.

8   Q.   Where is this photograph taken?

9   A.   In the front of the motorhome inside, up

10 towards the front.

11   Q.   Does that look about the same condition as

12 when you were there in --

13   A.   Yeah.

14   Q.   -- end of March of 2003?

15   A.   Correct.

16   MR. LAGATTUTA: I'm going to object to this

17 line of questioning, outside the scope of

18 cross-examination. It's as if we started the direct

19 all over again.

20   THE COURT: I agree, sustained.

21   MR. JENSVOLD: I believe that's all I have,

22 thank you.

23   THE COURT: Do the jurors have any questions

24 for Mr. Franks? Write them out and then Peter will

25 collect them. Counsel, approach, please.

SUPERIOR COURT, PIMA COUNTY

1   (The following proceedings took place at the
2   bench between Court and Counsel, out of the hearing of
3   the jurors:)
4   THE COURT: I'll mark them, four, five and
5   six. You can read them, have you read them, give them
6   back and I'll go over them with you.
7   I'm just going to read the last part, okay.
8   Questions number six really -- really are for you as
9   far as what you present. If you want me to say
10   something, it's up to the people who present things.
11   MR. LAGATTUTA: I don't think you can answer
12   that.
13   MR. JENSVOLD: This question here, well, at
14   this point if my witness is going to be a little late,
15   I can go ahead, they can see the handwriting samples.
16   THE COURT: Here is the thing, it's for you
17   to decide when to publish this. If you want me to say
18   anything, what I will say, you know, about it, you can
19   take it up with -- the jurors sometimes like to see
20   what it is you're talking about.
21   THE COURT: What -- can you -- can you
22   define what is possession, just going to have to leave
23   that in the instructions. I might say -- I might say
24   that you'll get, you know, additional instructions at
25   the end of trial. Any objections to those?

SUPERIOR COURT, PIMA COUNTY

```
 1              MR. LAGATTUTA:  No, that's fine.

 2              THE COURT:  Okay.  Now then, number five,

 3   any objections to me asking him these questions?

 4              MR. JENSVOLD:  No.

 5              MR. LAGATTUTA:  Can I look at that question

 6   one more time.

 7              THE COURT:  Any objections?  Come a little

 8   closer.  I'll rephrase it, if he can answer.

 9              MR. LAGATTUTA:  Okay.

10              THE COURT:  No objections.  And number six,

11   any objections?  I think it was just -- maybe it was

12   something that was heard, re-ask.

13              MR. JENSVOLD:  I don't have any objection.

14              THE COURT:  Any objections?

15              MR. LAGATTUTA:  No.

16              THE COURT:  Okay, going to ask questions

17   five and six.

18              (The following proceedings were held in open

19   court, in the presence of the jurors:)

20              THE COURT:  We have a couple questions here,

21   one has to do with the things the lawyers know about,

22   and they may get to address it at some point.  And

23   I'll remind you that you will get additional

24   instructions at the end of the case, preliminary

25   instructions are the instructions I gave you with
```

SUPERIOR COURT, PIMA COUNTY

1 regard to the -- some definitions and elements you can
2 peruse those as you go along and look at those.

3 Then, a couple other questions here. The
4 questions here is, if you were -- Mr. Franks, if you
5 were willing to tell your father perhaps a brother and
6 female friend about child pornography, why didn't you
7 call the police earlier about it?

8 THE WITNESS: Because I was in prison and I
9 learned -- I was -- I want to say schooled in prison,
10 like learned the ropes in there by older people,
11 convicts, you're not supposed to rat on nobody, you're
12 not supposed to tell on anybody, just keep your mouth
13 shut, mind your own business. So that was kind of
14 like the mentality I had to break away from, so that's
15 why it took me so long.

16 THE COURT: Did you ask to use the Go-ped
17 scooter on the 31st of March.

18 THE WITNESS: I don't believe I did.

19 THE COURT: Had you been previously given
20 permission to use it?

21 THE WITNESS: Yes, previously.

22 THE COURT: On that date.

23 THE WITNESS: I don't think I asked him that
24 day.

25 THE COURT: Did you ever counsel Mr. Coghill

1   about -- against using or against having child
2   pornography.
3   THE WITNESS: I just told him he shouldn't
4   have that stuff, it ain't right.
5   THE COURT: When do you recall doing that?
6   THE WITNESS: Just like numerous -- I don't
7   have any specific dates because I probably said that
8   more than once.
9   THE COURT: Was it during the time you were
10   living in Phoenix or during time you were in Tucson.
11   THE WITNESS: Phoenix.
12   THE COURT: Ever mention it in Tucson?
13   THE WITNESS: I don't believe I did, I don't
14   know.
15   THE COURT: This was I think to ask a
16   question, maybe someone didn't hear your complete
17   answer to -- in response to a question about whether
18   you ever clicked on a file with child pornography.
19   Did you say it wasn't your computer?
20   THE WITNESS: Like you mean actually like
21   clicked on the folder it had the stuff in it? You
22   don't even know.
23   THE COURT: I think there was a question
24   that asked about whether or not you ever clicked on
25   child pornography on the computer or on the internet

1   while you were in -- let me just try to narrow it

2   down.

3   Did you ever click on pornography, child

4   pornography on the computer through the internet or

5   what you -- while you were in the RV that belonged --

6   THE WITNESS: There was probably a couple of

7   occasions where I thought something was something but

8   it was named something else and it came up maybe two

9   or three times. I would just go, oh, God, and click

10 it off, you know what I mean.

11   THE COURT: Who's computer?

12   THE WITNESS: Jim Coghill's.

13   THE COURT: When you did that, was it here

14 in Tucson or up in Phoenix.

15   THE WITNESS: Both, it happened both.

16   THE COURT: Let me just ask you, did you own

17 the computer in the RV?

18   THE WITNESS: No, I did not.

19   THE COURT: Follow up questions from that?

20 The state, from any of the questions that I asked?

21   MR. JENSVOLD: Yes, Your Honor.

22

23   REDIRECT EXAMINATION

24 BY MR. JENSVOLD:

25   Q. On one of those occasions that you clicked

                SUPERIOR COURT, PIMA COUNTY

                                                    411

1   on the child pornography, do you recall telling --

2   what you told Detective Moretz? Do you remember

3   describing --

4   A.   I don't remember what I said to him in my

5   interview. When I looked at the transcript it comes

6   back to me, but it's a long transcript, I haven't sat

7   there and read it.

8   Q.   Take a look at page eight of your transcript

9   there probably should be line 27 or 28. How did you

10 describe --

11   A.   Oh, repulsive.

12   MR. JENSVOLD: That's all I have, thank you.

13   THE COURT: Mr. Lagattuta?

14

15   RECROSS EXAMINATION

16

17 BY MR. LAGATTUTA:

18   Q.   Mr.. Franks, you answered some questions

19 about having seen images on the computer screen that

20 repulsed you, I guess was your last phrase. Do you

21 recall in this same interview that you gave with

22 Detective Englander that says you haven't seen any --

23 any of these things recently, you haven't seen any

24 since you been back in Tucson?

25   A.   Since I been back in Tucson.

1   Q.   Take a look at page seven of that report

 2 right there, almost to the bottom about four or five

 3 lines up from the bottom?

 4   A.   Yeah. And your question?

 5   Q.   My question is, are you telling the

 6 investigator right there in that -- in that interview

 7 that you had not seen any child pornography images

 8 since you were in Tucson?

 9   A.   Yeah, actually that's what I did say.

10   Q.   Okay. And last you told us in response to

11 one of the last question was, you didn't report Jim

12 Coghill to the police because I think, what you

13 described as a prison code. Was that -- was that a

14 code of ethics that you learned in prison about being

15 fair to another person?

16   A.   Yeah, well --

17   Q.   Is it?

18   A.   I -- I didn't really --

19   Q.   Let me ask you a question so I understand.

20 Is this based deeply in the -- in the feelings of

21 other prison inmates, is that where the prison code --

22   A.   Honestly, stuff like this is quite frowned

23 on, anybody who is like that who actually held any

24 code of ethics like that would have killed him.

25   Q.   But let me ask you this ethical -- this

SUPERIOR COURT, PIMA COUNTY

413

1   ethical code of conduct that you relied on to make

2   your decision one way or another was -- was gleaned

3   from listening to people who had been in prison,

4   invented what they believed to be their code of honor,

5   is that right?

6   A.   In a sense, yeah.

7   MR. LAGATTUTA: That's all the questions I

8   have.

9   THE COURT: I have one follow-up question,

10   I'm sorry, you all can follow up on this.

11   I understand that what you said that you at

12   least clicked on an image. I understand it to be at

13   least in Phoenix. It was child pornography. Now what

14   I'd like to know, I'm demonstrating my knowledge of

15   computers, what have you, when you clicked on that,

16   was that something that was on the screen on the --

17   through the internet or was it -- or was it based on a

18   disc that had been placed in the computer somehow?

19   THE WITNESS: It was either -- it was either

20   something that was on a CD that was placed in the CD

21   drive in the computer or something that was on the

22   actual hard drive of the computer.

23   THE COURT: Okay. So it was either -- it

24   wasn't off the internet either on hard drive or it --

25   was it was on a CD that was put in?

                SUPERIOR COURT, PIMA COUNTY

1   THE WITNESS: I never surf, I don't really

2 surf the web for stuff like that, I don't do that.

3   THE COURT: Now, did you put the CD in and

4 have it come up?

5   THE WITNESS: I never -- the only time I put

6 a CD in if it didn't had no writing on it, I look, but

7 I don't actually remember any times I done that and

8 actually had that stuff come up. So I wouldn't -- if

9 it didn't have my music stuff on it, I didn't mess

10 with it usually unless it was like a movie, like a

11 regular movie like Ghoastbusters, whatever --

12   THE COURT: Okay.

13   THE WITNESS: -- something like that.

14   THE COURT: What I'm trying to figure out if

15 it was either on a hard drive or CD.

16   THE WITNESS: Either a CD or hard drive.

17   THE COURT: You put the CD in, then have it

18 come up?

19   THE WITNESS: CD would already be in there.

20   THE COURT: Follow up questions on this,

21 Counsel? State?

22

23   REDIRECT EXAMINATION

24 BY MR. JENSVOLD:

25   Q.   How the CD would have been in the CD drive,

SUPERIOR COURT, PIMA COUNTY

415

1   was that in the computer itself, would that be a

2   portable CD?

3   A.   Yeah, external portable, not really

4   portable, but it's not built into the machine, so it's

5   external, not an internal.

6   Q.   It's connected to the computer?

7   A.   Yes, through cables, USB, whatever.

8   Q.   But there would be specific icon on the

9   computer where you can access the files that are on

10   the CD?

11   A.   Yeah, you just go up to the internet, not

12   the -- the thing, you know, the Explorer for Windows,

13   whatever, you can access the drives that way.

14   Q.   And it would have been -- you would have

15   clicked on something on that CD?

16   A.   Would have clicked the CD itself. It would

17   have showed you what it was in it, either folders or

18   files or both, you know.

19   MR. JENSVOLD: Thank you.

20   THE COURT: Mr. Lagattuta.

21

22   RECROSS EXAMINATION

23   BY MR. LAGATTUTA:

24   Q.   Mr. Franks, would that mean you never

25   yourself have handled any of those discs that had the

1   KP put on them?

2   A.   Actually handled the disc?

3   Q.   Handled --

4   A.   I might have handled them a couple times,

5   yes.

6   Q.   And in the spindle, the stack where those

7   discs were, is it possible you also handled a lot of

8   discs that were there, too, right?

9   A.   Probably handled all the discs because the

10 fact they -- they were not organized very well.

11   MR. LAGATTUTA: That's all the questions I

12 have.

13   THE COURT: Any further juror questions?

14 Okay thank you, sir. Here is one more, I'm sorry.

15   (The following proceedings took place at the

16 bench between Court and Counsel, out of the hearing of

17 the jurors:)

18   THE COURT: Okay, there are three questions

19 on number seven and I think that you are saying he

20 wouldn't be the person to answer any of them.

21   MR. LAGATTUTA: Exactly.

22   THE COURT: Then response to this, I will

23 just tell them that you are aware of and there will be

24 other evidence presented at some point in time that

25 would perhaps -- some of the questions asked, then I'm

1 going to mark here eight, another question, nine, and

2 Peter has number ten.

3 THE COURT: Go back to eight. Let me look

4 at eight. Any objection to eight?

5 MR. LAGATTUTA: No.

6 MR. JENSVOLD: No.

7 THE COURT: Any objections to nine?

8 MR. LAGATTUTA: No can I see the second part

9 of number eight there.

10 I think that calls for some kind of

11 speculation, I didn't see that part, I thought it was

12 just who put it in there. You could ask him, why did

13 he do it, almost sounds -- he is asked to speculate

14 just saying why.

15 MR. JENSVOLD: Just say, was he asked.

16 MR. LAGATTUTA: Or say, why did you do it?

17 If he has his own personal knowledge of that.

18 THE COURT: I'll rephrase it. Any

19 objections to eight or nine if I rephrase?

20 MR. LAGATTUTA: No, you can ask that.

21 THE COURT: No objection to ten? Okay,

22 thanks.

23 (The following proceedings were held in open

24 court, in the presence of the jurors:)

25 THE COURT: A few more questions in here,

SUPERIOR COURT, PIMA COUNTY

1 Mr. Franks. With the CD that was labeled "dirty," can

2 you tell me who put it in the computer.

3   THE WITNESS: The CD, that was before it was

4 labeled or after it was labeled.

5   THE COURT: Let's go -- when did you first

6 -- what did you do with -- give us -- tell us what

7 happened with regard to the CD that was labeled

8 "dirty"?

9   THE WITNESS: There was some files that were

10 questionable to me and I didn't like them where my

11 files were, so I asked him, what can we do about this?

12 Can we get rid of them? He said, go ahead and put a

13 blank CD and then burn them to a CD.

14   THE COURT: I have to understand, there were

15 files -- you mean they were on the computer in the

16 hard disc?

17   THE WITNESS: Yes, they were -- they were in

18 the folder where I have my music stuff in, I just had

19 a bad attitude that day probably, it was like, get

20 this crap off my folder.

21   THE COURT: So there was things in the

22 folder on the computer that you were using that you

23 had not put there.

24   THE WITNESS: Exactly.

25   THE COURT: Okay. And so who did you ask?

SUPERIOR COURT, PIMA COUNTY

1   THE WITNESS: Mr. Coghill.

 2   THE COURT: He said what to do about it,

 3 what did he tell you?

 4   THE WITNESS: He instructed me to get a

 5 blank CD, put it in the CD, the burner, take all the

 6 files and put them into the area where they can be

 7 burned on to that disc, delete the files and I asked

 8 him what to label it, he told me to label it the word,

 9 dirty.

10   THE COURT: Did you tell him what was on

11 those files?

12   THE WITNESS: He knew, he was sitting right

13 there.

14   THE COURT: Had seen the file with him?

15   THE WITNESS: I didn't open them or nothing

16 but the titles were right there.

17   THE COURT: He saw the titles.

18   THE WITNESS: Yes.

19   THE COURT: Both in Phoenix and in Tucson,

20 was it normal practice for you to place your CD on the

21 spindle with Mr. Coghill's?

22   THE WITNESS: Honestly, no, I had my own

23 little spindle. I would keep my stuff separate from

24 him. However, there was things like music videos and

25 like, well, basically every "X" Files episode known to

1 man, stuff like that that he had fixed in with other

2 stuff. If I wanted to look for something specific,

3 you know, specified, I can't talk -- you know, say I'm

4 looking for some "X" Files, I'm looking through --

5 looking through, oh, God, I'm looking through, I'm

6 seeing some of the stuff mixed in with it, you know

7 what I mean?

8   THE COURT: You had access to his -- to

9 his --

10   THE WITNESS: Yeah, he didn't have it

11 hidden, it was just sitting right out next to the

12 computer.

13   THE COURT: Had you your own spindle with

14 your own documents?

15   THE WITNESS: Yes.

16   THE COURT: And then final question here is,

17 did you ever see Mr. Coghill use Nero or another

18 program to burn child pornography to -- to a disc?

19   THE WITNESS: Yes.

20   THE COURT: And when and where did you see

21 that? I mean general times, Phoenix, Tucson?

22   THE WITNESS: Both, and on numerous

23 occasions.

24   THE COURT: Follow-up on these questions,

25 counsel. First, the State?

SUPERIOR COURT, PIMA COUNTY

```
 1

 2                    REDIRECT EXAMINATION

 3   BY MR. JENSVOLD:

 4        Q.   Mr. Franks, would you recognize -- do you

 5   remember what your spindle looked like?

 6        A.   It was a small CD spindle, I don't know how

 7   many discs it held, probably 50.  It was -- there's

 8   probably something similar in your evidence over

 9   there, but the date this all went down, I took mine

10   with me.

11        Q.   You took yours with you?

12        A.   They let me get all the stuff out of there.

13        Q.   Sheriff didn't confiscate --

14        A.   I'm sure they looked through it, but they

15   didn't take nothing.

16        Q.   So I was going to ask you if this spindle

17   that I showed you yesterday, this is State's

18   Exhibit 20?

19        A.   That was the size of mine.

20        Q.   But this is not yours?

21        A.   No.

22        Q.   This was not your spindle in the RV?

23        A.   No.

24        Q.   But this was your handwriting on the Star

25   Trek CD?
```

```
 1        A.    On that particular disc, yeah.

 2              MR. JENSVOLD:  I have nothing further.

 3              THE COURT:  Mr. Lagattuta?

 4

 5                    RECROSS EXAMINATION

 6    BY MR. LAGATTUTA:

 7        Q.    Mr. Franks, in the interview that you gave

 8    here to Detective Englander, you never mentioned in

 9    there that you had seen Mr. Coghill actually burn

10    child pornography onto a disc, isn't that right?

11        A.    Did he ask me this question?

12        Q.    My question to you is, in the entirety of

13    that interview, the entirety of all the times that you

14    talked to the police throughout this investigation,

15    you never once stated to them that you saw Mr.

16    Coghill, actually witness him burn child pornography

17    onto a CD, isn't that correct?

18        A.    I was never asked that question.

19        Q.    Never asked that question.  And today is

20    first time that you have volunteered that information

21    to any law enforcement agency or anybody other than --

22    this is the first time in this investigation you

23    revealed that information?

24        A.    As far as I know.

25              MR. JENSVOLD:  Your Honor, may I follow-up
```

1 on that?

2   MR. LAGATTUTA: I'm not done yet.

3   THE COURT: Thank you. Sure, go ahead.

4 BY MR. LAGATTUTA:

5   Q. Are you going to tell us today that you saw

6 Mr. Coghill label those CD's KP?

7   A. Honestly, I don't know, I don't pay

8 attention to what he was doing.

9   Q. Okay. So you're not willing to tell us that

10 you didn't witness him after he burned them write

11 anything on them, right? You never saw him write

12 initials -- let me finish, you saw him write the

13 initials KP on any disc during the entirety of the

14 time you were around him, isn't that correct?

15   A. I have no idea.

16   Q. Okay. You don't know -- the answer is, you

17 never saw him write it on it, right?

18   A. I might have seen it, maybe, I don't

19 remember. I have no freaking clue, sir.

20   Q. You never told any police officers, through

21 the course of this investigation, that you ever saw

22 Mr. Coghill label those discs KP, did you?

23   A. I don't think so, unless it's in this

24 transcript, I don't know.

25   Q. Well, it's not.

SUPERIOR COURT, PIMA COUNTY

1   A.   All right then.

2   Q.   When you say then that you witnessed Mr.

3   Coghill download child pornography at -- how many

4   instances, how many CD's can you attest to today that

5   you actually saw him use a program on that computer to

6   download child pornography?

7   A.   There was a program on there that was

8   specifically for that stuff.

9   Q.   How many times -- how many discs did you see

10 him actually manufacture?

11   A.   How many discs did I see him actually

12 manufacture that I knew for a fact was illegal child

13 pornography?

14   Q.   Correct?

15   A.   Probably like four or five.

16   Q.   And, again, this is the first time you ever

17 reported that specific information to anybody with

18 respect to the investigation in the case, isn't it?

19   A.   I'm new at this, you know, they never asked

20 me.

21   Q.   Did you actually view, during the course of,

22 you know, when these discs are -- are created, does

23 there have to be an image on the screen for the

24 information to be transferred from the computer to the

25 disc?

SUPERIOR COURT, PIMA COUNTY

425

```
1        A.    No.

2        Q.    How do you know what's on the discs?

3        A.    When they are labeled you will assume, so

4   this is all -- I guess that's based on assumption.

5        Q.    Assumption?

6        A.    So --

7        Q.    During the course of the time that you are

8   telling us now that you saw Mr. Coghill created this

9   child pornography during the course of the creation

10  these discs, you never saw from -- an image on the

11  screen what was actually transferred to the disc,

12  correct?

13       A.    No, if you were to look at the file names,

14  you were to click them open.

15       Q.    I didn't say if you were -- my question was,

16  during the portion of what you're describing as him

17  performing this creation of these discs, you never saw

18  any images on the screen during the course of the --

19       A.    No, I did not.  If I were to look -- say if

20  that was going down right now, I were to look over his

21  shoulder, I would see names and titles of the file by

22  whoever named them.  That was all I would see.  I

23  would not see any images.

24       Q.    You never saw any images of child

25  pornography on the screen?
```

1   A.   That is correct.

2   Q.   And what you're saying, you saw names of

3 files on the screen that later went into a disc?

4   A.   Yeah.

5   Q.   Okay. And when you created a disc, how

6 quickly do the files leave the screen, go through the

7 burning process on to the disc itself?

8   A.   With his burner, not that fast.

9   Q.   Not that fast. So slow enough you could

10 probably read what, 40, 50 images in a minute there?

11   A.   I have no idea, I don't know.

12   Q.   Okay. Aside from the discs that you say you

13 took from the -- from the motorhome, there were other

14 discs that over the years of -- of yours were still

15 there in the motorhome when you left in April of 2004,

16 is that right, 2003?

17   A.   They were my specific discs, they were

18 something I may have labeled.

19   Q.   Something you may have created?

20   A.   Yeah, but they weren't mine, just general

21 collection of -- of movies, Star Trek crap. I never

22 watched "X" Files, left behind. Star Trek, stuff like

23 that.

24   Q.   Some of stuff had been in there you created

25 or worked with it prior to you living down in the

1 motorhome in Tucson?

2   A.   Only reason I would ever create anything

3 because the hard drives were full of files so --

4   Q.   During the course of time when you were

5 there, you want to make some stuff, you move out,

6 leave some of -- of the things there, when you moved

7 back, you wouldn't have to carry them back and forth?

8   A.   I'm sure you go through there discs with

9 movie videos I made in there, but I had no use for

10 them. I didn't have a computer, I didn't have a DVD

11 player. I left them behind.

12   MR. LAGATTUTA: That's all the questions I

13 have.

14   THE COURT: I just want to tell you that

15 there was at least one question that had several parts

16 to it that Counsel know about, but there are going to

17 be other witnesses to address certain things, so they

18 know about those questions.

19   MR. JENSVOLD: Your Honor, may I follow-up?

20   THE COURT: Well, kind of -- of had your

21 chance.

22   MR. JENSVOLD: Your Honor, I mean there's

23 factual errors on a couple of these things.

24   THE COURT: All right, one last time.

25   MR. LAGATTUTA: Your Honor, the witness

1   didn't give a factual contradiction.

2   THE COURT: We're really done, Mr. Jensvold.

3   MR. JENSVOLD: Factual errors.

4   THE COURT: You each get a chance after he

5   speaks and to do the follow-up. We're not going to go

6   on anymore. So without any further questions.

7   Thank you for your testimony, Mr. Franks,

8   you are excused for now. The State will tell you

9   whether they need to keep you available.

10   THE WITNESS: All right. Thank you, Your

11 Honor.

12   THE COURT: Hand me those exhibits, pass

13 them back. Thank you.

14   MR. JENSVOLD: The State calls Deputy Judd.

15

16   JACE JUDD,

17 having been duly sworn, was examined and testified as

18 follows:

19   DIRECT EXAMINATION

20 BY MR. JENSVOLD:

21   Q. Deputy, could you introduce yourself to the

22 jury?

23   A. Jace Judd.

24   Q. And it should be obvious, who do you work

25 for?

```
 1        A.    I work for the Pima County Sheriff's

 2   Department.

 3        Q.    And how long have you been there?

 4        A.    Since September of '95.

 5        Q.    And what are your general duties?

 6        A.    I work the San Xaiver District Patrol.

 7        Q.    And what district were you working in April

 8   of 2003?

 9        A.    San Xaiver.

10        Q.    Do you recall a call out around 7:30 in the

11   morning on April 1st of 2003?

12        A.    Yes.

13        Q.    What was the nature of the call?

14        A.    An anonymous male had called the -- oh

15   called 911 to report that someone he was living with

16   was in possession of child pornography.

17        Q.    Where did you go?

18        A.    I went to the Circle K located at Benson

19   Highway and Country Club, not sure of the exact --

20   where the anonymous male eventually agreed to meet us

21   there.

22        Q.    And who was there when you got there?

23        A.    Mr. Franks.

24        Q.    Anyone else?

25        A.    Deputy Schupbach.
```

```
 1      Q.   Had Deputy Schupbach arrived before you?

 2      A.   Yes.

 3      Q.   Did you talk to Mr. Franks?

 4      A.   Briefly, yes.

 5      Q.   What did Mr. Franks tell you?

 6      A.   He said that his roommate, James Coghill --

 7           MR. LAGATTUTA:  Objection, hearsay.

 8           THE COURT:  Sustained.

 9           MR. JENSVOLD:  Your Honor, may we approach?

10           THE COURT:  Sure.

11           (The following proceedings took place at the

12      bench between Court and Counsel, out of the hearing of

13      the jurors:)

14           MR. JENSVOLD:  Well, part of it is rebuttal

15      evidence because in Mr. -- Deputy Judd's report he

16      says that indeed Mr. Franks told him that he knew

17      about child pornography labeled KP.  Mr. Lagattuta

18      just inferred, implied in his questions to Mr. Franks.

19      Mr. Franks never told anyone that he did, that he knew

20      about KP, he told he -- told Deputy Judd.

21           MR. LAGATTUTA:  I asked Franks on the stand

22      if he ever saw Mr. Coghill label a disc.  It's

23      cumulative evidence.  We heard it three, four times.

24           THE COURT:  State your question again.

25           MR. JENSVOLD:  Mr. Lagattuta is changing the
```

SUPERIOR COURT, PIMA COUNTY

1 nature of -- of his questions at this point, in my

2 opinion, in his question to Mr. Franks during the

3 follow-up to the jurors questions, you never told

4 anybody about seeing discs labeled KP, seeing them

5 write KP, wasn't just write KP on the disc.

6   THE COURT: Follow this up with --

7 consistent of -- of Franks, you believe it was -- was

8 impeached by cross-examination by Lagattuta.

9   Well, on that basis jury is to determine the

10 nature of -- of the questions. I'll allow it. So

11 overrule the objection.

12   (The following proceedings were held in open

13 court, in the presence of the jurors:)

14 BY MR. JENSVOLD:

15   Q.   Deputy Judd, did Mr. Franks tell you?

16   A.   He told me that his roommate Coghill had

17 child -- child pornography in his RV.

18   Q.   Did he tell you anything specific about

19 labels or CD's?

20   A.   Yes. I asked him how he knew it was child

21 pornography, he stated that there were kids ranging

22 from four years old to 17 years old on the videos and

23 that the discs were labeled KP, letters K and P

24   THE COURT: Will counsel approach for a

25 minute, I want to ask counsel. Approach for a minute,

SUPERIOR COURT, PIMA COUNTY

432

1 please.

2   (The following proceedings took place at the

3 bench between Court and Counsel, out of the hearing of

4 the jurors:)

5   THE COURT: I'll give an omitting

6 instruction, he went farther in the question then I

7 expected. I'll give a limiting instruction, ages and

8 stuff like that aren't something that -- for him to

9 testify to, that's beyond, so do you want a limiting

10 instruction.

11   MR. LAGATTUTA: Yeah, you want to do it

12 right now?

13   THE COURT: Yeah, I think it's probably --

14 do it.

15   THE COURT: Okay. There's the question in

16 this case was asked for a limited.

17   (The following proceedings were held in open

18 court, in the presence of the jurors:)

19   THE COURT: I'm going to strike, you may not

20 consider the testimony of this officer that Franks

21 said that there were kids on the video the ages four

22 to 17. You may consider the testimony that the

23 officer gave only as to whether or not there was a

24 prior consistent or inconsistent statement to Mr.

25 Franks with regard to the label being of the discs KP.

1   BY MR. JENSVOLD:

2   Q.   After you talked to Mr. Franks, where did

3   you go?

4   A.   To Mr. Franks' address which --

5   Q.   Mr. Franks' address?

6   A.   I'm sorry, Mr. Coghill's address.

7   Q.   Where was that?

8   A.   I'm not sure of the exact numbers.

9   Q.   Did you write a report in this case?

10   A.   Yes, I did.

11   MR. LAGATTUTA: Stipulate to the address if

12   you want to give it to him.

13   THE COURT: Go ahead and stipulate to the

14   address, have him go ahead and testify to it.

15   BY MR. JENSVOLD:

16   Q.   Deputy, was the address 356 East Benson

17   Highway?

18   A.   Yes.

19   Q.   What was the area like, describe it to the

20   jury, please?

21   A.   It's a small trailer park where you can --

22   you can put RV's or small camp trailers and a little

23   maybe a one or two acre lot.

24   Q.   And did you speak with Mr. Coghill?

25   A.   Yes.

```
 1      Q.    How did you first see Mr. Coghill?

 2      A.    I knocked on his door of his RV and he

 3 answered the door.

 4      Q.    And is Mr. Coghill in the courtroom today?

 5      A.    Yes, he is.

 6      Q.    Can you point him out for the record?

 7      A.    Mr. Coghill is seated at the defense table

 8 wearing a gray suit and a red tie.

 9            MR. JENSVOLD:  Your Honor, may the record

10 reflect the witness has identified the defendant?

11            THE COURT:  Yes.

12 BY MR. JENSVOLD:

13      Q.    Now, what did you do when you first started

14 to speak with Mr. Coghill?

15      A.    I introduced myself and asked him if I could

16 speak with him inside his RV.

17      Q.    And did he say, yes?

18      A.    Yes.

19      Q.    And you and Officer Schupbach were there?

20      A.    Yes.

21      Q.    Then what happened?

22      A.    We walked inside his RV.  Mr. Coghill sat

23 down, and I asked him questions regarding his

24 relationship with Jacob Franks.

25      Q.    And what did he tell you?
```

SUPERIOR COURT, PIMA COUNTY

435

1   A.   He said that they were roommates and that he

2   had been living there for, I believe, a couple of

3   months.

4   Q.   Okay. Are you certain that he told you two

5   months?

6   A.   Yes, two months.

7   Q.   And just so when you're interviewing -- when

8   you interviewed Mr. Coghill then, were you taking any

9   notes?

10   A.   No.

11   Q.   And what did you do as far as writing a

12   report from your involvement in the case?

13   A.   The notes that I took in this case were

14   simply Mr. Coghill's name, date of birth, address,

15   social security number, things of that nature,

16   identifying information, the rest of the information

17   in my report was from memory.

18   Q.   Okay. Do you know when you dictated your

19   report?

20   A.   I don't, it should be at the top of the

21   report though.

22   Q.   I'm going to show you what is marked State's

23   Exhibit Four, does that help to refresh your memory

24   about when you dictated the report?

25   A.   At 11 minutes after 10:00.

1   Q.   A.M.?

2   A.   A.M.

3   Q.   Is that on what date?

4   A.   April 1st, 2000 -- correction, April 3rd,

5   2003. Correction -- yeah, April 1st.

6   Q.   Okay. So you dictated it April 1st, 2003 at

7   10:11 A.M.?

8   A.   Yes.

9   Q.   Okay. And you arrived at Mr. Coghill's

10 place about what time?

11   A.   At approximately 7:30.

12   Q.   Now, was the time that you were dispatched

13 to the call?

14   A.   I believe I was dispatched about 7:30; yes.

15   Q.   Okay. Then how much time between the time

16 you were dispatched to the time you went to Mr.

17 Coghill's place?

18   A.   I can't say for sure, I know I had to -- if

19 I had a radiolog, an actual radiolog of my activity I

20 could give you a better idea. But I had to first

21 respond to the Circle K at Country Club and Benson

22 Highway. I had to speak with Jacob Franks, and then I

23 had to respond further east to Benson Highway to Mr.

24 Coghill's home.

25   Q.   Okay. If you could just give a rough

SUPERIOR COURT, PIMA COUNTY

1   estimate how much time you think that took?

2   A.   Rough estimate is maybe 15 or 20 minutes.

3   Q.   Now, what else did you ask Mr. Coghill?

4   A.   I asked if he was in possession of any child
5   pornography.

6   Q.   What did he tell you?

7   A.   He said, no.

8   Q.   Did you ask him specifically about the stuff
9   that you had been told by Franks about KP?

10   A.   Yes.

11   Q.   What did you ask him?

12   A.   I asked if he had any child pornography on
13   the discs on -- on the computer discs. He said, no.
14   I asked if I could look at his computer discs which
15   were in plain view. He said, yes. I asked him what
16   the KP meant on the disc that I could see which was on
17   a spindle, and he said he didn't know what that meant
18   and that he didn't write that KP on there.

19   Q.   Did he say anything else about who might
20   have written that on there?

21   A.   He said since some of them are Jacob's, I
22   assuming referring to Jacobs Franks, that he may have
23   written KP on there.

24   Q.   Did Mr. Coghill actually say that Jacob must
25   have written them on there?

SUPERIOR COURT, PIMA COUNTY

```
1              MR. LAGATTUTA:  Objection, leading.

2              THE COURT:  Sustained.

3    BY MR. JENSVOLD:

4         Q.   Are you confident about just the distinction

5    between, may, is that the correct word, if you

6    remember?

7         A.   He said some of them are Jacobs, and he must

8    have written KP on them.

9         Q.   Now, did you physically handle any of the

10   CD's themselves?

11        A.   I don't recall whether I handled them or

12   not.  I know I looked down on the top CD and saw the

13   KP was written on it.

14        Q.   And you didn't have to move any other CD's

15   around to see one that was labeled KP?

16        A.   No.

17        Q.   Did that case have like a little plastic

18   cover over it if you remember?

19        A.   I don't remember.

20        Q.   And did you make any decision about

21   arresting Mr. Coghill while you were there?

22        A.   No.

23        Q.   Did you basically turn over the

24   investigation to other detectives at some point?

25        A.   Yes.
```

```
 1        Q.    Deputy Judd, I want to show you a few

 2    photographs.  These have been marked as exhibits 1K

 3    and then 1GG, 1 --

 4             THE COURT:  Can you do one at a time because

 5    if you're going to have a description of each, it's

 6    easier for us to run it through that way, give us all

 7    the numbers just kind of hard to keep up with because

 8    then you're going back one, individually also.

 9    BY MR. JENSVOLD:

10        Q.    Let's start with 1K, do you recognize that

11    photograph?

12        A.    Yes.

13        Q.    And what is it?

14        A.    That is the interior of Mr. Coghill's RV.

15        Q.    And what specifically does it show?

16        A.    His computer area with the computer and disc

17    spindles.

18        Q.    Is that in the same condition as you

19    arrived?

20        A.    Yes.

21        Q.    And State's Exhibit 1GG, do you recognize

22    that?

23        A.    Not specifically.

24        Q.    Okay, we'll move on?

25        A.    I don't.
```

SUPERIOR COURT, PIMA COUNTY

1   Q.   How about 1HH?

2   A.   Yes.

3   Q.   Okay. What does that show?

4   A.   Also the interior of Mr. Coghill's RV.

5   Q.   Okay. And then 1II?

6   A.   Yes.

7   Q.   What is that?

8   A.   The interior of Mr. Coghill's RV leading

9   back to the bedroom area, kitchen and bedroom area.

10   Q.   And 1JJ?

11   A.   Yes.

12   Q.   What's that?

13   A.   That's the interior of Mr. Coghill's RV

14   looking from the bedroom up toward the living room

15   area.

16   Q.   And finally 1KK?

17   A.   Yes.

18   Q.   What's that?

19   A.   That's Mr. Coghill's RV parked in the RV

20   park.

21   Q.   Do all of those photographs look like they

22   are the same condition as when you saw them?

23   A.   Yes.

24   MR. JENSVOLD: The State moves for admission

25   of 1K, 1HH, 1II, 1JJ, and 1KK.

```
 1          THE COURT:  Any objection?

 2          MR. LAGATTUTA:  No objection at all, Your

 3   Honor.

 4          THE COURT:  Okay admit 1K, 1HH, 1II, 1JJ,

 5   and 1KK.  Thank you.

 6   BY MR. JENSVOLD:

 7      Q.   And did you have any other involvement in

 8   this case?

 9      A.   Other than an interview with Mr. Coghill's

10   attorney, no.

11          MR. JENSVOLD:  That's all I have, thank you.

12          THE COURT:  Cross?

13          MR. LAGATTUTA:  Thank you.

14                  CROSS EXAMINATION

15   BY MR. LAGATTUTA:.

16      Q.   Deputy Judd, how are you today?

17      A.   Well, thank you.

18      Q.   Good.  When you got this call you went down

19   to meet Jacob Franks, what was your first impression

20   of him when you saw him?  By that I mean, physically,

21   how did he look?

22      A.   Can you be more specific?

23      Q.   Well, Deputy Schupbach, you're familiar with

24   her, aren't you?

25      A.   Yes.
```

1   Q.   She arrived before you did to meet with Mr.

2   Franks?

3   A.   Yes.

4   Q.   Okay. She gave us a description what she

5   thought he looked like when she saw him. When you

6   first met him, this is person that you're meeting on

7   the street to report maybe a crime to you, what were

8   your impressions how he looked physically? Display

9   any outward motion, anything like that, just basic

10   physical description.

11   A.   You're asking for physical description and

12   emotional description?

13   Q.   Let's start with the physical description?

14   A.   Okay. Young, white man, not particularly

15   clean, which is not uncommon for the appearance of an

16   individual who lives where I work.

17   Q.   Well, okay. Did he appear agitated?

18   A.   He appeared a bit nervous.

19   Q.   Did he appear upset?

20   A.   Not particularly.

21   Q.   Did he appear desperate in anyway?

22   A.   No.

23   Q.   All right. In the course of speaking with

24   him, did -- did you understand that the reason he knew

25   that there was this illegal material in Mr. Coghill's

1 motorhome was because he himself had lived there for a

2 period of time? Did you ever understand that from

3 him?

4   A.   I assumed that by his statement that he was

5 a roommate that, yes, he had lived there.

6   Q.   You assumed that. Did you go into that in

7 any depth with him how long he had been a roommate,

8 what the terms of their living situation was?

9   A.   No, I just assumed that being a roommate

10 would connotate living together with someone.

11   Q.   Okay. All right. And did you make any

12 inquiry how long the two of them had been roommates?

13   A.   With Mr. Franks?

14   Q.   Yes.

15   A.   No.

16   Q.   No? Why didn't you do that?

17   A.   It wasn't the utmost pressing issue at that

18 time.

19   Q.   Okay. But it had been something that might

20 have been of a clue to provide you some other leads to

21 further investigations?

22   MR. JENSVOLD: Objection, speculation.

23   THE COURT: Overruled.

24   THE WITNESS: Can you restate your question?

25 BY MR. LAGATTUTA:

SUPERIOR COURT, PIMA COUNTY

```
 1      Q.    Might that have asking that question might
 2   that have proved later maybe to be a clue to finding
 3   out further information with respect to this
 4   investigation?
 5      A.    Actually, with the limited information that
 6   I had at that time, I was satisfied that they were
 7   roommates.
 8      Q.    Okay.  And the length of time that they
 9   lived together was not important to you?
10      A.    Not at that time.
11      Q.    Okay.  All right.  So you proceed over to
12   the motorhome where Mr. Coghill lives.  And when you
13   get there, you arrive -- you arrive on foot or you in
14   a squad car?  How do you get there?
15      A.    I drove.
16      Q.    Okay.  And so did Deputy Schupbach?
17      A.    Yes.
18      Q.    Drove separately?
19      A.    Correct.
20      Q.    And you entered -- when you entered the
21   motorhome, you knocked on the door and Mr. Coghill
22   came?
23      A.    Yes.
24      Q.    And when -- and he let you in freely?
25      A.    Correct.
```

SUPERIOR COURT, PIMA COUNTY

1   Q.   And when he came -- when you came in, did
2   you come in before Deputy Schupbach?
3   A.   I don't know.
4   Q.   Do you remember you have to step up, take a
5   couple steps up to get in this motorhome, do you
6   recall this at all?
7   A.   Yes, yes.
8   Q.   Okay. Well, do you recall once you got into
9   the motorhome where you, you know, stationed yourself
10   as far as -- where were you standing?
11   A.   As you enter, a motorhome space is limited,
12   and I stood, oh, a foot or two to the right of the
13   entry way of the motorhome.
14   Q.   All right. And did you think maybe Deputy
15   Schupbach might have been in the interior of the
16   motorhome more towards where the sleeping area is?
17   A.   I don't know.
18   Q.   You don't know?
19   A.   I don't remember where she was standing.
20   Q.   Okay.
21   THE COURT: I want to make a correction to
22   an exhibit marked yesterday. There was an exhibit I
23   think defense exhibit -- we called it H yesterday in
24   fact it was A. And so if you have in your notes
25   anything before Exhibit H it was K, we called it K

SUPERIOR COURT, PIMA COUNTY

446

1   yesterday and it is in fact A. It's been remarked as

2   A, and that was admitted yesterday.

3   BY MR. LAGATTUTA:

4   Q.   Okay. Deputy Judd, would you mind taking a

5   look at this photo?

6   A.   Sure.

7   Q.   And this is what the Court has just

8   described as Defense Exhibit A that's been remarked,

9   okay. What do you see there?

10   A.   I see the interior of Mr. Coghill's RV.

11   Q.   Okay, that's pretty -- pretty right up view,

12   you can see pretty much, you know, everything that's

13   looking ahead of you towards the front of the

14   motorhome?

15   A.   Yes.

16   Q.   Okay. You see those two stacks of discs in

17   there?

18   A.   Actually I see one, two, three, four, five

19   six.

20   Q.   Okay. Look over by the computer where --

21   you know what a scanner is, don't you?

22   A.   Yes.

23   Q.   Look on top of scanner, what do you see?

24   A.   Two spindles of CD's.

25   Q.   Aha, okay. Now, when you -- your testimony

1 was that you went over there because you had this

2 information that there might be a -- there was CD's

3 there or present in the motorhome that were marked

4 with the letters KP, correct?

5   A.   I'm sorry, could you re-ask the question?

6   Q.   Okay. Your testimony is that when you went

7 over -- went over to the motorhome, Jim Coghill's

8 motorhome, you've already been given information you

9 would find there, some CD's that were marked KP,

10 labeled with letters KP, right?

11   A.   That was the information that I received,

12 yes.

13   Q.   Okay. And I think you just told us that

14 when you went into the motorhome you saw in plain view

15 a stack of CD discs on the top the disc was labeled

16 KP, isn't that right?

17   A.   I testified that I could see the stacks of

18 discs.

19   Q.   Right.

20   A.   Now, until I asked if I could look at them,

21 I could not tell if they were labeled KP.

22   Q.   Okay. Tell us what he looked at?

23   A.   Which time?

24   Q.   When you found the disc that was labeled KP

25 I think you told us earlier you saw it sitting on top

1 of a stack of discs on a spindle?

2   A.   I asked Mr. Coghill if I could look at his

3 CD's.

4   Q.   Okay.

5   A.   He said, sure.

6   Q.   All right.

7   A.   I walk over, because I clearly wouldn't be

8 able to see them from where I was standing.

9   Q.   Exactly.

10   A.   So I walked over, looked down and there's KP

11 written on the disc.

12   Q.   The disc -- this disc is just sitting on top

13 of a spindle on top of a stack?

14   A.   Yes.

15   Q.   Okay. Where is the stack sitting, can you

16 find it in that picture?

17   A.   Are you asking me which stack had KP written

18 on it?

19   Q.   That's what I'm asking.

20   A.   I don't know, I don't know if it was this

21 stack, this stack or which one.

22   Q.   Okay. But you're sure that you walked over

23 and looked on top and this disc was sitting on top of

24 a stack?

25   A.   Yes.

```
 1       Q.   Okay.  Let me --

 2            MR. LAGATTUTA:  Your Honor, may I approach

 3  the witness?

 4            THE COURT:  Sure, sure.

 5  BY MR. LAGATTUTA:

 6       Q.   This is Defendant's Exhibit D, can I show

 7  you this?

 8       A.   Sure.

 9            MR. JENSVOLD:  Counsel, may I see the

10  photograph?

11            MR. LAGATTUTA:  Oh, I'm sorry.

12            THE COURT:  That's -- what exhibit is that?

13  Defense Exhibit D, okay.

14  BY MR. LAGATTUTA:

15       Q.   What -- okay tell -- tell me what you see

16  when you look at that?

17       A.   I see a spindle of CD's next to what appears

18  to be packaged evidence.

19       Q.   Okay.  And there's a disc on top of that

20  spindle of CD's, right?

21       A.   Correct.

22       Q.   Correct.  And can you read what's written on

23  top of the CD that's on top of that spindle?

24       A.   No.

25       Q.   Does it look like the word, dirty?
```

1   A.   Could be.

2   Q.   Okay. That's not the disc that you think

3   you saw that said KP?

4   A.   That's a confusing question.

5   Q.   I'm trying -- you know, I'm confused, I'm

6   trying to --

7   A.   Okay.

8   Q.   You told us you saw a disc that was sitting

9   on top of a spindle and that disc was labeled KP?

10   A.   Yes.

11   Q.   Right. Okay. Now, I'm showing you a

12 spindle of discs and on top of -- top CD is written

13 the word, dirty?

14   A.   Okay.

15   Q.   Okay. We already had testimony in the case

16 about that dirty disc, where it came from and the fact

17 that it was part of the discs in the motorhome, okay?

18   A.   Okay.

19   Q.   Now, what I'm going to tell you --

20   THE COURT: Now, wait a minute, wait a

21 minute, please ask a question. If your question is

22 whether or not he saw dirty on one of those, let's

23 just ask him that, we don't have to have your

24 testimony refreshing.

25 BY MR. LAGATTUTA:

SUPERIOR COURT, PIMA COUNTY

451

1   Q.   When you look at Defendant's Exhibit A,
2 again, the two -- I direct your attention to two
3 stacks of CD's that are on top of the scanner?
4   A.   Yes.
5   Q.   Okay. Does that stack of CD's that you're
6 looking at in that picture resemble this second stack
7 that's in the photo?
8   A.   Yes, it resembles that stack.
9   Q.   Can you tell us whether or not they are in
10 fact the same stack?
11   A.   No, I can not.
12   Q.   So can you, can you look in that photo and
13 show us any other stack that might be the stack of
14 CD's where you saw the one that was labeled KP on the
15 top?
16   A.   I want to make sure I understand your
17 question. You're asking me if this stack of CD's
18 might resemble any other stack in this photograph.
19   Q.   You know what I'm asking you, if that stack
20 of CD's with the dirty disc on top is in fact this
21 stack right here, the second taller one that's on top
22 of the scanner?
23   A.   I believe you just asked me that.
24   Q.   Yeah.
25   A.   I said, I don't know.

SUPERIOR COURT, PIMA COUNTY

1   Q.   You don't know that?

2   A.   I don't know if these -- if this stack of

3   CD's is -- is that stack, I don't.

4   Q.   You don't know that?

5   A.   I don't know that.

6   Q.   So now I'm asking you, when you look in the

7   defense picture here, Defense Exhibit A, you see other

8   stacks of spindles of CD's, right, in other areas in

9   the motorhome?

10   A.   I see six stacks of CD's.

11   Q.   Okay. Can you identify which of those six

12 had the disc marked KP sitting on top of it?

13   A.   No.

14   Q.   You can not?

15   A.   I can not.

16   Q.   Okay. Wouldn't that have been something you

17 would have written down in your report as being an

18 important element of the investigation in the case as

19 to which spindle that disc was found on?

20   MR. JENSVOLD: Objection, argumentative.

21   THE COURT: Overruled.

22   THE WITNESS: I don't recall exactly how

23 many discs or stacks of discs were in Mr. Coghill's

24 motorhome. I believe in our attorney interview I told

25 you I don't know how many discs were in there.

SUPERIOR COURT, PIMA COUNTY

453

1   BY MR. LAGATTUTA

2   Q.   Right.

3   A.   Now, with that information, not knowing

4   exactly how many discs there were, I wouldn't have

5   been able to label which spindle had the CD on it.

6   Q.   You can't even tell me where it was by

7   looking at that picture, can you?

8   A.   Where was?

9   Q.   The disc -- the stack of discs that you say

10 had the KP disc on top of, you can't --

11   A.   No, I can't -- I can't tell you which stack

12 had KP on it.

13   Q.   So, in the course of -- and when you go over

14 you believe this a disc labeled KP is -- is an

15 important piece of evidence, right?

16   A.   There was an allegation.

17   Q.   Right.

18   A.   That child porn was located on a disc with

19 KP written on it.

20   Q.   Okay. So now you go over into the motorhome

21 you find what you believe is a stack of discs with

22 this KP on it which is an allegation of the existence

23 of child pornography, and you don't write down in your

24 report exactly where you found it?

25   A.   No.

SUPERIOR COURT, PIMA COUNTY

1   Q.   Okay. So what did you do after you saw the

2   disc?

3   A.   I asked --

4   Q.   By the way, when you saw it, was it in Mr.

5   Coghill's hand or was it in your hand?

6   MR. JENSVOLD: Objection, compound question.

7   THE COURT: Sustained.

8   BY MR. LAGATTUTA:

9   Q.   Whose hand was it when you saw it? Where

10 was the disc when you saw it?

11   A.   In a spindle.

12   Q.   Okay. All right. What did you do when you

13 saw it?

14   A.   I -- if I can refer to my report I asked

15 what KP stood for.

16   Q.   Aha, and then what happened?

17   A.   Mr. Coghill said, I don't know, some of

18 those aren't mine.

19   Q.   All right. Okay, okay I understand that.

20 What did you do after that? He gives you an answer,

21 then what do you do?

22   A.   I said, okay, and I asked him other

23 questions.

24   Q.   Okay. And while you were doing this where

25 was the disc? Was it still in the same place? Did

SUPERIOR COURT, PIMA COUNTY

1   you touch it? Did you move it?

2   A.   I didn't move it.

3   Q.   Okay. You still even looked at that picture

4   then after these questions, don't remember where it

5   was?

6   A.   I remember all the spindles of CD's being in

7   this area of the motorhome.

8   Q.   Okay. All right. After your questioning

9   him, what did do you?

10   A.   After questioning Mr. Coghill?

11   Q.   Yeah.

12   A.   I asked him if he would be willing to speak

13   with detectives.

14   Q.   Okay. At any point in time did you take

15   this disc labeled KP and move it from the where you

16   saw it?

17   A.   No.

18   THE COURT: Actually this is probably a good

19   place to take a break and so we'll take our lunchtime

20   recess. It's 12:00 o'clock now, ask you all to be

21   back by 1:30. You can leave your books here, won't be

22   anybody in here during the -- during the lunch hour

23   and have you return at 1:30. See everybody back at

24   1:30.

25   I think what I'd like to do -- the jurors

SUPERIOR COURT, PIMA COUNTY

1 have left, I think that if we can come back at 1:20

2 and I could talk to Sergeant -- or Detective Englander

3 at that time I'll ask my questions of him and try to

4 sort out what he might go into later. I'd like to do

5 that without the jurors' presence.

6   MR. JENSVOLD: Your Honor --

7   THE COURT: Can you come back at 1:20?

8   MR. LAGATTUTA: I can.

9   MR. JENSVOLD: I believe so, I'll check with

10 Detective Englander. Defense counsel, I believe

11 opened the door here going into this -- how Deputy

12 Judd was supposed to know where this KP disc was. I

13 skirted around this based on the Court's rulings, but

14 Deputy Judd says in his report that he asked Mr.

15 Coghill about where the CD were and Mr. Coghill

16 pointed out to Deputy Judd, this one is pornography,

17 that's how he knew how to look for KP prior to that.

18 I think I skipped over what Mr. Coghill had told him.

19 Yeah, there's some adult pornography but no child

20 pornography, that's how Deputy Judd knew to look at

21 the disc, how he first saw it was KP.

22   THE COURT: Okay.

23   MR. LAGATTUTA: Your Honor, I didn't skirt

24 around anything. The reason I'm questioning Deputy

25 Judd, the other testimony in the case is that the disc

1   that's on top of the spindles is this dirty disc.

2   THE COURT: Well, you know --

3   MR. LAGATTUTA: I don't want to say this in

4   front of him because --

5   THE COURT: I don't want you to get into

6   saying that in front of him, he's out, I understand

7   you all have argument. You can go back and ask your

8   questions. I don't have the records to see what it is

9   that you're trying to get at. I'll make a ruling

10 after I talked to -- after I talked to Detective

11 Englander on questions you can ask him.

12   (The Court stood in recess.)

13   THE COURT: Let's see we're here with

14 defendant and counsel and Detective Englander is here.

15 I'd like you to come forward and be sworn and I need

16 ask you a couple questions. Actually, you can come

17 over here.

18

19   JEFFORD ENGLANDER,

20 having been duly sworn, was examined and testified as

21 follows:

22   THE COURT: Sir, I understand you're the

23 investigating officer in this case?

24   THE WITNESS: Yes.

25   THE COURT: What I'd like to know is whether

    1   names of files in this case that I found on the
    2   computer were very indicative of their contents
    3   potentially, they had words in them that would
    4   definitely lead one to believe there was child
    5   pornography there.
    6   THE COURT: Were they intermixed with files
    7   that would indicate they were just they were simply
    8   pornography?
    9   THE WITNESS: Yes, or files that by their
   10   name you couldn't make a determination.
   11   THE COURT: Knew it was pornography, but you
   12   didn't know whether this was child or not?
   13   THE WITNESS: Correct or maybe not even knew
   14   it was pornography, but it had a woman's name, a
   15   pornography star's name. I guess if you wouldn't --
   16   hadn't known that was a particular actress in
   17   pornography films, you wouldn't have known. There was
   18   some that you might not -- if you weren't familiar
   19   with the material, you might not have known it was
   20   pornography at all. I think that it probably would
   21   have been a fairly logical conclusion based on its
   22   surrounding contents the other files in the folder.
   23   THE COURT: When you talk about the
   24   surrounding contents in the file, what have you, I
   25   need to understand a little bit more about the kind of

SUPERIOR COURT, PIMA COUNTY

1   files you're talking about whether you're talking

2   about something that is on the internet, been

3   downloaded to the hard disc or is on a disc and

4   somehow added back to the computer to do from a disc.

5   Help me understand that in this case.

6   THE WITNESS: Okay. In this case there were

7   two different types of volumes that held files that I

8   was dealing, there were the hard drives on the

9   computer which were what the computer uses to hold all

10   of the files that are stored on the computer. And

11   then this computer had the ability to create CD's

12   which are also volumes, but they are much smaller in

13   size than these hard discs.

14   There were files on the hard drive, hard

15   drives, there were two on this computer, and then

16   there were files on the CD's. Child pornography files

17   were -- an indications of child pornography files were

18   in both places, on some of the CD's that we found, and

19   in some of the places on the hard drive. There were

20   also indications that files were on a hard drive that

21   had been deleted, but we can still see the indication

22   that the file was there. The file may not be there,

23   but it's title -- for example, if you have a book with

24   multiple chapters, table of contents there's the

25   actual chapter, you can remove the table of contents

1 and still see the chapter that's there or remove the
2 chapter and the main contents is still there.
3   So references to files may exist while the
4 file may not or the reference may not exist and the
5 file may, and that's specifically on the hard drive on
6 the CD, the files that were there were there. There
7 was no, no debate as to whether it was deleted or not.
8   THE COURT: Now, you found certain files on
9 discs also. Did you review the discs that you found,
10 you found either pornography or child pornography on?
11   THE WITNESS: I believe I reviewed all of
12 the discs, all the CD's.
13   THE COURT: Seen pictures, I think six
14 different sized cases with discs?
15   THE WITNESS: The vertical spindles. Yes,
16 each one that was labeled and I believe that was all
17 of them. There may have been a handful that were not
18 if they were commercially produced discs. Once you
19 write to most of these discs you can't change what's
20 on there. If it was commercially produced I don't
21 look at. All the others one that had potential to
22 have data put on there by a home user I looked at.
23   THE COURT: So you actually you -- did you
24 review just the titles or did you actually look at
25 what the contents?

1   THE WITNESS: The contents of the discs,

2   Judge.

3   THE COURT: And from that or any other way,

4   is there a way to -- to connect -- based on the

5   placement in the disc or otherwise, information that

6   would be differentiated between child pornography and

7   pornography? If somebody picked up one that was

8   pornography, would it lead to definite knowledge there

9   was child pornography associated with whatever area --

10   whatever it is you're look at?

11   THE WITNESS: Without putting a disc in the

12   computer and playing the files?

13   THE COURT: One way or other, I don't know.

14   THE WITNESS: If you put the disc and play

15   the file you saw a very young person engaged in sexual

16   activity, it probably be evident it was child

17   pornography. If you put it in and just looked at the

18   listing of the files on the CD, some of these files,

19   their names, that would be visible. Just by browsing

20   the contents of the disc would be indicative, some

21   would not necessarily, there were some, as I said, for

22   the hard drive, there are some file names that -- that

23   contained either ages or descriptions that would

24   indicate it was child pornography.

25   THE COURT: They were stored together?

1   THE WITNESS: Yes, yes. Now, just looking

2   physically at the compact disc you might or might not,

3   depending on the label, know what was on there. Some

4   of these were labeled with things that I think anyone

5   familiar with pornography could deduce.

6   THE COURT: Okay. I think I've asked the

7   questions I wanted to. I'll ask if either of you have

8   any questions with regard to what I'm getting at here.

9   I'm getting at the whole issue of intent and knowledge

10   and opportunity exceptions to misconduct under 404(B).

11   Mr. Jensvold?

12   DIRECT EXAMINATION

13   BY MR. JENSVOLD:

14   Q.   Mr. Englander, were there CD's that had both

15   adult and child pornography files on them?

16   A.   Yes.

17   Q.   Were the majority of the files, the CD's

18   that had child pornography, were they solely child

19   pornography?

20   A.   I believe so as far as the CD with the mix.

21   I would have to go back and look which once have -- I

22   know I made indications as to whether or not the files

23   had what I believed to be contraband on them. The mix

24   of them, I'm not entirely certain there may have been

25   files on the discs that contained child pornography

SUPERIOR COURT, PIMA COUNTY

463

1 that I wasn't able to determine if they were in fact

2 what I considered child pornography. I don't remember

3 if there was blatant adult pornography mixed with

4 blatant child pornography on the CD's.

5   Q.   Now, you reviewed the KaZaA log as well that

6 was left -- can you explain the KaZaA registry that

7 prints out in part of your report?

8   A.   KaZaA is as program used to trade files with

9 other people. It's along the line of Napster which

10 was publisized for his music sharing. KaZaA allows

11 you to share any kind of file. And one of the things

12 that it is used for is sharing video and picture

13 files. And through my experience as an online

14 investigator, we found that people were using KaZaA to

15 share and trade images of adult and child pornography.

16   When you utilize KaZaA to download movie

17 files or images to your computer, KaZaA keeps track of

18 the last, however many it's got a size of the file

19 where it's keeping track of what you download. And

20 when you download it and whether it's still available,

21 and it maintains a few different log files. Those

22 were included in this report.

23   However, those log files as new information

24 comes in, once that log file reaches it's maximum

25 size, it drops the last -- the oldest record off so it

1   only maintains a certain number of records or that's a

2   way to put certain number of records. As it receives

3   a new one, if it's full, it with will drop the oldest

4   record off. You don't have a complete history of the

5   downloads of KaZaA, you have a history of downloads of

6   KaZaA until that log file filled up and the oldest one

7   was deleted out.

8   Q.   And what was the oldest date on the KaZaA

9   registry, if you remember?

10   A.   I believe it was beginning of March '03 was

11 the oldest date I found, maybe 3/2, I would have to

12 check my notes but --

13   Q.   Do you have notes or would your report?

14   A.   I -- I had basic notes for the proceedings

15 today. If I looked at the actual databases

16 themselves, given a few minutes.

17   Q.   Okay. This is State's Exhibit 12A, does

18 that -- is that what you need?

19   A.   Yes, these are the KaZaA databases and I

20 believe -- I believe the latest date I found was March

21 31st and the earliest was March 2nd. And, again, that

22 has to do -- the dates have less to do with the log

23 file then the total size of the records. Once this

24 file reaches its maximum size, it will begin to drop

25 the oldest entries out.

SUPERIOR COURT, PIMA COUNTY

465

1 necessarily, so I don't know from the KaZaA database

2 files.

3   MR. LAGATTUTA: So the answer is, I don't

4 know?

5   THE WITNESS: Correct.

6 BY MR. JENSVOLD:

7   Q. And Detective -- Mr. Englander, the burn

8 dates on the CD's that you found that contain child

9 pornography, did that weigh into your decision as to

10 whether to charge Mr. Coghill or not?

11   A. Absolutely.

12   Q. How did it do so?

13   A. Well, I had relative timeframe of when Mr.

14 Franks and Mr. Coghill were living in the trailer

15 together and when they were not, and several of the

16 discs had burn dates that were outside of the time

17 range that my understanding that Jacob Franks was

18 living.

19   Q. Some of the dates that you got were -- you

20 got dates from Mr. Coghill as to when Mr. Franks was

21 there?

22   A. I did personally, yes.

23   Q. And did just the mere volume of both adult

24 pornography and child pornography files that you found

25 indication of or actual files, did that weigh on your

1   decision to charge this case?

2   A.   Absolutely.

3   Q.   How?

4   A.   Tremendous volume on the discs, on the burn

5   CD's and, you know, it occurred to me in the timeframe

6   of my understanding that Mr. Franks had been there for

7   approximately two weeks that one would have had to

8   have sat and done and nothing but download and create

9   CD's for an entire two weeks. Even then, I don't

10 think it would have been possible to create the

11 volumes of CD's that I found that contained child

12 pornography to -- to search for, download and then

13 burn and compile discs. I think it would have been

14 outside the scope of what any normal person could do

15 in the normal course of using a computer.

16   THE COURT: Let me make sure I understand,

17 that's related only to child pornography, not to

18 pornography.

19   THE WITNESS: Sorry?

20   THE COURT: Not to adult pornography the

21 burn dates on the CD's. The burn dates and the time?

22   THE WITNESS: Correct.

23   THE COURT: Would have -- would be the

24 volume of child pornography such -- alone not with

25 regard to the any other pornography?

SUPERIOR COURT, PIMA COUNTY

```
 1          THE WITNESS:  That -- I don't think that's a
 2     statement I would make.  The entire collection as a
 3     whole was of such a large proportion, the volume of
 4     child pornography, you know, I don't have a good feel
 5     right now for the total volume of child pornography.
 6     I know what we ultimately generated these proceedings
 7     based on, but I just don't have a great feel for the
 8     total.
 9          THE COURT:  I understand.
10          Anything else, Mr. Jensvold?
11          MR. JENSVOLD:  No.
12          THE COURT:  Mr. Lagattuta, anything you
13     would like to say -- ask?
14          MR. LAGATTUTA:  Yeah.
15                    CROSS EXAMINATION
16     BY MR. LAGATTUTA:
17          Q.   Mr. Englander, I have a copy of your report
18     here that is the one where you identify the different
19     discs that you looked at, right?
20          A.   Correct.
21          Q.   And data, contraband, description, right?
22          A.   Yes.
23          Q.   Okay.  And on the first two pages, these
24     discs are marked things like SG1 and Voyager, things
25     like that?
```

1   A.   Those were the titles that were written, not

2   by me, on those discs.

3   Q.   And you looked at all of those?

4   A.   Yes.

5   Q.   There's a whole full page, those are just

6   like commercial movies and T.V. things -- things like

7   that?

8   A.   Yes.

9   Q.   They are not contraband, they are not --

10   they are not adult pornography?

11   A.   Correct.

12   Q.   Okay. Then we move into the second page and

13   then this one has the ones where you have listed the

14   discs that have the -- what you consider to be

15   contraband, right?

16   A.   I'm going to agree with you, I'm not looking

17   at the form you're looking at.

18   Q.   Oh, do you have this? Can you --

19   MR. JENSVOLD: It's State's 13, I believe.

20   THE WITNESS: Some spindles did not contain

21   pornography, they contained --

22   MR. JENSVOLD: State's Exhibit 13.

23   THE WITNESS: Thank you.

24   BY MR. LAGATTUTA:

25   Q.   Okay. So the first portion of these, the

SUPERIOR COURT, PIMA COUNTY

1   ones that are charged discs from which the indictment

2   comes in the case, then underneath there is just a

3   list of other CD discs that you found, right?

4   A.   Which page are you looking at.

5   Q.   Looking at JE3, it's probably --

6   A.   Yes.

7   Q.   Okay. And exception of one about midway

8   down there's a checkmark that says contraband, the

9   rest of them, these X's to me indicate there's no

10 contraband on there, right?

11   A.   Correct, an X in the contraband would

12 indicate, no contraband, the checkmarks do.

13   Q.   The next thing, the same thing the whole

14 page is full of X's?

15   A.   Correct.

16   Q.   No contraband on any of those discs?

17   A.   Correct.

18   Q.   You looked at all of those?

19   A.   Correct.

20   Q.   Okay. And the next page, the same thing?

21   A.   Yes.

22   Q.   Then we go to the next page, it's the same

23 thing I'm looking at them. There's -- at the top disc

24 describe first A through Z, these are call "X" Files.

25 You watched that, is that like the T.V. show?

1   A.   I didn't watch the entire -- it was a T.V.

2   show.

3   Q.   No contra -- there's no -- there's no adult

4   pornography, so far we haven't run into it yet?

5   A.   Contraband would indicate child pornography,

6   adult pornography is not illegal.

7   Q.   So far what we discussed we still haven't

8   run into any adult pornography yet, have we?

9   A.   Not on these discs, correct.

10   Q.   Okay. Turn on the next page, you looked at

11   those discs right there at the top YY ZZ, triple A?

12   A.   If you look in the description, you will

13   notice the top one YYT, movies is that the one you're

14   looking at?

15   Q.   The one that follows the page I just

16   directed your attention to?

17   A.   I'm sorry at the top of right-hand side

18   beginning of each spindle, there's number JE3.

19   Q.   JE4, okay, the full page right there from A

20   to double X, none of those discs contain any adult or

21   child?

22   A.   JE4 did not contain child or adult

23   pornography.

24   Q.   Okay. How many discs have we looked at so

25   far?

1   A.   You would have to count.

2   Q.   A 100 so far?

3   THE COURT: Let's focus --

4 BY MR. LAGATTUTA:

5   Q.   My point is, this is -- he's made mention

6 that there's a volume of adult pornography in the disc

7 collection and through what we been disclosed, I don't

8 see it here. Well --

9   A.   Sir, I apologize --

10   THE COURT: Let go ahead, we're not with the

11 jury, he -- I want get this out, you can ask your

12 question if you're trying to get where that is.

13 BY MR. LAGATTUTA:

14   Q.   Good, tell me where?

15   A.   JE, item NN100 and 18 adult movies item PP.

16   Q.   Slow down. Item NN?

17   A.   If you look in the description, it is not

18 contraband, it is adult pornography, 118 adult movies,

19 item PP121, adult movies, item SS --

20   THE COURT: Slow down, one person at a time.

21 BY MR. LAGATTUTA:

22   Q.   When you say 121 adult movies, that's on one

23 disc?

24   A.   One CD rom.

25   Q.   One CD rom?

1   A.   Yes.

2   Q.   Okay, go ahead?

3   A.   Item SS11; item TT22; item VV70; item WW35;

4 item X123; item YY72; item ZZ56 --

5   THE COURT: Stop for a minute, I think we

6 got the point here. And those are all adult porn

7 movies?

8   THE WITNESS: Correct.

9   THE COURT: But not contraband?

10   THE WITNESS: Correct.

11   MR. LAGATTUTA: All right. Okay.

12 BY MR. LAGATTUTA:

13   Q.   On JE12 from A through RR, do you see any

14 adult --

15   A.   No adult pornography there.

16   Q.   Item JE13, item A through G?

17   A.   Item A, C, D, and F contained deleted files

18 that were in some cases child pornography and in -- in

19 other cases, I don't have indicated whether they were

20 child or adult. The description column where I'm

21 referring to, sir.

22   Q.   You're on GE14 right now?

23   A.   JE13, A through G.

24   Q.   It says 89 deleted files?

25   A.   Continue reading you'll see six deleted C.P.

1   movies.

2   Q.   Have they been deleted, that means you can't
3   see them, right?

4   A.   That means that they exist; however, a user
5   placing that disc into a normal machine would not see
6   it. The software we use to use or examination allows
7   us to see items that have been deleted.

8   Q.   So you were able to see what was in these 89
9   deleted files?

10   A.   In some cases, I believe so. I don't know
11   sitting here looking at this form, though, I would
12   have to look at the disc. It's not a disc that we
13   took images or movies from and charged with, so I
14   don't have the file names for you.

15   Q.   So you don't really know what they are?

16   A.   I know what they are, sir, I know six of
17   them were deleted child pornography movies.

18   Q.   How can you have a record of a deleted file
19   on a CD?

20   A.   It -- tell you what, let's take the picture
21   of that disc, take a look at disc CD RW, the CD could
22   have been formatted CD RW are unique, they allow to
23   you write and erase and rewrite to them. That may be
24   why this is a small grouping, it was a small grouping
25   of CRW. Off the top of my head, sir, I don't know, we

1 have to look at the individual disc. It is possible

2 to erase and delete, even format a CD, look like a CD

3 RW if you didn't know the difference.

4   Q.   Having been either erased or deleted, you

5 can't view it again?

6   A.   You can't. I can, I have software that

7 allows me to.

8   Q.   All right.

9   A.   However, a normal user who has deleted that

10 would not necessarily have access to that without a

11 tool to recover the deleted file.

12   Q.   So if I had -- if you have these actual CD's

13 somewhere in here, in the courtroom or whatever, and a

14 person had one without having your computer

15 capability, they put it in, nothing comes up?

16   A.   Correct.

17   Q.   Okay. And you can't tell whether any of

18 these CD's on JE13 were, either when they were made --

19   A.   I don't have an indication of that, no.

20 Sitting here right now I can't tell you, if I could or

21 not. I would have to look at the -- examine the CD

22 again.

23   Q.   They virtually -- useless to a user like on

24 a regular computer, put them in there and see any of

25 this information you think was on there at some time?

1   A.   The -- it says -- you would not see them as
2   normal user of a computer.

3   MR. LAGATTUTA: Your Honor, I don't want to
4   ask any more questions, I want to point Mr. Englander
5   on -- you asked something whether this adult
6   pornography was intermixed. The reason I ask those
7   questions is, because, this. You know, this list is
8   basically a diagram of all those CD's that's in that
9   giant bag right over there. And if you look at them,
10 gone through page by page, the reason I had the former
11 detective point out whether they were adult
12 pornography or not was to suggest that given the vast
13 number of CD's, the ones that he describes for -- in
14 here as containing actual adult pornography as a very
15 small percentage.

16   THE WITNESS: I think -- I'm sorry, there
17 are two different ways to represent the volume, the
18 number of discs or the number of files that contain
19 the adult and child pornography. I was referring to
20 the number of files contained the adult and child
21 pornography. It matters not to me as a forensic
22 examiner whether they are all on hard drive or each
23 unbroken up over 15 floppy disc, number of volumes
24 they are contained is are irrelevant to me, it's
25 number of files I was referring to.

                    SUPERIOR COURT, PIMA COUNTY

```
 1          MR. LAGATTUTA:  I'm talking about number of
 2    discs.
 3          THE COURT:  I think that I heard enough.
 4    The issue here really -- and I think that the
 5    defendant in his statement to Deputy Judd, when he was
 6    asked about child pornography it's intertwined as far
 7    as I'm concerned on the identification of what was
 8    where.  And I think that the evidence here with regard
 9    to pornography -- first of all, I can't even say
10    pornography, is fits the definition of misconduct
11    under 404(b) because it is not illegal and therefore,
12    it is intertwined what was on all these discs and
13    where it came from and how it's connected.
14          It seems to me it's almost impossible to
15    talk in some cases about child pornography without
16    also talking about pornography that is listed with it
17    based on the testimony, what I heard here from
18    Detective Englander.  I think as I say, it's so
19    intertwined what is on the computer, that I'm going to
20    allow the testimony with regard to pornography that
21    has been testified to.
22          You can go back into it with regard to
23    Mr. -- or Deputy Judd after the cross-examination, and
24    I'm ruling that the testimony here that the defendant
25    gave to Detective Englander is admissible, the
```

SUPERIOR COURT, PIMA COUNTY

1 objectionable parts, there were some parts that were
 2 not objected to that -- which included the terminology
 3 of pornography and I think it needs to be made clear
 4 and I will make clear that pornography is not illegal
 5 and that the jury can't consider that and I'll
 6 consider a limiting instruction on that, but because
 7 it is innerconnected, I think it does go to the issue
 8 of the defendant's intent and also opportunity having
 9 a computer and his knowledge of what is -- was in fact
10 on the various discs and his computer.
11   And so I do find that this evidence has --
12 is not prejudicial then it is probative under the
13 circumstances. So I don't believe it is to impune his
14 character, rather for relevant evidence in the case.
15 I will say, however, that I don't expect it to be gone
16 into voluminously. There will be a point where it
17 gets to be cumulative and unnecessary and the focus
18 should be on, very clearly on the contraband and
19 allegations in the complaint as it fits into the
20 discussion, not going to approve the mentioning of the
21 term pornography.
22   MR. JENSVOLD: Then I just want to ask one
23 follow-up question about uncharged child pornography,
24 I don't want to belabor that either, but we do have at
25 least the dirty CD that has been talked about because

1   of the handwriting analysis and Mr. Franks' own

2   testimony that -- Detective Englander -- contain child

3   pornography. However, none of the charged files are

4   from that disc, what limits do you want to set on that

5   and -- and I mean Mr. Englander could testify the

6   reason that he didn't charge any files from the dirty

7   CD because of the questionable possession since Mr.

8   Franks acknowledged writing and the handwriting

9   analysis supported that.

10   MR. LAGATTUTA: Your Honor, I'd like to

11   respond.

12   THE COURT: Sure.

13   MR. LAGATTUTA: I'm not sure I really

14   understand what -- what the question or the objection

15   was. The disc, the dirty disc, that's already been

16   talked about was clearly a disc that Mr. Franks -- he

17   admits he makes it, by his own testimony he believes

18   it's illegal, he writes his name on it. Everything is

19   all good. Detective Englander at the time the --

20   Detective Englander knows about it for some reason

21   gives him a free pass. I don't see how that crosses

22   the line into, you know, opening the door about any --

23   THE COURT: I think you're right, the fact

24   that that did have child pornography on it and wasn't

25   charged, it belongs totally to somebody else. So I

1 think that the fact that it's been basically admitted
2 tomorrow he could testify to the fact that it did in
3 fact include child pornography on that particular
4 dirty disc.

5   So let me say this, I don't think that
6 opens the door to -- to allow the State to say, you
7 know, we only charged Mr. Coghill with 15 counts, but
8 there's 300 and 400 other counts laying around out
9 there. I don't think that's appropriate. We've not
10 -- been we can't defend against that.

11   THE COURT: I agree. But the fact that it
12 did contain what was written on by Mr. Franks and the
13 testimony that's already out that it did in fact
14 contain it can be verified by the testimony of the
15 witness, although you have to make clear that none of
16 that is charged.

17   MR. JENSVOLD: I just -- that's going to
18 come out because there are specific CD's from which
19 the charged files are derived.

20   THE COURT: Okay. I'm sure we'll hear more.
21 Okay. Sir, thank you. You can just -- let us have
22 these things now and you can bring in --

23   Peter, I hope you checked to see if the jury
24 is there.

25   MR. JENSVOLD: I had one chain of custody

1   issue before the jury comes in.

2   THE COURT: They are not in yet.

3   MR. JENSVOLD: If we get to that point,

4   today. I don't know how far we're going to get.

5   Detective Gideny copied the contents of the hard

6   drives to the laptop that Mr. Englander brought in I

7   wanted to have Mr. Englander testify first, but he

8   wanted to hear from -- I was going to have Detective

9   Gideny come back tomorrow to testify.

10   THE COURT: It's your order, what have you,

11 I'm trying to be orderly here. I think we need to do

12 that. You just call him when you have them and need

13 them.

14   MR. JENSVOLD: I was going make an offer of

15 proof, Detective Gidney was going to take off.

16   THE COURT: Why don't you talk to -- why

17 don't you talk to -- to Mr. Lagattuta and see if you

18 all can agree to something.

19   MR. LAGATTUTA: If you want to do it, then

20 bring him back, offer that, you're going to bring him

21 back later to fill it in, if it's all good, then I'll

22 be fine with that.

23   MR. JENSVOLD: All right. Thank you.

24   THE COURT: Sir, you can come back up and

25 take the stand.

SUPERIOR COURT, PIMA COUNTY

481

1   (The following proceedings were held in open

2   court, in the presence of the jurors:)

3   THE COURT: Thank you, please be seated.

4   We're here with defendant, counsel, and the jurors and

5   we are continuing the cross-examination of Deputy

6   Judd.

7   Mr. Lagattuta?

8   MR. LAGATTUTA: Thank you, Your Honor.

9   BY MR. LAGATTUTA:

10   Q.   Deputy Judd, excuse me I don't want to be

11   repetitive, I want to ask you a couple quick things

12   then I'll go back to -- on what we first said, but it

13   is my understanding that when you -- when you entered

14   the trailer, the motorhome, Jim Coghill's motorhome,

15   your testimony is that you observed at least one disc

16   that was marked KP and it was on a top stack of a

17   spindle?

18   A.   Yes.

19   Q.   Okay. But today looking at the photographs,

20   you can't recall the certainty which spindle that disc

21   was on, is that right?

22   A.   Correct.

23   Q.   Okay. You also mentioned when I asked you

24   if you had made any notation in your report about

25   where the spindle was and you responded that you did

SUPERIOR COURT, PIMA COUNTY

482

1   not make a notation where the spindle was in the body

2   of your report?

3   A.   You mean the location of the spindle inside

4   the motorhome?

5   Q.   Correct.

6   A.   I would have to review my report briefly.

7   THE COURT: What's exhibit number is it, ,

8   Four?

9   THE WITNESS: Yes.

10   THE COURT: Thank you.

11   THE WITNESS: My report states that there

12 was spindles next to his computer.

13 BY MR. LAGATTUTA:

14   Q.   Okay. All right. Going back -- okay, so

15 then after you located this -- located this disc, you

16 had a conversation with Mr. Coghill, what did you do

17 after that?

18   A.   Directly after we talked about the --

19   Q.   About the CD's and anything else in the

20 trailer -- the motorhome, what -- how did you exit the

21 place?

22   A.   Through the door.

23   Q.   Okay. And did that conclude your

24 investigation in this matter?

25   A.   It did not conclude my involvement.

SUPERIOR COURT, PIMA COUNTY

483

1   Q.   Okay. What did you do when you exited the
2   motorhome? Did you take Mr. Coghill with you?
3   A.   No.
4   Q.   Did you leave him inside the motorhome?
5   A.   Yes, I left and picked up Jacob and took him
6   to 1750 East Benson Highway.
7   Q.   Okay.
8   A.   Which is the Sheriff's Department
9   administration building.
10   Q.   In fact that's right down the street from
11   where the mobile home park is?
12   A.   It's a ways -- it's on the -- it's on Benson
13   Highway.
14   Q.   All right. What did you do there?
15   A.   I dropped him off so that Jacob could speak
16   with detectives.
17   Q.   Okay. Did you do anything to secure the
18   contents of the motorhome before you left?
19   A.   I did not leave until detectives were there
20   to maintain some order.
21   Q.   Okay. You basically turned it -- you waited
22   until the detectives came then turned the
23   investigation over to them, is that correct?
24   A.   Correct.
25   Q.   Had you written a report -- and you did

1   write a report in the case, you would have turned that

2   into what the investigating -- the -- who did you turn

3   your report into?

4   A.   We don't return -- turn our reports to

5   anyone, we gave a dictation system which means I pick

6   up the telephone, dial a number and I dictate into the

7   telephone. Then we have people that listen to my

8   recording, transcribe it and it's entered into a

9   database that can be retrieved.

10   Q.   Okay. But I guess what I'm getting at, does

11 your report then send on to another detective or

12 somebody else who may be involved in further

13 investigation of the case?

14   A.   In a sense a detective can access my report,

15 it was under the same case number that they would

16 dictate reports under.

17   Q.   Okay. Did you know at that time Detective

18 Englander was also involved in the investigation of

19 the case?

20   A.   Yes.

21   Q.   And would you have turned your -- would you

22 have made your report accessible to him?

23   A.   Not necessarily. My report is simply there,

24 the detective would know he would be working under the

25 same case number that I was, so Detective Englander

1 would make a report under the same case number.

2   Q.   Okay, very good. And I'm done with it.

3   I want to take you back in the very

4 beginning when you and Detective Schupbach first

5 encountered Jacob Franks, okay, you with me?

6   A.   Yes.

7   Q.   You had a conversation with him, right?

8   A.   Correct.

9   Q.   Okay. She told us that he said that he had

10 always told Jim that he better not make him mad and

11 that he was just mad enough now that he wanted to

12 report this to the police. Were you present when that

13 statement was made?

14   A.   No.

15   MR. LAGATTUTA: That's all the questions I

16 have.

17   THE COURT: Redirect?

18   MR. JENSVOLD: Thank you, Your Honor.

19

20   REDIRECT EXAMINATION

21 BY MR. JENSVOLD:

22   Q.   Deputy Judd, was your purpose in talking to

23 either Mr. Franks or Mr. Coghill to do a forensic

24 interview?

25   A.   No.

SUPERIOR COURT, PIMA COUNTY

```
1       Q.    What is forensic interview?

2       A.    I'm not sure.

3       Q.    Have you ever done one?

4       A.    No.

5       Q.    Okay.  Is there specific training that

6  you're aware that goes into being able to perform one?

7       A.    Yes.

8       Q.    Now, we had a lot of discussion about the CD

9  spindle.  Did you ask Mr. Coghill about child

10 pornography files?

11      A.    Well, I told him that there was an

12 allegation that he possessed child pornography.

13      Q.    Then did he tell you anything about

14 pornography around the computer?

15      A.    Yes.

16      Q.    What did he tell you?

17      A.    Regarding the stacks of spindles, I asked if

18 he could break them down and tell me what was on each

19 spindle.  He said that one stack was "X" Files, one

20 was a Star Trek Trilogy, one was blank and he said

21 this one is pornography.

22      Q.    Now, had he told you that it was -- what did

23 he tell you, what kind of pornography?

24      A.    No, he did not, not regarding the CD's.

25      Q.    But he denied it was child pornography?
```

SUPERIOR COURT, PIMA COUNTY

1   A.   Yes.

2   Q.   Were you present when all the CD's were

3   packaged and placed into bags?

4   A.   No.

5   Q.   And do you recall if you ever put latex

6   gloves on during your initial encounter to handle the

7   CD or the cases?

8   A.   I don't remember whether I put gloves on or

9   not.

10   Q.   Do you remember if Mr. Coghill handled the

11   CD at all to show you where stuff was?

12   A.   No, I don't.

13   MR. JENSVOLD: That's all I have.

14   THE COURT: Do the jurors have any questions

15   for Deputy Judd? Okay, I see none. Thank you, sir,

16   very much for your time and testimony and you are

17   excused. Give me your exhibit, I'll pass it over

18   here. Thank you.

19   Next witness?

20   MR. JENSVOLD: It's going to be Englander.

21   THE COURT: He's the sworn case agent?

22   MR. JENSVOLD: Yes, Your Honor.

23   THE COURT: Sir, just come up here and be

24   sworn.

25

SUPERIOR COURT, PIMA COUNTY

```
 1                    JEFFORD ENGLANDER,
 2    having been duly sworn, was examined and testified as
 3    follows:
 4                    DIRECT EXAMINATION
 5    BY MR. JENSVOLD:
 6         Q.   Could you please introduce yourself to the
 7    jury?
 8         A.   My name is Jefford Englander.
 9         Q.   And who do you work for presently?
10         A.   Right now I work for company called the
11    Spinelli Corporation, it's a litigation support
12    company in Phoenix.
13         Q.   What do you do for them?
14         A.   I am a computer forensic investigator for
15    them.
16         Q.   And so what kind of -- who are your clients?
17         A.   Mainly companies involved in lawsuits
18    against other companies and employees, law firms hire
19    us to assist them with their cases, insurance claims,
20    things of that nature.
21         Q.   And how long have you been there?
22         A.   Coming up on a year, about eight months.
23         Q.   And who did you work for before then?
24         A.   Prior to that I worked for the Pima County
25    Sheriff's Department.
```

SUPERIOR COURT, PIMA COUNTY

1   Q.   And in what capacity did you work for

2 Sheriff's Department?

3   A.   I was a deputy, a detective with the

4 Sheriff's Department.

5   Q.   And did you have any specific duties as a

6 detective?

7   A.   I did. I wore a few different hats. I was

8 a detective assigned to the Crimes Against Children

9 squad. As part of those duties, I received a regular

10 caseload of investigations. I was also assigned to an

11 Online Investigations Task Force that was headed by

12 the F.B.I., and I was also a computer forensic

13 investigator for the Sheriff's Department with respect

14 to the electronic evidence.

15   Q.   Can you explain to the jury your education

16 and experience regarding forensic analysis of

17 computers?

18   A.   Sure. I have all tolled in excess of about

19 400 hours of training with respect to computer

20 forensics and electronic investigations. I am

21 certified by the International Association of Computer

22 Investigative Specialists as a certified forensic

23 computer examiner. I am certified by a company called

24 MEGA Software that produces the preeminent forensic

25 computer examination program. I'm certified to use

1   their program, both certifications requires both a

2   written test as well as practical examinations.

3   I'm also a member of the High Technology

4   Crime Association Training, National White collar

5   Crime Center, basic data recovery and advanced data

6   recovery analysis. I also attended trainings from a

7   variety of other providers of computer forensic

8   training in respect to retrieval and analysis of

9   digital evidence.

10   Q.   How long in total were you with the

11   Sheriff's Department?

12   A.   Ten years.

13   Q.   And how did you start out with them? What

14   were you doing when you first started?

15   A.   I started like every other deputy. I was a

16   patrol officer. I worked on the northeast side of

17   town as well as the south side of town.

18   Q.   Did you have some of your computer

19   experience before you even started?

20   A.   I did not. I had very little, I had sent

21   e-mail, had an AOL account.

22   Q.   Just developed your experience as you were

23   with the Sheriff's Department?

24   A.   I was a patrol officer for about three and a

25   half years, the remainder of my time was as a

                    SUPERIOR COURT, PIMA COUNTY

1 detective and that was where I developed computer

2 experience.

3   Q.   And before this case, how many cases -- when

4 you're with the Sheriff's Department had you been

5 involved in analyzing computers?

6   A.   It had been about three years since I had

7 started working with electronic evidence. I started

8 in about November of '99 handling those type of cases,

9 maybe a 100 involving a different -- different variety

10 of electronic evidence, be it floppy discs, computer

11 thumb drives, online investigations, 100, 200,

12 somewhere in that line.

13   Q.   About how many of those involved allegations

14 or possible child pornography?

15   A.   A majority of them. Every now and then

16 because of my assignment to the Crimes Against

17 Children Squad and task force I worked on specifically

18 focused on child exploitation, that tended to be the

19 wide share of cases I was assigned as an electronic

20 crime investigator as well.

21   Q.   Have you had further training on specific

22 issues regarding to child pornography images?

23   A.   I have.

24   Q.   Can you describe to the jury what that is?

25   A.   Part of the training, the initial training

1 for the task force, Innocent Images Task Force I

2 participated here in Tucson which is called the Safe

3 Team was training with respect to how to conduct

4 online investigations training with respect to child

5 pornography, training with respect to online personas

6 and online predictors, things of that nature.

7   Q.   Have you had any specific training on how to

8 evaluate the age of a child on an image?

9   A.   I had the lux -- I called it luxury from a

10 training prespective, it's a bell that can't be

11 unrung. Nonetheless, I had the opportunity

12 professionally to view hundreds of thousands of images

13 and movies of child pornography. In addition, I had

14 the ability to reference several federal data basis

15 that Department of Justice and F.B.I. maintains, and I

16 think Immigration and Customs maintains ones that --

17 contain images of known child pornography where the

18 images were found and the child was actually located

19 and was interviewed and it was determined that at the

20 time the images were taken, that child was in fact a

21 minor, so it's almost a standard to hold things,

22 again, generally speaking. Obviously, if we ever came

23 across those specific images, typically they are in

24 series or movies that seven or eight different movies

25 were created, obviously we know these are definitively

SUPERIOR COURT, PIMA COUNTY

1 child pornography, I've been able to use the

2 character -- physical characteristics of those images

3 and movies to hone my skills to determine whether or

4 not images in movies, of what I believe to be minors,

5 are in fact minors.

6   Q.   And can you explain to the jury, you know,

7 briefly what kind of things you look for to -- to

8 judge in age?

9   A.   Typically the first determination I make

10 when I look at a male or female on a movie is, is this

11 person pre or post-pubescent, have they entered that

12 realm, the gray area during puberty which is always a

13 little difficult to determine. Things that I look

14 for, obviously, development of pubic hair, development

15 of the sexual genitals, loss of childhood baby fat,

16 for lack a better term, pudginess that comes with

17 pre-adolescents. Typically I deal more with female

18 victims in imaging movies than with male victims; tend

19 to be more prevalent, with female victims.

20   I'll look for definition of facial

21 structure, the bones, the cheekbones, definition in

22 the clavicle area, the arm muscles. Muscle structure

23 develops before and after puberty, as well as

24 definition of muscle tone in the legs and abs as well

25 as things like body hair, arm hair, leg hair that's

1 begun to develop. Typically, it's kind of the entire

2 package. I would never base a decision on one or two

3 characteristics, it's an overall impression based on a

4 multitude of characteristics.

5   Q. Slow down, so the jury can hear you.

6   A. I'm sorry.

7   THE COURT: And maybe be -- slow down a

8 little bit that might be difficult with your

9 background to do that, but the court reporter is

10 probably typing pretty quickly.

11   THE WITNESS: My apologies.

12   THE COURT: If you can slow down a little

13 bit from your natural gait, thank you.

14   Mr. Jensvold?

15   MR. JENSVOLD: Thank you.

16 BY MR. JENSVOLD:

17   Q. Okay. Mr. Englander, then are there

18 particular -- you mentioned like known series of child

19 pornography, ask you -- what are some of those that

20 you see common?

21   A. Probably the most common series, and it's

22 typically seeing, well, as of late has been -- was

23 seen more in a still image series, oftentime movies

24 are made then still images are drawn from those movies

25 or the still images are created at the same time.

SUPERIOR COURT, PIMA COUNTY

1 Before everyone got onboard with high speed internet,

 2 and even subsequent to that, some people still prefer

 3 images as opposed to movies. The Vicky series is one

 4 that stands out as virtually anyone working in the

 5 field of child pornography would immediately recognize

 6 through the name or the images -- images from the

 7 Vicky series. There are also movies made that involve

 8 the young girl and she is what is known as a known

 9 victim. She has been -- based on the still images she

10 had been interviewed and is known to have been a minor

11 at the time those were created, so that's an example

12 of a series that is a known -- a known series.

13   Some of them -- on occasion, you will see

14 images or movies on the internet that contain the word

15 Vicky in the title that could not have true Vicky

16 series images or movies. People are just trying to

17 increase the downloads of that for whatever reason or

18 dupe people who are surfing for Vicky movie images

19 into downloading it. Typically, if it has the name in

20 it, then it's going to be either the actual contents

21 or something very, very similar.

22   Q.   There's -- is there also an issue about

23 whether a child is an actual child as posed to virtual

24 child?

25   A.   That is a non-issue in movie files with

1 still images. If any portion of the child is there,
2 then that is a portion of child being depicted as a
3 minor involved in sexual activity. With movie files,
4 in order to have life-like motion, you need to have a
5 certain number of frames per second. And if anyone
6 has ever seen some of Hollywood's best creations,
7 their animated film such as the Final Fantasy movie,
8 Hollywood can do very, very well. But even with
9 hundreds of digital animators working for thousands of
10 hours on five to ten seconds each of work, you, as an
11 individual, can put that movie in the VCR or DVD
12 player and know it's not truly a human being, it's a
13 digital creation. You'll be -- probably be impressed
14 how good a job they have done. You would be able to
15 tell.
16   When we view movie files of child
17 pornography or that we suspect to be child
18 pornography, we obviously look for things like changes
19 in skin tone, appropriate shadows, appropriate facial
20 and body muscle, movement, things of that nature to
21 determine whether or not it's a really good attempt
22 or -- or a true video.
23   I have yet to actually see on the internet a
24 digitally created movie of child pornography. I have
25 never seen that.

1   Q.   Let's move into your investigation in this

2   case.   Mr. Englander, when did you first become

3   involved in the case?

4   A.   I became involved, I believe it was

5   April 1st, I was assigned to the Crimes Against

6   Children Squad and also was handling the electronic

7   evidence cases. My supervisor, Sergeant Pesqueira

8   contacted me, asked me if I would conduct an

9   investigation based on information that our

10 dispatchers and patrol officers had received.

11   Q.   And what information were you given to start

12 off with?

13   A.   I believe I was told that there was a person

14 who had made a phone call from a convenience store,

15 was reporting another person that had child

16 pornography.

17   Q.   And what did you do?

18   A.   I went to -- my understanding was that a

19 patrol officer had already talked to both individuals

20 and I believe I discovered that the person making the

21 report was going to be taken to our main station to

22 give a more detailed report to be done with a

23 detective and give a lengthy report. I went to the

24 location where the child pornography had been reported

25 as being located.

1   Q.   And where was that?

2   A.   It was a small mobilehome park on Benson

3 Highway, I don't recall the specific address.

4   Q.   Okay. And who was there when you got there?

5   A.   When I got there, there was -- Deputy Judd

6 was there and Mr. Coghill was there, I believe that

7 there was another deputy there as well, I don't

8 remember who that was. It may have been a female

9 deputy?

10   Q.   What did you do?

11   A.   When I got there, the first thing I did was

12 I asked just for a quick synopsis of what had

13 happened. Sometimes when my sergeant gives us a quick

14 rundown where we're going, it doesn't turn out to be

15 the right thing, so I asked for a rundown of what the

16 patrol officers had been dispatched to, had found out,

17 and I was told that basically, the information my

18 sergeant had given me was correct, that I was now at

19 the location where the reportee, the person making the

20 report had been staying for a short period of time and

21 that this was in fact someone else's trailer. This

22 was where the child pornography was supposed to be

23 located.

24   Q.   Okay. Then what did you do?

25   A.   At that point I asked the owner of the

SUPERIOR COURT, PIMA COUNTY

499

1   trailer, Mr. Coghill, if he would be willing to sit

2   down in my car and talk to me. I believe I had stood

3   near the opening or gone inside to talk to Mr.

4   Coghill. I don't know where I first encountered him.

5   I know the trailer had a very, very strong odor of

6   cigarette smoke. It was also -- it was warm in there.

7   I didn't want to sit in there and talk to Coghill, I

8   asked him if he would be willing to sit in my car,

9   air-conditioning on. It was parked right out outside

10   his trailer. I asked if he was would be willing to

11   talk to me.

12   Q.   Was he?

13   A.   Yes, yes.

14   Q.   And at any time prior to talking to him, did

15   you place him under arrest?

16   A.   Absolutely not.

17   Q.   Did you have a basis to place him under

18   arrest?

19   A.   Absolutely not.

20   Q.   Did you ever draw your gun or handcuff him

21   in any way?

22   A.   Not at all.

23   Q.   Did you threaten to take him to jail in

24   anyway?

25   A.   Not at all.

SUPERIOR COURT, PIMA COUNTY

1   Q.   And so where specifically did you sit in
2 your patrol car -- in your patrol car?
3   A.   Just a regular 2002 Dodge Stratus. It
4 wasn't a patrol car. As detectives, we were given
5 just regular vehicles. There's no screen, no lights,
6 there's no star, nothing. I didn't even have a police
7 radio or anything in the car except for my hand-held.
8 I sat in the driver's seat and Mr. Coghill sat in
9 front seat, passenger side.
10   Q.   Okay. We're going get to specific on the
11 issue of the statements made during the interview a
12 little bit later. How long did your interview take?
13   A.   I don't know maybe 20 minutes, give or take.
14   Q.   Okay. So after you interviewed Mr. Coghill,
15 what did you do?
16   A.   After I interviewed Mr. Coghill, I asked a
17 patrol officer, uniformed officer to stay at the
18 trailer, at the mobilehome, to secure the location so
19 that no one could disturb the contents of the
20 mobilehome, and I left to go back, five minute drive
21 to where our main station is to obtain a search
22 warrant for the trailer.
23   Q.   And did you get the search warrant?
24   A.   Yes.
25   Q.   And who did you get that from, a judge?

SUPERIOR COURT, PIMA COUNTY

501

1   A.   Correct.

2   Q.   Okay. Did anyone else participate in the
3 search warrant procedure with you?

4   A.   I'm sure I had a witness, I don't recall
5 who. It was typically whoever you can grab that has
6 five minutes to sit and listen to you talk to a judge
7 on the telephone. It's documented there somewhere on
8 the form.

9   Q.   After you got the search warrant, what did
10 you do with it?

11   A.   Then I went back to the trailer with a few
12 other detectives and executed the warrant, actually
13 conducted a search of the mobilehome.

14   Q.   Okay. And what kind of materials did you
15 take from the search warrant?

16   A.   We took a computer, we took a host of CD
17 Roms from a variety of locations. We took I believe
18 some VHS tapes, paperwork, a lot of photographs. We
19 took photographs; we didn't take photographs. We took
20 some other peripheral computer equipment. I probably
21 left something out. I would have to look at the
22 property sheet to know exactly what we took.

23   Q.   Was there a cable bill or slip of some sort?

24   A.   Yeah, the paperwork that we took there was a
25 Cox Cable bill.

SUPERIOR COURT, PIMA COUNTY

502

1   Q.   Now, from your understanding of the RV

2   itself, where did you come to find out that Mr.

3   Coghill was sleeping?

4   A.   I guess I misstated. When I said a

5   mobilehome, this was a drive-it-away-type Winnebago, I

6   don't know, 36 feet. I don't know the dimensions of

7   it. You could get in and drive it. There was one

8   area in the back of the vehicle that was a bedroom

9   had -- had -- it had a curtain you could pull across

10   the doorway. It had a bed in there. My understanding

11   was that was Mr. Coghill's bedroom and there was a

12   bathroom and a living area towards the front then,

13   obviously, the very front are the driver and front

14   passenger seat.

15   Q.   Where was the computer located within the

16   RV?

17   A.   A computer was located on the passenger side

18   behind the passenger front seat, there was a small

19   desk area there.

20   Q.   And besides just the computer tower itself,

21   what other types of equipment were there associated

22   with the computer?

23   A.   Well, there was an almost empty shell of

24   another computer that didn't have any storage devices

25   in it. There was an external CD burner, CD drive, can

1   data onto CD's. There was, I believe it was a one 100

2   megabyte disc, external disc. It looks like a big

3   floppy disc. It's not computer, it's attached to it.

4   I believe there was also a printer and a monitor,

5   obviously a keyboard and a mouse. I'm not sure if it

6   was a scanner or printer, if it was just a printer. I

7   think it was just a printer.

8   Q.   What was the internet connection there?

9   A.   Cox Cable internet.

10   Q.   Okay. Cable modum is a separate piece of

11   equipment from the computer also?

12   A.   Correct. The cable line ran into the cable

13   modum. I believe there was a network cable running

14   from the modum to the back of the PC.

15   Q.   And the computer itself, what kind of

16   equipment was installed within -- within the computer?

17   A.   The computer had two physical hard drives

18   inside of it. Aside from that, it wasn't a brand

19   name, it was kind of a home built PC, a variety of

20   different -- there was a video card in there, just

21   some other standard computer equipment.

22   Q.   And what kind of software did this computer

23   -- well, do you know what kind of software was on it

24   when you first got there?

25   A.   Not from looking at it, no.

SUPERIOR COURT, PIMA COUNTY

1   Q.   You found out later?

2   A.   Correct.

3   Q.   Let's go to the -- oh the Cox bill, who's

4   name was on it?

5   A.   Mr. Coghill's.

6   Q.   Did you see any materials that appeared to

7   be -- to belong to Mr. Franks?

8   A.   You know, I remember that there -- I

9   remember either discussing or seeing maybe a bag that

10   that was his. I don't recall if that was through

11   discussion or through seeing it, so I don't recall

12   whether or not I saw the items that were his -- his

13   personal possessions or if I learned that through

14   discussion.

15   Q.   And the CD's that you saw, where were those?

16   We seen some pictures already, but where were they and

17   about how many of them were there?

18   A.   There were -- you can buy CD's in individual

19   cases and buy them in these large spindles where they

20   are stacked 25 or 50 or 100 high. There were a few of

21   those spindles on the desk that the computer keyboard

22   and things were -- were on. I believe there were a

23   few to the left of it in the common area or right near

24   the passage way to the front seats and there were some

25   CD's that were located in a vinyl -- a nylon CD holder

1   with the slots near the driver's seat area.   The
2   majority them were from directly around the computer
3   area.
4   Q.   And did you take all of those CD's?
5   A.   Yes.
6   Q.   Okay.   So what did you do with the computer
7   and the CD and what you had?
8   A.   Initially they were packaged, they were
9   photographed, packaged into either brown paper sacks
10   or our Sheriff's Department evidence envelopes,
11   labeled and placed into our property and evidence
12   section a warehouse with specific control procedures
13   for storing and handling evidence.
14   Q.   Eventually, did you write an inventory of
15   all the CD's?
16   A.   Yes, I did.
17   Q.   When did do you that?
18   A.   That was during my forensic examination of
19   the computers and the CD's.
20   Q.   And as you were there you saw the CD's, did
21   anybody else handle the CD's and switch the order
22   around while you were there?
23   A.   No, not at all.
24   Q.   Do you know if the order was switched at all
25   from the way that, you know, Deputy Judd and Schupbach

SUPERIOR COURT, PIMA COUNTY

1 would have seen them when you arrived?

2   A.   I don't have any information that it was or

3 was not. Not being there, there is no way I would

4 know that.

5   Q.   So you photographed the CD's as you found

6 them when you got there?

7   A.   Correct.

8   Q.   Okay. So after you gathered up all the

9 materials that you needed, what did you do?

10   A.   After we had collected everything that we

11 considered important or evidence, we take photographs

12 as we leave to document the condition that we are

13 leaving the residence or the vehicle in, leave a copy

14 of the items that -- a receipt for the property we're

15 taking basically and a copy of search warrant and then

16 I left.

17   Q.   What happened to Mr. Coghill?

18   A.   He was left at his residence.

19   Q.   Was he under arrest?

20   A.   No.

21   Q.   Why not?

22   A.   At that time all I had was a report and an

23 indication that there was evidentiary items on his

24 computer or CD's. I needed to look at those items,

25 the digital evidence to determine whether there was

1 any validity to the reports aside from what validity I

2 had determined in obtaining the search warrant.

3   Q.   And so did you participate at all in an

4 interview with Mr. Franks?

5   A.   Very briefly. He was still talking to

6 detectives after we had concluded or after I had

7 concluded collecting items that were some other people

8 at the mobilehome. When I got back to the main

9 station, he was still talking to a co-worker and I

10 believe I asked a couple of brief questions.

11   Q.   Now, while we're on that, forensic

12 interviewing, can you tell the jury what that is?

13   A.   Forensic interviewing is a technique used by

14 interviewers to elicit information from someone in a

15 way that begins with very open-ended questions and

16 ends with pointed or leading questions. It allows for

17 the greatest flow of information that is accurate.

18 Typically inaccuracies in an interview of this type

19 are errors of omission where something is accidentally

20 forgotten as opposed to intentionally or

21 unintentionally misstated. It begins with questions

22 such as, I understand something happened today, tell

23 me about that or -- I'm not providing information to

24 you about what I would like to hear, just that I

25 understand something happened and whatever information

SUPERIOR COURT, PIMA COUNTY

1   you provide to me, I will use to create further

2   open-ended questions such as that.

3   Now, if at the conclusion of that and the

4   information desired has not been obtained and I think

5   -- it's still is something that you may have

6   information about, I may ask more pointed questions

7   such as, did something happen today at the mobilehome,

8   where I provide a little bit of information which I

9   had initially tried not to do and now I focused

10   questioning a little bit. Now you are aware I'm

11   looking for information about what happened in the

12   mobilehome. If that still does not elicit

13   information, I may provide a little bit more

14   information, go to a more leading question. I

15   understand you had an argument or I understand that

16   you decided to call the police today about something

17   at the mobilehome, tell me about that, leading you a

18   little bit, giving you a little more direction what

19   kind of information I'm looking for. Where as that

20   initially, I just open it up and said, give me

21   whatever information you got that you think is

22   pertinent all the way down to the most pointed and

23   certainly avoided questions if possible. I understand

24   that you made a report today about possession of child

25   pornography, tell me what you know about that, where

1   I've given you all details what I'm looking for in a

2   formed response and hoping you will provide me a

3   specific information on what I'm looking for. If not,

4   then the interview would probably be over. That's the

5   general basis of a forensic interview, elicit

6   information without tainting your -- your mindset as

7   to what I'm looking for.

8   Q.   Did you have specific training on doing

9   these type of interviews before you were allowed to do

10 them?

11   A.   Yes.

12   Q.   About how much?

13   A.   There's a beginning class that is maybe a

14 four or five-day class then there's a class I had

15 attended, the beginning class of forensic

16 interviewing, it's either four or five days of class

17 instruction and practicals with actual persons.

18   Q.   Okay. So you gathered up the search warrant

19 materials then you participated briefly in Mr. Franks

20 interview?

21   A.   Yes. It was -- it had progressed

22 considerably. I had some specific questions after

23 having left the mobilehome that I wanted to ask Mr.

24 Franks?

25   Q.   Then after that -- you when you were done

1   with that, what did you do?

2   A.   After that, it was a period of time, I don't

3   recall how long between that activity and there's a

4   document procedure we have to go through with the

5   search warrant to bring it back to the courts after

6   that. There was period of time between that and my

7   forensic examination of the CD's and the computer

8   where I retrieved them from our property in evidence

9   and brought them to a my office and conducted an

10 examination.

11   Q.   Are there procedures in place to prevent,

12 you know, electronic contamination of these computer

13 CD's and/or the hard drives?

14   A.   They are stored in a controlled facility.

15 There's very rigid access to them. You have to sign

16 in an sign out. If you would like to view or handle

17 any of the evidence, you have to sign that -- a sheet

18 specific to that evidence that you are checking out

19 and checking it back in. Again, it's a very

20 controlled access area.

21   Q.   Are there specific areas within the

22 Sheriff's Department main building where computer

23 analysis is conducted?

24   A.   There is, there are now. At that time, I

25 was conducting the exams at my federal task force

1   office which also does examinations of that nature.

2   Q.   Okay. So if at that time at your federal

3   office, was there -- was it like limited access to

4   these areas?

5   A.   Absolutely. It's -- it's inside the F.B.I.

6   offices and as an employee there, I had difficulty

7   getting in some times.

8   Q.   When did you start your analysis in this

9   case?

10   A.   I don't know the exact date. I know it was

11 not that day or shortly thereafter. Having a caseload

12 from three, four different types of jobs, it took a

13 little while to get to. I don't remember the exact

14 date that I started the exam.

15   Q.   Okay. Were you in any particular rush to

16 get this done?

17   A.   Not necessarily. I didn't have any

18 indication that there were any extenuating

19 circumstances that would cause me to rush to do it.

20 Obviously, like to get things done as soon as

21 possible, but just the volume of the electronic

22 evidence that had been taken, I knew it would take a

23 fair amount of time to conduct the examination.

24   Q.   Okay. So if you can approximate when did

25 you think you started the analysis?

1   A.   A couple weeks later, maybe a month, I don't

2   really recall.

3   Q.   Do you know how long it took you to finish

4   it?

5   A.   It took me several -- it took me at least a

6   week, two weeks just because of the volume of CD's

7   that we had taken. It was -- it was a fairly lengthy

8   process to go through all of them.

9   Q.   Which one did you do first, did you anaylze

10   the computer hard drives first or the CD?

11   A.   I looked at the computer hard drives first,

12   then I -- then I moved onto the CD's.

13   Q.   Okay. Then how do you go back analyzing the

14   hard drives?

15   A.   Typically, what we do with the hard drives,

16   the one overriding principle we abide by is not to

17   change any data on that disc. If I were to take your

18   home computer, bring it to my office, plug it in and

19   turn it on, just by turning it on, by activating the

20   file system, the operating system on the computer, I

21   would change hundreds of files. I may not change the

22   contents of your word document that has your resume,

23   but if I open that file and looked at it, I would

24   change the date that the computer associates that file

25   having last been opened or accessed. Or if I changed

SUPERIOR COURT, PIMA COUNTY

513

1   it, it would change a modified date. There are a

2   multitude of different items that a computer will

3   change that we don't allow to happen on the computers

4   that we seize. The way we do that is by never

5   actually working our examination on the hard drive, we

6   make an exact forensic duplicate of the hard drive

7   using special certified software that we have

8   validated to correctly image the drive.

9   Typically, digital evidence added to root

10   level consists of ones and zeros or magnetic bits on

11   an on and off state. The hardware and software we use

12   goes to that first bit and says, is it a one or zero.

13   If it's a one, it copies a one over. If it's a zero,

14   copies, and it literally goes through the entire disc

15   or CD or floppy disc and does that exact same thing

16   without ever making any changes to those dates and

17   times or the file system or any of the items that

18   would be changed if we booted up that PC.

19   I made a duplicate, forensic duplicate, of

20   the drive and that's verified through a -- what's

21   called a hash value. It's kind of like fingerprints

22   for the data on there. If you changed any of those

23   ones and zeros, the hash value would change. If I

24   don't get a matching hash value, I don't get a

25   duplicate. I did receive a matching hash value in

1   this case hard drive.

2   Once though a duplicate is made, I'll use

3   that duplicate to conduct my examination on, then I

4   don't risk the possibility of making any changes or,

5   you know, the silly spilling a cup of coffee on it,

6   the original digital evidence is -- is touched only to

7   make its duplicate, then the duplicate is what we work

8   with. If need be, we could always go back and make

9   another duplicate. As a safety precaution we don't

10   work on the original evidence though, unless the

11   evidence is of a nature that it cannot be changed.

12   For example, once a CD is written and

13   closed, if we examine it and a CD drive that does not

14   have the capability of writing to a CD, only reading

15   from it, then I don't need to duplicate it, I can look

16   at the original item, my equipment physically cannot

17   make a change to that device.

18   So after completing that, I will use a

19   forensic examination program and at the time I was

20   using Guidance Software Encase, and I believe it was

21   version 3.22 which was the latest version I had access

22   to. They are very expensive programs. I believe

23   there was an update available, but for budget reasons

24   I didn't have the ability to use the updated version.

25   It didn't fix any significant problems in the earlier

SUPERIOR COURT, PIMA COUNTY

1   version, it just added some functionality, would have

2   been --

3   THE COURT: We need to sort of get to the

4   questions and answers here. We need to have a little

5   bit of direction.

6   MR. JENSVOLD: Thank you, Your Honor.

7   BY MR. JENSVOLD:

8   Q.   Mr. Englander, was that software validated?

9   A.   Yes.

10   Q.   What does validated mean?

11   A.   Validated means that it has been put through

12   a set of rigorous tests either by myself or the

13   computer forensic community as a whole or the vendor

14   or all or any combination to determine that the

15   product works as it is supposed to.

16   In other words, not changing any data,

17   showing the appropriate data in the appropriate

18   places. It's a procedure that we use with virtually

19   all of our equipment hardware and software, otherwise

20   we wouldn't know for sure that it does in fact work

21   the way it's supposed to.

22   Q.   Then what specific purposes, besides just

23   copying data, is that its only purpose?

24   A.   I believe in order to copy this data I used

25   what's called a logic cube, it's a physical device

1   that duplicates the drives, only allows for one way

2   flow of information. It takes the first one, puts it

3   on the other drive, takes the second bit, if it's zero

4   or one, such as that, then I use Encase to do the

5   examination of that duplicate.

6   Q.   So then what -- then what examinations are

7   -- are you performing with this Encase software?

8   A.   Encase software allows to us see every file

9   and folder on the computer, additionally allows us to

10 see a host of other data. For example, if you had a

11 file on your computer and you deleted it and you had

12 deleted it the day before you provided the computer, I

13 would be able to see that file still on the drive as a

14 deleted file.

15   If a file is on a computer and the file has

16 been deleted and the data perhaps has been

17 overwritten, but the indication that a file was there

18 has not, I will be able to see with Encase that this

19 file existed, this is where it existed, the data isn't

20 there anymore, kind of like a book where you have the

21 chapter index and the actual text. Text can be gone

22 and the table, you can tear the text out, table of

23 index is still there, you can tear out the index, the

24 text is still there. The two don't necessarily go

25 hand in hand, the file name or really it's indication

SUPERIOR COURT, PIMA COUNTY

517

1   in the operateing system. Encase allows us to see

2   both of those, if they're present or whichever one is

3   present necessarily. We can also see --

4   THE COURT: Okay, we're getting, again, a

5   little bit further. I'd like Mr. Jensvold to either

6   -- direct testimony, what evidence you want to get

7   from the witness, please.

8   BY MR. JENSVOLD:

9   Q.   All right. Have you gone through all the

10   specific procedures that this software analyzes as far

11   as the hard drive and file dates?

12   A.   I think it would probably take me weeks to

13   go through the manual with everyone but --

14   Q.   That's fine, I don't want to you do that.

15   Let's talk about the files. You mentioned

16   it can detect whether files were created. Can you

17   discuss how it does that?

18   A.   When you have a file on your computer, the

19   computer keeps track of several dates, depending on

20   the operating system and a few other factors, when the

21   file was created on the computer is the date that the

22   computer maintains when the file was last accessed,

23   accessed means kind of touched in any way, you don't

24   have to open it. If you move it, that may cause you

25   to access when the file was last written.

1   So in other words, not just moved, but

2   actually written to, if you change something in the

3   file and sometimes you have the ability to see when

4   files are deleted, the actual date that it was deleted

5   in accordance to the computer/s clock. Those are --

6   those are -- that's information that Encase will allow

7   us to see that you may or may not be able to see as a

8   traditional user of your computer.

9   Q.   Were there also ways for this software to

10   see when files were transferred specifically to the CD

11   burner?

12   A.   Computers can keep track of that. Typically

13   those types of storage areas only keep a very small

14   number of recent transferred files, if any at all. It

15   simply depends on the mechanism used to transfer.

16   Q.   Now, how many hard drives -- you said this

17   computer had two hard drives?

18   A.   Yes.

19   Q.   Okay. And did you analyze both of those?

20   A.   Yes.

21   Q.   Using the Encase software?

22   A.   Yes.

23   Q.   And did you also analyze electronically the

24   CD's specifically?

25   A.   Correct. In the same fashion using Encase,

1   however, I did not need to duplicate them because I

2   used the procedure I mentioned earlier.

3   Q.   And what things -- when you analyze the CD.

4   what is happening there?

5   A.   What I'm able to see on the CD's are

6   obviously the files that have been placed on the CD.

7   Additionally, most of common software used to burn a

8   CD to put data on them imbeds in the beginning of the

9   CD the date and time according to the computer clock

10   that the CD was burned. Oftentimes you, as a user,

11   may not be able to see that data. Encase allows me

12   see it because I can see the raw data that is put on

13   the computer.

14   Q.   Can -- can that data be -- that file burn

15   date be changed?

16   A.   Once it's been burned on the CD, no, not to

17   my knowledge.

18   Q.   Okay. Let's talk about specifically the

19   hard drives. There were two evidence numbers for

20   these hard drives, do you remember what they were?

21   A.   I don't off the top of my head.

22   Q.   All right. Mr. Englander, I want show you

23   State's Exhibit 10A, do you recognize that?

24   A.   That is Pima County Sheriff's Department

25   property and evidence sheet and it's -- it looks like

SUPERIOR COURT, PIMA COUNTY

1   it was completed at the scene, copy of receipt,

 2   property and evidence.

 3   Q.   Is that from this case?

 4   A.   Yes.

 5   Q.   What materials are indicated on the property

 6   sheet?

 7   A.   There is a white computer tower with a P2MX

 8   sticker spindle with multiple -- several entries for

 9   spindles with multiple CD roms. There is an

10   indication of one Omega zip 100 drive with cords,

11   indication of one QUE Exclamation point, fire CD RW

12   burner with cables. There's an indication of one

13   surfboard cable modum,, an indication of one Soho

14   five port Ethernet, and a black a single black Case,

15   Logic CD holder with multiple CD's.

16   Q.   What's the evidence number for the computer

17   itself?

18   A.   JE1, my initials and the number one.

19   Q.   And J stands for Jeff Englander?

20   A.   Yes.

21   Q.   Handing you State's Exhibit 12A, what is

22   that?

23   A.   This is the portion of my computer forensic

24   report.

25   Q.   And --

SUPERIOR COURT, PIMA COUNTY

521

1   THE COURT: So -- what's the exhibit.

2   THE WITNESS: 12A.

3   BY MR. JENSVOLD:

4   Q.   And does that report also indicate specific

5   evidence numbers for the two hard drives?

6   A.   It does JE1A, and JE1B.

7   Q.   Now, there was -- what were the -- were

8   there different purposes for these two hard drives?

9   A.   You know, they were two different hard

10 drives and it looked like the smaller hard drive may

11 have initially been used as an operating system drive,

12 then the larger drive was purchased that was used as a

13 operating system drive. They both contained data,

14 both contained a directory structure associated with

15 an operating system, My Documents folders, things of

16 that nature. But one was -- one computer with this

17 kind of a drive, you can set one up to be the primary

18 drive, the master drive and you can set other drives

19 to be just kind of storage drives, called slave

20 drives. One was set as a master and one was set as a

21 slave.

22   Q.   Which one was which?

23   A.   The JE1A was set as master, and I believe

24 that was an approximately 15 gigabyte drive was set as

25 the mater and JE1B which is around five gigabyte was

1   set as the slave.

2   Q.   And now, did you find any evidence of --

3   correct me if my terminology is wrong here, any

4   evidence of child pornography files on either one of

5   these hard drives?

6   A.   I found indications.

7   Q.   Okay. Now, was -- did you find actual movie

8   files that you can play and see on a computer screen

9   from the hard drive itself?

10   A.   I believe that several of the files were

11   found on the drive. I would have to refer to the

12   actual drive report or the -- I correct myself in my

13   summary, it does indicate that I did find files on the

14   drive.

15   Q.   Which files, what files did you find?

16   A.   Let's see. The drive was JE1B and it looks

17   as though the files were -- I'll be honest, it was

18   listed in an attachment that I don't have.

19   Q.   I have other sections of your entire report.

20   Let me, I have State's Exhibits 12B C, D and E?

21   Okay, I broke your report down in sections

22   just for manageability.

23   Mr. Englander, I'll show you what is marked

24   as 12B, what is that?

25   A.   This is an indication of files from the hard

SUPERIOR COURT, PIMA COUNTY

1   drives or hard drive that were found to contain child

2   pornography or indications of those files.

3   Q.   Okay.   Can you explain the difference

4   between actual files and indication of files?

5   A.   Files would be a movie file or a still image

6   file that was child pornography, an indication would

7   be, as I said earlier about having a table of contents

8   and a chapter.   If the data is not present, the file

9   name alone is and the file name is indicative of child

10   pornography or I found the data somewhere else and I

11   only have the listing of the file name on the hard

12   drive that would be an indication of the file.

13   It's not the actual data, it's not a

14   playable movie, it may be a file listing the name of

15   or the path to the file where it may have existed

16   previously or where it was moved from or copied from,

17   things of that nature.   It's not the actual data, the

18   indication is just it existed at some point in time.

19   Q.   Okay.   Now, the files that were charged in

20   this case, the 15 different files, were those found on

21   CD's?

22   A.   Yes.

23   Q.   Okay.   Then were some of those files you

24   could play all of those files?

25   A.   Correct playable movie files.

1   Q.   Okay. Were some of those files found on

2 either JE1A or JE1B?

3   A.   Yes.

4   Q.   Okay.

5   A.   An indication of some of them as well.

6   Q.   Okay. Can you tell from your report which

7 ones were files that you could play and which -- which

8 ones were indication?

9   A.   I can, yes.

10   Q.   Okay. From which document are you looking?

11   A.   Looking at 12B.

12   Q.   Looking at 12, which files did you find

13 actual files that you could play, is that a correct

14 question?

15   A.   Correct.

16   Q.   And which ones did you find there?

17   A.   I guess I should make a distinction. I can

18 play as using forensic software because I can access

19 files that have been deleted as opposed to what you as

20 a user could play. There is a file, it existed then

21 was overwritten by itself. I believe it was

22 downloaded twice that existed in a deleted state. I

23 was able to play it because I have the ability to

24 restore a deleted file using this program. As a user,

25 none of the files in this report were playable by a

```
1    tradtional user.

2         Q.    Okay.  So those hard drives were placed in
3    the tower as you found it, without your software, you
4    could not play those?

5         A.    Correct.

6         Q.    You didn't find any files of child
7    pornography that you could actually play in its
8    existing state as you found it?

9         A.    Correct.  I'm sorry, that was my mistake,
10   I'm making that distinction.

11        Q.    How many of those did you find, the actual
12   file itself using your software that you could play?

13        A.    Of these?

14        Q.    Of these, right, the charged files?

15        A.    How many did I find on the hard drive?

16        Q.    Yes.

17        A.    There are -- I guess the answer to your
18   question would be none using my software.

19        Q.    Using --

20        A.    Using my software I found one in -- in two,
21   I believe one in -- on the drive.

22        Q.    And what file name was that?

23        A.    The file name is it's Baby J, the letter J
24   hyphen, babycum.mpeg.

25        Q.    And that's the only one --
```

1   A.   Correct.

2   Q.   -- that you could actually play using your

3   software?

4   A.   Correct.

5   Q.   Okay. Was there a creation date for that

6   file that your examination discovered?

7   A.   There is.

8   Q.   What was that?

9   A.   March 4th, 2003.

10   Q.   Could a user on the computer as you found

11   it, before you analyzed it, could a normal user

12   manipulate that creation date?

13   A.   I never say no because people -- you can

14   manipulate a computer date by changing the system

15   clock and things of that nature, but it's fairly rare

16   to find that having happened. Within this, it would

17   have to have been done prior to the downloading and

18   creating of this file. Once the file is on the

19   computer, that created date remains irrespective of

20   what happens to the computer.

21   Q.   Now, you found -- based on your previous

22   testimony, you found other indications of files on the

23   hard drives?

24   A.   Yes.

25   Q.   Which of the charged files did you find

SUPERIOR COURT, PIMA COUNTY

527

1 indications of?

2   A.   I found an indication of a file called --

3 I'm going use this term a few times so I'm going to

4 spell it first, it's R, at symbol, YGOLD, R@YGOLD

5 style, hyphen, Lucy.mpg. Another file R@YGOLD or the

6 at symbol, R@YGOLD style, BabyJ, the letter J, 3yo

7 girl eats cum2.mpg. Another file was R@YGOLD,

8 underscore, then all one word Ilikeit.mpg. File

9 called BabyJ hyphen Lol hyphen 01.avi.

10   MR. LAGATTUTA: Your Honor, could I enter an

11 objection and may I approach the bench for a moment

12 with Counsel?

13   THE COURT: Sure.

14   (The following proceedings took place at the

15 bench between Court and Counsel, out of the hearing of

16 the jurors:)

17   MR. LAGATTUTA: I am not certain at this

18 point if he is not testifying to uncharged areas or

19 other uncharged either files or data, and I thought we

20 had an understanding then Mr. Coghill having been

21 charged with 15 counts, we were going to refer to

22 those 15 counts, not to everything else in the world.

23   THE COURT: Okay. Well, kind of going down

24 what they are, I think we should limit these. I think

25 the question was, which of the counts were charged

```
 1   so --

 2            MR. JENSVOLD:  That was the question.

 3            MR. LAGATTUTA:  But, I don't recognize a lot

 4   of those as being listed in the Indictment.

 5            THE COURT:  This would be a good time for a

 6   break, why don't you take that and take a few minutes

 7   at the break.  You all look at this get, you know,

 8   somehow or other the charges up there, list them, what

 9   they are that he found based on the charges so that we

10   smooth it out a little bit because no one is going to

11   understand this anyway.

12            MR. LAGATTUTA:  Okay.

13            (The following proceedings were held in open

14   court, in the presence of the jurors:)

15            THE COURT:  Folks this is a good time for

16   our break.  We'll take until about quarter after.

17   It's just few minutes before 3:00 right now, and so

18   we'll take until 3:15, we'll be in recess until then.

19            (The Court stood in recess.)

20            THE COURT:  Thank you, please be seated

21   we're here now with the jurors, counsel, the defendant

22   and we're continuing the direct examination of Mr.

23   Englander.

24       Mr. Jensvold?

25       MR. JENSVOLD:  Thank you, Your Honor.
```

SUPERIOR COURT, PIMA COUNTY

1   BY MR. JENSVOLD:

2   Q.   Okay. Detective Englander, before we got

3   this equipment set up here, you opened up a piece of

4   evidence. I'm going to show it to you. I'll show you

5   what is marked as State's Exhibit Number 23, this was

6   opened in your presence during the break?

7   A.   Yes.

8   Q.   What is it?

9   A.   It is Pima County Sheriff's Department

10 evidence envelope and description is CD rom for Grand

11 Jury.

12   Q.   Okay. And how did you make this CD rom?

13   A.   The CD rom I made by taking the -- the movie

14 files that were to be charged, placing them from the

15 locations on the CD's that I had located them on the

16 actual files and simply copying them out of the

17 forensic software onto the CD. They are exact

18 duplicates.

19   Q.   All right. And has anybody else handled

20 this CD rom besides yourself and when we opened it

21 today?

22   A.   I believe Matt Gidney did, but it's the

23 right one, CK so --

24   Q.   Detective Matt Gidney is a detective with

25 the Sheriff's Department?

SUPERIOR COURT, PIMA COUNTY

1   A.   Yes.

2   Q.   He has sort of taken over chain of custody

3   issues in this case since you left the Sheriff's

4   Department?

5   A.   Correct.

6   Q.   Okay. Now, do you remember specifically

7   which CD's, which files that are charged were found on

8   which CD's?

9   A.   I don't. Off the top of my head I don't

10   recall, but I believe it was documented at some point

11   in time.

12   Q.   Now, this is a copy -- I discussed this with

13   defense counsel, this is State's Exhibit 24. These

14   are a copy of notes taken from your interview with Mr.

15   Lagattuta and the State's representative also. Turn

16   to the last page here, it has specific counts tied up

17   with specific CD names?

18   A.   Yes.

19   Q.   Okay. Does that look like -- does that look

20   accurate to you?

21   A.   Yes.

22   Q.   Okay. If you could, without giving the file

23   names, if you could just write Count One through 15 on

24   the left-hand portion of the board there and then tie

25   up which CD name, evidence number, is associated with

1 that?

2   A.   Sure.

3   Q.   For the record, you listed Count One through

4 15 on the left-hand margin. And let's see Count One

5 and Two and Three are associated with CD number JE3N?

6   A.   Yes, I apologize that's not very straight.

7   Q.   And four is associated with JE3Q?

8   A.   Q.

9   Q.   And Five and Six are associated with JE3O?

10   A.   Yes. Seven, Eight are 3E 3L, nine, JE3J.

11   Q.   Ten through 15 are JE3B?

12   A.   Yes.

13   Q.   Now, have you verified that on State's

14 Exhibit 24?

15   A.   Three.

16   Q.   Twenty-three -- State's Exhibit 23, the

17 Grand Jury disc, have you verified all of those files

18 that you indicated came from the various CD's under

19 the JE3 designation are on this CD?

20   A.   Yes.

21   Q.   Okay. And this CD is same one that you used

22 in preparing it and presenting it to the Grand Jury?

23   A.   Correct.

24   Q.   What I'd like to do, we're going to play

25 each one of these in order from Count One through 15

SUPERIOR COURT. PIMA COUNTY

1   What I'm going do for the jury purpose and everyone

2   else here, as soon as, for my perspective I see what's

3   been described in the file, I'm going to ask you to

4   forward through that unless someone in the jury has

5   some reason not to.

6   A.   Okay.

7   MR. JENSVOLD: Your Honor, is that

8   acceptable?

9   THE COURT: Why don't all approach for a

10 minute.

11   (The following proceedings took place at the

12 bench between Court and Counsel, out of the hearing of

13 the jurors:)

14   THE COURT: I'm not sure exactly -- you want

15 to turn this over to the jury, they can ask questions

16 or something?

17   MR. JENSVOLD: Maybe I'll just play it and

18 then ask them if they have any -- if they want

19 anything played back if they're not satisfied.

20   THE COURT: I think we can -- well, what's

21 your position?

22   MR. LAGATTUTA: My position, we're willing

23 to stipulate that every one of these items are

24 identical to the charged items in the Indictment and

25 constitutes a violation of statutes, not to play

```
 1   record, the -- Count One is R@YGOLD Style-Lucy, is

 2   that correct?

 3       A.   Yes.

 4                      (MOVIES PLAYING)

 5       Q.   All right.  Detective, you can move on to

 6   the next file.

 7            Count Two would be R@YGOLD Style babyJ 3yo,

 8   etc.?

 9       A.   Yes.

10       Q.   Okay, Detective, you can move to the next

11   one.

12            Count Three would be R@YGOLD with an under

13   score, ilikeit?

14       A.   Yes.

15       Q.   Detective, is there a way to forward through

16   part of this?

17       A.   Sure.

18       Q.   Okay.  That's okay, you can go to the next

19   one, please.

20            And Count Four, would be Vicky complete?

21       A.   Yes.

22       Q.   You can move to the next one, please.

23            Count Five starts with R@YGOLD russian 2

24   preteen boys?

25       A.   Yes.
```

```
 1       Q.    You can move on to the next one.

 2             And count Six is reel, R-E-E-L, kiddy

 3    K-I-D-D-Y?

 4       A.    Yes.

 5       Q.    You can move on to the next one, please.

 6             And Counts Seven is Vicky_ good daughter 2 ?

 7       A.    Yes.

 8       Q.    You can go on to the next one, please.

 9             And Count Eight would be R@YGOLD Style RCA3?

10       A.    Correct.

11       Q.    You can move on to the next one.

12             Count Nine is R@YGOLD_tvg013 bound, is that

13    correct?

14       A.    Yes.

15       Q.    Can you forward through this one?

16       A.    Certainly.

17       Q.    You can move on to the next one.

18             Count Ten is BabyJ-babycum, C-U-M?

19       A.    Yes.

20       Q.    You can move on to --  Count 11 is

21    BabyJ-captive?

22       A.    Yes.

23       Q.    You can move on to the next one.

24             And Count 12 is BabyJ-1OL.  You can move on

25    to the next one, please.
```

1   Count 13 is BabyJ-Teddy, T-E-D-D-Y?

2   A.   Correct.

3   Q.   You can move on to the next one.

4   Count 14 is R@YGOLD BabyJ compilation,

5   numbers and letters after that?

6   A.   Correct.

7   Q.   Can you forward through a little bit. Move

8   on to the next one, please.

9   And finally Count 15 is R@YGOLD Style- Open

10   11, some other words after that, is that correct?

11   A.   Correct. Can you forward through some of

12   this, Detective?

13   A.   Sure.

14   Q.   I think that's good, thank you.

15   Mr. Englander, while we're here on this

16   particular laptop that you have, have you been -- has

17   there been downloaded copies of files that were

18   present from the hard drive of the JE1A A and B onto

19   this laptop?

20   A.   Yes.

21   Q.   How did that happen?

22   A.   Detective Gideny created a duplicate image

23   of the hard drives for use in the Encase program and

24   that duplication was verified through the use of hash

25   values.

1   Q.   Do you have State's Exhibit 12E up at the

2   witness chair?

3   A.   No, I have 12A here.

4   Q.   Detective, I'm going to hand you what is

5   12E. What is 12E, I think we discussed it earlier,

6   maybe it was with Mr. Franks. Have you seen this

7   before?

8   A.   Yes.

9   Q.   What is it?

10   A.   This is a printout of a series of database

11   files that are maintained by a peer to peer file

12   sharing program called KaZaA. In this case I believe

13   it was KaZaA Lite which just means it doesn't have

14   some of the other features.

15   THE COURT: Let me just ask, can we turn

16   this off?

17   MR. JENSVOLD: I was going to lay a little

18   bit of foundation, go ahead lay some more, do it all

19   at once.

20   THE COURT: Sure.

21   THE WITNESS: The database files are

22   maintained by the program. They are a fixed sized

23   file and as files are downloaded through the use of

24   this peer to peer program which is like Napster used

25   to be for music, this can kind of do any files. As

SUPERIOR COURT, PIMA COUNTY

1   files are downloaded this data files, an entry is made

2   for each file. Since it's a fixed sized file, once

3   that file is full of entries, a new one is added, the

4   oldest one is dropped off, so it goes back to a

5   certain date based on the size of file and number of

6   entries in here. These are database files of the

7   files that are -- that were used with the KaZaA

8   program.

9   Q.   There are page numbers on the bottom, bottom

10 middle of 12E?

11   A.   Yes.

12   Q.   Starting with page one, what appear to be

13 records of mp3 that were downloaded?

14   A.   Correct.

15   Q.   There's a file date designation, what does

16 that mean?

17   A.   That's the date that it was downloaded on.

18   Q.   And then there's also indication of file not

19 present, last available, what does that mean?

20   A.   The program and most of the ones similar to

21 it, there are a variety of them. When you initially

22 set up the program, it designates a folder on your

23 hard drive for where it's going to put these files.

24 The idea of these files is that you are -- once you

25 have them, going to share them with everyone else. It

1 needs to know where to look for them.

2   If the file is downloaded to that folder,

3 then is moved from that folder somewhere else or

4 deleted or the name of it is changed, it will show in

5 the log as not present for sharing or not present

6 anymore so that the program itself knows I can't offer

7 this to other people using this program because it's

8 not here anymore.

9   Q. Now, have you -- if I didn't ask you already

10 have you gone through this the hard drive, and scanned

11 anything within this, My Shared folder KaZaA Lite, My

12 Shared folder, look for child pornography?

13   A. Yes.

14   Q. Did you find any?

15   A. No.

16   Q. Did you find any adult pornography files?

17   A. Yes.

18   Q. Okay. Can we -- well, let's go -- let's go,

19 can you turn to page 47 now. Is there a way that you

20 can look at what's on your laptop and compare it to

21 what is indicated to State's Exhibit 12B?

22   A. I can look for the file name, I can look for

23 that on the hard drives of the computers that we

24 examined to see if that file name exists or I can go

25 to the folder that this is pointing to and see if this

```
 1  file exists in that location as opposed to anywhere on
 2  the drive, yes.
 3       Q.  All right.  Let's start with -- there's one
 4  that appears to the top of page 48, there's a file
 5  name that says wet horny latin brazil (1)(4)?
 6       A.  Correct.
 7       Q.  Can you check to see on your duplicate copy
 8  of the hard drives whether that file is present?
 9           MR. LAGATTUTA:  Objection, Your Honor, as to
10  relevancy.
11           THE COURT:  Counsel approach, please.
12           (The following proceedings took place at the
13  bench between Court and Counsel, out of the hearing of
14  the jurors:)
15           MR. JENSVOLD:  This is based on Mr. Franks'
16  testimony that he recognized -- he admitted to being
17  on the computer on KaZaA downloading pornography as
18  pm3 on March 26th, the dates are specifically
19  toward --
20           THE COURT:  Tell me again.
21           MR. JENSVOLD:  The reason is because there
22  were no -- there were no adult pornography files or
23  child pornography files anywhere during this time Mr.
24  Franks admits he was on the computer while he was in
25  Tucson.  I'm not going play all these, I just -- it's
```

1 important that the jury see clear distinction, there's

2 some of these files based on their descriptions that

3 could, you know, be -- could be adult, child

4 pornography. But when you see them, these were files

5 he would never -- the difference is so clear.

6   THE COURT: I don't think we need to get

7 into the computer -- what's your objection.

8   MR. LAGATTTUA: You're going to use this to

9 show that Jacob Franks admitted to downloading

10 pornography here, now is the record of that, how is

11 that relevant to the crime.

12   MR. JENSVOLD: It's relevant because the

13 defense that this was Jacob Franks, the fact that

14 Jacob Franks was alone in this RV in Tucson, he was

15 not downloading child pornography even with

16 descriptions that are -- the indication that none of

17 these files are.

18   THE COURT: I think -- I think I'm going to

19 sustain the objection right now. I think it's

20 misleading right at this point to deal with something

21 like that.

22   One of the things we don't have here is

23 where these different exhibits came from, the dates

24 they were downloaded, that is probably important with

25 regard to the defendant in this case. So I think

SUPERIOR COURT, PIMA COUNTY

1 that -- I don't know what additional questions you're

2 going to have, but that's -- that's the thing that I

3 don't see downloading, you know, this was a concern

4 that the defense had. I understood the reason to

5 connect up some of the pornography as opposed to child

6 pornography, but I think it's very confusing to go --

7 at this point go back with what you're trying to do.

8 Maybe on cross-examination, depending on where they go

9 to you can do that, but right now, I'm going sustain

10 the objection.

11   MR. JENSVOLD: Okay.

12   (The following proceedings were held in open

13 court, in the presence of the jurors:)

14 BY MR. JENSVOLD:

15   Q.   Detective Englander, can you shut off the

16 equipment?

17   A.   Sure.

18   Q.   Mr. Englander, keep going back and forth.

19 Did you examine, in other words, view some of these

20 files, file names that are indicated on State's

21 Exhibit 12B starting like page 46?

22   A.   Yes.

23   Q.   Did any of those, in your opinion,

24 constitute child pornography?

25   A.   Some of them by their name would seem to

SUPERIOR COURT, PIMA COUNTY

1　indicate because they include an age in the name.

2　Typically that's why we don't simply go by a file

3　name, there's no way to know and oftentimes in that

4　border area 15, 16, 17 years old that description is

5　given to entice people to download it thinking it's

6　something that it's not. It may very well be, but

7　it's so difficult to tell from looking at an image or

8　movie of someone that age to determine once they're at

9　that level of maturity.

10　　　　　I saw files here, by their file name could

11　potentially be, but the age was so high but, yet, you

12　know, in that range, the number of those was very

13　small. The number of just standard run of the mill

14　pm3 and adult pornography files were much, much

15　greater. I didn't really see anything that -- I

16　didn't see anything with the word like R@YGOLD or

17　BabyJ or anything that was definitively indicative to

18　me that it was potential child pornography, no.

19　　　　　MR. LAGATTUTA: Excuse me, Your Honor, could

20　I just ask for a point of clarification.

21　　　　　Was that a "yes" or "no" answer?

22　　　　　THE WITNESS: That was for the most part,

23　no.

24　　　　　MR. LAGATTUTA: Okay.

25　BY MR. JENSVOLD:

1   Q.   Would you, as a forensic examiner and a

2   detective in cases such as this, have charged anyone

3   with child pornography possession for these files that

4   were found within records of which are indicated on

5   State's Exhibit 12E?

6   A.   I doubt it. I didn't necessarily see some

7   of them because they were deleted, but, no, if it's --

8   if it's something that -- the answer to your question,

9   I wouldn't have.

10   Q.   Is that based upon some of your testimony

11   earlier looking at the -- you being able to tell the

12   age differences between --

13   A.   Yes.

14   Q.   -- people that are depicted?

15   A.   Yes.

16   Q.   And were -- can you play any of these mp3

17   that are indicated to here?

18   A.   I did.

19   Q.   And did they appear to be what they say they

20   are?

21   A.   They did.

22   Q.   Did any of them not appear to be what they

23   say they are?

24   A.   No.

25   Q.   I want to go back to where we started then

1   with the charged files. You found each of those files

2   that we discussed in particular, CD under JE3?

3   A.   Correct.

4   Q.   Were all of those CD's within the same

5   spindle?

6   A.   Yes, hence the JE3 designation and then each

7   CD within that spindle was given a label of A through

8   seven and then when I got to seven, I went to double A

9   through double Z.

10   Q.   And you testified earlier you made a log of

11 all the CD's that were present?

12   A.   Correct.

13   Q.   Mr. Englander, I'm going to hand you what is

14 State's Exhibit 13, do you recognize that?

15   A.   I do.

16   Q.   What is it?

17   A.   This is the hand filled-in spread sheet I

18 made with that log of the different CD spindles.

19   Q.   Okay. And how many different spindles were

20 there?

21   A.   Nine.

22   Q.   All right. And before we get to JE3, was

23 there JE4, did that indicate "X" Files episodes at

24 least the starting CD's at the top?

25   A.   Yes.

1   Q.   And then JE5, for example, started with Star
2 Trek?
3   A.   Correct.
4   Q.   Then there were other spindles that had
5 various pm3's?
6   A.   Yes.
7   Q.   For example, JE12?
8   A.   Correct.
9   Q.   Now let's go to JE3. When you first saw
10 this spindle, what was the CD that was placed on the
11 top, what was it labeled?
12   A.   The label was the word, dirty.
13   Q.   And during your investigation, you were
14 given information that Mr. Franks admitted to writing
15 the label on that CD?
16   A.   Correct.
17   Q.   And did he -- he told you that there was
18 child pornography on that CD?
19   A.   Correct.
20   Q.   Now, the charged files -- what is the
21 evidence number for the CD labeled dirty?
22   A.   That is JE3A.
23   Q.   Okay. And did you analyze that CD to see
24 what the burn date was?
25   A.   I did.

SUPERIOR COURT, PIMA COUNTY

```
 1      Q.   Okay.  You did that using Encase software
 2  you talked about earlier?
 3      A.   Yes.
 4      Q.   What was the burn date?
 5      A.   March 25, 2003.
 6      Q.   Okay.  Now, we have several -- let's see
 7  Counts Ten through 15.
 8      A.   Correct.
 9      Q.   On JE3B was that the second CD in the -- in
10  that particular spindle?
11      A.   Yes.
12      Q.   And what was the label on that CD?
13      A.   It was two letters KP.
14      Q.   Was there anything else written on the top?
15      A.   No.
16      Q.   And did you analyze that CD for a burn date?
17      A.   Yes.
18      Q.   What was the burn date on that one?
19      A.   March 6th, of 2003.
20      Q.   And then we also looked at JE3J?
21      A.   Yes.
22      Q.   And that would be the tenth one on the
23  stack?
24      A.   Correct.
25      Q.   And what was the label on that one?
```

SUPERIOR COURT, PIMA COUNTY

1   A.   Also the letters KP.

2   Q.   And what was the burn date on that one?

3   A.   The burn date was December 28th, 2002.

4   Q.   I'm sorry J -- I'm sorry?

5   A.   I'm sorry, November 12th of 2002, for J, and
6 the label was also KP.

7   Q.   And that corresponds to Count Nine, is that
8 correct?

9   A.   Yes.

10   Q.   We also -- the next one in order would have
11 been JE3L?

12   A.   Yes.

13   Q.   And you performed the same burn date
14 analysis on that one?

15   A.   Yes.

16   Q.   What was the burn date?

17   A.   October 27, 2002.

18   Q.   And then we had JE3N?

19   A.   N?

20   Q.   I'm sorry. What was the label on that one?

21   A.   KP.

22   Q.   Okay. Then we have JE3N?

23   A.   Yes.

24   Q.   That corresponds to Count One through Three?

25   A.   Yes.

SUPERIOR COURT, PIMA COUNTY

1   Q.   And what was the burn date on that one?

2   A.   March 6th of 2003 and that label also was

3   KP.

4   Q.   Okay. Then, finally, we have JE3O, and what

5   that corresponds to Count Four through Six?

6   A.   Five and Six.

7   Q.   Five and six?

8   A.   Four is Q.

9   Q.   So five and six were JE3O?

10   A.   Yes.

11   Q.   What was the label on that one?

12   A.   The word, porn, and then the letters KP.

13   Q.   And then what was the burn date on that one?

14   A.   For O, the burn date was January 21st, 2003.

15   Q.   And then finally we have JE3Q, which

16   responds to Count Four?

17   A.   Correct.

18   Q.   What was the label on that?

19   A.   That one.

20   A.   Label on Q was letters KP, the word, movies,

21   the word, porn.

22   Q.   And then what was the burn date on that one?

23   A.   May 5th, 2002.

24   Q.   Okay, now, you already heard -- you said

25   there was child pornography found on JE3A with, dirty,

SUPERIOR COURT, PIMA COUNTY

549

1   A.   I submitted a variety of the CD's themselves

2   that had been hand-labeled with a sharpie, I believe.

3   Q.   How did you select which ones to submit for

4   analysis?

5   A.   Initially I talked to an individual that I

6   would be submitting them to and asked him what would

7   be the best to submit for him to be able to make a

8   determination. I don't recall the gentleman's name.

9   He indicated the more writing the better, so I

10   selected some that had the KP because I was interested

11   in those as they had files that I intended on

12   charging. And then some with more prolific writing on

13   them, either a full title of a movie or something to

14   that effect. I did make sure that some of them were

15   the ones that I was charging.

16   Q.   And you also submitted JE3A, that has,

17   dirty, to the label?

18   A.   Correct.

19   Q.   That you -- were you someone who directed to

20   have Mr. Franks do a handwriting sample?

21   A.   Yes.

22   MR. JENSVOLD: Your Honor, may we approach

23   at this point?

24   THE COURT: Sure.

25   (The following proceedings took place at the

SUPERIOR COURT, PIMA COUNTY

1   bench between Court and Counsel, out of the hearing of
2   the jurors:)
3   MR. JENSVOLD: Based on cross-examination
4   yesterday from Mr. Dreitl, I spoke -- to handle about
5   why he didn't get a writing sample from Mr. Coghill.
6   His explanation is that once somebody asked for an
7   attorney, they typically don't do that based on his
8   training and experience. Obviously that creates an
9   issue with invocation. That's the explanation. I
10 don't think it's really fair to leave that impression
11 for defense to be able to argue they just didn't do it
12 for no reason whatsoever.
13   THE COURT: Well, what kind of question do
14 you want to ask?
15   MR. JENSVOLD: I can ask the question what
16 the --the answer I want to get, I don't want a
17 mistrial, I don't know how to --
18   THE COURT: What's your position?
19   MR. LAGATTUTA: Well, my position he's going
20 to give a lousy answer anyway, so let's have it.
21   THE COURT: You're not going to object?
22   MR. LAGATTUTA: No, but I would like to
23 cross-examine him on it. I didn't Coghill, during the
24 interview, I want to talk to a lawyer, I should be
25 able to ask him that question. Why don't you call his

1 lawyer up and ask him if you could do -- I mean, if he

2 gives that as an answer, I'm not going to object that

3 he's commenting on my client implication of his

4 rights, but I do want to be able --

5 THE COURT: I don't think we want to get

6 into the whole issue of rights. You already had

7 testimony out that this is what it is and I think that

8 that's already been dealt with another witness. I

9 think you're in an dangerous area that goes into

10 constitutional rights, you know what the answer is

11 going to be.

12 MR. JENSVOLD: For -- can I ask for a

13 limitation based on that. I think that's fair in --

14 in his case because then the jury is left with the

15 impression this was just, oh, we didn't think about

16 it, he did think about it. He -- he chose not to do

17 it for this particular reason.

18 THE COURT: Well, argue they didn't do it.

19 MR. LAGATTUTA: Well, not only that, let's

20 face it, he could have applied to the court for, you

21 know, my client to give exemplars, he could have done

22 different things.

23 THE COURT: You can take an analysis without

24 having -- without any kind of assertion of

25 constitutional rights.

```
1            MR. LAGATTUTA:  Yeah, so --

2            THE COURT:  Well --

3            MR. LAGATTUTA:  If he wants to say it, I

4   won't object to the grounds --

5            THE COURT:  You're not --

6            MR. LAGATTUTA:  We're not.

7            THE COURT:  Go ahead and ask your question,

8   there's no objection.

9            MR. JENSVOLD:  Okay.

10           (The following proceedings were held in open

11  court, in the presence of the jurors:)

12  BY MR. JENSVOLD:

13       Q.   Mr. Englander, did you ever request a

14  handwriting sample from Mr. Coghill?

15       A.   No.

16       Q.   Why not?

17       A.   Because when I had talked to him initially

18  in my car outside of his RV, he had told me that he

19  didn't want to talk to me any more without counsel,

20  without an attorney.  And as far as I was concerned,

21  that was -- that was him indicating he didn't want to

22  participate in the investigation with me anymore.  I

23  have, in my experience as an investigator with the

24  Sheriff's Department, never had a situation where an

25  attempt --
```

SUPERIOR COURT, PIMA COUNTY

```
 1          MR. LAGATTUTA:  Objection, nonresponsive.

 2          THE COURT:  Let's finish with the question

 3  and answer.

 4  BY MR. JENSVOLD:

 5      Q.   Was it -- is it, well, procedures in your

 6  mind or the department that lead you not to pursue --

 7      A.   Correct.

 8      Q.   -- the handwriting sample?

 9      A.   Correct.

10          THE COURT:  Counsel do want you to approach

11  for a minute?

12          (The following proceedings took place at the

13  bench between Court and Counsel, out of the hearing of

14  the jurors:)

15          THE COURT:  I can offer a limiting

16  instruction for limited purposes, you didn't object to

17  it, you knew it was coming so I think that basically

18  waives the issue.  But, you know, I still think that

19  -- could tell the court -- tell the jury they are not

20  to consider the fact that the defendant asserted his

21  rights.

22          MR. LAGATTUTA:  That's fine.

23          MR. JENSVOLD:  Yeah.

24          THE COURT:  You both agree I should do that?

25          MR. JENSVOLD:  I agree.
```

```
 1            MR. LAGATTUTA:  That's fine.

 2            MR. LAGATTUTA:  As long as -- I mean, I

 3  still have to be allowed to cross-examination around

 4  the idea because I don't want the jury to get the

 5  impression that once he thinks my client asserts his

 6  right there's literally nothing else he can do.  I

 7  should be able to ask him, couldn't you have come to

 8  court, couldn't you have done this?

 9            THE COURT:  I think that's legitimate, I'll

10  let you do that.

11            MR. JENSVOLD:  Did you make a determination

12  based on the interview, I know --

13            THE COURT:  Yeah, I did, I said that could

14  come in.

15            MR. JENSVOLD:  The way that we had it, the

16  way I had a stop point on it.

17            THE COURT:  Oh, yeah, I am past the stop

18  point.

19            MR. JENSVOLD:  So I -- if that's okay, I'll

20  play it tomorrow instead of going into

21  cross-examination.  I don't want to break things up.

22            THE COURT:  Are you about ready to --

23            MR. JENSVOLD:  I'm getting close, I don't

24  have a whole lot more.  Is it okay if I do that

25  tomorrow based on he's laid the foundation for the
```

SUPERIOR COURT, PIMA COUNTY

1   interview already so --

2   THE COURT: You can do that tomorrow. Do

3   you want to come back tomorrow?

4   MR. JENSVOLD: I don't need a witness to do

5   that necessarily, he's already described he

6   interviewed him.

7   THE COURT: You want to go get that in your

8   case in chief?

9   MR. JENSVOLD: I don't need to do it during

10   Mr. Englander's testimony. I can lay the foundation

11   now, he's going to be here tomorrow any way. I can

12   just play it and let it go, I don't need --

13   THE COURT: I think --

14   MR. LAGATTUTA: If that's part of what

15   you're going to do with him.

16   THE COURT: Do it today, let's not get out

17   of order.

18   MR. LAGATTUTA: If I can cross-examine after

19   all that stuff.

20   MR. JENSVOLD: Okay.

21   MR. LAGATTUTA: Is that what you're saying.

22   THE COURT: I'm just saying you should

23   finish whatever you're bringing, any evidence so -- we

24   have to get a taperecorder.

25   MR. JENSVOLD: That's what I need, a little

1 time to get a taperecorder.

2   THE COURT: How far do you have to get the

3 taperecorder.

4   MR. JENSVOLD: I can have it in five

5 minutes, if that's okay.

6   THE COURT: Well, go ahead and if we need to

7 take a break in place, but we'll do that.

8   MR. JENSVOLD: Okay. Why don't we do that,

9 you don't need them sitting around here for five

10 minutes.

11   THE COURT: Finish your questions here.

12   MR. JENSVOLD: Okay.

13   (The following proceedings were held in open

14 court, in the presence of the jurors:)

15   THE COURT: Just want to advise the

16 court(sic) you're not to consider the defendant

17 asserted his rights to counsel is any way indicating

18 any kind of admission of guilt with regard to the

19 defendant.

20 BY MR. JENSVOLD:

21   Q. And Detective Englander, what was the --

22 when, if you remember, did you finally make the

23 decision to charge the files that you charged?

24   A. It was many months after serving the search

25 warrants, maybe even a year later. It was -- it was a

1   long time later.

2   Q.   And what evidence did you have at that point

3   when you made your decision?

4   A.   At that point I had an idea of the timeline

5   of when people were in and were not at the RV. I had

6   an idea of the results of the handwriting analysis. I

7   had been able to look back over statements that had

8   been collected. I basically had everything to a point

9   where I felt like it had been refined as much as I was

10 going to be able to examine all the CD's, examine the

11 hard drive.

12   Q.   Then you brought that to the County

13 Attorneys Office for evaluation?

14   A.   Correct.

15   Q.   Were there other programs besides KaZaA that

16 were capable of downloading information off the

17 internet that were present on this hard drive?

18   A.   Absolutely.

19   Q.   What programs were that?

20   A.   Well, at a basic level there was Internet

21 Explorer, comes with Windows, just a browser. If you

22 go to a web page that has links to files, you can

23 download that way.

24   Additionally there was a program, FTP

25 program. It's a file transfer program. It's a very

1   rudimentary program for downloading and uploading to

2   and from specific other people. There was also a

3   program that's traditionallly used for chatting all

4   M-R-I-C or MRIC has features built in that allow for

5   transfer to and from kind of older method of file

6   sharing known as F serves which are another way to

7   upload and download files.

8   So there were several programs that could

9   send and/or receive files.

10   Q.   Mr. Englander, I'm going hand you what is

11 State's Exhibit 19. Do you recognize that?

12   A.   This is a Pima County Sheriff's Department

13 property envelope, the description is Cox Cable bill.

14 The item is BK4.

15   Q.   And do you recognize the package?

16   A.   Yes.

17   Q.   Did you place that into evidence or were you

18 involved in --

19   A.   Yes.

20   Q.   Okay. And if you could open that, please.

21   A.   I believe the court evidence tag has been

22 stapled through the item.

23   MR. LAGATTUTA: Your Honor, we will be

24 willing to stipulate, if that's the Cox Cable bill

25 from my client's motorhome or from --

```
 1          THE COURT:  If you want to discuss whether
 2    you want to stipulate, do it together then talk about
 3    it up here.  If there is not to be any objection, why
 4    don't you talk about it without doing it in front of
 5    the jury.
 6    BY MR. JENSVOLD:
 7          Q.  Detective, if we could open it.  Does that
 8    appear to be the Cox bill that you retrieved and the
 9    defendant's RV?
10          A.  It does.
11          Q.  Are there any dates associated with that
12    bill?
13          A.  There are.  There is a drop replacement date
14    of 2/27 of '03.  There is a tag number or type date of
15    2/25/03.  I think that initial 2/27 is actually an
16    install date, install is printed, but it looks like it
17    printed over a different block.
18          Q.  Whose name appears to the bill?
19          A.  Jim Coghill.
20          Q.  Is Jacob Franks appear on the bill?
21          A.  No.
22          MR. JENSVOLD:  Your Honor, at this point the
23    State would move to admit State's Exhibits 19 --
24          THE COURT:  Why don't you refresh my memory.
25          MR. JENSVOLD:  Nineteen is the Cox bill.
```

SUPERIOR COURT, PIMA COUNTY

```
1          THE COURT:  Any objection to 19?

2          MR. LAGATTUTA:  No, Your Honor.

3          THE COURT:  Admit 19.

4          MR. JENSVOLD:  And 10A which is property

5    sheet.

6          MR. LAGATTUTA:  That's fine, too, Your

7    Honor.

8          THE COURT:  Admit 10A.

9          MR. JENSVOLD:  Your Honor, may we approach?

10         THE COURT:  Sure.

11         (The following proceedings took place at the

12   bench between Court and Counsel, out of the hearing of

13   the jurors:)

14         MR. JENSVOLD:  This might be a good time to

15   give them -- to publish the photographs, handwriting

16   sample, I can get the tapeplayer.

17         THE COURT:  You want to call them to get the

18   tape, you can use the phone.  Here, publish the

19   photos.

20         MR. JENSVOLD:  And handwriting sample and

21   the Cox bill which is stuff that's been admitted.

22         THE COURT:  All right.  That's fine you can

23   do that.

24         MR. LAGATTUTA:  Finish with that and play

25   the tape, then that will finish out the day, start
```

1   cross-examination tomorrow.

2   THE COURT: Let see how long that goes.

3   (The following proceedings were held in open

4   court, in the presence of the jurors:)

5   THE COURT: Ladies and gentlemen, at this

6   time I'd like to show you State's Exhibit 10A, 19 and

7   several photographs which is the writing sample,

8   photographs 1K, 1HH, II, JJ and KK and State's

9   Exhibit 21 which is the handwriting sample. I'll tell

10   you, you will have the exhibit that you have with you

11   in the jury room. This is an opportunity for to you

12   look at them and have them published. I want to make

13   sure you had a chance to look at them before we

14   continue on with direct.

15   Counsel approach again, please.

16   (The following proceedings took place at the

17   bench between Court and Counsel, out of the hearing of

18   the jurors:)

19   THE COURT: In deference to the court

20   reporter since we already have a transcription of what

21   is on the tape, wonder if you all agree Kristi doesn't

22   have to record what's on the tape as it's being

23   played.

24   MR. JENSVOLD: That's fine. I think the

25   only error I saw was like an -- or it was supposed to

SUPERIOR COURT, PIMA COUNTY

```
 1  be F instead of -- I think that's the only error.

 2          MR. LAGATTUTA:  I'm fine with that.

 3          THE COURT:  I want to make sure both of you

 4  agree she doesn't have to try to type what's on there,

 5  she needs to make a transcript.

 6          Have this admitted as a transcript.  If you

 7  want to make any objection --

 8          MR. JENSVOLD:  I'm okay everything to where

 9  I said --  I don't have to edit it or anything.

10          THE COURT:  You're going to be playing pages

11  one through --

12          MR. JENSVOLD:  I'm going to start right

13  there at page 18.

14          THE COURT:  One through 17?

15          MR. JENSVOLD:  Correct.

16          THE COURT:  And so if there's any

17  corrections to any of that, before that, that you're

18  aware of otherwise --

19          MR. JENSVOLD:  I listened to it again

20  yesterday and it was -- there may be one or two little

21  minor things, but for the most part it was right on.

22          THE COURT:  Well, with that understanding,

23  no objection to having Kristi not have to type -- take

24  the transcription of what's going to be played.

25          MR. LAGATTUTA:  Right.
```

1   THE COURT: Do you have a copy of this for

2 the jurors to --

3   MR. JENSVOLD: I can make it for them, I

4 don't have copies for all of them.

5   THE COURT: So they will have to listen.

6 That's fine, I just want to make sure --

7   MR. LAGATTUTA: And to the extent that any

8 of that covers areas I marked in blue pen, I renew my

9 objection. I don't know if that's been --

10   THE COURT: I understand. We'll use this

11 copy that I have and I'll just state for the record

12 that we should have this marked as an exhibit and that

13 Mr. Lagattuta has objections to areas particularly

14 beginning on page ten -- so you won't be submitting

15 this copy?

16   MR. JENSVOLD: Admitted for the file

17 purposes.

18   THE COURT: There are some areas on page ten

19 beginning on line 25 and the better part of page 11

20 and a couple of questions and answers on page 12 that

21 are marked in blue that he's objecting to that I'm

22 overruling the objections on, at least based on my

23 prior rulings stated for on the record. I'm

24 influenced by some of 404(b) cases I mentioned, but

25 also a case by 512 Utah Advanced, Reporter 29 -- it's

1   Miller Utah -- it's State of Arizona vs Miller which

2   discusses a very similar situation.

3   MR. JENSVOLD: And if it's okay, you

4   stipulate to the foundation for all of these, just to

5   save time.

6   MR. LAGATTUTA: Those pictures, yeah.

7   MR. JENSVOLD: Just, that's not the bedroom

8   stuff.

9   THE COURT: Okay. Now if you're going --

10   MR. JENSVOLD: I'll offer these though.

11   THE COURT: Are you going to try to --

12   MR. JENSVOLD: I'll publish these today,

13   they can look at them later.

14   THE COURT: I'm going to have this statement

15   here marked the next exhibit for the State,

16   Plaintiff's 25 will be -- the taped statement will be

17   substituted, might check on where your exhibits are,

18   see where they are.

19   (The following proceedings were held in open

20   court, in the presence of the jurors:)

21   MR. JENSVOLD: For the record, we're

22   stipulating for foundation State Exhibits 10, all the

23   way from U to 1Z as well as 1AA and 1BB.

24   THE COURT: So without objection -- any

25   objection to that?

1   MR. LAGATTUTA: No objection.

2   THE COURT: Will admit State's 10 to seven

3   and 1AA and 1BB.

4   THE COURT: Mr. Jensvold picked up your

5   exhibits the one that have made it around.

6   MR. JENSVOLD: Your Honor, I think this is

7   only 20 minutes, perhaps I can play it. If somebody

8   hasn't looked at the writing sample, they could look

9   at it afterwards. How many people haven't seen it

10   yet? Okay.

11   BY MR. JENSVOLD:

12   Q.   Mr. Englander, while we're in here, can you

13   put in the different color a red or orange asterisks

14   next to the counts in which you found some indication

15   or evidence on the hard drives going back to the

16   beginning of the testimony?

17   MR. LAGATTUTA: Your Honor, I'm going to

18   object at this point. I thought -- I thought his

19   answer was that there were no files found on the hard

20   drive.

21   THE COURT: You want to approach, let's come

22   on up and talk about it.

23   (The following proceedings took place at the

24   bench between Court and Counsel, out of the hearing of

25   the jurors:)

```
 1            THE COURT:  You got an objection so --

 2            MR. JENSVOLD:  With this qualification I

 3    think he said there was only one file that he could

 4    play using his software, none of the files could he

 5    play with the computer as it existed when they --

 6            THE COURT:  I'm going to sustain on

 7    foundation right now.  You can rephrase to see whether

 8    or not there's a name that's associated with something

 9    he's related between the hard disc and one of the

10    discs.  Tighten it up.

11            (The following proceedings were held in open

12    court, in the presence of the jurors:)

13    BY MR. JENSVOLD:

14       Q.    Mr. Englander, actually I think we were sort

15    of interrupted when we were going through this back

16    awhile there because if I recall correctly, there was

17    one file in which you stated that you could play the

18    movie using your software, your Encase software or

19    something else?

20       A.    Correct.

21       Q.    Not Encase?

22       A.    Encase -- well Encase would be able to

23    access the file then standard media player would play

24    the file.

25       Q.    So that particular file, if it was as it
```

SUPERIOR COURT, PIMA COUNTY

1 existed on the computer when you found it at Mr.

2 Coghill's RV, he would not be able to play it?

3   A.   Correct.

4   Q.   Then there were other files that you merely

5 saw indications of their existence on the hard drives?

6   A.   Correct.

7   Q.   Okay.   And which file, based on the count

8 number, did you -- were you able to play using the

9 Encase software?

10   A.   I don't know if I have the document in front

11 of me, that would --

12   Q.   I have it in my hand, it's State's

13 Exhibit 12B?

14   A.   Thank you.   I have the file name, I don't

15 have the count number associated with it though.

16   Q.   Okay.   What's the file name?

17   A.   It is BabyJ--babycum, C-U-M .mpg.

18   Q.   And based --

19   A.   I'm sorry -- no, that's correct.

20   Q.   Okay.   I believe that corresponds to Count

21 Ten?

22   A.   I'm sorry, give me one second, I want to

23 make sure I give you the correct -- yes, I'm sorry

24 that is correct.

25   Q.   Okay.   And that corresponds to Count Ten.

1   Can you circle that count number in purple or whatever

2   color you have up there?

3   Q.   Now, looking at your -- in reviewing your

4   State's Exhibit 12B there are other files that you say

5   you couldn't even play with your Encase software, you

6   saw through your analysis indications that those files

7   were present at one time on one of the two hard

8   drives?

9   A.   Yes.

10   Q.   Is there any distinction between the rest of

11   those files, are they basically all the same?

12   A.   They are all the same.

13   Q.   Could you then -- which -- let's just start

14   in order. What other files did you see indications of

15   on either of the hard drives?

16   MR. LAGATTUTA: Your Honor, I'm going to

17   object as to foundation and relevancy.

18   THE COURT: I'm going to sustain right now.

19   I'm not sure what the question is. Why couldn't you

20   try to ask the question so I can understand, so I

21   understand at least what it is you're asking.

22   BY MR. JENSVOLD:

23   Q.   Mr. Englander, back when you were testifying

24   about what how the Encase software finds indication

25   files have been overwritten by other files?

1   A.   Correct.

2   Q.   Those files you couldn't play but you know

3   those files existed based on your experience and your

4   involvement with the Encase software?

5   A.   Correct.

6   Q.   Now what other files did you see indications

7   of that you weren't able to play?

8   A.   R@YGOLD style-Lucy.mpg.

9   Q.   Okay. That corresponds with Count One.

10   Could you circle that count in orange?

11   MR. LAGATTUTA: I'm going to enter the same

12   objection how these are relevant to the case at hand.

13   THE COURT: Mr. Jensvold, I don't want you

14   testifying. If you all come up here to the bench.

15   (The following proceedings took place at the

16   bench between Court and Counsel, out of the hearing of

17   the jurors:)

18   THE COURT: If you want to get in -- your

19   testifying, you're telling me where it is.

20   MR. JENSVOLD: He's testified to all this.

21   THE COURT: He hasn't testified what's

22   connected up with what with all this, he somehow

23   indicated that -- that he's found these files

24   somewhere and, quite honestly, at this point I don't

25   know whether they were simply found on the discs -- I

SUPERIOR COURT, PIMA COUNTY

1 think were played on discs but, you know, they are

 2 downloaded, he had record having been downloaded on

 3 the computer on the hard drive or something to a disc.

 4 I haven't heard that evidence yet. I think that's

 5 what you're trying to get at. If you want to ask him

 6 whether a particular one up there is related to a

 7 count, you know, what the status of that particular

 8 one, where it was found, then I can understand the

 9 questions but, you know --

10   MR. JENSVOLD: Okay.

11   MR. LAGATTUTA: What he's talking about

12 images that don't exist at all, are not -- nobody can

13 even turn them on Mr. Coghill's computer. We don't

14 know when, how, at what point they ever existed. They

15 don't exist now. They didn't exist for the common

16 user to turn them on. What are they? It's an

17 indication that only through his advanced software he

18 can find that something happened that's been

19 overwritten, it's been replaced. We don't know when

20 it's been replaced. It may have been replaced on Mr.

21 Coghill owning the computer.

22   THE COURT: I know you are going to have

23 those computers, I understand that. What I'm sitting

24 here -- I had understood at least up to now that the

25 evidence was that what was on those discs is what was

1 played and you're trying to establish some kind of

2 connection what was on the computer at one time and

3 what's on those discs.

4 MR. JENSVOLD: Exactly.

5 THE COURT: And -- and you have had evidence

6 which it seems you can ask him where -- based on Count

7 One, did you find the items was it on a disc in a

8 particular exhibit, I think you got exhibits.

9 MR. JENSVOLD: Those -- we already

10 established which disc came from which count.

11 THE COURT: Well, go back and trying to

12 establish that -- what was found on that disc was at

13 one time on the computer.

14 MR. JENSVOLD: Yes.

15 MR. LAGATTUTA: But when and how and why.

16 MR. JENSVOLD: We went through the Encase

17 software he was getting bored with that, so I moved

18 on.

19 MR. LAGATTUTA: He never -- these things

20 that are just indications that don't exist at all that

21 have been overwritten. We don't know when that took

22 place. It may have been before he even bought this

23 thing. It's not even relevant to the time period.

24 THE COURT: That's for you to argue, that's

25 for you to argue. If they are found on the disc which

1   is one of these items that appear, 3E, and it's on the

2   disc and it's been on the computer, I think the State

3   is entitled to present that, just ask the right

4   question to get that so we know which exhibit, which

5   one of these things we're dealing with.

6   MR. JENSVOLD: He doesn't have a copy of the

7   Indictment. I was reading off the indictment just to

8   -- we already -- I mean, we already correlated the

9   counts to the file names when we were playing them.

10   THE COURT: It's your case, so I'm going --

11   MR. LAGATTUTA: Go over it again.

12   MR. JENSVOLD: You interrupted me and we

13   stopped because you objected based on --

14   THE COURT: All right. I don't know whether

15   you're going to do this or that, you got about

16   25 minutes before we take our recess, sort out which

17   one you're going to do. Do you want to do the

18   statement then come back finish this up tomorrow on

19   direct?

20   MR. JENSVOLD: I was going to try to do

21   both, but --

22   THE COURT: I don't think you're going to

23   get both done in 20 minutes, I think --

24   MR. JENSVOLD: I just thought we went

25   through all the --

SUPERIOR COURT, PIMA COUNTY

1   THE COURT: You leave it where you want it,
2   if this is where you are, it's the State's case.
3   MR. JENSVOLD: I think I rather do this and
4   if we have time to play the tape, if not, I'll play
5   the tape first thing tomorrow.
6   THE COURT: All right. Go ahead ask your
7   questions.
8   (The following proceedings were held in open
9   court, in the presence of the jurors:)
10   BY MR. JENSVOLD:
11   Q.   All right. Mr. Englander, I thought we went
12   through all this earlier. What indications being how
13   the software, your Encase software evaluates this and
14   gives you some indication that there were -- that
15   these files exist on one of the hard drives at one
16   time. Do you -- besides -- besides Count Ten, are
17   there other counts which in your forensic analysis of
18   two hard JE1A, JE1B indicated they are some point
19   where some of the charged files were on either one of
20   those two hard drives?
21   A.   Yes.
22   Q.   Okay. Let's start with JE1 -- JE1A. Are
23   there any of the files that were, through your
24   analysis, associated with JE1A were present on JE1A at
25   one time?

1   A.   Yes.

2   Q.   The files names?

3   A.   Yes.   JE1A contained R@YGOLD style-Lucy.mpg.

4   Q.   We established already while when we were

5   playing the files that's Count One. Could you circle

6   that one in orange, please?

7   MR. LAGATTUTA: Objection. Was that a

8   question to the witness?

9   THE COURT: That's the problem that we're

10 having here. I'm not going to let you correlate it.

11 You can ask him to correlate which count you're trying

12 to deal with without relating it to the counts

13 yourself. He's the one that has to testify with

14 regard to these things, not the State. He's testified

15 that it's R@YGOLD style Lucy.mpg, that's fine. If you

16 want to relate it to a particular count, you're going

17 to have to have him do that.

18 BY MR. JENSVOLD:

19   Q.   All right. Mr. Englander, I'm going to hand

20 you what is marked as State's Exhibit 17 a copy of the

21 Indictment in this case.

22   A.   Yes.

23   Q.   Okay. So looking through that, which count

24 corresponds to the file that you just mentioned

25 R@YGOLD style Lucy?

               SUPERIOR COURT, PIMA COUNTY

1   A.   Count One.

2   Q.   That -- okay. Did you then circle that

3 count in orange, please.

4   What other files have you found in

5 indication on JE1A?

6   A.   R@YGOLD style BabyJ 3yo girl eats cum,

7 C-U-M, 2.mpg.

8   Q.   And which count is that?

9   A.   Count two.

10   Q.   Can you circle that one also. Any other

11 files associated with JE1A.

12   A.   R@YGOLD_ilikeit.mpg

13   Q.   Which count is that?

14   A.   Count Three.

15   Q.   Would you circle that one also.

16   Any others on JE1A?

17   A.   BabyJ-Lol-01.avi.

18   Q.   Which count is that?

19   A.   That is Count 12.

20   Q.   Any others JE1A?

21   A.   I believe all of the remnants were from JE1A

22 babyJ-Teddy-mpg as well --

23   Q.   What -- what count is that?

24   A.   That's Count 13.

25   Q.   Circle that one also, please?

1   A.   Did you want me to circle 12?

2   Q.   Yes, please. And any others?

3   A.   R@YGOLD Style-Open_11, then other text.

4   Q.   Which count is that?

5   A.   That is Count 15.

6   Q.   Could you circle that one also. Are there

7 any others?

8   A.   Bear with me. No, I don't believe.

9   Q.   What about BabyJ captive?

10   A.   I'm sorry, I missed that.

11   Q.   And what file count number is that?

12   A.   That is count 11.

13   Q.   Would you circle that one also.

14   Now, in the analysis that your Encase

15 software went through in this case, were there file

16 created dates that you got for those?

17   A.   Yes.

18   Q.   What does that mean?

19   A.   That is the date and time that a file was

20 first created on a computer according to the system's

21 log.

22   Q.   Do you have corresponding dates to the files

23 you just circled on the board behind you?

24   A.   What I have is the created date of the file

25 that took its place which means the created date of

SUPERIOR COURT, PIMA COUNTY

577

1   the file that took its place, that date has to be at

2   or after when that file existed.

3   Q.   Okay. Does that give you any indication

4   when this file was present on the --

5   A.   Up until that date, but I can't tell you

6   starting when, I can tell you up until that date.

7   Q.   And do you have corresponding dates for each

8   of the items, each of the file names associated with

9   count numbers you circled on the board behind you?

10   A.   Yes.

11   Q.   Okay. Could you just sort of go in order

12   and just for the sake of expediency, just state them

13   and write them on the board next to the counts?

14   A.   Sure. For Count One, the overriding --

15   overwrote on 3/30/03.

16   Q.   You can just go ahead and stand up, if you

17   can just go in order. How about Count Two?

18   A.   Count Two was overwritten on 3/28/03. Count

19   Three was overwritten on 3/30/03. Count 11 on 3/4/03.

20   Count 12 on 3/19/03. Count 13 on 3/19/03 and Count 15

21   on 3/30/03.

22   Q.   Now, based on those dates and your -- the

23   way the Encase software works, a report is generated,

24   can you make any conclusions about user access with

25   those files based on those dates?

SUPERIOR COURT, PIMA COUNTY

1   A.   They certainly weren't accessed after that

2   date because they didn't exist according to the -- the

3   user wouldn't have seen them in existence after that

4   date. Before that date, there's really know way to

5   make determination as to what was done with them prior

6   to that, aside from the fact that in some way, shape

7   or form, the user of the computer told the computer, I

8   don't need this file anymore. It's available to be

9   overwritten either by deleting it or by physically

10   removing it, copying it to something else in some way,

11   shape or form. It was removed from the drive either

12   by deletion or by copying it out.

13   Q.   Now the file BabyJ-Lol, that was overwritten

14   by a particular -- each one of these has another file

15   that overwrote it, right?

16   A.   Correct.

17   Q.   What file name was that?

18   A.   Which --

19   Q.   For the BabyJ-Lol-01?

20   A.   That was written -- overwritten by an mp3, a

21   music file or an audio file that was found. The file

22   itself is Alan Watts, W-A-T-T-S Transcending

23   Duality.mp3.

24   MR. LAGATTUTA: Which one is that, what is

25   he talking about?

1   MR. JENSVOLD: Count 12.

2   BY MR. JENSVOLD:

3   Q.   Detective Englander, do you still have

4   State's Exhibit 12E?

5   A.   Pardon me?

6   Q.   E?

7   A.   Yes.

8   Q.   Can you turn to page 23, for me, please?

9   A.   Okay.

10   Q.   Do you see that file that you just

11   mentioned, the Alan Watts?

12   A.   I do.

13   Q.   Indicated on KaZaA?

14   A.   I do.

15   Q.   And what date what's the file date under the

16   KaZaA log?

17   A.   March 19th, 2003.

18   Q.   Does that corresponds to your indication

19   from the Encase software the same March -- March 19th,

20   2003?

21   A.   Yes.

22   MR. JENSVOLD: Your Honor, at this point I'm

23   ready to play the tape or play it tomorrow.

24   THE COURT: Yeah, I think if we have that

25   tape to go, it's going to last after 5:00. It's ten

SUPERIOR COURT, PIMA COUNTY

1 to 5:00 now, good time for the evening recess. Have a

2 good evening and remember the admonition not to talk

3 about the case please store your books back with Peter

4 in the deliberation room and -- the jury room that is,

5 and we'll see you tomorrow at 10:30.

6   (JURY NOT PRESENT)

7   THE COURT: Let me just ask Mr. Jensvold.

8 Do you expect to start at 10:30. You have a little

9 bit more then you're going to be a while with this

10 witness I suspect?

11   MR. LAGATTUTA: Not too long, Your Honor. I

12 would like to schedule -- like to think that we could

13 begin tomorrow afternoon.

14   THE COURT: Okay. And just so that I'm

15 anticipating, you know, how long it will take to deal

16 with that. My guess is right now that if you have

17 witnesses, are we going to need instructions tomorrow,

18 any chance of dealing with that, just your best guess

19 on it.

20   MR. LAGATTUTA: I'm sorry, what was the

21 question?

22   THE COURT: Your best guess on how long it

23 will take you tomorrow before you would be ready to

24 close might you goal into next week.

25   MR. LAGATTUTA: I would like to think that I

                SUPERIOR COURT, PIMA COUNTY

1   would like to finish tomorrow late afternoon.

2   THE COURT: Okay. So I'm going to prepare

3   some jury instructions tonight.

4   MR. JENSVOLD: Depending on what Mr. Green

5   says, I may want to bring Mr. Englander to rebut. I

6   was actually planning on putting Detective Moretz on

7   briefly to talk about his interview with Mr. Franks.

8   THE COURT: I'm not rushing you at all. I

9   am trying to anticipate -- we have to talk about

10 instructions. Are you going to look at any lesser

11 includeds, will you anticipate -- assume you -- you go

12 to the jury, I'm not making any pre-determinations,

13 I'm just trying to have things prepared so that we can

14 move along smoothly if we get to that point.

15   MR. LAGATTUTA: Judge, honestly, I don't

16 have an answer on that at this point. I'm not

17 thinking anything lesser included at this moment.

18   THE COURT: I'm going to go ahead -- I'll

19 prepare things as if we're ready best I can, and maybe

20 during lunch tomorrow we would spend some time to look

21 at instructions if it looks like we might get to it.

22 I'll need some time with the attorneys to do that.

23   MR. LAGATTUTA: If you're -- I'm trying to

24 schedule --

25   MR. JENSVOLD: Finish up with Jeff, real

SUPERIOR COURT, PIMA COUNTY

```
1   short, then I was going to bring Moretz in, just
2   briefly talk about his interview with Jacob then that
3   was going to be it.
4            THE COURT:  You can talk, sounds like we'll
5   be going into tomorrow afternoon, certainly, on the
6   testimony.  See you next -- have a nice evening.
7            (The Court stood in recess.)
8
9
10
11
12
13
14
15
16
17
18
19
20
21
22
23
24
25
```

SUPERIOR COURT, PIMA COUNTY

1

2

3   C E R T I F I C A T E

4

5

6   I, Kristine B. Valdez do hereby certify that

7   as an Official Court Reporter for the Pima County

8   Superior Court I reported the foregoing proceedings to

9   the best of my skill and ability; and that the same

10   was transcribed under my supervision via

11   computer-aided transcription; and that the foregoing

12   pages of typewritten matter are a true, correct, and

13   complete transcript of all the proceedings had as set

14   forth in the title page hereto.

15

16

17   _____

18   KRISTINE B. VALDEZ, RPR
                            CERTIFIED COURT REPORTER #50182
19   Pima County Superior Court
                            Tucson, Arizona 85701
20

21

22

23

24

25

                    SUPERIOR COURT, PIMA COUNTY

Day 3, March 30, 2006

Page 391-22: How can a person not on the police force, who left the police force for employment in the private sector, be a case agent? Is he receiving compensation for it?

Page 394-20: How can a document provided by the prosecutor, Jake's record of incarceration, be hearsay?

Page 395-23: Court erred in not admitting the document as evidence. The information it contained became crucial at numerous points in the trial. Because it was not entered as evidence, the jury could not use it to deliberate.

JAKE

Page 396-17 Jake states on CR-0320195 he was tried in Maricopa Superior Court on December 2, 2003. So is it Maricopa or Pena County?

Page 397-8. Prosecutor uses Defense exhibit B. after the court refused to admit the document as evidence, because the prosecution had the court declare it was hearsay. Prosecutorial misconduct.

Page 398-5: Jake told me he had never lived anywhere outside Phoenix.

Page 410-5: Jake caught lying to police.

Page 411-19: Jake answers judge's question by stating contraband was on CD and hard drive only. No mention of downloading from the Internet.

Page 412-7: Jake just got through testifying he clicked on a file and saw it. Now he doesn't remember.

Page 413-11. If what Jake's says is true a record of the event would be in the Windows Explorer open/safe cash and cash by file extension. There is nothing there. Perjury.

Page 414-4: Jake might have handled KP disks.

Page 414-6: Jake probably handled all the disks in the spindle where KP disks came from.

Page 417-22: Now that's a lie. Where in all the evidence is this spindle?

Page 418-15: Another lie.

Page 418-19: Jake states he witnessed defendant using Nero to burn contraband files to a CD Another lie.

Page 418-22: Perjury. Page 409-25.

Page 419-12: The sheriff's Department, in particular, Detective Englander, allowed Jake to get his possessions out of what Englander identified as a crime scene.

Page 421-7: Jake doesn't know if Defendant labeled KP on contraband disks. Contradicts statements to the police on April 01, 2003.

Page 421-18: Now Jake might have seen Defendant label disks with KP.

Page 422-7: Jake states Defendant used a special program to download contraband.

Page 422-15: Jake states he saw Defendant manufacture four or five contraband CD's.

Page 423-3: Jake states his testimony is based on an assumption.

Larrison v. U.S., 24 F.2d 82 (7th CIR 1928)
"A new trial should be granted when (a) the court is reasonably well satisfied that the testimony given by a material witness is false; (b) that without it the jury might have reached a different conclusion; and (c) that the party seeking the new trial was taken by surprise when the false testimony was given and was unable to meet or did not know of its falsity until after the trial.:
(NOTE: As discussed in the above case, was the basis for the Larrison standard followed by many circuits. See following for further information:

U.S. V. Natanel, 938 F.2d 302 (1st CIR 1991)
U.S. V. Nixon, 881 F.2d 1305 (5th CIR 1989)

U.S. V. Mass., 867 F.2d 174 (3rd CIR 1989)
U.S. V. Butler, 567 F.2d 885 (9th CIR 1978)
U.S. V. Anderson, 509 F.2d 312 (1975)
U.S. V. Johnson, 487 F.2d 1278 (4th CIR 1973)
and many more.)

Page 423-13: Jake never saw any images of contraband files played on the screen.

Page 423-19: Same as Item 20.

Page 424-1: Same as Item 20.

Page 424-8: Defendant had the fastest burner money could buy at the time with an IEEE 1394 firewire connection.

Page 424-17: Jake states over the years living with Defendant, he left CD's belonging to him in Defendant's motor home. Perjury. Day 3, Page 424-20.

Page 424-20: Now Jake states the disks lefty time to work his. Perjury. Day 3, Page 424-17.

Page 425-8: Jake states he doesn't own a computer.

JUDD

Page 432-2: Defendant was raking debris outside his motor home, not inside the motor home.

Page 433-10: Judd is recalling all this from memory. He did not take notes. Perjury. Day 3, Page 51-13.

Page 433-13: Judd just said he took no notes. Perjury. Day 3, Page 433-10.

Page 436-11: Judd states he saw KP as the top disk.

Page 440-11: Judd states Jake appeared nervous.

Page 451-11: Judd can't identify stack that had KP disk on top of it from photographic evidence.

Page 451-25: Judd didn't write in his report which spindle had KP on it.

Page 453-17: Judd states he never handled disks.

ENGLANDER

Page 456-14: Englander states to the judge adult pornography and contraband was, "fairly interspersed in the folders on the computer" yet his own forensics report reveals no files present on the hard drives. Perjury.

Page 457-9: Same as page 526. Perjury.

Page 457-13: Same as page 526. Perjury.

Page 458-14: Same as page 526. Perjury.

Page 465-11: Englander states CD burn dates figured prominently in investigation.

Page 466-4: Englander states that, "Mr. Franks had been there for approximately two weeks."

Page 473-4: Englander states in Day 4 a CD can't be modified after it's burnt.

Page 476-18: Judge states, "Adult pornography is so intertwined on the computer." There was no adult pornography on the computer. None! It was all on CD's.

Page 480-3: Prosecutor reveals the contents of Defendant's hard drives were copied to a laptop.

ARS 13-35.1
(J) Except as provided below, nothing in this rule shall be construed to require the prosecutor to reproduce or release for testing or examination any items listed in Rule 15.1(b)(5) if the production or possession of the items is otherwise prohibited by ARS 13-351. Reproduction of or release for examination and testing shall be subject, in addition to such other terms and conditions ordered by the court in any particular case, to the following restrictions: (1) the item shall not be further reproduced or distributed except as allowed in the courts order.

ARE 1003 Admissibility of duplicates
A duplicate is admissible to the extent as an original unless:
(1) a genuine question is raised as to the authenticity of the original.

Lambright v. Lewis, 932 F. SUPP. 1547 (ARIZ. 1996)
State trial courts violation of state law constitutes violation of federal constitutional right to due process.

U.S. v. Deters, 143 F.3d 577 (10th CIR. 1998)
When government action deprives a person of life, liberty or property without fair procedures it violates procedural due process.

Page 487-12: Englander states he doesn't remember Defendant handling the CD's.

Page 495-25: Not according to US Congress statements about child pornography. Congress has said it can be done.

Page 501-19: Englander states he didn't take Defendant's photographs, yet photo albums are on the list of material taken. Perjury.

Page 503-12: Wrong. The cable modem was connected to a hub because Defendant's computer was being used as an Internet server to provide Internet access via 10-Base-T cable to his next-door neighbor.

Page 506-18: Defendant was not at place of residence when search warrant was served.

Page 510-6: A period of 1.5 years to be precise.

Page 512-1: Englander did not begin examination of digital information until 11/17/04, Day 4, Page 453-1, not a couple of weeks later. Perjury.

Page 512-15: Englander talks about how activating the operating system (O/S) changes many files on a hard drive and that this is why they duplicate the hard drives onto another set of hard drives inside a computer with a running O/S and use a separate computer to examine the copied data. If what Englander says is true in regard to his imaging of Defendant's hard drive, then none of the files contained on the hard drives would be accessed and modified by the operating system and would remain unchanged and intact and as they were originally on the hard drives. However, this is not the case in regard to the Kazaa database logs that record every

589

file transaction. All file transactions are recorded in Kazaa via the DATA 1024.DBB and DATA 256.DBB files. At the top of the pages for each of these files in Englander's computer forensics report, the last date these files began recording information was 12/6/2004 – 20 months after Defendant's computer had been seized. In addition, what can be determined from the record of the Log On to the Kazaa network is that the database files were located on the A: Drive which is the floppy disk drive of an IBM computer. This means that this record was copied from its original location on C: Drive to a floppy disk where it was then used on another computer with Kazaa installed and access to the Kazaa network was obtained using Kazaa which had been reconfigured to look for these files on A: Drive. It is possible to reconfigure Kazaa to look for these database files on any drive capable of being read or written to using the configuration option on the menu bar. Also a confirmed connection to the Morpheus, Kazaa and Grokster networks is recorded in the Log On header. According to sworn testimony given by Englander on Day 4 of the trial, Page 71, Line 1, computer forensics began on 11/17/04 at 4:55 pm and concluded on 02/01/05. Therefore the following can be deduced:

1.   These are not the Kazaa database logs from Defendant's computer.
2.   These logs were modified on 12/06/04 while Englander was doing the computer forensics in his lab.
3.   Perjury, evidence tampering and fraud – Englander is the only one who could have done it.

ARS 13-2407 Tampering with public record; classification.
A.   A person commits tampering with a public record if, with the intent to defraud or deceive, such person knowingly:
1.   Makes or completes a written instrument, knowing that it has been falsely made, which purports to be a public record or true copy thereof or alters or makes a false entry in a written instrument which is public record or a true copy of a public record; or
2.   Presents or uses a written instrument which is or purports to be public record, knowingly that it has been falsely made, with intent that it be taken as genuine; or
3.   Records, register or files in a governmental office or agency a written statement which has been falsely made, completed or altered or in which a false entry has been made or which contains a false statement or false information, or
4.   Destroys, mutilates, conceals, removes or otherwise impairs the availability of any public record; or

5. Refuses to deliver a public record in such persons possession upon proper request of a public servant entitled to receive such record for examination or other purposes.

B. In this section" public records" means all official books, papers, written instruments or records created, issued, received or kept by others for the information of government.

C. Tampering with a public record is a class 6 felony.

ARS 13-2409 Obstructing criminal investigations or prosecutions; Classification. A person who knowingly attempts by means of bribery, misrepresentation or force or threats of force to obstruct, delay or prevent the communication of information of testimony relating to a violation of any criminal statute to a peace officer, magistrate, prosecutor or grand jury or who knowingly, injures another in his person or property on account of the giving by the latter or by any other person of any such information or testimony to a peace officer, magistrate, prosecutor or grand jury is guilty of a Class 5 felony.

USC § 556(d), 557, 706
Once due process is denied all jurisdiction ceases. The above U.S. code is made applicable in the state by instrumentality rule with:

28 USC § 3001/3002 (15)(A)(C)
Wherefore any alleged jurisdiction has already been voided by the denial of due process.

Page 522-16: Englander states the contraband file titles were for the 5GB secondary drive. Take note he keep saying files. They are not files. They are deleted file titles. Also, since deleted file titles were found primarily on secondary drive JEIB and not the primary drive JEIA which had the O/S on it, it tends to indicate these files were not downloaded from the internet because all internet programs are set by default to store files on the primary drive JEAI, because most computers don't have more than one hard drive.

Page 525-17: Englander states no intact files were found on either hard drive. They all had been deleted and that a normal user could not have known they were there.

Page 526-2: Englander states only Count 10 was playable. Yet on Day 4, Page 499-7, he states Count 11 was played yet provides no proof of his claim. Perjury.

Page 526-2: Englander, against court instructions, begins to list file indications that were uncharged.

Page 529-13: Court plays CD manufactured by Englander for the grand jury. Violation of ARS 13-35.1(J), "The evidence shall not be further reproduced or distributed without court order." There was no court order.

Lambright v. Lewis, 932 F. SUPP. 1547 (ARIZ. 1996)
State trial courts violation of state law constitutes violation of federal constitutional right to due process.

Page 533-4: Court allows files to be played.

Page 539-15: Englander states he found no contraband files in the "My Shared" folder of Kazaa.

Page 546-19: Jake told Englander the dirty disk had contraband on it.

Page 547-5: Burn date of dirty disk – March 25, 2003.

Page 547-9: JE3B burn date March 6, 2003 – Counts 10-15.

Page 548-5: JE3F burn date November 12, 2002 – Count 9.

Page 548-17: JE3L burn date October 27, 2002 – Counts 7 and 8.

Page 549-2: JE3N burn date March 6, 2003 – Counts 1-3.

Page 549-3: JE3O burn date January 21, 2003 – Counts 5 and 6.

Page 549-23: JE3Q burn date May 5, 2002 – Count 4.
Counts 4, 5, 6, 7, 8 and 9 transpired outside the dates Defendant was living in Tucson. Therefore, they do not fall under the jurisdiction of Pima County and should have been dropped. Also, indictment is flawed because it covers offenses outside the jurisdiction of the Grand Jury, which had no authority to decide on matters outside their venue. Thus Defendant was denied due process.

<u>Lambright v. Lewis</u>, 932 F.SUPP. 1547 (ARIZ. 1996)
State trial courts violation of state law constitutes violation of Federal constitutional right to due process.

<u>U.S. v. Deters</u>, 143 F.3d 577 (10th CIR. 1998)
When government action deprives a person of life, liberty or property without fair procedures it violates procedural due process.

<u>U.S. v. Gatto</u>, 746 F. SUPP. 432 (D.N.J. 1990)
To extent that government is able to do so, precise date and place of each event alleged in indictment should be provided to defendant.

Page 550-6: Englander states he didn't arrest Jake because he "didn't feel as though he would be able to make a determination as to who had downloaded the files and created the disk". Englander seems to have forgotten the wording of the law. A crime is committed by knowing possession. There is no higher form of evidence of knowing than a confession of knowing.

ARS 13-3559 Reporting suspected visual depictions of sexual exploitation of a minor; immunity.
A.   Any communications service provider, remote computing service, system administrator, computer repair technician or other person who discovers suspected visual depictions of sexual exploitation of a minor on a computer, computer system or network or any other storage medium may report that discovery to law enforcement officer.

B.   A person who on discovery in good faith reports the discovery of suspected visual depictions of sexual exploitation of a minor is immune from civil liability.

C.   It is an affirmative defense to a prosecution of ARS 13-3553 that on discovery a person in good faith reports the discovery of unsolicited suspected visual depictions involving the sexual exploitation of a minor.

Jake obviously knew because he told Englander he knew 1.5 years before this event. He therefore does not fall under the cloak of immunity provided by ARS 13-3559. Why didn't they prosecute Jake? What kind of deal did they make with him?

U.S. v. Deters, 143 F.3d 577 (10th CIR. 1998)
When government action deprives a person of life, liberty or property without fair procedures it violates procedural due process.

Once due process is denied all jurisdiction ceases per 5 USC § 556(d), 557, 706.

Page 553-12: In a sidebar, Jensvold states Defendant "Chose not to submit a handwriting sample". How can you make a choice about something you were never asked for?

Page 559-4: Englander states he finished his examination of the hard drives before he decided to pursue Defendant as the sole person responsible for the crime. This would have had, by natural course of events, to have been prior to his appearance before the grand jury to have Defendant indicted on July 15, 2004. Computer forensics did not begin until 11/17/04. Volume II Day 4, Page 79-1. Perjury.

Page 560-2: Englander states MIRC is installed on Defendant's computer. Volume II Day 4, Page 93-5. Perjury.

Page 568-20: Englander states only one file for Count 10 was recovered by his forensics software and was playable. Yet on Volume II Day 4, Page 121-7, he states Counts 10 and 11 were recovered and playable, using his forensics software. Perjury.

Page 571-21: Judge believes deleted file titles that were overwritten by the O/S were downloaded from the internet even though this conclusion is not supported by facts in evidence and has not been presented by prosecution. Judge has already formed an opinion of this case and it's a sure bet the jurors have too and it's not based on the facts. Could the playing of the files have something to do with this since it happened moments ago?

State v. Mills, 196 ARIZ. 269, 275 28, 995 P.2d 705 (APP 1999)
Evidence is unfairly prejudicial if it has an undue tendency to suggest decision on an improper basis, commonly, though not necessarily an emotional one.

State v. Mott, 187 ARIZ. 536, 545, P.2d 1046, 1055 (1997)
Improper basis include emotion, sympathy or horror.

Page 575-15: Prosecutor says, "that these files exist on the hard drive." They don't. Prosecution's questioning, the witnesses answers lead the jury to believe they are talking about tangible, useable, playable files and they aren't.

Page 580-1: The user wouldn't have seen the files before that date either because they were deleted.

Page 580-10: This is a lie. A copy command copies. The file winds up in two places, not one. A move command moves the data from one place to another resulting in one file. Copying does not remove file, only deleting does that.

About The Author

My career began in the United States Coast Guard. My first unit was Coast Guard Station Saginaw River. There I was responsible for search and rescue in Saginaw Bay and Lake Huron, where I performed numerous rescues. Earned Coast Guard Good Conduct Award, Meritorious Unit Commendation with Operational Designator and Meritorious Unit Commendation I was also responsible for standing a radio watch, listening for distress calls on the VHF-FM marine radio. I was transferred to Coast Guard Cutter Bristol Bay WTGB 102 where I worked as a Fireman and Oiler. I advanced to the rank of Machinery Technician Third Class at Yorktown, Virginia and spent my last two years of enlisted service at Search and Rescue Station Panama City Florida. Honorably Discharged after 4 years active duty service.

I obtained my FAA Airframe and Powerplant mechanics license in 1988 and began working as a mechanic for the Midway Commuter, which was a wholly owned subsidiary of Midway Airlines. From there I worked for Midway Aircraft Engineering in Miami, Florida working as a mechanic on DC-9 and B-737 aircraft. I advanced to the Position of Senior Aircraft Maintenance Planner where I was responsible for scheduling both routine overnight maintenance and heavy maintenance for one third of Midway's fleet. After Midway went out of business I moved to California and began working as a mechanic on B-747 aircraft which was something that I had always wanted to do. Later I began working in Phoenix, Arizona at Sky Harbor Airport and various repair stations throughout the region.

I obtained a Bachelor of Science Degree in Legal Study's from Kaplan University in 2011 while on the President's List. In 2013, I studied Computer Numeric Control at Glendale Community College and earned a position on the Dean's List and a Certificate of Completion in that program. I was released in 2017 after fighting my case for 14 years and obtained my Certificate of Absolute Discharge from the Arizona Department of Corrections in 2018. My only remaining requirement is to register for life and abide by all local SO laws as well.

www.ingramcontent.com/pod-product-compliance
Lightning Source LLC
Chambersburg PA
CBHW081506220526
45467CB00010B/2810

* 9 7 8 1 7 1 7 5 4 5 0 8 4 *